Decolonizing the Study of Palestine

Decolonizing the Study of Palestine

Indigenous Perspectives and Settler Colonialism after Elia Zureik

Edited by
Ahmad H. Sa'di and Nur Masalha

I.B. TAURIS
LONDON • NEW YORK • OXFORD • NEW DELHI • SYDNEY

I.B. TAURIS
Bloomsbury Publishing Plc
50 Bedford Square, London, WC1B 3DP, UK
1385 Broadway, New York, NY 10018, USA
29 Earlsfort Terrace, Dublin 2, Ireland

BLOOMSBURY, I.B. TAURIS and the I.B. Tauris logo are trademarks of Bloomsbury Publishing Plc

First published in Great Britain 2023

Copyright © Ahmad H. Sa'di and Nur Masalha, 2023

Ahmad H. Sa'di and Nur Masalha have asserted their right under the Copyright, Designs and Patents Act, 1988, to be identified as Editor of this work.

For legal purposes the Acknowledgements on p. xii constitute an extension of this copyright page.

Cover design: www.paulsmithdesign.com
Cover image: Tabula Rogeriana Muhammad al-Idrisi map of Syria, Palestine, Sinai, ca. 1154. (© Bibliothèque nationale de France)

All rights reserved. No part of this publication may be reproduced or transmitted in any form or by any means, electronic or mechanical, including photocopying, recording, or any information storage or retrieval system, without prior permission in writing from the publishers.

Bloomsbury Publishing Plc does not have any control over, or responsibility for, any third-party websites referred to or in this book. All internet addresses given in this book were correct at the time of going to press. The author and publisher regret any inconvenience caused if addresses have changed or sites have ceased to exist, but can accept no responsibility for any such changes.

A catalogue record for this book is available from the British Library.

A catalog record for this book is available from the Library of Congress.

ISBN: HB: 978-0-7556-4834-4
        PB: 978-0-7556-4835-1
        ePDF: 978-0-7556-4831-3
        eBook: 978-0-7556-4832-0

Typeset by RefineCatch Limited, Bungay, Suffolk

To find out more about our authors and books visit www.bloomsbury.com and sign up for our newsletters.

Contents

List of Contributors	vii
Acknowledgments	xii
Introduction *Ahmad H. Sa'di & Nur Masalha*	1

Part 1 Colonial and Decolonial Conceptualizations of Palestine

1	Towards a Decolonization of Palestinian Studies *Ahmad H. Sa'di*	13
2	Indigenous versus Colonial-Settler Toponymy and the Struggle over the Cultural and Political Geography of Palestine: The Appropriation of Palestinian Place-Names by the Israeli State *Nur Masalha*	37
3	What's the Problem with the Jewish State? *Raef Zreik*	73

Part 2 Zionist Settler-Colonialism: Tenets and Practices

4	The Epistemology of Zionist Settler Colonialism and the Ontological Securitization of Palestinians *Amal Jamal*	93
5	Al-Naqab: The Unfinished Zionist Settler-colonial Conquest of its Elusive "Last Frontier", and Indigenous Palestinian Bedouin Arab Resistance *Ismael Abu-Saad*	115
6	The Paradox of Settler Colonial Citizenship in Israel: The Dialectics of Dispossession and Palestinian Resistance *Areej Sabbagh-Khoury*	149
7	Celebrating Survival: Palestinian Epistemes and Resisting Anti-Palestinian Racism *Yasmeen Abu-Laban*	169

Part 3 Zionist Settler-Colonialism: Surveillance

8	Secrecy as Colonial Violence: The Case of Occupied East Jerusalem *Nadera Shalhoub-Kevorkian and Abeer Otman*	185
9	Israel's Telecommunications Lines and Digital Surveillance Routes *Helga Tawil-Souri*	207

Part 4 Palestine: Connections, Ruptures and Popular Resistance

10 Settler Colonialism in Palestine: Connections and Ruptures
    Magid Shihade 229
11 Popular Resistance in Palestine *Marwan Darweish* 247

Part 5 Issues of Bio-power

12 The Effect of the Separation Wall on the West Bank Labour Market
    Sami Miaari and Đorđe Milosav 269
13 Palestinian Refugee Archives: UNRWA and the Problem with Sources
    Salim Tamari and Elia Zureik 295

In lieu of Afterword

14 Liminal Lights in Dark Places: Elia Zureik's Sociological and Critical
    Contribution to Palestinian and Surveillance Studies *David Lyon* 323

Index 337

Contributors

Yasmeen Abu-Laban is Professor of Political Science and Canada Research Chair in the Politics of Citizenship and Human Rights at the University of Alberta. Her published research addresses themes relating to: ethnic and gender politics; nationalism, globalization and processes of racialization; immigration policies and politics; surveillance and border control; and multiculturalism and anti-racism. She has served as President of the Canadian Political Science Association (2016–17) and Vice-President of the International Political Science Association (2018–21).

Ismael Abu-Saad is a Professor of Educational Policy and Administration in the Department of Education, founding director of the Center for Bedouin Studies and Development, and the holder of the Abraham Cutler Chair in Education at the Ben-Gurion University of the Negev in Beer-Sheva. He holds a Ph.D. from the University of Minnesota, USA. Professor Abu-Saad received the *Outstanding Achievement Award* from the University of Minnesota in 2004. His research interests include inequality in education and access to higher education among indigenous societies, management and culture in multicultural societies, settler colonialism and indigenous resistance, and Arab education in Israel. He has authored and edited over one hundred publications, including the books (co-edited with D. Champagne) *Indigenous Education and Empowerment: International Perspectives*, Walnut Creek, CA: AltaMira Press, 2006 and *The Future of Indigenous Peoples: Strategies for Survival and Development*, American Indian Studies Center, UCLA, 2003; and (co-authored with K. Abu-Saad, and T. Horowitz) *Weaving Tradition and Modernity: Bedouin Women in Higher Education*. Beer-Sheva: Ben-Gurion University of the Negev Press, 2011.

Marwan Darweish is Associate Professor in Peace Studies at the Centre for Trust, Peace and Social Relations, Coventry University, UK. His research focuses on nonviolent resistance, social movements, cultural heritage and folk-singing and resistance. His latest book, *Popular Protest in Palestine: Uncertain future of unarmed resistance*, was published by Pluto in 2015 and translated into Arabic in 2018 by the Institute of Palestine Studies, Beirut.

Amal Jamal is a Professor in the School of Political Science, Government and International Affairs at Tel Aviv University. He served as the head of the Political Science Department in the years 2006–09 and is currently the head of the Walter Lebach Institute for the Study of Jewish–Arab Coexistence at Tel Aviv University. His scholarly interest focuses on political theory, politics and culture, political communication, civil society, postcolonial studies, politics of resistance and subaltern studies. He has published over one hundred articles in five languages in leading academic journals. He has also published over twenty books that include *Between National Consciousness and Civil Experience: The Political Realism of Palestinians in Israel* (2020), *Reconstructing the Civic: Palestinian Civil Activism in Israel* (2020) and *Arab Minority Nationalism: The Politics of Indigeneity* (2011).

Nadera Shalhoub-Kevorkian, a Palestinian feminist, is the Lawrence D. Biele Chair in Law at the Faculty of Law-Institute of Criminology and the School of Social Work and Public Welfare at the Hebrew University of Jerusalem and the Global Chair in Law, Queen Mary University of London. Her research focuses on trauma, state crimes and criminology, surveillance, gender violence, law and society and genocide studies. She is the author of numerous academic articles and books, among them *Militarization and Violence Against Women in Conflict Zones in the Middle East: The Palestinian Case Study* (2010), *Security Theology, Surveillance and the Politics of Fear* (2015); *Incarcerated Childhood and the Politics of Unchilding* (2019), all by Cambridge University Press. She has also co-edited two books, the latest entitled: *When Politics are Sacralized: Comparative Perspectives on Religious Claims and Nationalism* (Cambridge University Press, 2020).

David Lyon is Professor Emeritus, Sociology and Law, at Queen's University, Kingston, Canada. Ironically, in view of Orwell's famed novel, he was first in touch with Elia Zureik in 1984, not knowing that he would become his colleague and co-researcher on several major projects from 1991. His best-known book is probably *The Electronic Eye: The Rise of Surveillance Society* (1994) and his latest books are *Pandemic Surveillance* (2021) and *Surveillance: A Very Short Introduction* (2022). With Zureik he co-edited *Surveillance, Privacy and the Globalization of Personal Information* (2010) and *Surveillance and Control in Israel/Palestine* (2011).

Nur Masalha is a Palestinian historian and academic; he is currently a member of the Centre for Palestine Studies, SOAS, University of London. He is also editor of the international academic *Journal of Holy Land and Palestine Studies*, published by Edinburgh University Press (Scotland). Professor Masalha is the author of many books on the history of Palestine and the Palestinians. His books include *Expulsion of the Palestinians: The Concept of 'Transfer' in Zionist Political Thought 1882–1948*" (Washington DC and Beirut: Institute for Palestine Studies, 1992); *A Land without a People: Israel, Transfer and the Palestinians, 1949–1997*" (London: Faber and Faber, 1997); *Imperial Israel and the Palestinians: The Politics of Expansion* (London: Pluto Press, 2000); *The Politics of Denial: Israel and the Palestinian Refugee Problem* (London: Pluto Press, 2003); *Catastrophe Remembered: Israel and the Internal Palestinian Refugees* (London: Zed Books, 2005); *The Bible and Zionism: Invented Traditions, Archaeology and Post-Colonialism in Palestine-Israel* (London: Zed Books, 2007); *The Palestine Nakba: Decolonising History, Narrating the Subaltern, Reclaiming Memory* (London: Zed Books, 2012); *The Zionist Bible: Biblical Precedent, Colonialism and the Erasure of Memory* (London: Routledge, 2013); *Theologies of Liberation in Palestine-Israel: Indigenous, Contextual, and Postcolonial Perspectives* (Eugene, OR: Pickwick Publications, 2014); *An Oral History of the Palestinian Nakba* (co-edited with Nahla

Abdo (London: Zed Books, 2018); *Palestine: A Four Thousand Year History* (London: Zed Books, 2018); *Palestine Across Millennia: A History of Literacy, Learning and Educational Revolutions* (London: Bloomsbury, 2022).

Sami Miaari is currently a Lecturer at the Department of Labor Studies in Tel-Aviv University and a Research Fellow at the Blavatnik School of Government, Oxford University. He earned his PhD and MA degrees in Economics from the Hebrew University of Jerusalem as well as a BSc in Mathematics and Economics from the same University. Dr Miaari's research focuses on labor economics, the economic causes and consequences of conflict, including the economic costs of political instability and the relationship between economic shocks and conflict (focusing on the Israeli–Palestinian conflict), discrimination against ethnic minorities, economic inequality, and applied econometrics. His researches on the economics of conflict and the labour market received major external recognition following publication in leading journals in the field of economics, including the *Journal of Population Economics*, the *Journal of Public Economics*, the *Journal of Conflict Resolution*, the *Journal of Economic Behavior & Organization*, *Labor Economics*, the *Journal of the European Economic Association* and the *Review of Economics of the Household, Defense and Peace Economics*.

Đorđe Milosav is a PhD candidate at Trinity College Dublin. He received his Masters degree in political science at the University of Gothenburg, Sweden and his Bachelors degree in political science at the University of Belgrade, Serbia. In his dissertation, he is examining why some citizens express high levels of state legitimacy in countries with lower levels of quality of government from a political psychology perspective.

Abeer Otman has a doctorate in social work from the Hebrew University of Jerusalem. Her doctoral research focused on fathers and fatherhood in a settler-colonial context: the case of occupied East Jerusalem (OEJ). She holds a master's degree in social work from the Hebrew University of Jerusalem, for which her thesis investigated bilingual and multicultural civil society organizations in Jerusalem. Her experience in studying the OEJ community includes researching child arrest, women's access to justice and the socio-economic impacts of the annexation wall with local NGOs and the United Nations. As a community and social worker in East Jerusalem for more than ten years, Abeer engages in local activities concerning fulfilment of socio-economic rights, improving physical spaces, developing social and educational services.

Areej Sabbagh-Khoury is senior lecturer of sociology and anthropology at the Hebrew University of Jerusalem. Her research interests lie in political and historical sociologies, colonialism, indigenous studies and critical social theory. Her forthcoming book Colonizing Palestine: The Zionist Left and the Making of the Palestinian Nakba (Stanford University Press) examines encounters between kibbutz settlers and Palestinian inhabitants in Northern Palestine's Jezreel Valley before, during and after 1948. Drawing on resources uncovered in the settler-colonial archives, it demonstrates the coloniality of socialist Zionist settlers' practices of purchase, expropriation and accumulation by dispossession and how their representation of the past facilitated disavowal of the indigenous right to sovereignty. Sabbagh-Khoury's research has been generously supported by institutions like Fulbright; PARC; New York, Columbia, Brown, and Tufts universities; and, recently, the H.F. Guggenheim Foundation. Recent publications include: "Tracing Settler Colonialism: A Genealogy of a Paradigm in the Sociology of Knowledge Production in Israel" in *Politics and Society* (2021); "Citizenship as Accumulation by Dispossession: The Paradox of Settler Colonial Citizenship" in *Sociological Theory* (2022), "Memory for Forgetfulness: Conceptualizing a Memory Practice of Colonial Disavowal" in *Theory and Society* (2022), and Settler Colonization and the Archives of Apprehension in Current Sociology (2022). She is a member of the board of Mada al-Carmel, the Arab Center for Applied Social Studies, and its academic research committee.

Ahmad H Sa'di is an Associate Professor in the Department of Politics and Government at Ben-Gurion University of the Negev. He is the co-editor of *Nakba: Palestine, 1948, and the Claims of Memory* (with Lila Abu-Lughod), and the author of *Thorough Surveillance: The Genesis of Israeli Policies of Population Management, Surveillance & Political Control towards the Palestinians*. His publications have appeared in English (mainly), Arabic, Hebrew, Japanese, German, Spanish, Farsi and Portuguese. He was formerly a Visiting Professor at the Universities of Waseda, Tokyo, Japan; The National University of Singapore; and Columbia, New York.

Magid Shihade, PhD, is Vice President for Academic Affairs at Dar Al-Kalima University. His research and publications have engaged with aspects of modernity, violence, colonialism, settler colonialism, decolonization, Ibn Khaldun and the socio-cultural-political transformations of Palestinian society through the rural/village lens.

Helga Tawil-Souri is a media scholar whose work focuses on the overlaps between spatiality, technology and politics with a particular focus on Palestine/Israel. She is an Associate Professor in the Department of Media, Culture and Communication and the Department of Middle Eastern and Islamic Studies at New York University.

Salim Tamari is Professor of Sociology (Emeritus), Birzeit University; Research Associate, Institute for Palestine Studies; Editor, *The Jerusalem Quarterly*. His recent books include *Mountain Against the Sea: A Conflicted Modernity*; *The Storyteller of Jerusalem: The Life and Times of Wasif Jawhariyyeh* (with Issam Nassar); *Year of the Locust: A Soldier's Diary and the Erasure of the Ottoman Era in Palestine*; *The Great War and the Remaking of Palestine* (Berkeley, CA: University of California Press, 2018); *Landed Property and Public Endowments in Jerusalem* (with Munir Fakhr Ed Din, 2018). *Camera Palaestina: Photography and Displaced Histories of Palestine* (with Issam Nassar and Stephen Sheehi, Berkeley, CA: University of California Press, 2022); *The Palestinian City: Issues in Urban Transformations* (ed. with Majdi Maliki, Beirut: IPS, 2021).

Elia Zureik (1939-2023), was Emeritus Professor, Department of Sociology, Queen's University, Canada, has published ten books, most notably *The Palestinians in Israel: A Study in Internal Colonialism*, International Library of Sociology (London: Routledge and Kegan Paul, 1979); *Surveillance and Control in Israel/Palestine: Population, Territory and Power* (London: Routledge, London, 2011); *Israel's Colonial Project in Palestine: Brutal Pursuit* (London: Routledge, 2016; *Surveillance and The Globalization of Personal Data: International Comparisons* (McGill-Queen's University Press, 2008). He has also published more than 37 articles and chapters in collective volumes. Zureik was granted the Palestine prize in the social sciences in 1997 and Queen's University Research Excellence Award, 2008.

Raef Zreik earned his LLB and LLM degree magna cum laude from the Hebrew University in Jerusalem. He practised law for about ten years and then earned another LLM from Columbia Law School. In 2001 started his SJD studies at Harvard Law School and earned his degree in 2007, for which his dissertation dealt with Kant's legal theory. From 2010 till now he has been academic co-director of the Minerva Center for the humanities at Tel Aviv University, and an associate professor at Ono Academic College where he teaches jurisprudence, property law, law and culture. He is senior researcher at Van Leer Institute in Jerusalem. Fields of interest include legal and political theory, citizenship and identity, legal interpretation. Recent publications include 'The Ethics of the Intellectuals: Rereading Edward Said' in *Philosophy and Social Criticism* (2020); 'Historical Justice: On First and Second Order Arguments for Justice' in *Theoretical Inquiries in Law* (2020); 'Ronald Dworkin and Duncan Kennedy: Two Views on Interpretation', *Canadian Journal of Law and Jurisprudence* (2019), 'Subject, Subjectivity and Subjugation', *Comparative Literature and Culture* (2019), 'Kant, Time and Revolution', *Graduate Faculty Journal of Philosophy* 39(1): 197–225 (2018); 'When Does the Settler Become Native?' in *Constellation*, 2016. Raef is on the editorial board of several journals: *Theory and Criticism* (Hebrew), *Maftiah –Lexical Review of Political Thought* (Hebrew and English), *Journal of Palestine Studies* (Arabic) and the *Journal of Levantine Studies* (English).

Acknowledgments

Sadly, our friend and colleague Elia Tawfik Zureik, whose great academic scholarship inspired this book, passed away suddenly on 15 January 2023, ten days before the copy-editing of this manuscript was completed. Sadly, he will not be able to read the book, but we the editor are extremely grateful for his encouragement and advice without which this book would not have been published.

This volume is a product of collective and collaborative efforts. We would like to thank all the kind contributors who responded enthusiastically to our original call to this project and made huge efforts to meet the necesasry deadlines. We also wish to thank those colleagues who could not contribute for various reasons but helped with ideas and advice.

Throughout this project we also benefited from the kind advice and moral support of many colleagues and friends. In particular, we would like to thank Professors Lila Abu-Lughod and Andre Mazawi for their immense encouragement and professional advice. At I.B.TAURIS, we wish to thank Sophie Rudland and Yasmin Garcha for accompanying this project from the start and for kindness and for helping to bring about the successful completion of this book

The book also benefited from the professional copy-editing work at RefineCatch. These copyeditors managed to systematize the style throughout the book which has multiple contributors. We are also grateful to Merv Honeywood, the Client Manager, who responded to our request with great patience and understanding.

Last but not least, both editors wish to thank their families for their love and support. Nur Masalha wishes to thank his wife Stephanie and daughter Maryam for their constant inspiration. Ahmad Sa'di wishes to thank his family members – Sylvia, Yara, Sari, Abed el-Aziz, Emily, and Joud - for their constant support and for creating a warm and cheerful family environment that makes the stressful life in Israel bearable.

Introduction

Ahmad H. Sa'di and Nur Masalha

Political Jewish Zionism emerged in Europe in the late nineteenth and early twentieth centuries as a late form of European settler-colonialism. Paradoxically this political Zionism embarked on a settler-colonial project in Palestine at a time when the world was supposedly edging slowly towards decolonization and the establishment of new international world order. However, despite its apparent anachronism, political Zionism gained enormous international support from the colonial (and what soon became ex-colonial) Western powers. This raised questions regarding the commitment of these Western states to new and more equitable and humane post-Second World War arrangements and International Law. This anomaly became the focus of the lifelong academic work of Professor Elia Zureik, a Palestinian sociologist from Akka (Acre), an ancient port city in historic Palestine, who worked and lived throughout much of his life in exile in Canada. The life and works of Professor Elia Zureik epitomized the scholar-activist and an exiled Palestinian academic, in this case a self-imposed exile, and prominent scholar and engaged academic. Indeed, as David Lyon, Elia Zureik's close colleague, observes in the concluding chapter of this book: anyone can see Elia Zureik's impressive curriculum vitae, but this CV gives only a limited picture of the person in context, an exilic context that the late Palestinian intellectual Edward Said describes as follows:

> Exile is strangely compelling to think about but terrible to experience. It is the unhealable rift forced between a human being and a native place, between the self and its true home: its essential sadness can never be surmounted. And while it is true that literature and history contain heroic, romantic, glorious, even triumphant episodes in an exile's life, these are no more than efforts meant to overcome the crippling sorrow of estrangement. The achievements of exile are permanently undermined by the loss of something left behind forever.[1]

This collection of fourteen chapters, written in honour of Elia Zureik's life achievements, constitutes a dialogue and, indeed, an extended conversation with Elia Zureik's highly original research and seminal works on Zionist colonization of Palestine, in particular, and Palestine studies, in general. It also represents an attempt to rethink the losses the Palestinians have endured, and to usher in formulating a decolonial epistemology that would free Palestine and the Palestinians from the colonial power/knowledge web. The chapters dealing with a wide range of themes pertaining to this settler enterprise's methods, tactics, strategies, and intellectual rationalizations address two broad questions central to Elia Zureik's intellectual endeavor. The first is: what are the mechanisms that settler-colonial regimes institute to ensure settlers' dominance over time in the face of counteractive forces such as natives' resistance, market forces and international conscientious public opinion? The second question is: How do communication technologies affect political power, social relations and ordinary citizens' perception of their world? While this question is universal, communication technologies have played a pivotal role in colonial and settler-colonial conquests as well as in facilitating their control of the territories they occupied, particularly in Palestine. Indeed Zureik devoted considerable efforts to discerning the many ways Israel has used these means to subdue the Palestinians and their sympathizers.

The majority of these chapters are by scholars of Palestinian descent whose oeuvres have been influenced or inspired by Elia Zureik's scholarly output and theorization. This collection aspires not merely to give a Palestinian counter-narrative to the hegemonic Zionist one, but principally to lay the foundations for decolonial social science research on Palestine. In Chapter 1, Ahmad Sa'di illustrates the banality of the Zionist enterprise and its representations of Palestine and its indigenous inhabitants – representations which include terms such as the 'white man's burden'; the reference to Palestine as *terra nullius* or in the Zionist slogan 'a land without a people for a people without a land', as well as the use of utilitarian arguments to justify colonization and the erasure of the heritage of Palestine. Although such colonial premises have lost much of their credibility and even came to be considered offensive in many countries of the West in the last half-century, Zionist leaders, scholars and celebrities, including former Prime Minister Shimon Peres – a Nobel prize peace laureate – and Israel's foremost novelist Amos Oz continued to rehearse these offensive slogans for Western audiences.

More troubling, however, Sa'di argues, the Zionist colonial project has been elevated in recent decades from a relatively peripheral European colony to which an unwanted European population – the Jews – were directed, to an entity that claims to embody the ideal image and values of the neoliberal securitized international order. This shift in the projection of Israel and Zionism has not been articulated through a new philosophical or conceptual paradigm, but rather made by the repackaging of nineteenth-century ideas of racism and the hierarchical ordering of human beings and communities. This new shift and the internationalization of the Palestinian reality has been described by Magid Shihade, in Chapter 10, as 'global Israel and global Palestine', suggesting that decolonial research should look at the colossal implications of Zionist colonization globally and certainly far beyond Palestine's borders. Indeed, the rise of Israel as a leading producer of surveillance technology and equipment, which has been widely and globally used against human rights organizations as well as champions of progressive causes and a variety of democratic oppositional leaders, represents one grim aspect of this new reality.

Moreover, as part of this globalization trend, anti-Palestinian racism has not been confined to Palestine but, as Yasmeen Abu-Laban argues in Chapter 7, it is widely practised in the US, Canada and elsewhere:

[it] makes sense to begin to name and identify the key elements of anti-Palestinian racism as a specific form of racism operating in local and global contexts. Of course, as an Arab grouping comprised of both Christians and Muslims, Palestinians are subjected to Orientalism, as well as anti-Muslim racism (also called Islamophobia) and anti-Arab racism. But there is a relevance of naming anti-Palestinian racism as a form of racism distinctly experienced by Palestinians. This perspective gains some further depth when considering how it is becoming a key contemporary site of mobilization against Palestinian oppression in ways that parallel and bolster the BDS movement and the naming and challenging of the practice of apartheid directed at Palestinians.

According to Zionism and its supporters, the Palestinians should not only be kept under control but also muted. Amal Jamal, in Chapter 4, cites Elia Zureik's argument that one main goal of Zionism was to rob Palestinians of their humanity by stressing that 'the universal laws of humanity do not apply to them'. In this regard, a global campaign has been waged in the liberal West, led by Zionist lobbies and powerful Western elites, against Palestinian activists, their supporters and sympathizers, particularly on university campuses and against students and staff. All this highlights the limits of liberal values, such as free speech and the right to oppose oppression and apartheid. These new resurgent Zionist campaigns feed into and legitimize a growing current of anti-democratic populism, racism and xenophobia, and anti-democratic social movements worldwide. Indeed, as Shihade says, the question of Palestine has become the centre and an epitome of the struggles for the desired world order.

Nevertheless, Zionist politicians, scholars and theorists have always endeavoured to cover the Zionist project and Israel with a liberal camouflage. This led to their engagement in an enterprise of large-scale cover-up and the silencing and falsification of facts. Raef Zreik shows, in Chapter 3, how the violent and ethno-religious characteristics of Zionism have been submerged. Zreik traces these attributes to Theodor Herzl, the founder of political Zionism. For example, his novel *Altnueland* (1902) depicts the transformation of Palestine by European Zionist settlers over twenty years through the eyes of a liberal Jewish protagonist from a miserable place, poor, primitive and full of 'backward' Palestinians to a modern, vibrant and 'universal' country where a multitude of European theatres and opera houses – German, Italian, Spanish – flourish. Meanwhile, native Palestinians effectively disappeared. Discussing such perception with regard to the French colonization of Algeria, French historian Pierre Nora argues that the disappearance of the natives and the development of a so-called higher European culture/civilization in the colonies are complementary:

> Europeans have repressed the violence of their feelings through a collective decision not to recognize the Arabs. Because of the colonial situation, they act simply as if the Arabs did not exist.[2]

Nora further argues that the cultural 'refinement' of the colonists and their mannerisms – such as overt friendliness and openness – constitute no more than a veil to hide their terrible feelings of aggression, barbarism, repressed racist hatred and the desire to eliminate the natives.³

This desire for elimination and erasure as illustrated by Raef Zreik provides the key to understanding Israel's self-definition as *Jewish and democratic*. Zreik argues that:

> Now that the Jews are a majority in the country, they even can allow Palestinians who survived the transfer to become citizens and to have the right to vote. The dark side of the right to vote for Palestinian citizens in Israel is the statelessness of their sisters and brothers who became refugees. Transfer is the precondition for the limited liberalism Israel offers its citizens.

The theme of citizenship of Palestinians in Israel has been the subject of many academic publications. Areej Sabbagh-Khoury, in Chapter 6, explores in new ways the nature of the citizenship which has been awarded to those Palestinians who remained in Israel. Unlike T. H. Marshall's (1963) description of the status of citizenship as empowering and as forming the bases for social integration and equality, the Palestinians within Israel, she argues, have mostly experienced this status, as embodying dispossession, discrimination and marginalization. The expropriation of their property, mainly lands, particularly those owned by internally displaced the Palestinians who are classified in the Israeli legal-bureaucratic apparatus as *present-absentees* and the Palestinian Bedouin population in the Naqab (Negev) and its transfer to Jewish settlers is part of a process of settler colonial accumulation by dispossession.

Yet, Zreik argues Zionist settler-colonialism is unique in one respect. Unlike the French in Algeria, for example, where more than one-half of the *pied-noir* were not French but an assortment of Southern Europeans including Italians, Spanish, Maltese etc., and unlike the British in Australia, where the settlers migrated from all over Europe, the Zionist project in Palestine is ethno-religious: the settlers must be Jews. This ethno-religious character has defined the contours of Palestinian citizenship in Israel.

The cultural dimensions of Zionist settler-colonialism in Palestine and its particulars have been given less scholarly attention. Nur Masalha, in Chapter 2, explores the products of the Israeli official naming committees, which were set up to give Hebrew names to spaces and sites of Palestine as part of an effort to produce a space that would endow the Zionist colonization with an aura of authenticity and historical roots. The result, as Masalha shows, is an odd collage of Hebrew-sounding names, Hebraized Arabic names, ancient Hebrew names and European names. However, the new names represent a poor guide to the places they signify. For example, on the road signs pointing to the city of Akka (Acre), the words in Arabic and English are transliterated from Hebrew. Palestinians and foreign travellers with international maps might not understand the transliteration, which raises a question regarding their intent: do they mean to aid the passenger or underscore his/her foreignness? Moreover, Arabic names signify one feature of the place, highlighting its uniqueness in its milieu, but Hebrew names do not, on the whole, convey such attributes.

Symbolic and bureaucratic violence is another key theme in this collection. This symbolic violence or erasure and inscription reflects the continuing process of colonization: the removal of the indigenous population and the settlement of settlers on their land. Ismael Abu-Saad discusses, in Chapter 5, the process of forced eviction of the Palestinian Bedouin population in the Naqab (Negev) and its increasing concentration and ghettoization in poor townships. Indeed, as Abu-Saad illustrates, this population is ranked at the bottom of the socioeconomic scale in the country. The plans of ghettoization, often dubbed by state officials 'modernization', have not brought any worthwhile improvements to the conditions of this community. The confiscation of the Bedouins' lands has followed the colonial logic of non-recognition of the natives' modes of land ownership. Indeed, a fleeting glance at the Israeli laws used to expropriate the Bedouins' property would show their uncanny resemblance to the colonial laws that the French used in Algeria.

Although, since the nineteenth century, the Bedouins have been relying upon both seasonal agriculture and livestock for their living, Zionist publicists and Israeli spokesmen have tended to overstate the Naqab Bedouins' nomadism both in order to invoke Orientalist images of a community that is living outside history and to legitimize the expropriation of their land. However, as Magid Shihade and Ismael Abu-Saad illustrate in Chapters 10 and 5 respectively, the new Jewish settlers are the real nomads. They travel across countries and continents, build new settlements on Palestinian lands, acquire nationalities in many countries and constantly establish new frontiers to eliminate the natives. Moreover, while they enjoy travelling all over the world with multiple passports and with little hassle (due to their citizenship(s) in white-listed countries), the natives of Palestine are ghettoized and their movement is constantly monitored, delayed, obstructed and under constant surveillance.

Movement restrictions are just one element in a multitude of official policies, tactics, strategies and regular modes of behaviour by Israeli officials and bureaucrats towards the Palestinians, aimed at making their lives unbearable. In this regard, Amal Jamal, in Chapter 4, following C. Wright Mills' (2000) notion of sociological imagination, illustrates how an ordinary request by an Arab citizen for a permit to construct a terrace of rocks on his land becomes not only a bureaucratic nightmare but also a cause to subject the individual to an intrusive examination by the Israeli authorities. By contrast, Jewish settlements are built nearby, irrespective of the damage caused to the natural environment. To Jamal, this trivial case epitomizes a wider reality in which the Israeli state promotes an exclusivist and racist colonization of Palestinian territories and a calculated population management project that dehumanizes Palestinians. All this aims at the establishment of Jewish racial and demographic superiority and Palestinian subjugation, not only in the Palestinian areas occupied in 1967 but in the entire area of historic Palestine between the Jordan River and the Mediterranean Sea. The procedural democracy of Israel and the supposed rationality of its bureaucracy, Jamal argues, constitute a veil hiding anti-Palestinian racism and the drive to eliminate them. This leads Jamal to two conclusions: first, Israeli colonization is not 'a fact in the past' but an unfolding process of racist and brutal colonization; second, regardless of the political identity of Israeli leaders or governing coalitions, all Israeli governments wish to reduce the number of Palestinians and enhance the colonization project, and to this end they employ all sorts of biblical, security, 'greenwashing' and other spurious justifications.

The general themes of power and knowledge which are central to Edward Said's seminal work *Orientalism* are widely known. Yet, the centrality of Orientalist images and constructions to Israeli colonialist methodologies have attracted less scholarly attention. A key Orientalist image discussed by Ismael Abu-Saad in Chapter 5 is that the settlers often invoke the native's supposed barbaric nature. Also, Ahmad Sa'di, in Chapter 1, cites, for example, Shimon Peres's characterization of the Palestinians in the initial stages of the Zionist colonization of Palestine as a small violent population. However, Marwan Darweish, in Chapter 11, shows that non-violent popular methods of resistance have been a key feature of the Palestinian struggle against Zionist colonization in Palestine since the late Ottoman period. Also, during the First Palestinian Intifada, which began in December 1987, such non-violent popular methods of struggle reached their peak through the mobilization of the population in the West Bank and Gaza Strip, resulted in increasing worldwide sympathies for the Palestinians. However, these peaceful methods did not prevent settlers' violence against the Palestinians. Darweish also alludes to the failure of the Palestinian national leadership which – like many Third World leaders – pinned its hopes on persuading Western countries and their political establishments to support Palestinians under occupation. It seems the Palestinian national leadership failed to comprehend the deeply rooted colonialist and Orientalist currents in the West – and that Western liberal values, often touted a great deal in the international arena, deploy this rhetoric to ensure Western hegemony. Until now, the majority of Western political establishments have tended to support Israel and its Zionist colonial project in Palestine and the apartheid system Israel has created between the Jordan River and the Mediterranean Sea. Meanwhile many critical, liberal and progressive-minded audiences in the West have opposed Israeli policies and supported Palestinians' rights. It is worth remembering that the Jewish settlers' leaders originated from Europe; they spoke European languages, understood and shared European attitudes and cultures which were imbued with colonialist rhetoric.

Israeli surveillance is a major theme in the works of Elia Zureik as well as in this collection. Surveillance is a crucial tool for systemic ghettoization and the fragmentation of the Palestinians. These processes are not carried out through spatial planning and population management only, but also, through old orthodox and new digital means of surveillance. The new methods of surveillance are geared to render Palestinians visible, fracture their society by destroying the local networks of trust and solidarity, with the aim of further dismember and uproot the society. Nadera Shalhoub-Kevorkian and Abeer Otman, in Chapter 8, characterize some of the tactics used by Israel in East Jerusalem as *psychological warfare* and a politics of fear. They focus on the Israeli technology and terminology of 'secrecy', a widely used technology of surveillance. Shalhoub-Kevorkian and Otman maintain that the unremitting feelings of insecurity and helplessness that the technology of surveillance spawns have had a devastating effect on the local Palestinians. In the name 'secret information', Israeli security services raid homes and offices in East Jerusalem, publicly humiliate local Palestinians and apprehend many of them – Palestinians, who in the absence of clearly defined factually based charges find it difficult to defend themselves or fashion ways to face the often violent and brutal interrogations conducted by Israeli security services. Meanwhile, some relatives and friends of those under interrogation would distance themselves from the suspects fearing that they could be targeted or even incriminated by association. In some cases, arrests and detentions are carried out to intimidate other community members, while in other cases they are carried out to gather data and intelligence; all these methods are absurdly and arbitrarily used to justify arrests. One such case was that of an elderly Palestinian couple engaged in baking cakes and collecting donations to buy clothes for needy children during the Eid celebrations. The Israeli secret services interpreted the making of cakes as code for raising money for 'terrorists'. This illustrates how in the colonizers' minds, there is no room for kindness or empathy that might be extended to the colonized population, not even to the most vulnerable and needy members of Palestinian society. Such cases also epitomize Elia Zureik's notion – a notion that Amal Jamal expands on in Chapter 4: the racialization and dehumanization of Palestinians lead to a reality in which 'the universal laws of humanity do not apply to them'. Nadera Shalhoub-Kevorkian and Abeer Otman, in Chapter 8, comment on this Israeli politics of fear and report that the resultant environment of suspicion and fear has given rise to diverse psychological and psychosomatic illnesses among local Palestinian Jerusalemites. In comparative terms, and as in the case of colonized Algeria that Frantz Fanon (1963) famously describes, the colonialization of East Jerusalem by Israel since June 1967 has produced all sorts of psychological hardships among local Palestinians. However, Nadera Shalhoub-Kevorkian and Abeer Otman also found that in many cases, Israeli abuses have, paradoxically, spurred resilience, connectedness, solidarity and empowerment among local Palestinians.

Helga Tawil-Souri, in Chapter 9, traces the role communication infrastructure has played in the production of colonized spaces in Palestine, in bolstering hierarchies of power, in connecting as well as separating territories and communities and in rendering Palestinians hyper-visible in some areas and invisible and silenced in many areas. Tawil-Souri further argues that the British Mandatory authorities' uneven modernization and development of the transport and communication infrastructure in Palestine had largely shaped Jewish colonization in pre-1948 Palestine, and this unevenness eventually defined the areas upon which Israel was established in 1948. Tawil-Souri powerfully argues that:

> If the land could speak, it would tell us where the State of Israel would emerge: the cities of Haifa, Jaffa and Tel Aviv (when the Partition Plan was proposed in 1947), and Akka, Nazareth, Safad and Beer Sheba (when those Lines were drawn in 1949): each a city from which collectively hundreds of thousands of Palestinians would be expelled, and each a city wired and connected with more robust and expansive infrastructure than would be found in, say, Nablus, Jericho, Bethlehem, Hebron, and Gaza at that time.

Tawil-Souri's chapter makes an important contribution to the debate on Israeli surveillance culture and strategies. Her analysis goes beyond the assertion that the settlers were directed by the official Zionist colonization bodies to the more modern areas upon which they established the Jewish state in 1948, to explore the intricate relationships between Zionist settler colonialism and modern means of communication. Separate telephone directories were created for the Jewish residents of Tel-Aviv, Jaffa and other cities by 1939, and the whole infrastructure in Palestine was directed in such a way as to facilitate the establishment of a 'Jewish homeland' (under the pro-Zionist Balfour Declaration of 1917). Furthermore, not satisfied with the close collaboration with British intelligence, the Zionist-Jewish intelligence organizations in Mandatory Palestine began as early as 1940 to collect information on British political and military personnel and Palestinian leaders by bribing British officers and wiretapping.

The 1948 War produced great advantages for the Jewish state in one major area. The transport system and telecommunication infrastructure within the newly created boundaries of Israel in 1949 were far more developed than in the rest of Palestine, and Israel in 1949 had most of the telephone switches, terminals and connections to the outside world. This disparity in development has been accentuated since the Israeli occupation of the rest of Palestine in 1967. Nowadays, Palestinians in the West Bank and Gaza are not allowed to purchase communication equipment without Israeli approval, and such equipment has to be acquired through Israeli contractors, making it easy to implant in it Israeli surveillance devices. Furthermore, the existing aging infrastructure in the occupied territory, such as 2G and 3G cellular networks, could easily be monitored and cheaply controlled by Israel. Additionally, all incoming and outgoing telephone calls within these areas and between these areas and other destinations are routed through centres in Israel.

This tight surveillance of the Palestinians by Israel is carried out in the name of security. However, as Shalhoub-Kevorkian and Otman and Tawil-Souri illustrate, in their respective chapters, the security of the settlers always entails insecurity, disempowerment, dislodging and often the elimination of the indigenous population of Palestine. The 'Wall' Israel has built inside the West Bank is a case in point. Besides destroying large agricultural swathes of lands along the Wall's path, separating communities and making the movement within the 1967 occupied territories and between these territories and Israel time-consuming, arduous, and often a humiliating experience, the 'Wall' is used to regulate the entrance of Palestinian workers to Israel, fulfilling a similar function to the entry points and the passes that were used in apartheid South Africa. Sami Miaari and Đorđe Milosav, in Chapter 12, explore the impact of the 'Wall' on the Palestinian labour market, reporting that it has a geographical and gender effect. Employees residing in localities closer to the 'Wall' are affected more than those living in distant localities and women's working hours have dropped by more than half. Interestingly, Palestinian workers who worked in Israel and had permits were more negatively affected than their colleagues who did not have such permits, a fact that raises doubts regarding the presumed security significance of the 'Wall'. More importantly, on average, Palestinian workers' monthly income has dropped by US $56 per month, not an insignificant sum for many Palestinian families.

While the impact of Zionist settler-colonialism on historic Palestine between the Jordan River and the Mediterranean Sea and on the Palestinians as a whole has been devastating, this colonialism has failed to rob the Palestinians of their humanity. However, a large proportion of the Palestinians, who became stateless refugees, were pushed to the margins of humanity and have become dependent for their livelihood on the goodwill of international donors and humanitarian agencies. Care for this vast Palestinian population cannot be provided by the community or a Palestinian nation-state – which does not exist – thus becoming the task of international organizations, including the International Red Cross and the United Nations Relief and Works Agency for Palestine Refugees (UNRWA). In Chapter 13, Salim Tamari and Elia Zureik, analyse these humanitarian organizations' archives and provide an important description of the data gathered about the Palestine refugee population. This data is invaluable because it encompasses considerable information, including health records, educational attainments, family number, city/village of origin, the cause that led the family to leave Palestine, property losses, etc., thus providing a profile of this population, but it does not bring the voices of the Palestinian refugees themselves.

This introduction does not intend by any means to summarize the book's contents or chapters, but we, the editors, hope the introduction gives a sense of direction to the reader, and, at the same time, contributes towards advancing decolonial social science research on the Palestinians – research that would focus on their burning issues and geared towards providing tools for further critical research on Palestine and the Palestinians. Furthermore, for analytical purposes, the book is divided into five parts, an introduction and an afterword. In addition to its contribution to the study of the Palestinians, the collection contains important insights for students and scholars of settler-colonialism, and on the overt and covert realities of this pernicious type of colonialism, on native studies, and for all indigenous communities around the globe seeking decolonization, empowerment and justice for all.

Notes

1 Said 2000: 173.
2 Quoted in Carroll 2007: 22–3.
3 Carroll 2007: 22–5.

References

Carroll, David (2007), *Albert Camus, the Algerian: Colonialism, Terrorism, Justice*, New York: Columbia University Press.
Fanon, Frantz (1963), *The Wretched of the Earth*, New York: Grove Press.
Marshall, Thomas H. (1963), 'Citizenship and Social Class', in *Sociology at the Crossroads*, 67–127, London: Heinemann.
Mills, C. Wright (2000), *The Sociological Imagination*, Oxford: Oxford University Press.
Said, Edward (2000), 'Reflections on Exile' in *Reflections on Exile and Other Literary and Cultural Essays*, 173–86, London: Granta Books.

Part One

Colonial and Decolonial Conceptualizations of Palestine

1

Towards a Decolonization of Palestinian Studies

Ahmad H. Sa'di

> *The propagandist's purpose is to make one set of people forget that certain other sets of people are human.*
>
> Aldous Huxley

Introduction[1]

There is little that sets the Zionist venture apart from many other colonial quests, other than its late appearance on the world's stage. The adherence of Zionism/Israel to the colonial and neo-imperialist script explains the support that elites and large audiences in the West provide for this living example – albeit in miniature form – of the faded glory and greatness the West possessed when it ruled the rest of the world and imposed its will and narrative on indigenous populations. The legacy of colonialism still pervades all aspects of Western cultures, through coded images and forms of language that are often difficult to trace, but 'The colonizer's model of the world' – to borrow Blaut's (1993) conceptualization – also survives. In fact, the colonizer's Manichean vision has suffused global discourse since the eighteenth century, and Zionism/Israel has claimed legitimacy on its basis.

In colonial discourse, the West is understood to be unique, and this belief is grounded, as Wisner and Mathewson (2005) explain, in the idea that the West is uniquely capable of progressing and modernizing naturally, without external influence; its ability to progress is attributed to a racial, intellectual or spiritual factor, understood as a system of values (rationality, Judaeo–Christian civilization etc.). Meanwhile non-European progress is understood to occur only through the diffusion of innovation and influence from Europe, and non-material reserve flows from non-European environments are characterized and stigmatized as ancient, savage, atavistic, uncivilized or even evil (Wisner and Mathewson 2005: 903).

Israel's cultural affinity with the West, in addition to shared global interests and grubby involvements in the global South,[2] has constituted its main source of strength but also its Achilles' heel. While this chapter will not deal with these material interests, they comprise a background that researchers of culture and epistemologies of knowledge in and about Israel/Palestine should bear in mind, not least because the articulation of the Zionist settler-colonial project through Western modernist and colonial prisms made it hard for generations of scholars (particularly Palestinians) to formulate a widely accepted critical theory of Zionist colonization. Indeed, until the late 1970s, mainstream Western approaches neither provided a perspective through which colonialism could be effectively challenged nor left room for such criticism. Audre Lorde's (2018) assertion that 'the master's tools will never dismantle the master's house' aptly expresses that reality. Critical scholarship published before then was often dismissed as 'political' (as opposed to scientific) and was either ignored or relegated to the margins of scholarly discourse.

In the first section of this chapter, I shall discuss the presentation of the Zionist project/Israel in the political language and social sciences and the relation of that presentation to prevalent Western narratives of colonialism. In the chapter's second section, I shall examine critical theoretical projects which have emerged since the late 1970s with a view to demystifying the considerable colonial knowledge on Palestine and uncovering the basic organizing principles of Zionist colonization. I will offer fresh perspectives on these projects by suggesting that through their refusals, affirmations and allusions they attempted to advance a decolonial horizon. In the chapter's final section, I shall assess emerging research that explores what it entails to be a Palestinian under Israeli rule.

The colonial paradigm

The Zionist colonial perspective, whether scholarly or political, has been built around three central myths: first, that the country was empty or sparsely populated before the advent of the Zionist colonization; second, that Zionism has moral claim over the land because it made the desert bloom; and, third, that Zionism/Israel has a modernizing effect on the Palestinians. These claims constitute epistemological violence, as I shall illustrate in this section, but they also preclude non-violent consequences: they are the premises that justify and position as inevitable the elimination of Palestinians.

A land without a people

The Zionist myth regarding the country's demography was summed up by the phrase 'a land without people for a people without land', coined by the British Zionist leader Israel Zangwill. The first interpretation given to this claim is literal, suggesting that the country was desolate. Several Zionist scholars tried to make something out of nothing by arguing that a considerable number of Palestinians were, in fact, Arab workers from adjacent countries who migrated to Palestine following the economic boom that Jewish immigration triggered (e.g. Gottheil 1973, Dershowitz 2003). Joan Peters (1984) made a last-ditch attempt to promote this claim politically and academically. However, successive population surveys conducted by the Ottoman Empire and the British Mandatory authorities unequivocally illustrate that the country was, by the standards of the time, densely populated by an indigenous Arab population (Muslim and Christian) living alongside a tiny Jewish religious minority. Furthermore, about one third of this population was already urban by the middle of the nineteenth century

(Schölch 1985). Given these facts, the claim that Palestine was empty in the literal sense has not been able to withstand evidence drawn from sound demographic scholarship (e.g. Abu Lughod, J. 1971; Schölch 1985; McCarthy 1990; with regard to Peters' misleading claims see, for example, Said 1988, Finkelstein 1995).

Nevertheless, a colonialist understanding of the country's desolation before the arrival of the Zionist settlers has been invoked by countless Zionist statesmen and scholars. For example, in October 1986, Shimon Peres – a long-standing Israeli politician, often hailed in the West as a man of peace and recognized as a Nobel Peace Prize laureate – argued in the *New York Times Magazine* that:

> The land to which they [Zionist settlers] came, while indeed the Holy Land, was desolate and uninviting; a land that had been laid waste, thirsty for water, filled with swamps and malaria, lacking in natural resources. And in the land itself lived another people; a people who neglected the land, but lived on it. Indeed, the return to Zion was accompanied by ceaseless violent clashes with the small Arab population.[3]

The triteness of this statement is striking, and it reiterates the conventional colonial narrative – used in relation to Algeria, Australia, Western Africa, South-East Asia and the homelands of indigenous nations in the United States – to suggest that White colonists benevolently tame the wild environment and its barbarian inhabitants through the application of science and technology. In line with this myth, Zionist settlers were instructed, even before their arrival, that they were the rightful owners of the land. This made their violence against the indigenous population unavoidable (Mandel 1976: 26–7, Feuerlicht 1983: 195). Describing the impact of this myth on Jewish settlers, Mandel (1976: 310) observed that:

> Most members of the Yishuv were genuinely taken aback to find Palestine inhabited by so many Arabs. Given that they believed that they were coming to barren, empty land, their surprise was understandable.

Indeed, the settler violence that resulted from the empty land claim was discussed at the eleventh Zionist congress (Ro'i 1968: 205). Furthermore, this notion of empty land or *terra nullius* – that is, a land inhabited by an uncivilized population (i.e. non-European) – provided the basis for eliminating the indigenous people. As Wolfe (2006) has suggested, this claim is, in fact, a self-fulfilling prophecy. It should be remembered that behind the propagation of this myth and its implementation stood institutions and leaders – often acclaimed in Western culture as heroes – that consciously and tirelessly contrived, planned and then engaged in mobilization, as well as the construction of tactics and strategies. In the case of Palestine, in 1895, two years before the First Zionist Congress was convened, Herzl outlined the following plan to eliminate the Palestinian population:

> We shall try to spirit the penniless across the border by procuring employment for it in the transit countries, while denying it any employment in our country... Both

the process of expropriation and removal of the poor must be carried out discreetly and circumspectly.[4]

As for the rich:

> Let the owner of immovable property believe that they are cheating us, selling things more than they are worth. But we are not going to sell them anything back.[5]

Winston Churchill, one of Britain's most influential twentieth-century politicians, bluntly supported the empty land myth and its eliminatory consequences, as his statement before the 1937 Palestine Royal Commission made clear:

> I do not admit for instance, that a great wrong has been done to the Red Indians of America or the black people of Australia. I do not admit that a wrong has been done to these people by the fact that a stronger race, a higher-grade race, a more worldly wise race to put it that way, has come in and taken their place.[6]

In the light of this perception, peace treaties or proposals for peaceful coexistence between colonizers and indigenous populations – whether Tasmanian, Māori, Algerian, Native American Nations, or Palestinian – turned out to be nothing more than fresh strategies to make their elimination possible. In the case of Palestine, the Arab Bureau of the Jewish Agency maintained informal relations with some 'moderate' Palestinian leaders before 1948, not to explore ways to achieve understanding, but to gather intelligence and 'maneuver to split Arab ranks'.[7]

Paradoxically, a considerable proportion of Western civilization's emissaries who settled 'empty lands' were unwanted citizens in their own countries (e.g. poor and criminal Parisians, French refugees from the German–French war of 1870 and British convicts). Herzl's idea of solving the problem of anti-Semitism by establishing a Western-affiliated state in Palestine was along these lines. In 1896, he wrote in *Der Judenstaat* (*the Jewish State*) that 'We should form there part of a wall of defence for Europe in Asia, an outpost of civilization against barbarism'.[8]

Making the desert bloom

Colonization had been, on the whole, justified by invoking lofty ideals, and utilitarianism has often been cited both as its cause and its effect. Allegedly, due to their supposedly unique characteristics, White settlers were more capable of developing a country than its inhabitants. This reasoning was outlined, for example, by President Andrew Jackson when he addressed the US Congress in December 1830 regarding the removal of 'civilized tribes' – native nations that adopted the American way of life, including Christianity – which culminated in the Trail of Tears.

> What good man would prefer a country covered with forests and ranged by a few thousand savages to our extensive Republic, studded with cities, towns, and prosperous farms, embellished with all the improvements which art can devise or

industry execute, occupied by more than 12,000,000 happy people, and filled with all the blessings of liberty, civilization, and religion?[9]

All leading Zionist figures turned very often to this logic, but they lacked until 1948 the power that undergirded Jackson's fierce rhetoric and determination.

Notwithstanding such rhetoric, Palestine's economy was booming before the arrival of the Zionist settlers. The country's incorporation in the world capitalist system began in the first half of the nineteenth century, half a century before the beginning of the Zionist colonization, and the process continued unabated after the First World War. What was then a large surplus of agricultural products was exported to Syria, Egypt, Asia Minor, Britain, France and Italy.[10] The port of Jaffa emerged, by the end of the nineteenth century, as the east Mediterranean's second busiest export-import port,[11] and railways – often regarded as the spearhead of capitalist development[12] – were constructed at the beginning of the twentieth century to connect Palestine to adjacent countries and link the major Palestinian cities of Jaffa, Jerusalem, Acre, Nablus, Haifa, Lid/Lydda and Beersheba. Moreover, Western institutions associated with Western capitalism, including banks and post offices, opened branches in several Palestinian cities.[13] The idea that Palestine could be described as a desert is clearly problematic.

Another interpretation of the colonial promise to 'make the desert bloom' involves the idea that hitherto uncultivated land was reclaimed through the application of technology. However, the land survey conducted by British authorities in 1920 and consequent official reports revealed that there was no such land.[14] Even before 1920, Zionist leaders knew that this was the case, as is clear from the lecture Yitzhak Epstein (1907) presented at the Seventh Zionist Congress in 1905 under the title 'A Hidden Question'.[15] The Zionist colonization strategy had to adapt to include the purchase of cultivated land from absentee owners in the country's most fertile areas,[16] and ways also had to be fashioned to compel Palestinians to sell their land. Strategies included, for example, the lobbying of the British authorities to close the Agricultural Bank that the Ottoman Empire had established to provide credit to peasants affected by natural disasters or bad seasons (Hadawi 1988: 25). Bribery was used, and collaborators and local middlemen were also employed to purchase land. While Zionist colonization did not increase the area available for cultivation, it aggravated the problem of Palestinian landless peasants. In fact, despite the considerable investment made in Jewish agriculture, it was unable to supply more than 15 per cent of the calorie intake required by the urban Jewish population (Warriner 1948: 71). Jewish agricultural colonies, on the whole, were not economically viable, despite the massive capital influx from which they benefited; instead, they were intended to achieve a political goal, namely, to retain a large number of settlers on the ground to sustain territorial control (Warriner 1948: 71). According to Abraham Granott, who was a leading figure in the Jewish National Fund (JNF) and later an Israeli politician and economist, this colonial strategy paid off:

> The frontiers [i.e. the 1949 armistice lines] of the new State, which march in so curiously winding a fashion, were largely determined by the success of the Jews in creating faits accomplis. All those parts to which the Jewish settlers had penetrated were included within the State.[17]

When taking over the land through these methods miserably failed, war made possible ethnic cleansing – an option that has been debated, valued and praised by Zionist leaders since the beginning of Zionism.[18] Indeed, planning for war and intelligence-gathering to establish a Jewish state was stepped up in the 1930s, soon after the British crushing of the Palestinian 1936–39 revolt.

After the establishment of the State of Israel, the myth of 'making the desert bloom' continued to serve both as a tool to legitimize the Zionist colonization/Israel and as a rationale for the hierarchical ordering of Jewish citizens along racial lines (Ashkenazim vs Sephardim). Statistical manipulation has often been used to support this myth. For example, official Israeli statistics indicate that Israel doubled the size of its cultivated land in the thirty years after the state was established. However, a thorough analysis of the statistics reveals that, in fact, the size of the physical area under cultivation decreased. Official statistics primarily defined reclaimed lands as those that had been previously cultivated by Palestinian refugees and were left barren after their expulsion.[19]

Another interpretation of the promise to 'make the desert bloom' involves turning desolate land into green oases through afforestation. The Jewish National Fund (JNF) played a major role in this endeavour. It claimed to have planted 240 million trees, mostly pine, since 1948.[20] While this planting was represented as an act of recovery, it was instead a form of ecological violence meant to hide, uncannily, the remains of Palestinian villages destroyed during and in the aftermath of the Nakba – the 1948 War.[21] Michal Katorza, a JNF official in charge of place signs, bluntly explained that 'a great part of our parks are on lands that were Arab villages, and the forests are a cover-up'. Indeed, more than two thirds of Israeli forests cover the ruins of one Palestinian village or more. The Martyrs' Forest, where six million trees were planted to commemorate victims of the Holocaust, is a case in point. It was established on the remains of the Palestinian villages of Aqqur, Dayr' Amr, Bayt Umm al-Mays, Khirbat al-'Umur, and Kasla.[22] Would the victims of Nazism have endorsed such a commemorative act? Questions of ethics inevitably arise in analyses of colonialism and settler colonialism, not least because these regimes often resort to moral considerations to legitimizse their existence and actions.

This ostensibly environmental drive has accelerated in the twenty-first century, as Israel has determined to end the Naqab frontier. The JNF has used afforestation to seize lands on which the Bedouin population has lived for generations, both before and after 1948, on the pretext that these are state-owned lands. Israel has reacted in two ways to stave off international criticism by human rights organizations regarding the eviction of natives. As well as adopting a globally endorsed ecological message, it has endeavoured to implicate international governments and other bodies, including Germany, a country Israel has often found it easy to influence; Li Xiaolin, president of the Chinese People's Association for Friendship with Foreign Countries; and the American evangelical God–TV Forest network; meanwhile, a more concentrated effort resulted in the collaboration of forty-nine foreign ambassadors in Israel.[23]

The only delegate who objected to this 'environmental colonialism' – which resembles the use of missionary Christianity to defend colonialism[24] – was the South African ambassador, who, given the legacy of his nation, was aware of the role that colonial morality plays in legitimizing the dispossession of indigenous populations.[25]

A modernizing tutelage

Although Jewish agriculture and an Eastern-European way of life were not really a model for the Palestinians, Zionist leaders (including Herzl, Ben-Gurion, Weizmann, and Jabotinsky), publicists, scholars and novelists have argued that Zionism has had a modernizing effect on the Palestinians.[26] Settlers often used the 'white man's burden' narrative to describe their mission, as the following extract from a 1920 essay by Yosef Haim Brenner illustrates. Brenner represents his fleeting encounter with a young Palestinian shepherd, in the kind of depressing local surroundings that Shimon Peres, among many other Zionists, depicted. While Brenner's stated aspiration is to enlighten and improve the boy, the shepherd arguably also serves as a metaphor for the land the settler feels it is his duty to elevate:

> At the moment I blamed myself for the serious fault of not teaching myself Arabic. Here was ... an orphan worker ... a young brother! Whether the theory of the scholars is right or not, whether you are related to me by blood or not, in any case responsibility for you rests on me. It was for me to enlighten you, to let you taste human relations.[27]

Is Brenner different, in this regard, from many White men who came to Palestine to describe it and claim to represent its inhabitants? Yes. Unlike many European tourists, administrators, evangelicals and soldiers who came to visit, rule or exploit, Brenner, Peres and all Zionist settlers came to eliminate.

The idea that the Jewish community's colonizing actions constitute a modernizing tutelage has been reproduced in the Israeli social sciences since 1948. The theory of modernization has been valorized in Israeli academia and for a long time it was considered to be the hegemonic scientific paradigm, for various reasons. First, it endows Ashkenazi Jews with a sense of superiority, humanism and entitlement (as they are placed at the top of modernity's hierarchy and embody a modernizing agenda) while annulling or concealing prevailing power relations, the violent history of colonization, modes of exploitation and oppressive policies. Second, it attributes the 'sluggishness' of Arabs' modernization to Palestinians' local structures and social norms. Indeed, such structures, especially the Hamula (extended family), have been widely researched, particularly by anthropologists, including Emanuel Marx, Abner Cohen and Joseph Ginat, who worked in the state's control and surveillance apparatus.[28] Third, due to their characterization as 'traditional/backward', Palestinians have been defined as being devoid of nationalist consciousness. According to this colonial logic, splitting them into an assortment of insular ethnicities – employing what Chatterjee (1993) called 'a policy of difference' – could be represented as a natural and valid step. Moreover, Palestinians' acts of resistance to colonial control and policies could be delegitimized and portrayed as criminal or terrorist. Fourth, it endows the researcher with an aura of neutrality and objectivity. The style of writing in which researchers use the third person adds to this mystification:

> By delinking ethnic/racial/gender/sexual epistemic location from the subject that speaks, Western philosophy and sciences are able to produce a myth about a

> Truthful universal knowledge that covers up, that is, conceals who is speaking as well as the geo-political and body-political epistemic location in the structures of colonial power/knowledge from which the subject speaks.[29]

This, however, does not mean that Palestinian scholars have, either on the whole or mainly, spoken from a subaltern position. Rather, many of them have played a similar role to that adopted by many Third World scholars in rehearsing colonial myths, thus contributing, as Fanon (1963) argued, to their community's mystification. Grosfoguel (2007) highlights the difference between epistemic and social locations as follows:

> It is important here to distinguish the 'epistemic location' from the 'social location'. The fact that one is socially located in the oppressed side of power relations, does not automatically mean that he/she is epistemically thinking from a subaltern epistemic location.[30]

Indeed, the power/knowledge symbiosis after 1948 has resulted in the publication of voluminous research from within Israeli academic institutions on 'Israeli Arabs'. The modernization theory, developed in the West during the decolonization era, was adopted principally to research three areas, namely, the socioeconomic and cultural development of Israeli Arabs, changes in their collective consciousness, and their incorporation into the Israeli political system. The extent to which this research, and particularly the exploration of Palestinians' national consciousness, influenced policy could hardly be exaggerated. It enabled policymakers to assess the level of success being achieved by their policy of difference. Besides its policy applications, this research also contributed to reaffirming the state's legitimizing myths.

A more recent mutation of this colonialist discourse has centred on the democratic nature of Israel. Israel has never been a democracy, as, after 1948, it imposed a military government on Palestinian citizens – a regime that is antithetical to democracy and the rule of law – and, since 1967, it has been in control of non-citizen Palestinians who do not enjoy rights. Nevertheless, it has been portrayed in Israeli and Western social science literature and media as democratic. As scholars scrutinized the Israeli political system, they increasingly became sceptical regarding its democratic nature, but the veneer of democracy has been vital to the colonial paradigm, as it constitutes a key principle for supporting Israeli Jews' claim to superiority. Democracy is the most recent variable among all the variables according to which humanity has been ranked:

> We went from the sixteenth century characterization of 'people without writing' to the eighteenth and nineteenth century characterization of 'people without history', to the twentieth century characterization of 'people without development' and more recently, to the early twenty-first century of 'people without democracy'.[31]

Following globalization, democracy (and the scholarly debates on the third wave of democratization) has substituted development as the key organizing principle for the hierarchical ordering of nations and communities. In the light of this shift, Sammy Smooha (1997) coined the term 'ethnic democracy' to denote the Israeli political system. Although he explicitly acknowledged that the term 'ethnic democracy' embodies biased state-citizen relations along racial lines and separate development (i.e. apartheid), he clung to the appealing term. The passing of the racist Nation State of the Jewish People's basic law in 2018 not only disproved Smooha's model but also underscored the spuriousness of all colonial interpretations.[32]

The colonialist discourse presented so far has had an immense impact on shaping the consciousness of Israeli Jews and Palestinians. For the settlers, it endows them with a heroic sense of fulfilling a larger-than-life, utopian mission, which they occasionally have to pursue in the face of resistance from the uncomprehending and unappreciative 'civilized world'. Only through achieving their utopia can they gain self-worth and develop as individuals and as a collective; hence, the messianic concept of 'redemption' is a common refrain in the Zionist narrative. Moreover, in the name of this mission, it is permissible to commit or silence crimes, racism and oppression, which would otherwise be considered unacceptable. The cover-up of the ethnic cleansing and massacres committed during the 1948 War, and the support that large sections of the Israeli public lend to the everyday oppression Israel is practising in the West Bank and Gaza, are cases in point. This imagined mission also made subsequent generations of Israelis adamant in their rejection or trivialization of facts that contradict the essence of their colonial utopia. The considerable literature based on declassified Israeli and Zionist archival documents that not only refuted the foundational myths of Zionism/Israel but also reported horrendous crimes committed by Jewish settlers and Israel[33] and their cover-up has therefore had little effect, if any, on Israelis' consciousness. Israeli public opinion continues to move to the right, as successive election results and growing support for the settlement movement in the West Bank show.

For the Palestinians who became citizens of Israel, the Zionist narrative implies that their history is dishonourable; they are backward and lack not only a national consciousness but also the other faculties and sensibilities that characterize modern and worthy human beings. Their only chance for improvement depends on them following the example and dictates of the Jewish tutelage they receive. Moreover, their claims and grievances (such as Bedouin claims for ownership of their lands) are mostly understood to be unjustified, as they stem from their archaic social structure and values. Palestinians who wished to develop within the Israeli system, particularly in academic institutions, had to implicitly or explicitly accept and reproduce this 'regime of truth'. Hence, several Palestinian academics played the role of native informants and articulated in their writings a sensibility which Alatas (2002) called a 'captive mind' (e.g. Sa'di, 2004). Such articulations do not always stem from a lack of alternative knowledge but rather result from calculated policies.

In this context, Israel carefully designed educational policies to captivate Palestinian students intellectually. From an early age, Palestinian pupils are instructed – through textbooks, tours, newspapers, magazines, ceremonies and other means – to value being steered towards modernity by the state and Jewish citizens. The drive to use the educational system as a tool for intellectual domination began soon after the end of the 1948 War, when the fate of the Palestinians who remained within Israel had not yet been decided.[34] Deep surveillance and the suppression of free speech became a hallmark of the state-run Arab educational system. Moreover, state officials in charge of Arab affairs sought to enlist Palestinian students and professionals to disseminate the modernization discourse in their communities in exchange for personal benefit.[35] This policy also found expression in the field of literature. Almost all of the novels by Palestinian writers under the military government regime (1948–66) were classified as 'modernization novels'.[36]

The categories of settlers and natives are not set in stone; rather, given the dynamic social reality, they must be continually reproduced, and different rationales are applied to natives and settlers in this reproduction. The 'backwardness' of the Palestinians has to be reproduced to maintain the Manichean vision of reality that undergirds the identity of the Jewish settlers and their sense of superiority. In addition to the policy of difference, strategies including racial policies, and racist public discourse, the confiscation of property, and the appropriation or destruction of Palestinians' heritage and material culture (including books, buildings and archives) have been used.[37] The image of the Palestinians has also been essentialized. Yitzhak Shamir – who served twice as Israeli prime minister – famously stated that 'the Arabs are the same Arabs and the sea is the same sea', a statement that fits within Israeli discourse.[38] A supposedly respectable and scholarly version of this essentializing rhetoric was offered by Israel's foremost political theorist, Shlomo Avineri, who stated that:

> Arab society is a truly baroque society, where manners and style, façade and imagination are all the outgrowth of an overripe culture. Such a society may have greater difficulties in coming to terms with the modern world than a purely tribal 'primitive' society of the African variety.[39]

By contrast, Jewish settlers' identity has been reproduced, like that of several settler communities, through hybrid means. This includes the shaping of social spaces to reproduce a European – specifically, an Eastern-European – milieu, by planting pine trees and giving Jewish and European names to places and streets, and the appropriation of indigenous cultural elements (like cuisine) which are then presented as authentic Israeli products, such as hummus.[40] This constant reproduction of hierarchical identities has contributed to a sense of entitlement and the upsurge of an extreme form of nationalism among Israeli Jews, which is manifested, for example, in the saturation of everyday Hebrew language with militaristic jargon and metaphors. More ominously, it has meant constantly reproducing the frontier with its ghastly violence against the indigenous population, as in the case of the Naqab and, more markedly, the West Bank and Gaza.

Anti-colonial discourse regarding the Zionist colonization and Israel was not accepted in academic discourse until 1979. Several factors contributed to this silencing, including the Cold War, and the dire conditions of Palestinians, particularly the refugees. However, beyond these particularities, the main obstacle had been the hegemony of modernization and political development theories in the academic discourse in social sciences at universities in the West. These theories underpinned American hegemony and obscured the devastating impact of a colonial past and post-Second World War imperialist policies on the global south. Given their association with Western colonialism, Zionism and Israel have been incorporated into European and US modernizing narratives.

Anti-colonial writings

Paraphrasing Spivak's (1992) famous question, 'Can the subaltern speak?', Jay Maggio (2007) asked, 'Can the subaltern be heard?' Palestinian and non-Palestinian novelists and poets,[41] social scientists, and legal scholars produced voluminous literature critical of Zionism/Israel before 1978. Major works were produced within the social sciences[42] but although all of these scholars had received a Western education, and most of them studied and taught at prestigious universities and published their works in European languages, they were barely heard. Their writings were acknowledged and cited by only a few. This bias illustrates the depressing state of the intellectual debates in the liberal West regarding scholarship on Palestine.

However, by the mid-1970s, global political, social and intellectual struggles had created the conditions for a paradigmatic change. Critical theories that had been sidelined in academia for a long time, such as Marxism, were being accepted as legitimate. Moreover, French post-structuralism, and particularly Foucault's writings, introduced novel insights regarding the structure of knowledge and its relations to sociopolitical realities and power relations. This changing terrain paved the way for the success of Edward Said's *Orientalism*, first published in 1978. Said gave eloquent and erudite expression to a volatile but persistent intellectual current among scholars in the global South and scholars of disadvantaged backgrounds in the West. More importantly, *Orientalism* helped demystify fundamental assumptions about how the production of knowledge in Europe and the US in the humanities and social sciences was interwoven with colonial domination. This paradigmatic shift cleared the ground for subaltern voices to demand equal attention alongside the official narratives.

In Palestinian studies, three books that became canonical were published a year after the publication of *Orientalism* – they were *The Question of Palestine* by Edward Said (1979); *Palestinians: From Peasants to Revolutionaries* by Rosemary Sayigh (1979); and *The Palestinians in Israel: A Study in Internal Colonialism* by Elia Zureik (1979). Said's book is an articulate presentation of the Palestinian cause in general and it focuses on the affirmation of Palestinian rights. Palestinians' struggle, Said maintained, is principally directed against their complete historical deletion as a people and their categorization as either a humanitarian case or terrorists. While he acknowledges the tragic history of the Jews as survivors of the most tragic destiny, he does not accept that rectification of their tragedy should be achieved by dislodging Palestinians from their homeland, property, dignity and humanity. Zionism, he maintained, should be viewed not only from the viewpoint of its supporters, who often equate anti-Zionism with anti-Semitism, but also from its victims' vantage point. The prevailing one-sided approach towards Zionism in the Western media and among elites has endowed Israel with immunity against criticism and freed it from accountability for its policies and behaviours. This attitude, he argued, prevents mutual recognition and eventual normalcy.

Sayigh's book, meanwhile, is about Palestinian refugees in Lebanon, whom the West has treated as collateral damage of the arrangements, made after the Second World War in the Middle East, that rendered them eligible for humanitarian aid. Through interviews with Palestinian refugees, Sayigh's book foregrounds their memories, hardships and dreams, and the endeavours to achieve dignity and agency of those who have been treated only abstractly as 'Palestinian refugees'. Their lived experiences underscore Said's demand that Zionism and Israel should be considered from the viewpoint of their victims. Following Sayigh's book, several research and documentation projects have focused on the Palestinian refugees, including studies conducted by Sayigh herself. Along the way, research on this community has benefited from a growing interest in refugees worldwide that has been reflected in the inauguration of dedicated academic departments, research centres and academic journals.

Zureik's book, like Sayigh's, is about one segment of the Palestinian people, and it focuses on those who were fortunate enough to evade ethnic cleansing and stay within the 1948 borders. I shall discuss Zureik's work at some length in the next section, given its reliance on a considerable body of social science theorizations.

Internal colonialism

Instead of adhering to the theory of modernization discussed above, Zureik characterized Israel as a state established by settlers who devised policies to reproduce their superior position by converting areas populated by indigenous people into an internal colony. According to this view, racial policies of land confiscation, exploitation, legal and extra-legal discrimination, structural racism, proletarianization and political oppression are the means through which the colonial reality is reproduced. Employing theoretical advances in the sociology of colonialism, development and racism, Zureik illustrated that apartheid South Africa is a fitting comparator for Israel. Zureik's book sparked strong criticism in Israel, prompting a review filled with insinuations and bad faith from Kimmerling, then the foremost Israel sociologist:

> While reading Zureik's book, the impression that comes out is that it represents a continuation of the war by other means (in this case, an academic publication). The fate of the Palestinians (whether in Israel, under Israeli occupation, or those who live in different Arab countries) is difficult, and the darkening of their prospects does not deliver benefits either to them or to the accumulation of social science knowledge on conflict management and the motivations and obstacles that the processes of nation-building entail.[43]

Like many colonial officials and scholars, Kimmerling blatantly appoints himself as the final authority on what is good and what is inadequate for the indigenous population.

Despite strong opposition to Zureik's thesis in Israeli social sciences departments, the hegemony of the modernization discourse had been irrevocably damaged.[44] Moreover, the use of anti-colonial models and other critical theories, such as dependency theory, was growing. Indeed, Zureik's intervention turned out to be crucial and influential in the longer term. Davis (1987) argued that the Zionist project is even more radical than apartheid, because while apartheid aimed to incorporate black South Africans into the system in the clearly stated interests of economic exploitation using patterns of legal segregation, successful implementation of the Zionist enterprise has always been envisaged as a complete transfer of the native Palestinian population. The designation of Israel as an apartheid regime has been fully or partially accepted by a growing number of scholars.[45] Moreover, in the last few years, it has also been adopted by major human rights organizations.[46]

The anti-colonial paradigm has taken a particular trajectory among Palestinian scholars in the West Bank, who have developed what might be called a 'sociology of the occupation',[47] a field of exploration that Palestinians and non-Palestinian scholars have pursued.[48] For example, checkpoints – one of the places where the system of oppression is given concrete manifestation as part of everyday reality – have become a focal research topic for many scholars of surveillance.[49]

Taking a broader view, Zureik, Lyon and Abu-Laban (2010) edited a book on Israeli methods of surveillance and control of the Palestinians that ushered in a new phase in Palestinian studies in two ways. First, these scholars treated Palestinians residing within historical Palestine as a single unit, within which various segments are subjected to different control methods. Secondly, they underscored the key role that Israeli surveillance plays in the growing complexity, ubiquity, and intrusiveness of digital surveillance under the neoliberal regime.

From this perspective, Zionist settler-colonialism is understood to have moved from playing an auxiliary role to colonial powers, as Herzl envisaged, to presenting itself as a pioneer and future image of the neo-imperialist order.[50] Thus, it has brought forth a repackaged version of nineteenth-century ideas that privilege the hierarchical ordering of groups, racial exclusivity and democracy for 'us' and the oppression of 'other/s'.

Settler colonialism

Zureik's last book[51] examined the Zionist project from its beginning to the end of the first decade of the twenty-first century, and its devastating impact on the indigenous Palestinian society. Before analysing the 'settler-colonial paradigm', it might be instructive to succinctly examine the Janus-faced concept of 'settler-colonialism' in Palestine. Arthur Ruppin,[52] a scholar who wrote many books on the sociology and demography of the Jewish people and who was also in charge of the implementation of the Zionist colonization in Palestine, adhered to the Darwinist biological theory of race. He adopted such concepts as 'racial purity' and eugenics, and expressed appreciation, in his writings and in private, of German theorists of race who influenced Nazism, including Hans Günther, Himmler's mentor. Meanwhile, Haim Arlosoroff (1899–1933), who headed the Political Department of the Jewish Agency, was the first to introduce the term 'settler colonialism' to describe the Zionist colonization. He argued that South Africa was 'almost the only case in which there is a similarity in the objective conditions and problems so as to allow us an analogy'.[53] These shared objective conditions and *Weltanschauung* led to long relationships between Zionism/Israel and apartheid South Africa, which found expression, for example, in the strong endorsement of the Zionist colonization in Palestine by the South African prime minister Jan Smuts, who had considerable influence in the UK, as well as in Israeli arms sales to South Africa, particularly during the most macabre stages of the apartheid regime.

On the other hand, Palestinian scholars[54] found in this model hope that, like settler regimes in places such as Algeria, Kenya, Rhodesia and South Africa, Zionist colonization would wither. They were writing in the heyday of Third-Worldism, in the 1960s and 1970s, when the defeat of Western imperialism seemed within reach. With the dashing of these hopes, the paradigm of settler-colonialism also faded, but it was revived in the first decade of the twenty-first century. Patrick Wolfe (e.g. Wolfe 2006) and Lorenzo Veracini (e.g. Veracini 2010) played a key role in this resumption, and an academic journal entitled *Settler Colonial Studies*, founded in 2011, has published many articles that use Israel/Palestine in their case studies. Much of this material has engaged with Wolfe's and Veracini's arguments, particularly with regard to the eliminatory drive inherent in settler-colonialism's attitudes and behaviours towards natives.

Reflecting on the evolution of settler-colonialism theory over time, Abu-Lughod (2020) argued that it has lost much of its critical bite, mutating from a theory of political liberation (i.e. praxis) to an analytical model used in relation to a specific social formation. Moreover, Barakat (2018) questioned the epistemology of the settler-colonial paradigm, suggesting that the later, tamed, version of the settler-colonial approach is not necessarily decolonial and could instead very well accommodate the narratives of both Palestinians and settlers.

Zureik (2016) used the settler-colonial model as an analytical tool without engaging much with its epistemology. Instead, he used Foucault's (2009) arguments as his main theoretical point of departure alongside insights from Foucault's critics. Thus, he dealt with questions pertaining to 'biopolitics', 'security', 'necropolitics', 'urbicide', 'incarceration', 'targeted assassinations', references to the killing of innocent Palestinians as 'collateral damage', 'digital occupation' and so on. The book also brings to light the polarized attitude of Zionism/Israel towards the surveillance of the Palestinians: they are either considered invisible (a land without people) or massive resources are invested to render them constantly visible. Various chapters in the book shed light on the meaning and implications of living under such a regime, a topic related to what Maldonado-Torres (2007) called 'the coloniality of being', a concept I shall discuss in the next section.

Of the coloniality of being

The concept of 'coloniality of being' is useful for decolonizing Palestinian studies, as it touches on the essence of Palestinians' existence. Maldonado-Torres defines it as 'the normalization of the extraordinary events that take place in war'.[55] This includes, for example, humiliation, 'killability', the confiscation of property, dehumanization and the imposition of structural determinants that make the colonized people's existence dystopian. In this section, I shall briefly discuss illustrative pieces of research that deal with the coloniality of being that were conducted in three Palestinian cities: Jerusalem, Jaffa and Al-Khalil (Hebron).

Jerusalem is a holy city, but it is also a place of residence for 335,600 Palestinians, who comprise 34 per cent of the city's population. The policies constructed to drive

Palestinians out of the city through bureaucratic means and racist laws have been widely documented and they will not be discussed here. In the following, I shall probe Shalhoub-Kervorkian's (2017) discussion of sensory effects of the occupation on the occupied, which she referred to as 'the occupation of senses' that occurs through the imposition of aggressive sights and sounds, as well as unpleasant smells, on Palestinians. This 'occupation of the senses' takes place during festivities, as well as in everyday life. For instance, during celebrations, including the annual state-sponsored Jerusalem Light Festival, illuminated displays and visual artworks are projected onto buildings in the old city. Although these displays are officially described as non-political and as part of a multicultural international event, they intend to legitimize Israel's annexation of the eastern part of the city. Moreover, through displays of Jewish images, dreidels, menorahs and other traditional Jewish symbols on Palestinian houses and public spaces, Israel unambiguously imposes its dominance. While Israelis and tourists flock to attend the festivities, Palestinians' movement is impeded by security arrangements in which every Palestinian is a suspect. More aggressive festivities include the mass nationalist parades that pass through the Palestinian neighbourhood, such as those which take place during the so-called 'Jerusalem Day' – an Israeli national holiday that celebrates the 'unification' of the city.

Meanwhile, on a daily basis, Palestinian inhabitants and visitors to the holy places encounter rampant graffiti sprayed on the walls of houses and passageways, which include such offensive slogans as 'Jesus, son of Mary the whore'; 'Muhammad is a pig'; 'Get out of here'; and 'The people of Israel live, death to Arabs'. Such acts are attributed to fringe groups, but, in fact, like the frontier rabble, they further the state's goals. Palestinians' protests are met with brutal suppression, which includes, among other means, the use of skunk water, the horrible smell of which stays for days or longer. This stifling atmosphere is accentuated by the omnipresence of heavily armed police and surveillance equipment.

While east Jerusalem is an occupied place and its residents are not Israeli citizens, Jaffa's Palestinians are. The realities in Jaffa are both complex and revealing. Jaffa is one of the places where Palestinians are supposed to have been modernized by the Israeli Jewish liberal elite due to their proximity to Tel-Aviv, the capital of Israeli culture and liberalism, yet the city's depressing reality reveals the oppressive nature of settler-colonialism. After the Nakba, only 3,500 residents out of 70,000 remained. They were concentrated in the neighbourhoods of Al-'Ajami and Jabaliah. During the military rule imposed on these areas until June 1949, looting of property and gross acts of cruelty were widespread. Moreover, within a few years, 45,000 Jewish immigrants were housed not only in refugees' houses but also with Arab families. One of the interviewees in Sa'di-Ibraheem's research stated that 'in my fathers' house a [Jewish] Turkish family was brought in; we had a shared kitchen. When they brought the Jewish family, we said nothing, we did not complain'.[56]

The worst was still to come. Entire neighbourhoods were demolished, and the city lost its municipal status and was annexed to Tel-Aviv. According to a 1956 urban renewal plan for evacuation construction, Palestinians were to be encouraged to leave. To this end, these neighbourhoods were 'frozen'. House repair was prohibited, infrastructure was neglected, the seashore became hazardous because debris from demolished houses was dumped there, and the use of drugs by Palestinian youth was tolerated and often encouraged by official bodies. While the Jewish residents left for new neighbourhoods built for them during the 1970s, the Palestinians remained in the crumbling houses. This depressing and hopeless reality, which Sa'di-Ibraheem calls 'empty time', led to the mass migration of Palestinian residents to Canada and Australia. Jaffa, once a dynamic cosmopolitan city, became like a war-ravaged place. Indeed, several films on war and ghetto life were filmed in Jaffa, including the American movie *Delta Force* (1986). Endeavours by Palestinians to organize themselves and ameliorate their conditions were met with suppressive tactics, including the buying off of activists, bureaucratic control and legalistic manipulation. By the end of the twentieth century, the companies which managed refugees' properties began to sell their houses on the open market. The prices of these 'authentic Mediterranean' buildings, which appeal to the taste of rich Jews, skyrocketed and went beyond the reach of ordinary Palestinian residents, as one activist who lived in the city recalled:

> I never forget, when walking on the promenade and open spaces in Jaffa, that these are built on the ruins of people's houses, many of whom are refugees ... although it is very painful to reach such a state, [but] ... it is time to think about how to keep the memory of Jaffa in a museum or a cultural institution.[57]

In several studies, Daher-Nashif has discussed how the Israeli occupation authority administers the burial of Palestinians who are killed in clashes with Israeli forces. I will refer in this section to her work based on interviews with martyrs' families from Al-Khalil. Through various practices, this management endeavours to achieve two results: first, to frighten bereaved families and to accentuate their pain, and second to erase the martyr from history and the ordinary societal processes and rituals of burial and bereavement. These tactics include, among others, the withholding of bodies in freezers for up to a year; late-night visits to bereaved families by soldiers and intelligence officers who carry out house searches and repeatedly threaten to demolish the family house; the supply of misleading information regarding the timing of a corpse's release; the stipulation that funerals must take place late at night, with few participants (family members) who should not have their cell phones with them; the release of bodies in vile weather to prevent the holding of proper funerals; the release of bodies in frozen and sometimes dismembered forms (with body parts sometimes placed in different bags) to obstruct post-mortem procedures and therefore impede insights into the direct causes of death and organ removal.

While these examples might endow the concept of coloniality of being with meaning and actuality, there is an additional need, I think, to frame Palestinians' experiences within a conceptual edifice and a broad narrative. In concrete terms, there is a need for an elaborate theory of history – along the lines suggested by Hayden White – that would constitute 'a kind of auto-analysis on a general cultural scale' to discern 'what acting morally *in the society of which we are members* [involves]'.[58] The Israelis are probably more in need than the Palestinians of such a theory. However, besides a few voices, I cannot envisage the emergence of a large group of Israelis with the moral courage exhibited by either Jean-Paul Sartre and 'Réseau Jeanson' (the Jeanson network) during the Algerian war of independence or the South African scholars who supported the boycott of their country during the apartheid era. Given current realities, I suspect that the reluctant critique of Zionism that some liberal Israeli scholars espouse, which practically calls for more 'civil colonization', might not be adequate.

Conclusion

The analysis presented so far illustrates that endeavours to decolonize knowledge about Palestine have been underway since the 1960s and have achieved some success since 1979. Meanwhile, colonial theories, upon which the Zionist/Israeli discourse has relied, that arrange human groups hierarchically, impose presentism, narrow the horizons of the scholarly inquiry and radically reduce the options for interpreting reality have lost their hegemonic status. Moreover, scholars researching Palestine have benefited from the growth in anti-colonial scholarship worldwide. This increasing success found expression in two principal ways. First, the research agenda changed, as scholars began to explore topics that have been ignored or sidelined in the past. Studies, including the research discussed in the previous section, that centre on social phenomena relating to the concerns of ordinary Palestinians and use rigorous ethical methodologies, have contributed to the de-alienation of academic research.

Secondly, an exploration of large-scale questions relating to the politics of knowledge and Palestinians' consciousness has ensued. Broadly speaking, this has taken two directions, the first of which is an inquiry relating to the large-scale moral, cultural and epistemological dimension of Palestinian history and the role, claims and obligations entailed in being a member of Palestinian society. The second direction is the research into the destructive impact of the Nakba – as an event – on the fabric of Palestinian society, its culture and physical environment, and the exploration of the Nakba's effects, as an ongoing process, on Palestinians as individuals, as members of families, of communities and of a nation, has also gathered pace. In both cases, history reflects Palestinian (rather than Zionist) actualities and temporalities. The growing volume of decolonized knowledge could open the horizons for a different understanding of the current realities and might give rise to novel insights regarding decolonization. Put differently, colonial theories, temporality, interpretations and research topics have lost their privileged status. Instead, the production of knowledge about Palestine has begun to draw on decolonial theorization, insights and presuppositions; most importantly, this research is conducted on and with rather than simply about the Palestinians.

Notes

1   There is a considerable amount of literature I cannot refer to for practical reasons. I shall only cite relevant works that are essential to the arguments I present.
2   *The Guardian* revealed the existence of collaboration between Israeli surveillance companies, including those working with the Israeli defense ministry, and European ones in manipulating the public opinion in many African and Latin American

companies. This is done to affect the election results. https://www.theguardian.com/world/2023/feb/15/revealed-disinformation-team-jorge-claim-meddling-elections-tal-hanan accessed on16 February 2023
3. Quoted in Said 1988:5.
4. Herzl 1960: 88.
5. Ibid.
6. Cited in Iggulden 2002.
7. Peretz 1991: 88.
8. Quoted in Polkehn 1975: 76.
9. Cited in Young 1958: 31.
10. Schölch 1981: 37–40.
11. Buheiry 1981: 78.
12. Lenin 1999.
13. e.g. Ruppin 1971: 91; Gozansky 1987: 33.
14. Tylor 1989: 124.
15. Epstein 1907.
16. Granott 1952: 277.
17. Cited in Lehn 1974: 91–2.
18. Masalha 2012.
19. George 1979: 98–100.
20. Braverman 2009: 318.
21. Falah 1996; Braverman 2009; Galai, 2017.
22. Cited in Galai 2017: 280.
23. Galai 2017: 283–7.
24. Nelson 2003: 67.
25. Galai 2017: 283.
26. Sa'di 1997.
27. Brenner 1978: 1834.
28. Rabinowitz 1998.
29. Grosfoguel 2007: 213.
30. Ibid.
31. Ibid.: 214.
32. Sa'di 2019.
33. Morris 2004; Pappé 2006.
34. Sa'di 2014: 121.
35. Ibid: 137–8.
36. Makhoul 2020: 15–56.
37. Amit 2014; Sela 2018.
38. Fyler 2012.
39. Avineri 1972: 306.
40. Sa'di 2002: 184–5; Hirsch and Tene 2013; Salaita, 2017.
41. Sa'di, 2015.
42. Sayegh 1965; Jiryis 1976; Hadawi 1967; Abu-Lughod 1971; Rodinson 1973; Abu Lughod and Abu-Laban 1974; El-Asmar 1975; Asad 1975; Davis and Mezvinsky 1975.
43. Kimmerling 1980: 77.
44. e.g. Shafir 1996.
45. Fully: Mazrui 1983; Quigley 1991; Agbaria 2018. Partially: Yiftachel 2005, 2009.
46. B'Tselem Nov. 2021; Human Rights Watch Jan. 2022; Amnesty International 1 Feb. 2022.

47 E.g. Tamari 1981.
48 E.g. Gordon 2008.
49 e.g. Tawil-Souri 2011; Griffiths and Repo 2018.
50 Sa'di 2021.
51 Zureik 2016.
52 Morris-Reich 2006.
53 Quoted in Degani 2016.
54 E.g. Sayegh 1965; Abu-Lughod and Abu-Laban 1974.
55 Maldonado-Torres 2007: 255.
56 Sa'di-Ibraheem 2020: 348.
57 Quoted in Sa'di-Ibraheem 2020: 356.
58 Quoted in Anderson 2020: 370.

References

Abu-Lughod, I., ed. (1971), *The Transformation of Palestine: Essays on the Origin and Development of the Arab–Israeli Conflict*, Evanston: Northwestern University Press.

Abu-Lughod, I. and B. Abu-Laban, eds (1974), *Settler Regimes in Africa and the Arab World: The Illusion of Endurance*, Wilmette, IL: Medina University Press International.

Abu-Lughod, J. (1971), 'The Demographic Transformation of Palestine', in I. Abu-Lughod (ed.), *The Transformation of Palestine: Essays on the Origin and Development of the Arab–Israeli Conflict*, 139–63, Evanston: Northwestern University Press.

Abu-Lughod, L. (2020), 'Imagining Palestine's Alter-natives: Settler Colonialism and Museum Politics', *Critical Inquiry* 47(1): 1–27.

Agbaria, A. (2018), 'Israeli Education and the Apartheid in South Africa: Ongoing Insights', *Intercultural Education* 29(2): 218–35.

Alatas, S. H. (2002), 'The Development of an Autonomous Social Science Tradition in Asia: Problems and Prospects', *Asian Journal of Social Science* 30(1): 150–7.

Amit, G. (2014), *Ex-Libris: Chronicles of Theft, Preservation, and Appropriating at the Jewish National Library in Jerusalem*, Tel-Aviv: Hakibbutz Hameuchad.

Amnesty International (2022), 'Israel's Apartheid Against Palestinians: Cruel System of Domination and Crime Against Humanity', *Amnesty International* 1 February. Available online: https://www.amnesty.org/en/documents/mde15/5141/2022/en/ (accessed 9 February 2022).

Anderson, W. (2020), 'Decolonizing Histories in Theory and Practice: An Introduction', *History and Theory* 59(3): 369–75.

Asad, T. (1975), 'Anthropological Texts and Ideological Problems: an Analysis of Cohen on Arab Villages in Israel', *Economy and Society*. 4(3): 251–82.

Avineri, S. (1972), 'Modernization and Arab Society: Some Reflections', in I. Howe and C. Gershman (eds), *Israel, the Arabs, and the Middle East*, 300–11, New York: Quadrangle Books.

Barakat, R. (2018), 'Writing/Righting Palestine Studies: Settler Colonialism, Indigenous Sovereignty and Resisting the Ghost(s) of History', *Settler Colonial Studies* 8(3): 349–63.

Blaut, J. M. (1993), *The Colonizer's Model of the World: Geographical Diffusionism and Eurocentric History*, New York: Guildford Press.

Braverman, I. (2009), 'Planting the Promised Landscape: Zionism, Nature, and Resistance in Israel/Palestine', *Natural Resources Journal* 49(2): 317–61.

Brenner, Y. H. (1978), *Writings*, vol. 2, Sifriate Poalim and Hakibbutz Hamiohad Press. (In Hebrew.)
B'Tselem (2021), 'A Regime of Jewish Supremacy from the Jordan River to the Mediterranean Sea: This is Apartheid'. Available online: https://www.btselem.org/publications/fulltext/202101_this_is_apartheid (accessed 25 February 2022).
Buheiry, M. (1981), 'The Agricultural Exports of Southern Palestine, 1885–1914', *Journal of Palestine Studies*, 10(4): 61–81.
Chatterjee, P. (1993), *The Nation and its Fragments: Colonial and Postcolonial Histories*, Princeton: Princeton University Press.
Daher-Nashif, S. (2021), 'Colonial Management of Death: To be or not to be Dead in Palestine', *Current Sociology* 69(7): 945–62.
Davis, U., and N. Mezvinsky, eds (1975), *Documents from Israel, 1967–1973: Readings for a Critique of Zionism*, London: Ithaca Press.
Davis, U. (1987), *Israel: an Apartheid State*, London: Zed Books.
Degani, A. (2016), 'Israel Is a Settler Colonial State – and That's OK', *Haaretz* 13 September. Available online: https://www.haaretz.com/opinion/.premium-israel-is-a-settler-colonial-state-and-that-s-ok-1.5433405 (accessed 11 February 2022).
Dershowitz, A. (2003), *The Case for Israel*, Hoboken, N.J.: John Wiley & Sons.
El-Asmar, F. (1975), *To be an Arab in Israel*, Beirut: Institute for Palestine Studies.
Epstein, Y. (1907), 'A Hidden Question', *Hasheloah* (July–December): 193–206. (In Hebrew.)
Falah, G. (1996), 'The 1948 Israeli–Palestinian War and its Aftermath: The Transformation and De-signification of Palestine's Cultural Landscape', *Annals of the Association of American Geographers* 86(2): 256–85.
Fanon, F. (1961), *The Wretched of the Earth*, Harmondsworth: Penguin.
Feuerlicht, R. S. (1983), *The Fate of the Jews: A People Torn Between Israeli Power and Jewish Ethics*, London: Quartet Books.
Finkelstein, N. (1995), *Image and Reality of Israel–Palestine Conflict*, London: Verso.
Foucault, M. (2009), *Security, Territory, Population*, eds M. Senellart, F. Ewald and A. Fontana, London: Palgrave Macmillan.
Fyler, B. (2012), 'Netanyahu: Shamir's Statements about the Arabs and the Sea are Accurate', *Ynet*, 1 July. Available online: https://www.ynet.co.il/articles/0,7340,L-4249494,00.html (accessed 21 February 2022).
Galai, Y. (2017), 'Narratives of Redemption: the International Meaning of Afforestation in the Israeli Negev', *International Political Sociology* 11(3): 273–91.
George, Alan (1979). '"Making the Desert Bloom": A Myth Examined', *Journal of Palestine Studies* 8(2): 88–100.
Gordon, N. (2008), *Israel's Occupation*, University of California Press.
Gottheil, F. (1973), 'Arab Immigration into Pre-state Israel: 1922–1931', *Middle Eastern Studies* 9(3): 315–24.
Gozansky, T. (1987), *Formation of Capitalism in Palestine*, Haifa: Al-Ittihad. (In Arabic.)
Granott, A. (1952), *The Land System in Palestine: History and Structure*, London: Eyre & Spottiswoode.
Griffiths, M., and J. Repo (2018), 'Biopolitics and Checkpoint 300 in Occupied Palestine: Bodies, Affect, Discipline', *Political Geography* 65: 17–25.
Grosfoguel, R. (2007), 'The Epistemic Decolonial Turn: Beyond Political–Economy Paradigms', *Cultural Studies* 21(2–3): 211–23.
Hadawi, S. (1967), *Bitter Harvest; Palestine Between 1914–1967*, New York: New World Press.

Hadawi, Sami (1988), *Palestinian Rights and Losses in 1948*, London: Saqi Books.
Herzl, T. (1960), *The Complete Diaries of Theodor Herzl*, R. Patai (ed.), New York: Herzl Press & Thomas Yosefloff.
Hirsch, D. and O. Tene (2013), 'Hummus: the Making of an Israeli Culinary Cult', *Journal of Consumer Culture* 13(1): 25–45.
Human Rights Watch (2022), 'Submission by Human Rights Watch to the United Nations Human Rights Committee in Advance of its Review of Israel', *Human Rights Watch*, January. Available online: https://www.hrw.org/news/2022/02/03/submission-human-rights-watch-united-nations-human-rights-committee-advance-its (accessed 9 February 2022).
Iggulden, A. (2002), 'The Churchill You Didn't Know', *The Guardian*, 28 November. Available online: https://www.theguardian.com/theguardian/2002/nov/28/features11.g21 (accessed 15 January 2022).
Jiryis, S. (1976), *The Arabs in Israel*, New York: Monthly Review Press.
Kimmerling, B. (1980), 'The Palestinians from Two Research Perspectives', *State, Government, and International Relations*, 16: 74–7.
Lehn, W. (1974), 'The Jewish National Fund', *Journal of Palestine Studies*, 3(4): 74–96.
Lenin, V. (1999), *Imperialism: The Highest Stage of Capitalism*, Broadway, Australia: Resistance Books.
Lorde, A. (2018), *The Master's Tools Will Never Dismantle the Master's House*, London: Penguin UK.
Maggio, J. (2007), '"Can the Subaltern be Heard?": Political Theory, Translation, Representation, and Gayatri Chakravorty Spivak', *Alternatives* 32(4): 419–43.
Makhoul, M. (2020), *Palestinian Citizens in Israel: A History Through Fiction, 1948–2010*, Edinburgh: Edinburgh University Press.
Maldonado-Torres, N. (2007), 'On the Coloniality of Being: Contributions to the Development of a Concept', *Cultural Studies* 21(2–3): 240–70.
Mandel, N. (1976), *The Arabs and Zionism before World War I*, Berkeley, CA.: University of California Press, 1976.
Masalha, N. (2012), *Expulsion of the Palestinians: the Concept of 'Transfer' in Zionist Political Thought*, Washington, DC: Institute for Palestine Studies.
Mazrui, A. (1983), 'Zionism and Apartheid: Strange Bedfellows or Natural Allies?', *Alternatives* 9(1): 73–97.
McCarthy, J. (1990), *The Population of Palestine*, New York: Columbia University Press.
Morris, B. (2004), *The Birth of the Palestinian Refugee Problem Revisited*, Cambridge: Cambridge University Press.
Morris-Reich, A. (2006), 'Arthur Ruppin's Concept of Race', *Israel Studies* 11(3): 1–30.
Nelson, R. (2003), 'Environmental Colonialism: "Saving" Africa from Africans', *The Independent Review* 8(1): 65–86.
Pappé, I. (2006), *The Ethnic Cleansing of Palestine*, Oxford: Oneworld.
Peretz, D. (1991), 'Early State Policy towards the Arab Population, 1948–1955' in *New Perspectives on Israeli History*, 72–102, New York: New York University Press.
Peters, J. (1984), *From Time Immemorial: The Origins of the Arab–Jewish Conflict over Palestine*, New York: Harper & Row.
Polkehn, K. (1975), 'Zionism and Kaiser Wilhelm', *Journal of Palestine Studies* 4(2): 76–90.
Quigley, J. (1991), 'Apartheid Outside Africa: The Case of Israel', *Indiana International and Comparative Law Review* 2: 221–51.
Rabinowitz, D. (1998), *Anthropology and the Palestinians*, Beit-Berl: Institute for Israeli Arab Studies. (In Hebrew.)

Rodinson, M. (1973), *Israel: A Settler-Colonial State*, New York: Anchor Foundation.
Ro'i, Y. (1968), 'The Zionist Attitude to the Arabs 1908–1914', *Middle Eastern Studies* 4(3): 198–242.
Ruppin, A. (1971), *Memoirs, Diaries, Letters*, ed. A. Bein, Jerusalem: Weidenfeld & Nicolson.
Sa'di, A. H. (1997), 'Modernization as an Explanatory Discourse of Zionist–Palestinian Relations', *British Journal of Middle Eastern Studies* 24(1): 25–48.
Sa'di, A. H. (2002), 'Catastrophe, Memory and Identity: Al-Nakbah as a Component of Palestinian Identity', *Israel Studies* 7(2): 175–98.
Sa'di, A. H. (2004), 'Trends in Israeli Social Science Research on the National Identity of the Palestinian Citizens of Israel', *Asian Journal of Social Sciences* 32(1): 140–60.
Sa'di, A. H. (2014), *Thorough Surveillance: The Genesis of Israeli Policies of Population Management, Surveillance and Political Control Towards the Palestinians*, Manchester: Manchester University Press.
Sa'di, A. H. (2015), 'Representations of Exile and Return in Palestinian Literature', *Journal of Arabic Literature* 46(2–3): 216–43.
Sa'di, A. H. (2019), 'The Nation-State of the Jewish People's Basic Law', *Journal of Holy Land and Palestine Studies* 18(2): 163–77.
Sa'di, A. H. (2021), 'Israel's Settler-Colonialism as a Global Security Paradigm', *Race & Class* 63(2): 21–37.
Sa'di-Ibraheem, Y. (2020), 'Jaffa's Times: Temporalities of Dispossession and the Advent of Natives' Reclaimed Time', *Time & Society* 29(2): 340–61.
Said, E. (1978), *Orientalism*, New York: Pantheon Books.
Said, E. (1979), *The Question of Palestine*, New York: Times Books.
Said, E. (1988), 'Conspiracy of Praise', in E. Said and C. Hitchens (eds), *Blaming the Victims: Spurious Scholarship and the Palestinian Question*, 23–31, London: Verso.
Salaita, S. (2017), '"Israeli" Hummus is Theft, not Appropriation', *The New Arab*, 4 September. Available online: https://english.alaraby.co.uk/english/comment/2017/9/4/israeli-hummus-is-theft-not-appropriation (accessed 9 February 2022).
Sayegh, F. (1965), *Zionist Colonialism in Palestine*, Beirut: Research Center, Palestine Liberation Organization.
Sayigh, R. (1979), *Palestinians: From Peasants to Revolutionaries*, London: Zed Books.
Schölch, A. (1981), 'The Economic Development of Palestine, 1856–1882', *Journal of Palestine Studies* 10(3): 35–58.
Schölch, A. (1985), 'The Demographic Development of Palestine, 1850–1882', *International Journal of Middle East Studies* 17(4): 485–505.
Sela, R. (2018), 'The Genealogy of Colonial Plunder and Erasure – Israel's Control over Palestinian Archives', *Social Semiotics* 28(2): 201–29.
Shafir, G. (1996), *Land, Labor and the Origins of the Israeli–Palestinian Conflict, 1882–1914*, Berkeley, CA.: University of California Press.
Shalhoub-Kevorkian, N. (2017), 'The Occupation of the Senses: The Prosthetic and Aesthetic of State Terror', *British Journal of Criminology* 57(6): 1279–1300.
Smooha, S. (1997), 'Ethnic Democracy: Israel as an Archetype', *Israel Studies* 2(2): 198–241.
Spivak, G. (1992), '"Can the Subaltern Speak?"' in P. Williams and L. Chrisman (eds), *Colonial Discourse and Post-colonial Theory*, 66–111, New York: Columbia University Press.
Tamari, S. (1981), 'Building Other People's Homes: the Palestinian Peasant's Household and Work in Israel', *Journal of Palestine Studies* 11(1): 31–66.

Tawil-Souri, H. (2011), 'Qalandia Checkpoint as Space and Nonplace', *Space and Culture*, 14(1): 4–26.
Tyler, W. (1989), 'The Beisan Lands Issue in Mandatory Palestine', *Middle Eastern Studies* 25(2): 123–62.
Veracini, L. (2010), *Settler Colonialism*, Houndmills, UK: Palgrave Macmillan.
Warriner, D. (1948), *Land and Poverty in the Middle East*, London: Royal Institute for International Affairs.
Wisner, B., and K. Mathewson (2005), 'Critical Assessments of James M. Blaut's Life and Work', *Antipode* Special Issue 37(5): 901–1050.
Wolfe, P. (2006), 'Settler Colonialism and the Elimination of the Native', *Journal of Genocide Research* 8(4): 387–409.
Yiftachel, O. (2005), 'Neither Two States nor One: The Disengagement and "Creeping Apartheid" in Israel/Palestine', *The Arab World Geographer* 8(3): 125–9.
Yiftachel, O. (2009), '"Creeping Apartheid" in Israel-Palestine', *Middle East Report* 39(253): 7–15.
Young, M. E. (1958), 'Indian Removal and Land Allotment: The Civilized Tribes and Jacksonian Justice', *American Historical Review* 64(1): 31–45.
Zureik, E (1979), *The Palestinians in Israel: A Study in Internal Colonialism*, London: Routledge & Kegan Paul.
Zureik, E. (2016), *Israel's Colonial Project in Palestine: Brutal Pursuit*, London and New York: Routledge.
Zureik, E., D. Lyon, and Y. Abu-Laban, eds (2010), *Surveillance and Control in Israel/Palestine: Population Territory and Power*, London: Routledge.

2

Indigenous versus Colonial-Settler Toponymy and the Struggle over the Cultural and Political Geography of Palestine

The Appropriation of Palestinian Place Names by the Israeli State

Nur Masalha

Place names and social and cultural memory

Cartography and toponymy – the term derives from the Greek words *topos* ('place') and *onoma* ('name') – were central to European empire building in the nineteenth century.[1] Place names (including human settlements such as villages, towns, cities, streets and countries and natural places such as mountains, hills, valleys, rivers, springs and *wadis*) are meant 'to provide clues as to the historical and cultural heritage of places and regions'.[2] Yet in reality place names are not just spatial references; they are rooted in power relations and struggles over land and resources and the identities of the people that inhabit these places.[3] Struggles over land, place names, naming and renaming between indigenous peoples and settler-colonists are common. Examples include Rhodesia/Zimbabwe, the Falkland Islands/Islas Malvinas, Constantinople/Istanbul, Northern Ireland/Ulster (the Six Counties); apartheid South Africa, Aotearoa/New Zealand and Palestine/Israel.[4]

In modern times the drive to rename geographical sites is also about staking claims to a territory. This focus on place names in the context of modern *nationalism* shows how hegemonic political elites and state authorities use the toponymic process as a way of constructing a new collective memory and 'inventing traditions'[5] and as a tactic of land grab as well as an ideological reversion to a supposedly ancient or mythical 'golden age'. State authorities deploy *renaming strategies* to erase earlier political, social and cultural realities and to construct new notions of national identity.[6] Often Israeli renaming projects, and official renaming committees, have been studied within the context of reinforcing Zionist nationalist ideologies.

This chapter, however, goes beyond the inadequacies of the traditional debate about *nationalism* to examine critically the Israeli transformation of the cultural geography of Palestine and its historic place names within the context of the emerging field of *Settler-Colonial Studies*. The work also makes a distinction between settler-colonialism as a *concept* and the *strategies, modalities* and *set of practices* of Zionist settler-colonization in Palestine which may vary (slightly or substantially) from other forms of modern setter-colonialism in Africa, Australia and the Americas.

Modern Zionism and the medieval Crusaders: the legendary toponymy of the Latin Crusaders

Israeli renaming committees followed the methods of Christian scriptural geographers and biblical archaeologists of the nineteenth century such as Victor Guérin and Edward Robinson, who were inspired by the social memory of the Latin medieval Crusader colonial-settlers and pilgrims in Palestine – colonial-settlers famously discussed in Halbwachs 1941 – 'discovered', produced and reproduced particular place names from the myth narratives of the Old Testament, Talmud and Mishna.

The invention of a usable past: modern Zionism and retrospective colonization of ancient Palestine

Palestinian place names attracted the attention of fundamentalist Christians and European imperialists in the nineteenth century. Toponymic projects and geographical renaming of place names in Palestine became powerful tools in the hands of the European colonial powers which competed to penetrate Palestine, the 'land of the Bible'. Yet in modern Palestine the Bible and biblical claims also became central to the 'redeeming' ideas of settler-colonialism and indigenous cultural elimination.[7]

The Israeli place-renaming projects had their roots in the British colonial biblical explorations in the 1870s by members of the Palestine Exploration Fund which combined biblical 'restorationist' thinking and missionary activities with the official British civil service and was typical of Western colonial and imperial toponymic schemes in nineteenth- and early twentieth-century Palestine.

European secular Zionism was a classic case of the invention of a people in late nineteenth-century Europe and a synthesizing of a nation project. This invented tradition of the nineteenth century reinvented the European Jews as a 'race' and a biological group, and borrowed heavily from romantic and racializing nationalisms in Central and Eastern Europe. Political Zionism mobilized an imagined biblical narrative and scriptural geography which were reworked in the late nineteenth century for the political purposes of a modern European movement intent on colonizing the land of Palestine.

Inevitably place names in Palestine became a site of fierce contest between the European Zionist settler-colonizer and the colonized Palestinians. Palestinian Arab names were (and continued to be) 'unnamed' and Hebraicized by the Zionists using a colonizing strategy based on Hebrew names. Indigenous Palestinian place names were deemed 'redeemed' and liberated when they were rendered from Arabic into Hebrew.[8] The genealogy of British colonial name commissions and the Zionist-Hebrew renaming project, which began in the nineteenth century, continued under the British colonial system in Palestine[9] and were accelerated dramatically after the Nakba with the expansion of biblical archaeology, scriptural geography and 'Land of Israel' departments at Israeli universities. The reinvention of both usable Jewish past and modern Jewish nationhood in Zionist historiography, 'nationalist' archaeological practice and the creation of a modern Hebrew consciousness have received extensive scholarly attention.[10] Remapping and renaming projects were also deployed extensively and destructively by the European colonial powers and European settler-colonial movements.

Despite the fall of biblical archaeology in the West[11] biblical archaeology and scriptural geography are still central to the educational system of Israel. Commenting on Israeli educational policies and the erasure of Palestinian history and cultural geography, Professor Ismael Abu-Saad, of Ben-Gurion University, writes:

> The education system is essential to making the displacement of indigenous history and presence 'official', through texts such as that quoted from the 6th grade geography curriculum in Israeli schools, which teaches Palestinian children that the history of the coastal plain began only a hundred years ago, with the advent of European Jewish settlement and their transformation of this previously 'abandoned area'. In the text, modern (Jewish) Tel Aviv overrides any mention of Arab Jaffa; modern (Jewish) Ashdod of (Arab) Isdud; modern (Jewish) Ashkelon of (Arab) Al-Majdal. Modern Jewish Rishon Litzion ('First in Zion') and Herzliya and numerous other new towns are superimposed upon an unacknowledged landscape of Palestinian villages emptied and demolished in 1948. The indigenous landscape is erased from the curriculum, while it is simultaneously being erased *by* the curriculum, because of its absence from the official historical and geographical materials being taught about the region.[12]

Today it is widely recognized that the Old Testament narratives are literary imagination and fiction, theology and officially sanctioned religious memory – not history or evidence-based historical facts.[13] Yet in Palestine the top-down Zionist-Hebrew renaming projects became central to the ethnicization of the European Jews and nationalization of the fictional narrative of the Old Testament.[14] They were inspired by and followed closely British, French and American archaeological and geographical 'exploration' expeditions of the second half of the nineteenth century and first half of the twentieth century. In line with the reinventions of European ethno-romantic nationalisms, Zionist ideological archaeology and geography claimed to 'own' an exclusive 'national' inheritance in Palestine; the 'land of Israel' was invented and treated as a matter of exclusive ownership. This process of ethno-nationalization and reinvention of the past intensified after the establishment of the Israeli state in 1948 as part of the general attempt to nationalize both the European Jews and the Old Testament and construct a Zionist modern Jewish identity.[15] The creation of settler-colonial 'facts on the ground' together with usable past and the instrumentalization of cultural heritage are central to all modern settler-colonial projects but they were fundamental to the Zionist colonial project in Palestine.

The appropriation of indigenous Palestinian place names and the cultural heritage of Palestine as a tool for Zionist settler purposes were (and still are) central to Israeli educational policies and the activities of Israel's biblical academy and the official Israeli government's renaming projects. The cultural biases of politicized Israeli biblical archaeology and biblical academy[16] and the creation and selective reconstruction of a 'usable past' are widely known.[17] This officially-sponsored biblical political enterprise by the Israeli educational system, Israeli universities' departments of archaeology and the Israeli biblical academy have been examined by several Israeli academics and authors.[18] A large number of 'Israeli experts' on biblical excavations – who served on the Government Names Committee (*Ya'adat ha-Shemot ha-Memshaltiyot*) – are practitioners of retrospectively colonizing biblical archaeology, the 'privilege' of Israeli science *par excellence*.[19]

Since the rise of the Zionist settler movement in the late nineteenth century, and especially since the establishment of Israel in 1948, the struggle over toponymic memory and the renaming of sites has developed as an integral part of the political conflict in Palestine. The indigenous Palestinians have insisted on their own comprehensive set of Arabic place names through which they see their own social memory and deep roots in the land of Palestine. On the other hand, since the ethnic cleansing of the 1948 Nakba and the creation of the Israeli state, a large number of Palestinian Arabic place names have been Judaized, Hebraicized. Indeed since 1948 the Israeli army and Israeli state have sought to rename systematically Palestinian Arabic place names, claiming priority in chronology and using modern archaeology, map-making, and place names as their proofs of Jewish roots in 'the land of Israel'.

Masculinization, Hebraicization and the myth of restoration

Although eastern European Jewish settlers claimed to represent an indigenous people returning to its homeland after two thousand years of absence, in fact Russian nationals formed the hard core of Zionist activism. This self-re-indigenization and copying from the Arabic language and Palestinian Arab toponyms required a great deal of effort to create the mythological 'New Hebrew Man' (the masculinized 'Sabra Man') and construct a new Jewish identity. No wonder, for the early Zionist settlers were intent not only on 'inventing a Land, and inventing a Nation',[20] but also on inventing a new language and self-reinvention. Reinventing their own new, masculine Hebrew-imagined biblical identity, the post-1948 period saw top Zionist leaders, army commanders, biblical archaeologists and authors changing their names from Russian, Polish and German to 'authentic' Hebrew-sounding (biblically-sounding) names. For early Zionist leaders, to build a state in Palestine required the invention of founding national myths and something altogether different – a new secular Hebrew language. Many early Zionists called themselves 'New Hebrews'. The founding fathers of modern Zionism and modern Hebrew were responsible for the construction of foundational myths:

- new Zionist collective memory;
- the myth of Hebrew restoration;
- masculine Hebrew identity and masculinization of settler place names;[21]
- the myth that modern Hebrew is a purely Semitic language;

In fact, modern Hebrew was a new hybrid, a new Semitic-European hybrid language.

Central to the invention and construction of new Zionist collective memory – and subsequently Israeli identity – based on invented 'biblical memory' and the de-signification and de-Arabization of historic Palestinian cultural geography[22] was the Zionist Yishuv's memorializing toponymy project which was established in the 1920s to 'restore' imagined biblical names or to create new biblical-sounding names.[23] In the 1920s the Palestinian land of 'Wadi al-Hawarith'[24] in the coastal region was purchased ('redeemed') by the Jewish National Fund set up in 1901 by the Zionist leadership to settle and colonize the land of Palestine – from Arab absentee landlords, subsequently leading to the eviction of many Arab farmers. The Jewish settlement of Kfar Haro'e was established in 1934 on these lands. The displacements and replacement of the Arabic names followed this pattern: Arabic name was rendered into the Hebrew-sounding 'Emek Hefer' (the Hefer Valley). In some cases the Zionist-Hebrew colonizing toponymy simply translated Arabic names into Hebrew.

In 1925 the Naming Committee of the Jewish National Fund was set up to name the newly established Jewish colonies in Palestine to compete with the overwhelmingly Arabic map of Palestine; its renaming efforts were appreciated by the British Mandatory authorities and were incorporated into the Palestine government's official gazette.[25] The Israeli Governmental Names Committee of the 1950s,[26] which was the continuation of the JNF Naming Committee of the Mandatory period, was generally guided by the biblical geography of Victor Guérin (1868–80; 1881–83) and Edward Robinson (1841), in which he had argued that the place names of Palestinian villages and sites, seemingly Arab, were modern Arabic renderings of old Hebraic names. An important part of the 'New Hebrew' identity was the Zionist-Hebrew toponymy and the Israeli maps which gradually replaced the Palestinian Arabic names.[27]

The top-down approach and the role of the Israeli army

Indigenous and historic Palestinian place names began to be replaced by biblical and Hebrew-sounding names during the late Ottoman period and Mandatory period and small Palestinian villages began to disappear from the map, although local Palestinians continued to use the indigenous names for the new Zionist colonies. These practices of 're-claiming by re-naming', while displacing the indigenous names, were pivotal to the colonization of the land of Palestine and as a language for creating an 'authentic' collective Zionist-Hebrew identity rooted in the 'land of the Bible'. Referring candidly to the gradual replacement of Arabic place names (and of Palestinian villages) by Hebrew place names (and Jewish settlements) during the Mandatory period, Israeli Defence Minister Moshe Dayan – author of *Living with the Bible* (1978) – had this to say in an address in April 1969 to students at the Technion, Israel's prestigious Institute of Technology in Haifa:

> Jewish villages were built in the place of Arab villages. You do not even know the names of these villages, and I do not blame you because geography books no longer exist. Not only do the books not exist, the Arab villages are not there either. Nahlal arose in the place of Mahlul; Kibbutz Gvat in the place of Jibta; Kibbutz Sarid in the place of Hunefis, and Kefar Yehoshua in the place of Tal al-Shumam. There is not a single place built in this country that didn't have a former Arab population.[28]

The most influential Israeli biblical archaeologist was the second Chief of Staff of the Israeli army, General Yigael Sukenik (1917–84), who Hebraicized his name to Yigael Yadin. In the post-1948 period, the Israeli army set up a Hebrew Names Committee within the army to propose new Hebrew names to replace the European and Russian names of serving officers and soldiers in the army. The third Chief of Staff, General Moshe Dayan (1915–81), presented himself as an amateur biblical archaeologist.[29] Later Defence Minister, Dayan was considered by his fellow European settlers as a typical Ashkenazi (European) *sabra*. He was born in Kibbutz Degania Alef in Palestine before his parents moved to Nahlal, founded in 1921. His father, 'Shmuel Kitaigorodsky' (who served in the first three sessions of the Israeli Knesset), was born in Zhashkov, modern day Ukraine, and migrated to Palestine in 1908 and Hebraicized his name to Dayan, Hebrew for a judge in Jewish religious courts. According to Zionist propaganda 'Nahlal' derived its name from a biblical-sounding village (Joshua 19:15). Yet Moshe Dayan knew and was prepared to acknowledge publicly that the name of his own settlement (*moshav*), 'Nahlal', was in fact a Hebrew rendering of the name of the Palestinian Arabic village name it had replaced, 'Mahlul'; however, to give it a 'biblical authenticity', the Hebrew-sounding 'Nahlal' was linked by the Zionists to a name mentioned in the Old Testament. Also, the 'Gvat' Kibbutz, set up in 1926, was a Hebrew rendering of the Arabic place name it had replaced: the Palestinian village 'Jibta', but Gvat also echoed the Aramaic name Gvata (meaning hill) and a biblical-sounding name.

In Israel the significance of place names lies in their potential to legitimize 'historical claims' asserted by the Zionist settler-colonial movement. Justifying the Judaization and Hebraicization of the Palestinian landscapes and place names as a state-promoted national project and describing the setting up and mode of operation in the 1950s of the Governmental Names Committee, Zionist authors argued that formation of the Hebrew map of Israel following the foundation of the State of Israel was an institutionalized measure of cultural engineering and a procedure of Zionist nation-building aimed at restoring the Hebrew toponymy of the land. The Hebraicization of the landscape was the geographical aspect of Hebrew revival, which predominated Zionist ideology and imagination and Zionist nation-building. The Hebrew names affixed to landscape features replaced – at least for Israeli Hebrew speakers – Arabic names rendered foreign from a Ashkenazi (European) Zionist perspective.[30] In reality, the new Hebrew names were not introduced side by side with the indigenous Arab names since colonial motives underlay the work of the Israeli Government Naming Committee: a conscious and illegitimate effort to obliterate Palestinian Arab rights and the reality a continuous and uninterrupted Palestinian presence on the land for many centuries.

Neolithic agricultural culture is considered to have begun in Palestine, in Jericho, about 10,000–8,800 BC. It is widely recognized by historians and archaeologists that Palestine had a remarkably stable population from the end of the Neolithic period, some 6,000 years ago, when the Mediterranean economy was first established in the region.[31] Long before the creation of the State of Israel in 1948, Palestine had a diverse and multicultural population and a multi-layered identity deeply rooted in the ancient past. In the 1980s critical biblical scholars Thomas Thompson, Francolino Goncalvez and Jean-Marie van Cangh (1988) completed a pilot toponymic project with two regions in the Holy Land: the Plain of Akka (Acre) and the Jerusalem Corridor. This tried to bring out the many names of hills, *wadis*, springs and wells, but only those on maps. However, this project was limited in its scope and has not directly worked with the oral tradition. Thomas Thompson (1975, 1979) gives very useful lists of antiquity sites with the corresponding Arabic and Hebrew names.

Furthermore, the *Tübingen Bible Atlas* – based on the Tübingen Atlas of the Near and Middle East (TAVO) – documents the historical geography of the biblical countries in a unique way in 29 high-quality maps and extensive indexes. Although the question of Palestine's Arabo-Islamic heritage in the toponymic memory of the region is one which the *Tübingen Bible Atlas* project never took up directly, many Palestine maps of the TAVO B series as well as the *Tübinger Bibelatlas* and TAVO archives, an important resource with an enormous range of critically evaluated structure and sources. Abu-Sitta (2010) also provides useful maps and indexes on the modern Palestinian Arabic place names of the region.

On the theme of the charting of maps and the production and dissemination of knowledge on the Holy Land in the medieval and ancient periods, North (1979) is an important source, having its basic foundation in the archives of the Vatican library, Rome. In addition, there are some cartographic materials on Palestine in the libraries of Istanbul. There are two kinds of maps:

- Maps such as the Carte Jacotin; The British Mandate map 1:20,000; the Map of Israel 1:10,000 (although many sheets are classified secret by the Israeli military) and 1:50,000 (this entire map (including Sinai) has been declassified).
- Scholarly geographically and historically analytical maps, such as those in the *Atlas of Israel* (1967 and later editions) and other atlas studies such as Abu-Sitta (2010).
- The TÁVO maps, both the A and B series.

Indigenous Palestinian Arabic toponyms and the Arab heritage of Palestine

Palestinian social memory and place names have evolved from the Neolithic Age into the modern period by embracing multiple traditions and preserving the diverse cultural heritage of the land. In a largely peasant society and fertile land, many

Palestinian Arab toponyms were based on food plants (such as variety of beans, lentils), fruit trees (olives, vines) and natural geographical sites (hills, springs, streams, valleys and mountains).

The term 'Palestine' (Greek: Παλαιστίνη; Arabic: Filastin) is the conventional name used between 450 BC and AD 1948 to describe a geographic region between the Mediterranean Sea and the Jordan River and various adjoining lands.[32] Biblical archaeologist and scriptural geographer Edward Robinson (1794–1863), writing in the early 1860s when travel by Europeans to the Levant became widespread, notes that 'Palestine, or Palestinae, [is] now the most common name for the Holy Land'.[33] A cognate of the toponym *Palestine*, 'Peleset', is found in five inscriptions referring to a neighbouring people or land starting from *c*.1150 BC during the twelfth Egyptian dynasty and the Assyrians called the same region 'Palashtu' or 'Pilistu', in *c*. 800 BC.[34] In the Middle Ages the Arabo-Islamic toponym *Filastin* referred to the region from the time of the earliest Arab administrators, geographers and translators who relied on the Greco-Roman-Byzantine name; it first occurred in a classical Greek text, the *Histories* of Herodotus, written near the mid-fifth century BC. Under Byzantine administrative subdivisions in Syria and Palestine produced *Palaestinae Prima*, *Palaestinae Secunda* and eventually *Palaestinae Salutaris* or *Palaestinae Tertia*. The Byzantine administrative/territorial toponym became the source from which the Arabic term *Jund Filastin*, the 'province of Palestine', was consolidated beginning with the Islamic period in the 630s. Arab administrators, historians and geographers preserved the ancient place names of Palestine. In AD 985 the Palestinian geographer Al-Muqaddasi gave a systematic account of all the place names, cities and towns he had visited in Palestine (Al-Mukaddasi 1994). According to another Muslim historian, the ninth-century al-Baladuri (2014), the principal towns of *Filastin* included Gaza, Nablus, Jaffa, Imwas, Rafah, Yibna, Sebastia, Caesarea, Bayt Jibrin and Lydda. The nearby city of Ramle was founded by the Arabs and became the capital of the province. In the ninth century, during the Abbasid rule, *Filastin* was the most fertile of *Al-Sham* (greater Syria). After the Fatimid conquered the province from the Abbasids, al-Quds (Jerusalem) became the capital of the province and the main towns included Asqalan, Gaza, Ramle, Arsuf, Jaffa, Bayt Jibrin, Nablus, Jericho, Caesaria and Amman.[35]

At its greatest extent, the Arab province of Palestine, which was one of many provinces of the Umayyad and Abbasid states, extended from the Mediterranean coast to the Jordan River and from Rafah in North Sinai to parts of lower Galilee in the north. Its predominantly Muslim towns included Gaza, Nablus, Jafa, Lydda, Ramle, Caesarea, 'Imwas (Emmuas), Yibna, Rafah, Sebastia and Bayt Jibrin. The medieval Arabic term was identical to the old French ('Frankish') term, *Philistin*, which came from Latin *Philistina* or *Philistinus*, which, in turn, derived from the Roman name of the province, *Palestinae*, which was based on the name mentioned in the Old Testament and a variety of ancient languages, the Akkadian *Palastu* and Egyptian *Parusata*. However today it is widely accepted that the Palestinians are a mixture of groups (including descendants of ancient Hebrew and Canaanite tribes) who remained in the land and converted to Christianity and Islam and were later joined by some migrants of Arab descent.[36]

The social and cultural importance of toponymic memory and geographical rendering of sites and terms in historical writing is evident in many histories from antiquity, medieval and modern Palestine. Herodotus (1987), writing from the 450s to the 420s BC, listed place-nations of ancient Palestine; he is believed to have visited Palestine in the fifth decade of the fifth century BC and refers to 'Palaistine' (Παλαιστί vη), Syria, or simply 'Palaistine' five times, an area comprising the region between Phoenicia and Egypt.[37] Herodotus also mentions the city of Ascalon (Arabic: 'Asqalan), an ancient seaport city which dates back to the Neolithic Age. At the time of Herodotus Palestine was deeply polytheistic and consequently, in contrast to the myth-narratives of the Old Testament, Herodotus does not mention Jews and monotheism but describes Ascalan as having a temple for Aphrodite and its polytheistic tradition.[38] Herodotus' *Histories* is now considered a founding work of history in Western literature. Also, Greek toponym for *Palestine* and Ascalan were preserved in indigenous Palestinian Arab tradition and by medieval Arab historians and travellers and 'Ascalan' became known to the ancient and medieval Palestinian Arabs as 'Asqalan'. Palestinian Al-Majdal-'Asqalan was completely depopulated between 1948 and 1950[39] and the historic and medieval Arab name, Asqalan, was replaced by the Hebrew-sounding Ashkelon.[40]

Zionist toponmyic methods and key features of Israeli renaming projects: disappearing Palestinian villages

During the pre-state period the European Zionist colonial *Yeshuv* in Palestine developed three key strategies:

- appropriation of Arab names, hybridization of names of Jewish settlements and indigenization of the settlers;
- instrumentalization of the myth-narratives of the Old Testament and 'restorationist' biblical archaeology: Hebrewization and biblicization of Palestinian Arabic toponyms;
- utilization of the toponymic lists of the Palestine Exploration Fund and the works of Western biblical archaeologists.

Until 1948 the Zionists were not in control of the toponymic processes in Palestine. Following the mass ethnic cleaning of the Nakba[41] and the Israeli assumption of full control of nearly eighty per cent of historic Palestine, the cultural politics of naming was accelerated radically. State toponymic projects were now used as tools to ensure the effectiveness of the de-Arabization of Palestine. One of these tools consisted of the official Israeli road signs, which are often in Hebrew, Arabic and English but both the Arabic and the English are *transliterations* of the new Hebrew place names rather than reflecting the original Palestinian Arabic name. Of course, the overwhelming majority of Israelis cannot read Arabic; this is partly to remind the indigenous Palestinians inside Israel of the need to internalize the new Hebrew place names or perhaps seek the express approval of the vanishing Palestinian Arab,[42] making Arabic complicit in the de-Arabization of Palestine.

Key features and methods of Israeli-Zionist renaming patterns and creation of new place name in the post-Nakba period included:

- the role of the Israeli Army: the Hebrew Names Committee of 1949 and Indigenizing of the European settlers;
- State-enforced projects: the Israeli Governmental Names Committee;
- the legendary toponymy of Zionist settlers and the medieval Crusaders;
- toponymicide and the appropriation of Palestinian heritage, silencing the Palestinian past: mimicry, the de-Arabization of Palestinian place-names and assertion of ownership;
- The creation of a 'usable past' to reinforce a hegemonic regime of power/knowledge in Palestine-Israel;[43]
- Judaization strategies and the assertion of ownership: the superimposition of biblical, Talmudic and Mishnaic names;
- fashioning a new European landscape as a site of amnesia and erasure;
- transliteration of new Hebrew place names and road signs into English and Arabic after the 1967 occupation.

The Army's Hebrew Names Committee of 1949 and indigenizing the European settlers

British Jewish historian Sir Lewis Bernstein Namier (1888–1960), who migrated to the UK in 1907, was a long-time Zionist and a close friend and associate of Chaim Weizmann. He also worked as political secretary for the Jewish Agency in Palestine (1929–31). Namier was born 'Ludwik Niemirowski' in what is now part of Poland and his devotion to Zionism did not prevent the Anglicization of his name. While name-changing among British or American Zionist Jews who emigrated from Eastern Europe became part of the process of Anglicization or Americanization, name changing in Palestine among Zionist settlers began during the Mandatory period and became an integral part of the Hebrewization and biblicization of the immigrant settlers.[44] The initiative begun by Yizhak Ben-Tzvi, the second President of Israel, and by a directive written by Ben-Gurion to army officers that it was their moral duty to Hebraicize their names as an example. As a result, the army set up a Hebrew Names Committee to propose Hebrew names to officers and soldiers. A booklet was compiled by Mordechai Nimtsa-Bi (1903–49), the head of the Names Committee. The compilers offered four groups of Hebrew suggested name: family names, names of Taanim[45] and Amoraim,[46] biblical names and Hebrew personal names. A similar list was compiled a few years later by Yaakov Arikha under the title, *behar likha shem mishpaha Ivri*: 'Select for Yourself a Hebrew Family Name'. The booklet, published in Jerusalem in 1954 by the Israeli Academy for the Hebrew Language (which had replaced the Hebrew language Committee of Eliezer Ben-Yehuda) included advice on how to change family names, lists of Hebrew names serving as an example.[47]

Institutionalized renaming and State-sponsored projects: the Israeli Governmental Names Committee

Post-1948 Zionist projects concentrated on the Hebraicization of Palestinian geography and toponymy through the practice of renaming sites, places and events. The Hebraicization project deployed renaming to construct new places and new geographic identities related to supposed biblical places. The 'new Hebrew' names embodied an ideological drive and political attributes that could be consciously mobilized by the Zionist hegemonic project. The official project began with the appointment of the *Governmental Names Committee (Va'adat Hashemot Hamimshaltit)* by Prime Minister Ben-Gurion in July 1949. A year later, in 1950, the *Governmental Names Committee* was given an official state institution and was strategically placed in the Office of the Prime Minister. Prime Minister Ben-Gurion himself had visited the Naqab/Negev in June and had been struck by the fact that no Hebrew names existed for geographical sites in the region. The 11 June 1949 entry for his War Diary reads: 'Eilat ... we drove through the open spaces of the Arava ... from 'Ein Husb ... to 'Ein Wahba ... We must give Hebrew names to these places – ancient names, if there are, and if not, new ones!'[48]

In the immediate post-Nakba period Israeli archaeologists and members of the Israeli Exploration Society on the Government Names Committee concentrated their initial efforts on the creation of a new map for the newly occupied 'Negev'.[49] Commissioned to create Hebrew names for the newly occupied Palestinian landscape, throughout the documents produced by this committee were reported references to 'foreign names'. The Israeli public was called upon 'to uproot the foreign and existing names' and in their place 'to master' the new Hebrew names. Most existing names were Arabic names. Charged with the task of erasing hundreds of Arabic place names and creating Hebrew names in the Naqab, the committee held its first meeting on 18 July and subsequently met three times a month for a ten-month period and assigned Hebrew names to 561 different geographical features in the Naqab (Negev) – mountains, valleys, springs and waterholes – using scriptural geography as a key resource. Despite the obliteration of many ancient Arabic names from the Naqab landscape, some Arabic names became similar-sounding Hebrew names, for example Seil Imran became Nahal Amram, apparently recalling the father of Moses and Aaron; the Arabic Jabal Haruf (Mount Haruf) became Har Harif (Sharp Mountain), Jabal Dibba (Hump Hill) became Har Dla'at (Mount Pumpkin). After rejecting the name Har Geshur after the people to whom King David's third wife belonged, as a Hebrew appellation for the Arabic Jabal Ideid (Sprawling Mountain), the committee decided to call it Har Karkom (Mount Crocus), because crocuses grow in the Naqab.[50] However the sound of the Arabic name Ideid was retained for the nearby springs, which are now called Beerot Oded (the Wells of Oded), supposedly after the biblical prophet of the same name.[51] In its report of March 1956 the Israeli Government Names Committee stated:

> In the summarised period 145 names were adopted for antiquities sites, ruins and tells: eight names were determined on the basis of historical identification, 16 according to geographical names in the area, eight according to the meaning of the Arabic words, and the decisive majority of the names (113) were determined by mimicking the sounds of the Arabic words, a partial or complete mimicking, in order to give the new name a Hebrew character, following the [accepted] grammatical and voweling rules.⁵²

According to Hanna Bitan, the coordinator of the Governmental Names Commission, altogether 7,000 new Hebrew names were officially determined between the 1950s and 1992, incuding some 5,000 geographical locations, several hundred historical names and over 1,000 names of Jewish settlements (Bitan 1992: 369; 1998). New Hebrew place names have been added since then and the total figure since 1948 may be as many as 9,000 new place names, including the names of some 900 new Jewish settlements established between 1948 and 1998 often on lands belonging to the Palestinian refugees of 1948.

Palestinian scholar Basem Ra'ad shows the Israeli toponymy committees went far beyond their original mandates:

> There was simply not enough [biblical] tradition to go by, so [the project] could only continue by picking out Biblical or Jewish associations at random. It had to Hebrewise Arabic names, or in other cases translate Arabic to Hebrew to give the location an ideologically consistent identity. For example, some locations were rendered from Arabic into the Hebrew phonetic system: Minet el-Muserifa became Horvat Mishrafot Yam and Khirbet el Musherifa was changed to Horvat Masref. Sometimes, in this artificial process, the committees forgot about certain genuine Jewish traditions, as in the case of the total cancelling of the Arabic name Khirbet Hanuta, not recognizing that it probably rendered the Talmudic Khanotah. This forced exercise of re-naming often even went against Biblical tradition, most notably in erasing the Arabic names Yalu and 'Imwas [after 1967]. Yalo became Ayallon, while 'Imwas, Western Emmaus, associated with the Christ story, was one of the three villages, along with Beit Nuba, razed in 1967. The old stones from the villages were sold to Jewish contractors to lend local tradition and age to new buildings elsewhere, and the whole area was turned into the tragic Canada Park, made possible by millions from a Canadian donor.⁵³

Memoricide and toponymicide: the appropriation of Palestinian heritage and erasure of the Palestinian past

The Palestinians share common experiences with other indigenous peoples who had their self-determination and narrative denied, their material culture destroyed and their histories erased, retold or reinvented or distorted by European white settlers and colonizers. In *The Invasion of America* (1976), Francis Jennings highlighted the hegemonic narratives of the European White settlers by pointing out that historians for generations wrote about the indigenous peoples of America from an attitude of cultural superiority that erased or distorted the actual history of the indigenous peoples and their relations with the European settlers.

Maori scholar Linda Tuhiwai Smith argues that the impact of European settler-colonization is continuing to hurt and destroy indigenous peoples; that the negation of indigenous views of history played a crucial role in asserting colonial ideology, partly because indigenous views were regarded as incorrect or primitive, but primarily because 'they challenged and resisted the mission of colonization'.[54] She states:

> Under colonialism indigenous peoples have struggled against a Western view of history and yet been complicit with the view. We have often allowed our 'histories' to be told and have then become outsiders as we heard them being retold ... Maps of the world reinforced our place on the periphery of the world, although we were still considered part of the Empire. This included having to learn new names for our lands. Other symbols of our loyalty, such as the flag, were also an integral part of the imperial curriculum. Our orientation to the world was already being redefined as we were being excluded systematically from the writing of the history of our own lands.[55]

In Palestine settler-colonial toponym projects have been described by Israeli historian Ilan Pappe as cultural *memoricide*, a concept which encapsulates the systematic attempts of post-1948 renaming projects in Palestine. The concept of cultural memoricide is deployed by Pappe and myself to highlight the systematic scholarly, political and military attempt in post-1948 Israel to destroy the culture heritage of the Palestinians and de-Arabize and 'ecologicide' the Palestinian terrain.[56]

Although continuing some of the pre-Nakba patterns, Zionist toponymic strategies in the post-Nakba period pursued more drastically memoricide and erasure and the detachment of the Palestinians from their history. With the physical destruction of hundreds of Palestinian villages and towns during and after 1948, the Israeli state now focused on the erasure of indigenous Palestinian toponymic memory from history and geography. The physical disappearance of Palestine in 1948, the deletion of the demographic and political realities of historic Palestine and the erasure of Palestinians from history centred on key issues, the most important of which is the contest between a 'denial' and an 'affirmation'.[57] The deletion of historic Palestine from maps and cartography was not only designed to strengthen the newly created state but also to consolidate the myth of the 'unbroken link' between the days of the 'biblical Israelites' and the modern Israeli state. Commenting on the systematic silencing of the Palestinian past, historian Ilan Pappe deploys the concept of cultural memoricide, where he highlights the systematic scholarly, political and military attempt in post-1948 Israel to de-Arabize the Palestinian terrain, its names, spaces, religious sites, its village, town and cityscapes, and its cemeteries, fields and olive and orange groves, and the fruit called Saber (cactus), the prickly pears famously grown in and around Arab villages and cultivated in Arab gardens in Palestine. Pappe conceives of a metaphorical palimpsest at work here, the erasure of the history of one people in order to write that of another people over it; the reduction of many layers to a single layer.[58]

In the post-Nakba period, some of the features of the Israeli renaming strategy followed closely pre-1948 practices of appropriation of Palestinian Arabic toponyms and mimicry. The historic Arabic names of geographical sites were replaced by evoking biblical or Talmudic names and coining new Hebrew names, some of which vaguely resembled biblical names. It has already been shown that the replacement of Arabic places and the renaming of Palestine's geographical sites followed roughly the guidelines suggested in the nineteenth century by Edward Robinson.[59] The obsession with biblical archaeology and scriptural geography transformed Palestinian Arabic place names, Palestinian geographical sites and Palestinian landscape into subjects of Zionist mimicry and camouflaging.[60] From the mid-nineteenth century and throughout the first half of the twentieth century Western colonialist imagination, biblical landscape painting, fantasy and exotic travel accounts, Orientalist biblical scholarship, Holy Land archaeology and cartography and scriptural geography have been critical to the success of the Western colonial enterprise in the Middle East, recreating the 'Biblelands', reinventing ahistorical-primordial Hebrew ethnicity, while at the same time silencing Palestinian history and de-Arabizing Palestinian toponymy.[61]

Israel's settlement activities and official Hebrew renaming projects were embedded in this richly endowed and massively financed colonial tradition. Israeli historian Ilan Pappe remarks:

> [In 1948–49 the land] changed beyond recognition. The countryside, the rural heart of Palestine, with its colourful and picturesque villages, was ruined. Half the villages had been destroyed, flattened by Israeli bulldozers which had been at work since August 1948 when the government had decided to either turn them into cultivated land or to build new Jewish settlements on their remains. A naming committee granted the new settlements Hebraized [sic] versions of the original Arab names: Lubya became Lavi, and Safuria [Saffuriya] Zipori [Tzipori]... David Ben-Gurion explained that this was done as part of an attempt to prevent future claim to the villages. It was also supported by the Israeli archaeologists, who had authorized the names as returning the map to something resembling 'ancient Israel'.[62]

Jewish settlements were established on the land of the depopulated and destroyed Palestinian villages. In many cases these settlements took the names of the original Palestinian villages and distorted them into Hebrew-sounding names. This massive appropriation of Palestinian heritage provided support for the European Jewish colonizers' claim to represent an indigenous people returning to its homeland after two thousand years of exile. For instance, the Jewish settlement that replaced the large and wealthy village of Bayt Dajan (the Philistine 'House of Dagon') (with 5,000 inhabitants in 1948) was named 'Beit Dagon', founded in 1948; Kibbutz Sa'sa' was built on Sa'sa' village; the cooperative *moshav* of 'Amka on the land of 'Amqa village.[63] Al-Kabri in the Galilee was renamed 'Kabri'; al-Bassa village renamed 'Batzat'; al-Mujaydil village (near Nazareth) renamed 'Migdal Haemek' ('Tower of the Valley'). In the region of Tiberias alone there were 27 Arab villages in the pre-1948 period; twenty-five of them – including Dalhamiya, Abu Shusha, Kafr Sabt, Lubya, al-Shajara, al-Majdal and Hittin

– were destroyed by Israel. The name 'Hittin' – where Saladin (in Arabic: Salah al-Din) famously defeated the Latin Crusaders in the Battle of Hattin in 1187, leading to the siege and defeat of the Crusaders who controlled Jerusalem – was renamed the Hebrew-sounding 'Kfar Hittim' ('Village of Wheat'). In 2008 the Israel Land Authority, which controls Palestinian refugee property, gave some of the village's land to a new development project: a $150 million private Golf resort, which was to have an 18-hole championship golf course, designed by the American Robert Trent Jones Jr. Nearby, the road to Tiberias was named the 'Menachem Begin Boulevard' and heavy iron bars were placed over the entrance to Hittin's ruined mosque; the staircase leading to its minaret was blocked.[64]

In Marj Ibn Amer Kibbutz Ein Dor ('Dor Spring') was founded in 1948 by members of the socialist Zionist Hashomer Hatza'ir (later Mapam) youth movement and settlers from Hungary and the United States. It was founded on the land of the depopulated and destroyed village of Indur, located 10 kilometres southeast of Nazareth. Whether or not the Arabic name preserved the ancient Indur, a Canaanite city, is not clear. After 1948 many of the inhabitants became internal refugees in Israel ('present absentees', according to Israeli law) and acquired Israeli citizenship – but were not allowed to return to Indur. In accordance with the common Zionist practice of bestowing biblical names on modern sites and communities, the atheist settlers of Hashomer Hatza'ir appropriated the Arabic name, claiming that 'Ein Dor was named after a village mentioned in Samuel (28:3–19). However, it is by no means certain that the kibbutz's location is anywhere near to where the 'biblical village' stood. An archaeological museum at the kibbutz contains prehistoric findings from the area.

In the centre of the country the once thriving ancient Palestinian town of Bayt Jibrin (or Bayt Jubrin), 20 kilometres northwest of the city of al-Khalil, was destroyed by the Israeli army in 1948. The city's Aramaic name was '*Beth Gabra*' which translates as the 'house of [strong] men'; in Arabic *Bayt Jibrin* also means 'house of the powerful', possibly reflecting its original Aramaic name; the Hebrew-sounding kibbutz of Beit Guvrin ('House of Men'), named after a Talmudic tradition, was established on Bayt Jibrin's lands in 1949, by soldiers who left the Palmah and Israeli army. Today Byzantine and Crusader remains survive and are protected as an archaeological site under the Hebrew name of Beit Guvrin; the Arabo-Islamic heritage of the site is completely ignored.

Judaization and Israelification strategies: the superimposition of biblical, Talmudic and Mishnaic names

Fifty-six years after the Nakba, in March 2004, Israeli journalist Gideon Levy wrote:

The Zionist collective memory exists in both our cultural and physical landscape, yet the heavy price paid by the Palestinians – in lives, in the destruction of hundreds of villages, and in the continuing plight of the Palestinian refugees – receives little public recognition.... Look at this prickly pear plant. It's covering a mound of stones. This mound of stones was once a house, or a shed, or a sheep pen, or a school, or a stone fence. Once – until 56 years ago, a generation and a half ago – not that long ago. The cactus separated the houses and one lot from another, a living fence that is now also the only monument to the life that once was here. Take a look at the grove of pines around the prickly pear as well. Beneath it there was once a village. All of its 405 houses were destroyed in one day in 1948 and its 2,350 inhabitants scattered all over. No one ever told us about this. The pines were planted right afterward by the Jewish National Fund (JNF), to which we contributed in our childhood, every Friday, in order to cover the ruins, to cover the possibility of return and maybe also a little of the shame and the guilt.

A monumental 1992 study by a team of Palestinian field researchers and academics under the direction of Palestinian historian Walid Khalidi details the destruction of hundreds of villages falling inside the 1949 armistice lines. The study gives the circumstances of each village's occupation and depopulation, and a description of what remains. Khalidi's team visited all except 14 sites, made comprehensive reports and took photographs. Of the 418 depopulated villages documented by Walid Khalidi (1992), 293 (70 per cent) were totally destroyed and 90 (22 per cent) were largely destroyed. Seven survived, including 'Ayn Karim (west of Jerusalem), but were taken over by Israeli settlers. A few of the quaint Arab villages and neighbourhoods have actually been largely preserved and gentrified. But they are empty of Palestinians (some of the former residents are internal refugees in Israel) and are designated as Jewish 'artistic colonies'.[65] While an observant traveller can still see some evidence of the destroyed Palestinian villages, in the main all that is left is a scattering of stones and rubble. But the new state also appropriated for itself both immovable assets, including urban residential quarters, transport infrastructure, police stations, railways, schools, books, archival and photo collections, libraries, churches and mosques, and personal possessions, including silver, furniture, pictures and carpets.[66]

'In many of the JNF sites', Pappe – who analyses several sites mentioned by the JNF website, including the Jerusalem Forest – observes:

> bustans – the fruit gardens Palestinian farmers would plant around their farm houses – appear as one of many mysteries the JNF promises the adventurous visitor. These clearly visible remnants of Palestinian villages are referred to as an inherent part of nature and her wonderful secrets. At one of the sites, it actually refers to the terraces you can find almost everywhere there as the proud creation of the JNF. Some of these were in fact rebuilt over the original ones, and go back centuries before the Zionist takeover. Thus, Palestinian bustans are attributed to nature and Palestine's history transported back to a Biblical and Talmudic past. Such is the fate of one of the best known villages, Ayn al-Zeitun, which was emptied in May 1948, during which many of its inhabitants were massacred.[67]

In 1948 'Ayn Zaytun was an entirely Muslim farming community of one thousand, cultivating olives, grain and fruit, especially grapes; the village name was the Arabic for 'Spring of Olives'; Khalidi described the site as follows:

The rubble of destroyed stone houses is scattered throughout the site, which is otherwise overgrown with olive trees and cactuses [cacti]. A few deserted houses remain, some with round arched entrances and tall windows with various arched designs. In one of the remaining houses, the smooth stone above the entrance arch is inscribed with Arabic calligraphy, a fixture of Palestinian architecture. The well and the village spring also remain.[68]

Today the old stone mosque, parts of which are still standing, is not mentioned by the JNF website. In 2004 the mosque was turned into a milk farm; the Jewish owner removed the stone that indicated the founding date of the mosque and covered the walls with Hebrew graffiti.[69] Other mosques belonging to destroyed villages were turned into restaurants, in the case of the town al-Majdal and the village of Qisarya (currently the archaeological, Roman–Crusader theme park of Caesarea); a shop in the case of Beersheba; part of a tourist resort in the case of al-Zeeb; a bar/restaurant (called 'Bonanza') and a tourist site in the case of 'Ayn Hawd.[70]

In eastern Galilee, *Lavi*, near Tiberias, a religious kibbutz founded in 1949 on the fertile lands of the Palestinian village of Lubya, depopulated during 1948 by the Haganah forces, is another example of the appropriation of Palestinian place-names by Israel. Anyone can tell that the source of the Hebraicized name *Lavi* is the Palestinian village 'Lubya';[71] the Zionists, however, claimed that *Lavi* comes from the Mishana and Talmud. Yet the appropriation of the Palestinian toponym and choice of the new Hebrew name *Lavi* ('Lion') – rather than *Levi*, the ancient Jewish last name; and a Levite member of the priesthood – reflected the self-identity construction of the European Jewish colonists, the 'New Jews', and Zionism's new relationship to nature, political geography and tough masculinity.[72] Moverover at Lubya the JNF put up a sign: 'South Africa Forest. Parking. In Memory of Hans Riesenfeld, Rhodesia, Zimbabwe'. The South Africa Forest and the 'Rhodesia parking area' were created atop the ruins of Lubya, of whose existence not a trace was left.

Commenting on the gentrification of several former Palestinian villages (like 'Ein Karim) and neighbourhoods (like those of Lydda and Safad) and their transformation into Jewish built environments, Israeli architect Haim Yacobi, of Ben-Gurion University, writes:

> The Palestinian landscape is a subject of mimicry through which a symbolic indigenization of the [Zionist] settlers take place. As in other ethnocentric national projects, such mimicry may be described as 'an obsession with archeology', which makes use of historical remains to prove a sense of belonging ... The obsession with archeology and history, as well as with treating them as undisputable truths, is clearly evident in the texts that accompanied the design and construction of the Arab villages and neighborhoods. In this process, the indigenous landscape is uprooted from its political and historical context, redefined as local and replanted through a double act of mimicry into the 'build your own home' sites.[73]

In present-day Israel the claim is obsessively made that the Old Testament is materially realized thanks to secularizing biblical archaeology, giving Jewish history flesh and bones, recovering the ancient past, putting it in 'dynastic order' and 'returning to the archival site of Jewish identity' (Said 2004: 46). Biblical archaeology was always central to the construction of Israeli-Jewish identity and the perceived legitimacy of the Israeli state. The debate about 'ancient Israel', secularist and nationalist biblical scholarship and biblical archaeology is also a debate about the modern State of Israel, most crucially because in the eyes of many people in the West, the legitimacy of Zionist Jewish 'restorationism' depends on the credibility of the biblical portrait. One facet of that debate is the argument in the public domain over the use of the term 'Israel' to denote the land west of the Jordan, both in ancient and modern times.

The inevitable outcome of the obsession with the Old Testament in Western biblical scholarship calling the land 'biblical' and with its exclusive interest in a small section of the history of the land – has resulted in focusing on the Israelite identity of a land that has actually been non-Jewish in terms of its indigenous population for the larger part of its recorded history.[74] This state of affairs would not in any other part of the planet. It is due to the Old Testament and its influence in the West where an inherited Christian culture supported the notion that Palestine has always been somehow essentially 'the land of Israel'. Traditional biblical scholarship has been essentially 'Zionist' and has participated in the elimination of the Palestinian identity, as if over fourteen hundred years of Muslim occupation of this land meant nothing. This focus on a short period of history a long time ago participates in a kind of retrospective colonizing of the past. It tends to regard modern Palestinians as trespassers or 'resident aliens' in someone else's territory.

The obsession with the sacred artefacts of biblical archaeology has been central to the formation of Israeli collective identity and Zionist nation-building since in 1948. To make European Jewish identity rooted in the land, after the establishment of Israel the science of archaeology was summoned to the task of constructing and consolidating that identity in secular time; the rabbis as well as the university scholars specializing in biblical archaeology were given sacred history as their domain.[75] Abu El-Haj (2001) explores the centrality of selective biblical archaeology in the construction of Zionist Jewish collective identity before and after 1948. The work examines colonial archaeological exploration in Palestine, dating back to British work in the mid-nineteenth century. Abu El-Haj focuses on the period after the establishment of Israel in 1948, linking the academic practice of archaeology with Zionist colonization and with plans for the Judaization and repossession of the land through the renaming of Palestinian historic and geographic names. Much of this de-Arabization of Palestine is given archaeological justification; the existing Arab names are overwritten by newly coined Hebrew names. This 'epistemological strategy' prepares for the construction of an Israeli-Jewish identity based on assembling archaeological fragments – scattered remnants of masonry, tables bone, tombs – into a sort of special biography out of which the European colony the Yishuv emerges 'visible and linguistically, as Jewish national home'.[76]

Around Jerusalem thousands of acres of pine forests were planted by the Jewish National Fund, forests which are intended both to destroy Palestinian villages and fashion a new pastoral 'biblical landscape', create a new collective memory and give the impression of an 'authentic' timeless biblical landscape in which trees have been standing forever. But this 'natural landscape' is a carefully constructed scene to camouflage the systematically expropriated land of Palestinian villages, the destruction of cultivated olive groves and the ethnic cleansing of the Nakba. The underlying intention is to obscure the locations of the Palestinian villages and prevent any cultivation of the land by non-Jews. The Israeli architects Rafi Segal and Eyal Weizman, commenting on Israeli settlement and the creation of a pastoral biblical landscape, wrote:

> In the ideal image of the pastoral landscape, integral to the perspective of colonial traditions, the admiration of the rustic panorama is always viewed through the window frames of modernity.... the re-creation of the picturesque scenes of Biblical landscape becomes a testimony to an ancient claim on the land. The admiration of the landscape thus functions as a cultural practice, by which social and cultural identities are formed. Within this panorama, however, lies a cruel paradox: the very thing that renders the landscape 'Biblical' or 'pastoral', its traditional inhabitants and cultivation in terraces, olive orchards, stone buildings and the presence of livestock, is produced by the Palestinians, who the Jewish settlers came to replace. And yet, the very people who came to cultivate the 'green olive orchards' and render the landscape Biblical are themselves excluded from the panorama. The Palestinians are there to produce the scenery and then disappear ... The gaze that sees a 'pastoral Biblical landscape' does not register what it does not want to see, it is a visual exclusion that seek a physical exclusion. Like a theatrical set, the panorama can be seen as an edited landscape put together by invisible stage hands ... What for the state is a supervision mechanism that seeks to observe the Palestinians is for the settlers a window on a pastoral landscape that seeks to erase them. The Jewish settlements superimpose another datum of latitudinal geography upon an existing landscape. Settlers can thus see only other settlements, avoid those of the Palestinian towns and villages, and feel that they have truly arrived 'as the people without land to the land with people'.[77]

There are dozens of biblical and archaeological parks in Israel run by the Israel Nature and Parks Authority (*Rashut Hateva'Vehaganim*), a government organization set up in 1998. Many of these archaeological (biblical and Crusader) 'national heritage' parks have been constructed on the ruins of Palestinian villages and towns destroyed in 1948. The negation of both the Canaanite and Islamic heritage of the land by Israel's heritage industry of archaeological theme parks is very evident today in Palestinian Saffuriya (destroyed by Israel in 1948) – the heritage industry geared towards both the retrospective colonization of the past and the fashioning of modern Israeli collective identity.

Settler-colonial mimicry: examples of systematic appropriation of Arabic place names

In the post-Nakba period, some surviving Palestinian villages and towns within the Green Line were given Hebrew names, based on colonial mimicry; the Arab town of

Shefa-'Amr, in the Galilee, became officially Hebraicized to *Shfar'am*. In the Naqab, *Rahat*, the new Arab township created in recent decades by the concentration of Palestinian Arab Bedouin, was given officially the Hebrew sounding name *Rahat*, instead of the Arabic *Raht* ('group'). The appropriation and Hebraicization of indigenous Palestinian Arabic toponyms in a mimicking process designed to coin new Hebrew place names and new collective cultural memory are clear in loan Arabic place names, translations of Arabic place names and morphological patterns of renaming. In lower Galilee the Palestinian Arab village al-Sajara, depopulated in 1948, was replaced by the new Hebrew toponym 'Ilaniya', a place name which was based the Arabic dialect of the destroyed Palestinian 'al-Sharaja' ('tree' in Arabic). The following are new Hebrew-sounding toponyms based on, derived from or modelled on the Arabic toponyms of Palestinian villages depopulated and destroyed before or in 1948:

Palestinian villages and place names depopulated before or in 1948	Israeli settlements with toponyms derived from the names of destroyed Palestinian villages
Lubya depopulated July 1948, Arabic: 'Bean'	**Lavi** (kibbutz); founded 1948; Hebrew: 'lion'
Al-Kabri (in western Galilee), depopulated on 21 May 1948	**Kabri** (kibbutz); founded in 1949
'Alma (in the Sadad district); depopulated on 30 October 1948	**'Alma** (moshav); founded in 1949
Biriyya; depopulated on 2 May 1948	**Birya** (moshav); founded in 1971
'Amqa (in the Acre area), depopulated in October 1948	**Amka** (moshav); founded in 1949
Sajara (lower Galilee); depopulated July 1948, Arabic: 'tree'	**Ilaniya**, Hebrew: 'tree'
'Ayn Zaytun (Western Galilee) Arabic 'Spring of Olives'	**'Ein Zeitim** (kibbutz). Hebrew: 'Spring of Olives', originally founded in 1891 north of the Arab village **'Ayn Zeitun**; abandoned during the First World War; Six Muslims and one Jew were recorded there in 1931, living in four houses; the Jewish settlement was re-established in 1946
Indur (Ibn Amer valley), depopulated in 1948. Arabic toponym possibly preserves Canaanite site: Endor	**Ein Dor** (kibbutz) founded 1948: Hebrew: 'Dor Spring'
Fuleh; depopulated 1925, Arabic: 'Fava Bean'[78]	**Afula** (town) founded in 1925
Tal al-'Adas, Arabic: 'Lentils Hill'	**Tel 'Adashim** (moshav) established in 1923, *Hebrew* 'Lentils Hill'
Al-Mujaydil (village) depopulated in July 1948	**Migdal HaEmek** (town) founded in 1952; Hebrew: 'Tower of the Valley'
'Ayn Hawd; depopulated in 1948; Arabic: 'Spring Basin'	**'Ein Hod** (Artists colony); founded in 1953: Hebrew: *'Spring of Glory'*[79]
Eshwa, or Ishwa, depopulated in July 1948	**Eshtaol** (moshav); founded December 1949
'Aqir; depopulated on 6 May 1948	**Kiryat 'Ekron** (town), founded in 1948

Indigenous versus Colonial-Settler Toponymy

'Ayn Karim, or *'Ein Karim* (West of Jerusalem), depopulated in 1948, 'Generous Spring'	*'Ein Karem* (Jewish neighbourhood in West Jerusalem); Hebrew: 'Vine Spring'
Kafr Bir'im (northern Galilee) depopulated in October 1948; Arabic: 'Budding Village'	*Bar'am* (kibbutz); established in June 1949; Hebrew: 'Son of the People'
Mahlul; depopulated in the 1920s	*Nahlal;*(moshav) founded in 1921
Jibta; depopulated in the 1920s	*Gvat* (kibbutz) founded in 1926
al-Bassa (Western Galilee); on 14 May 1948	*Batzat* (nature reserve); renamed after 1948
Wadi al-Hawarith; Arabic: 'Valley of Plouging'	*'Emek Hefer*; Hebrew: 'Vally of Digging'. *Ein Ha-Horesh* (kibbutz) founded in 1931; was one of the first Zionist settlements in the northern part of *Wadi al-Hawarith*; Hebrew: 'the Plowman's Spring'; notable residents included Israeli historian Benny Morris
Wadi Sarar or *Wadi Surar* (west of Jerusalem; Arabic: 'Pebble Stream'	*Nahal Sorek*; Nahal Sorek Nature Reserve created in 1965 Hebrew: 'Stream of fruitless tree'derived from the Arabic toponym made to sound like a name from the Midrash, the body of exegesis of the Torah
Seil Imran (Naqab); Arabic 'Stream of Imran'	*Nahal Amram*; Hebrew: 'Stream of Amram' recalling the Biblical name of the father of Moses and Aaron
Jabal Haruf (Naqab); Arabic 'Mount Haruf'	*Har Harif*; Hebrew: 'Sharp Mountain'
Jabal Dibba (Naqab); Arabic: 'Hump Hill'	*Har Dla'at*; Hebrew: 'Mount Pumpkin'.
Tall as-Safi; (northwest of al-Khalil); depopulated in July 1948; Arabic: 'the white hill'	*Tel Tzafit* National Park
Bayt Dajan (southeast of Jaffa); depopulated in April 1948	*Beit Dagan*; founded in 1948; Hebrew 'House of Grain'
Sa'sa' (upper Galilee); depopulated October 1948	*Sasa*; kibbutz; founded in January 1949
Hittin (Eastern Galilee); depopulated in July 1948	*Kfar Hittim* (moshav); established in 1936; Hebrew: Village of Wheat'
Al-Khadra, or *al-Khdeira* (central Palestine): Arabic: the 'Green'	*Hadera;* established in 1891 as a farming Zionist colony; today a major Israeli city; Israeli toponmym makes no sens in Hebrew
Meiron or Mayrun (5 kilometres west of Safad) depopulated in 1948; the name associated with the ancient Canaanite city of *Merom* or *Maroma*	*Meron* (moshv), founded in 1949
Al-Majdal (a coastal town in the south); depopulated between November and June 1950	Israeli city; renamed to the Hebrew-sounding *Migdal 'Ad* in 1949 and subsequently to the biblical-sounding *Ashkelon*
Zir'in (village) in the Jezreel valley, depopulated in the summer of 1948; (Arabic: sowing)	*Mizra* (Kibbutz) in the Jezreel valley, founded in 1923; (Hebrew: sowing); Mizra hosted the Palmah headquarters, until 1946. *Yizre'el* (Kibbutz), established in August 1948 by to the west of the remains of the depopulated Ziri'n

Fashioning a European landscape as a site of amnesia and erasure: new Israeli place names and the landscape

In the first two decades of the state Israelis had a deep anxiety about the discovery of the truth about the 1948 Nakba and the 'nightmarish' prospect of Palestinian refugees returning to their towns and villages in what had become Israel. *Facing the Forests*, one of novelist A. B. Yehoshua's first major works, was published in 1963. It opens with the destruction of a Palestinian village in 1948 and the planting of a JNF forest on its ruins. The novel recounts the story of an Israeli student who is 'obsessed' with the history of the Latin Crusaders. The student, looking for a break and solitude, finds a job as a forest ranger. When he arrives at the watch house in the JNF forest he finds an Arab man (whose tongue had been cut out) and the man's daughter. Shortly after his arrival the student begins to suffer from nightmares and this is constantly anticipating a catastrophe. As the summer continues the student begins to desire the man's daughter. The tension between the two escalates and suddenly the man sets fire to the forest and the whole forest burns down. At dawn the student 'turns his gaze to the fire-smoking hills, frowns. There out of the smoke and haze, the ruined village appears before his eyes; born anew, in its basic outlines as an abstract drawing, as all things past and buried'.[80] While the student fails to see the truths unearthed by his research on the Crusades, the fire reveals it. The novel ends with the destruction of the forest and the re-emergence of the Arab village.

The JNF's forests, such as the Carmel National Park, became an icon of Zionist national revival in Israel and in Israeli Hebrew literature, symbolizing the success of the European Zionist project in 'striking roots' in the ancient homeland and sacred landscape. Children were often named after trees and children's Hebrew literature described young trees as children.[81] Names such as Ilan ('tree'), Oren ('pine tree') Tomer and Tamar (male and female for 'palm tree'), Amir ('tree top'), or Elon or Allon ('oak tree') are very common in Israel. Natural woodlands of oaks covered many areas of historic Palestine, especially in upper Galilee, Mount Carmel, Mount Tabor and other hilly regions. Some local Palestinian Muslim traditions in Galilee have even attributed holiness to ancient oak trees. The ancient oak tree and its leaves have been seen as a symbol of strength and endurance not only in Palestine but in many countries across the world. European pre-Christian and medieval Christian traditions of veneration of oak trees are well known. The leaves of the oak were also traditionally an important part of German Army regalia and symbolise ranks in the US army. In ancient Palestine this tree had its own cult in Biblical mythology – mythology derived from Canaanite religious traditions; a tree which is associated with life and supposed to have grown since the beginning of the world.

But the worship of the JNF (European-style) forests in Israel has also become central to an invented Zionist secular collective memory. Israeli historian and journalist Amos Elon, who was born in Vienna as 'Amos Sternbach' and migrated to Palestine in 1933, changed his name to 'Amos Oak'. In similar vein General Yigal Allon, commander of the Palmah in 1948, was born 'Yigal Paicovitch' and changed his name to the Hebrew-sounding Allon ('oak' tree). As we have seen above this tradition of the 'ancient woods' and wood worship was derived from central European notions of romantic nationalism.

In 2004 Amos Elon moved to Italy, citing disillusionment with developments in Israel since 1967. '[F]ew things are as evocatively symbolic of the Zionist dream and rationale as a "Jewish National Fund Forest", he wrote.[82] Israel's European-style forests and reforestation policies enjoy Western support. Planting a European-style forest in the 'sacred soil' and 'sacred landscape' confirms the undeniable ethical value of Israel's (and by extension the West's) project in the East. Afforestation is also linked, materially and symbolically, to the European Holocaust, and thousands of trees have been planted in memory of the lost communities and individual victims.[83] For Palestinians, however, few things better encapsulate the most notorious role of the JNF since the Nakba.[84]

Israel's ideological struggle over the 1967 Occupied Territories: transliteration of New Hebrew toponyms and road signs into English and Arabic

The official Judaization, Hebraicization and biblicization schemes which began after 1948 continued into the post-1967 era[85] and efforts at de-Arabization of Palestine have continued until present day. More recently, in July 2018, the Israeli Nationality Law, adopted by the Israeli Knesset, stripped the Arabic language spoken by twenty per cent of Israeli citizens of its official status as Israel's second official language.

Almost immediately after June 1967 Israel began interfering with Arabic road signs and toponyms in occupied East Jerusalem. In that year it coined a new word, *Orshalim*, that was supposed to be the Arabic form of the Hebrew word for Jerusalem, *Yerushalayim*.[86] In recent years thousands of road signs became the latest front in Israel's battle of accelerating the erasure research Palestinian Arab toponymic heritage of the land. The pattern, which began before 1967, included the transliteration of newly-coined Hebrew toponyms and road signs into both English and Arabic. In July 2009 the Israeli Transport Minister Yisrael Katz announced a new road signs scheme for all major roads in Israel, occupied East Jerusalem and even parts of occupied West Bank to be 'standardized' by converting the original Arabic place names into straight transliteration of the new Hebrew name. Traditionally some road signs in Israel included names that were rendered in three languages top-to-bottom: Hebrew (first), English and Arabic. Under the 2009 scheme of the Transport Ministry, which was open about the political motivation behind its policy, Jerusalem, or *al-Quds* in Arabic, would be standardized throughout occupied East Jerusalem as *Yerushalayim* and transliterated into Arabic *Orshalim*; Nazareth, or *al-Nasra* in Arabic, would be standardized as *Natzrat*; and Jaffa, the Palestinian port city after which Palestine's oranges became famous as Jaffa oranges, would be *Yafo*. As for Palestinian *Nablus*, the ministry was also looking for ways to spell the Hebrew/biblical-sounding name *Shechem* in Arabic.[87] Today all major international airlines which fly to Ben-Gurion Airport (formerly Lydda airport which was created in 1936 during the Palestine Mandate period and later renamed after Israel's first prime minister) use the Hebrew transliteration of the Arabic toponym *Yafa* (Jaffa) by drawing the attention of their passengers on arrival to weather in the *Yafo-Tel Aviv* region.

Today there are about 200 Jewish colonial settlements in the occupied West Bank and East Jerusalem, established on confiscated Palestinian lands in the West Bank after 1967, and more than 200 outposts mostly given biblical-sounding or claimed Talmudic names. However, clearly not enough biblical names to go by, so the table below[88] shows dozens of these sites that were given Hebrew names which either mimic or translate indigenous local Arabic names:

1	Jewish settlement name	Indigenous Arabic names	District
2	*Adora*	*Doura – Tarqumia*	Al-Khalil
3	*Almog*	*Al- Mukalak*	Jericho
4	*Ateret*	*Atara*	#Ramallah
5	Barkan	El- Buraq	Salfit
6	Beit El	Beitin	Ramallah
7	Beit Horon	Beit Or al –Foqa	Ramallah
8	Bruchin	Burqin	Salfit
9	Enav	Enaba	Tulkarm
10	Geva Benjamin (Adam)	Jaba'	Jerusalem
11	Gilo	Beit Jala	Bethlehem
12	Giv'at Ha-Radar	Tal Al-Raddar	Jerusalem
13	Har Gilo	Beit Jala	Bethlehem
14	Har Homa	Jabal Abu Ghnaim	Bethlehem
15	Karmel	El-Karmel	Al-Khalil
16	Kedar (Old Kedar)	Wadi el qudeira	Jerusalem
17	Kedumim	Kafr Qaddum	Qalqiliya
18	Kokhav Ya'acov	Kafr Aqab	Jerusalem
19	Ma'ale Adumim	Al-Khan al-Ahmar	Jerusalem
20	Ma'ale Levona	Al-lepan	Ramallah
21	Ma'ale Mikhmas	Mikhmas	Ramallah
22	Ma'on	Ma'in	Al-Khalil
23	Migdalim	Majdal Bani Fadil	Nablus
24	Mishr Adumim	Al-Khan al-Ahmar	Jerusalem
25	Mod'in Illit	Al-Midya	Ramallah
26	Mshoki Dargot	Um al-Darajat	Bethlehem
27	Nili	Ni'lin	Ramallah
28	No'omi	Nu'ema	Jericho
29	Pesagot	Jabal Al-Taweel	Ramallah
30	Peza'el	Fasayel	Jericho
31	Rimonim	Rammon	Ramallah
32	Sa Nur	Ajja	Jenin

33	Sal'it	Kafr Sur	Tulkarm
34	Shaked	Loza	Jenin
35	Shilo	Silon	Nablus
36	Shim'a	Shama	Al-Khalil
37	Teko'a	Taqu'	Bethlehem

After the 1967 conquests the Israeli State was bound to base its conception of occupied Jerusalem upon a mythologized entity, 'Jerusalem of Gold', and to involve abstract historical and ideological rights in the newly acquired territories, as well as resting its claim on territorial expansion and domination and the 'redemption of land' through settler-colonization. The same process of appropriation and erasure of Palestinian heritage and the superimposition of Zionist colonizing toponymy on Palestinian sites continued after 1967. Almost immediately after the conquest of East Jerusalem the 'Palestine Archaeological Museum', which represented the multi-layered identity and heritage of Palestine, was renamed the 'Rockefeller Museum'. Some items were taken to the Shrine of the Book' ('Heikhal Hasefer'), a wing of the Israel Museum in West Jerusalem. Until 1966 the museum was run by an international board of trustees; it was then taken over by the Jordanian state. Since 1967 the museum has been jointly managed by the Israel Museum and the Israel Department of Antiquities and Museums (later renamed Israel Antiquities Authority). The site is now the headquarters of the Israeli Antiquities Authorities. While the 'Palestine Archaeological Museum' of the Mandatory period still represented the positive diversity of religions and ethnicities that characterized Jerusalem and Palestine for many centuries, the Israel Museum and Shrine of the Book represent that single-minded determination by the Israeli Antiquities Authorities and Israel's heritage industry to Judaize and colonize both the ancient and modern histories of Palestine.

Epilogue: decolonization and indigeneity as resistance: reclaiming Palestine's multi-layered cultural identity

Several indigenous Palestinian scholars, who are also fluent bi-lingual (Arabic and Hebrew) and graduates of Israeli universities, have produced several critical studies comparing indigenous Arabic place-names with the new Hebrew names superimposed on the cultural and physical geography of Palestine.[89] Comparing indigenous Palestinian (Arabic) with the new superimposed Israeli (Hebrew) names, Dahamshe (2021) argues that despite the dominance of the new Israeli Zionist nationalist narrative, the persistence of Palestinian place names within Israel attests to the subversive linguistic practices of the Palestinian citizens of Israel and their bottom-up indigenous linguistic and communication practices.

Within the context of the debate on Zionist settler-colonialism and the elimination of Palestinian cultural geography and place names, it has been suggested that *indignity* can be a key resistance and decolonization strategy in the case of Palestine-Israel.[90] The only indigenous Palestinian and Arab citizen of Israel to serve on the Israeli Government Names Committee was Dr Shukri 'Arraf, who joined briefly the committee in May 1995, at the height of the Olso process, but resigned shortly after failing to make an impact on the actual activities of this committee. Born in Mi'ilya in the Upper Galilee in 1931, 'Arraf wrote over twenty monographs on indigenous Arab cultural and geographical sites in Palestine. But his magnum opus is *Geographic Sites in Palestine: Arabic Names and Hebrew Denominations* (2004). Supplying their original Arabic place names as well as the new Hebrew replacements, this is a major reference work for researchers and for anyone interested in decolonization of Palestine's geography and history. The book also provides a systematic survey tracking changes on the ground, preserving for posterity the original Arabic place names of historic Palestine, including the names of destroyed villages and towns and names of valleys, mountains and rivers; the works also ensure that these place names remain alive in the minds and collective memory of the people of Palestine.

There were other Palestinian responses to forced depopulation and ethnic cleansing from their villages and towns and other forms of resistance to Israeli renaming strategies and these responses are 'discursively rich, complex and protean'.[91] In recent decades novels, poems, films, plays, ethnographic and photographic documentation, maps, oral history archives, online websites and a wide-range array of activities in exiled and internally displaced communities have been and are being produced, many with the aim of countering Israeli denial and correcting distortions of omission and commission that eradicate the Palestinian presence in the land. Also a large number of books have been produced both inside Israel and at Birzeit University, all dedicated to villages depopulated and destroyed. These form part of a large historical and imaginative literature in which the destroyed Palestinian villages are 'revitalised and their existence celebrated'.[92] Since 1948 Palestinians have maintained the multiple meaning of their Arabic names and the multi-layered Palestinian identity embedded in ancient names.[93]

Palestinian nationalism (both secular and religious) however – like all other modern nationalisms – with its construction of national consciousness and identity, is a modern phenomenon.[94] But this must not be automatically conflated with the Palestinians' social, cultural and religious identities which are deeply rooted in the land as well as in the ancient history and memory of Palestine. Furthermore the Palestinians, until the 1948 catastrophe, were predominantly peasants, deeply rooted in the physical and cultural landscapes of Palestine. The local dialect and the names of their villages and towns preserved a multi-layered identity and diverse cultural heritage in Palestine.

Today the Palestinians are culturally and linguistically Arab and largely but not exclusively Muslim. The Palestinian Muslim population was mainly descended from local Palestinian Christians and Jews who had converted to Islam after the Islamic conquest in the seventh century and inherited many of the social, cultural, religious and linguistic traditions of ancient Palestine, including those of the Israelites, Canaanites and Philistines.[95] Furthermore the similarities between their Arabic language and Ugaritic suggests that Arabic was not a late intruder into Palestine from AD 638 onwards, following the Arabo-Muslim conquest.[96] Also many Palestinians are Christian Arabs who have historic roots in Palestine and a long heritage in the land where Christ lived. Commenting on the multi-layered cultural identity and diverse heritage of the Palestinians, Palestinian sociologist Samih Farsoun (1937–2005) writes:

> Palestinians are descendants of an extensive mixing of local and regional peoples, including the Canaanites, Philistines, Hebrews, Samaritans, Hellenic Greeks, Romans, Nabatean Arabs, tribal nomadic Arabs, some Europeans from the Crusades, some Turks, and other minorities; after the Islamic conquests of the seventh century, however, they became overwhelmingly Arabs. Thus, this mixed-stock of people has developed an Arab-Islamic culture for at least fourteen centuries.[97]

The development of Palestinian nationalism research in recent decades has brought with it a much greater awareness of critical archaeology and historical writing based on critical biblical studies and the question of the shared historical heritage of Palestine and the Palestinians.[98] Also interestingly, Palestinian scholar Mazin Qumsiyeh has suggested a more realistic and less dichotomous approach to the debate on Canaanites–Israelites. He argued for coexistence in Palestine–Israel based on shared historical heritage and cultural and genetic affinities between the 'Canaanitic people': Mizrahi Jews and Palestinian Christians and Muslims.[99]

Indeed it would not be unreasonable to argue that the modern Palestinians are more likely to be the descendants of the ancient Israelites (and Canaanites) than Ashkenazi Jews, many of whom were European converts to Judaism. Certainly historically – in contrast to the myth of 'exile and return' – many of the original Jewish inhabitants of ancient Palestine remained in the country but had accepted Christianity and Islam many generations later. Today, however – in contrast to the Ashkenazi Zionist and Arab nationalist historiographies – more and more archaeologists and biblical scholars are convinced that the ancestors of the Israelites had never been in Egypt and that the biblical paradigm of a military conquest of Canaan was completely fictional. Indeed, the archaeological evidence undermined, in particular, the Book of Joshua. If the Exodus from Egypt and the forty years' desert journey around Sinai could not have happened and the military conquest of the 'fortified cities' of Canaan (according to Deuteronomy 9:1: 'great cities with walls sky-high') were totally refuted by archaeology, who, then, were these Israelites, Philistines or Canaanites?

Palestinian digitally-archived oral histories and toponymic memories of the hundreds of destroyed villages and towns have emerged in recent decades as a significant methodology not only for the construction of an alternative history of the Palestinian Nakba and memories of the lost historic Palestine but also for an ongoing indigenous life, living Palestinian practices and a sustained human ecology. In contrast with the Israeli hegemonic heritage-style industry and an orthodox biblical archaeology, with its obsession with assembling archaeological fragments, remains and traces of the ancient past – scattered traces of history, remnants of pottery, masonry, tables, bones, tombs – and officially approved historical and archaeological theme parks of dead monuments and artefacts destined for museums, Palestinians have devoted much attention to the 'enormously rich sedimentations of village history and oral traditions' as a reminder of the continuity of native life and living practices.[100] Reclaiming and preserving the ancient heritage and material culture of Palestine and the Palestinians is vital. The ancient history of Palestine and the Palestinians (Muslims, Christians and Jews included), teaching of the Palestinian textbooks, schools and universities, is urgently needed. This understanding and teaching should encompass the new critical archaeological scholarship of Palestine and the new critical understanding of the ancient history and memories of the land.

Notes

1   Bassett 1994: 316–35.
2   Kearns and Berg 2002: 284.
3   Kearns and Berg 2002.
4   Benvenisti 2002; Zerubavel 1995, 1996; Yacobi 2009; Masalha 2007, 2012, 2014; Gann 1981; Nyangoni 1978; Abu El-Haj 2001; Ra'ad 2010; Berg and Kearns 1996; Berg and Vuolteenhaho 2009; Nash 1999; Housel 2009; Kadmon 2004.
5   Hobsbawm and Ranger 1983.
6   Guyot and Seethal 2007; Nash 1999; Azaryahu and Kook 2002; Azaryahu 1996; Azaryahu 1997.
7   Prior 1997, 1999.
8   Slyomovics 1998, 2002.
9   Al-Shaikh 2010.
10 Abu El-Haj 1998; Myers 1995; Ram 1995: 91–124; Broshi 1987; Piterberg 2001; Raz-Krakotzkin 1993, 1994.
11 Davis 2004.
12 Abu-Sa'ad 2008: 24–5.
13 Masalha 2018: 32.
14 Ibid.
15 Rabkin 2010: 130.
16 Glock 1999.
17 Peled-Elhanan 2012: 12.
18 Peled-Elhanan 2012: 12–47; Beit-Hallahmi 1992: 119; Sand 2009, 2011: 159–60; Benvenisti 1986, 2002; Piterberg 2001, 2008; Zerubavel 1995: 25.
19 Said 2004: 45–6; Kletter 2003.
20 Rabkin 2010: 130.
21 Dahamshe 2021.
22 Falah 1996.
23 Ra'ad 2010: 189.
24 Wadi al-Hawarith was also the name of a Palestinian village depopulated in 1948.
25 Benvenisti 2002: 26.
26 For Israeli archival reports on the activities of the Governmental Names Committee in the 1950s, see 'Report on the Accomplishments of the Governmental Names Committee for the beginning of the year 5719 (1958–1959), September 1958', 1, ISA C/5551/3787; 'Report on the activities of the Governmental Names Committee, the Negev Committee 1949–1950', 4 April 1952, ISA C/5551/3788.
27 Cohen and Kliot 1981, 1992; Azaryahu and Golan 2001; Azaryahu and Kook 2002.
28 Reported in *Haaretz*, 4 April 1969.
29 Kletter 2003.

30 Azaryahu and Golan 2001; Cohen and Kliot 1981.
31 Thompson 1992: 171–352; 1999: 103–227.
32 Masalha 2018.
33 Robinson 1865: 15.
34 Schrader 1878, 2012.
35 Masalha 2018.
36 Doumani 1995; Yiftachel 2006: 53; Ateek 1989: 16.
37 Rainey 2001; Jacobson 1999.
38 Masalha 2018: 42–5.
39 Masalha 1997: 9.
40 Levy 2000.
41 Masalha 1992.
42 Shohat 2010: 264.
43 Peled-Elhanan 2012; Foucault 1969, 2002; 1980.
44 Brisman 2000: 129.
45 Rabbinic sages whose views were recorded in the Mishnah.
46 Jewish Oral Torah scholars.
47 Brisman 2000: 129.
48 Ben-Gurion 1982: 3.989.
49 Abu El-Haj 2001: 91–4.
50 Don C. Benjamin, 'Stories and Stones: Archaeology and the Bible, an introduction with CD Rom', 2006, at: http://www.doncbenjamin.com/Archaeology_&_the_Bible.pdf, note 78, p.254.
51 Yadin Roman, at: http://www.eretz.com/archive/jan3000.htm.
52 Quoted in Abu El-Haj 2001: 95. Approximately one-fourth of all geographical names were derived from the Arabic names on the basis of the similarity of sounds.
53 Ra'ad 2010: 188–9, citing Thompson, Goncalves and van Cangh 1988.
54 Smith 1999: 29.
55 Ibid.: 33.
56 Pappe 2006; Masalha 2012, 2014.
57 Said 1980.
58 Pappe 2006: 225–34.
59 Robinson 1841; Robinson, Smith *et al.* 1860.
60 Yacobi 2009: 115.
61 Masalha 2007; Whitelam 1996; Long 1997, 2003.
62 Pappe 2004: 138–9.
63 Wakim 2001a, 2001b; Boqa' Nihad 2005: 73.
64 Levy 2004.
65 Benvenisti 1986: 25; Masalha 2005, 2012.
66 Khalidi 1992.
67 Pappe 2006: 230.
68 Khalidi 1992: 437.
69 Pappe 2006: 217.
70 Pappe 2006: 217; Khalidi 1992: 151.
71 'Issa 2005: 179–86.
72 Massad 2006: 38.
73 Yacobi 2009: 115.
74 Whitelam 1996.
75 Said 2004: 45.

76 Abu El-Haj 2001: 74; Said 2004: 47–8; Bowersock 1988.
77 Segal and Weizman 2003: 92.
78 The Palestinian Arab village 'al-Fuleh, which in 1226 Arab geographer Yaqut al-Hamawi mentioned as being 'a town in the Province of Palestine'. The Arabic toponym al-Fuleh is derived from the word *foul*, Arabic Fava Bean'.
79 Echoing the same glorification of the Zionist settler-colonization, the two new settlements built on the lands of the destroyed Palestinian vilage Miar (in northern Galilee) were called: *Segev* (greatness or exaltation) and *Ya'ad* (destiny, goal).
80 Quoted in Gover 1986.
81 Zerubavel 1996: 60–99.
82 Elon 1983: 200.
83 Ibid.
84 Jamjoum 2010.
85 Cohen and Kliot 1992.
86 Jonathan Cook (2009 'Israel's plan to wipe Arabic names off the map', *The Electronic Intifada* (17 July), at: http://electronicintifada.net/content/israels-plan-wipe-arabic-names-map/8351
87 Cook (2009 'Israel's plan to wipe Arabic names off the map'.
88 For the full list, see 'Arraf (2004).
89 Dahamshe 2021; Falah 1996; Abu-Sa'ad 2008; Boqa' 2005.
90 Pappe 2021.
91 Slyomovics 2002.
92 Ibid.
93 Ashrawi 1995: 132–4; Doumani 1995.
94 Khalidi 1997.
95 Shaban 1971: 25–161; Donner 1981; Nebel and Oppenheim 2000; Rose 2010.
96 Ra'ad 2010.
97 Farsoun 2004: 4.
98 Thompson, 2003: 1.
99 Qumsiyeh 2004: 28–30; see also Nebel and Oppenheim 2000.
100 Said 2004: 49; Masalha 2008.

References

Abu El-Haj, Nadia (1998), 'Translating Truths: Nationalism, Archaeological Practice and the Remaking of Past and Present in Contemporary Jerusalem', *American Ethnologist* 25 (2): 166–18.

Abu El-Haj, Nadia (2001), *Facts on the Ground: Archaeological Practice and Territorial Self-fashioning in Israeli Society*, Chicago: University of Chicago Press.

Abu-Sa'ad, Ismael (2008), 'Present Absentees: The Arab School Curriculum in Israel as a Tool for De-educating Indigenous Palestinians', *Holy Land Studies* 7 (1): 17–43.

Abu-Sitta, Salman (2010), *Atlas of Palestine 1917–1966*, London: Palestine Land Society.

Al-Baladuri (2014), *Kitab Futuh al-Buldan* [Book of the Conquests of Lands], trans. Philip Hitti, *The Origins of the Islamic State*: being a translation from the Arabic, accompanied with annotations, geographic and historic notes of *Kitab Futuh al-Buldan*, Charleston, SC: Nabu Press.

Al-Muqaddasi (1994), *The Best Divisions for Knowledge of the Regions. Ahasan al-Taqasim Fi Ma'rifat al-Aqalim*, trans. Basil Anthony Collins, Reading: Garnet Publishing.

Al-Shaikh, Abdul-Rahim (2010), 'Last Year in Jerusalem', *This Week in Palestine* 141 (January). Available at: www.thisweekinpalestine.com/details. php?id=2969&ed=177&edid=177.

'Arraf, Shukri (2004), *Geographic Sites in Palestine: Arabic Names and Hebrew Denominations*, Beirut: Institute for Palestine Studies. [Arabic.]

Ashrawi, Hanan Mikhail (1995), *This Side of Peace: A Personal Account*, New York: Simon & Schuster.

Ateek, Naim Stifan (1989), *Justice, and Only Justice: A Palestinian Theology of Liberation*, New York: Orbis.

Azaryahu, Maoz (1996), 'The power of commemorative street names', *Environment and Planning D: Society and Space* 14: 311–30.

Azaryahu, Maoz (1997), 'German reunification and the politics of street names: the case of East Berlin', *Political Geography* 16 (6): 479–93.

Azaryahu, Maoz, and Arnon Golan (2001), '(Re)naming the landscape: The formation of the Hebrew map of Israel 1949–1960', *Journal of Historical Geography* 27 (2): 178–95.

Azaryahu, M. and R. Kook (2002), Mapping the nation: street names and Arab-Palestinian identity: three case studies, Nations and Nationalism 8 (2): 195–213.

Bassett, Thomas J. (1994), 'Cartography and empire building in nineteenth-century West Africa', *Geographical Review* 84: 316–35.

Beit-Hallahmi, Benjamin (1992), *Original Sins: Reflections on the History of Zionism and Israel*, London: Pluto Press.

Ben-Gurion, David (1982), *Yoman Hamilhamah* [War Diary], vols 1–3, Tel Aviv: Misrad Habitahon Publications. [Hebrew.]

Benvenisti, Meron (1986), *Conflicts and Contradictions*, New York: Villard.

Benvenisti, Meron (2002), *Sacred Landscape: The Buried History of the Holy Land Since 1948*, Berkeley, CA: University of California Press.

Berg, L. D., and R. A. Kearns (1996), 'Naming as norming: "race", gender, and the identity politics of naming places in Aotearoa/New Zealand', *Environment and Planning D: Society and Space* 14 (1) 99–122.

Berg, L. D., and J. Vuolteenhaho (eds) (2009), *Critical Toponymies: The Contested Politics of Place Naming*, Burlington, VT: Ashgate Publishing.

Bitan, Hanna (1992), 'The Governmental Names Commission', *Eretz Israel: Studies in the Knowledge of the Land* 23: 367–70.

Bitan, Hanna (1998), *Sefer ha-yishuvim yeha-meḳomot be-Yiśraʾel: ḥamishim shenot hityashvut 1948–1998*, Jerusalem: Vaʿadat ha-Shemot ha-Memshaltiyot, Miśrad Rosh ha-Memshalah. [Hebrew.]

Boqa' Nihad (2005), 'Patterns of Internal Displacement, Social Adjustment and the Challenge of Return', in Masalha (ed.) 2005: 73–112.

Bowersock, Glen W. (1988), 'Palestine: Ancient History and Modern Politics', in Edward W. Said and Christopher Hitchens (eds), *Blaming the Victims: Spurious Scholarship and the Palestinian Question*, 181–91, London: Verso.

Brisman, Shimeon (2000), *A History and Guide to Judaic Dictionaries and Concordances*, New Jersey: Ktav.

Broshi, Magen (1987), 'Religion, Ideology and Politics and Their Impact on Palestinian Archaeology', *Israel Museum Journal* 6: 17–32.

Cohen, Saul B., and Nurit Kliot (1981) 'Israel's Place Names as Reflection of Continuity and Change in Nation Building', *Names* 29: 227–48.

Cohen, Saul B., and Nurit Kliot (1992), 'Place-names in Israel's ideological struggle over the administered territories', *Annals of the Association of American Geographers* 84: 653–80.

Dahamshe, Amer (2021), 'Palestinian Arabic versus Israeli Hebrew Place-Names: Comparative Cultural Reading of Landscape Nomenclature', *Journal of Holy Land and Palestine Studies* 21 (1): 62–82.

Davis, Thomas W. (2004), *Shifting Sands: The Rise and Fall of Biblical Archaeology*, New York: Oxford University Press.

Dayan, Moshe (1978), *Lehyot 'Im HaTamakh'* [*Living with the Hebrew Bible*]. Jerusalem: 'Edanim. [Hebrew.] Published in English as *Living With the Bible*, London: Weidenfeld & Nicolson.

Donner, Fred McGraw (1981), *The Early Islamic Conquests*, Princeton: Princeton University Press.

Doumani, Beshara (1995), *Rediscovering Palestine: Merchants and Peasants in Jabal Nablus, 1700-1900*, Berkeley, CA: University of California Press.

Elon, Amos (1983), *The Israelis: Founders and Sons*, New Orleans: Pelican.

Falah, Ghazi (1996), 'The 1948 Israeli-Palestinian war and its aftermath: the transformation and de-signification of Palestine's cultural landscape', *Annals of the Association of American Geographers* 86: 256–85.

Farsoun, Samih K. (2004), *Culture and Customs of the Palestinians*, Westport, CT: Greenwood Press.

Foucault, Michel (1969, 2002), *The Archaeology of Knowledge*, London: Routledge.

Foucault, Michel (1980), *Power/Knowledge*, New York: Pantheon.

Gann, Lewis (1981), *The Struggle for Zimbabwe*, New York: Praeger.

Glock, Albert E. (1999), 'Cultural Bias in Archaeology', in Tomis Kapitan (ed.), *Archaeology, History and Culture in Palestine and the Near East: Essays in Memory of Albert E. Glock*, 324–42, Atlanta: Scholars Press and American Schools of Oriental Research.

Gover, Yerach (1986), 'Were You There, or Was It a Dream? Militaristic Aspects of Israeli Society in Modern Hebrew Literature', *Social Text* 13/14: 24–48.

Guérin, Victor (1868–80), *Description géographique, historique et archéologique de la Palestine*. 7 vols, Paris: Imprimé par autorisation de l'empereur à l'Impr. Impériale.

Guérin, Victor (1881–83), *La Terre Sainte : Son histoire, ses souvenirs, ses sites, ses monuments*, 2 vols, Paris: Imprimeurs-Éditeurs.

Guyot, S., and C. Seethal (2007), 'Identity of place, places of identities: change of place names in post-apartheid South Africa', *South African Geographical Review* 89 (1): 55–63.

Halbwachs, Maurice (1941), *La Topographie légendaire des évangiles en terre sainte : étude de mémoire collective*, Paris: Presses Universitaires de France.

Herodotus (1987), *The History*, trans. David Grene, Chicago: University of Chicago Press.

Hobsbawm, Eric, and Terence Ranger (1983), *The Invention of Tradition*, Cambridge: Cambridge University Press.

Housel, Jacqueline A. (2009), 'Geographies of Whiteness: the active construction of racialized privilege in Buffalo, New York', *Social and Cultural Geography* 10 (2): 131–51.

'Issa, Mahmoud (2005), 'The Nakba, Oral History and the Palestinian Peasantry: The Case of Lubya', *Masalha*: 179–86.

Jacobson, David M. (1999), 'Palestine and Israel', *Bulletin of the American Schools of Oriental Research* 313: 65–74.

Jamjoum, Hazem (2010), 'Challenging the Jewish National Fund', *Electronic Intifada*, 21 July. Available at: http://electronicintifada.net/v2/article11406.shtml.

Kadmon, Naftali (2004), 'Toponymy and geopolitics: The political use – and misuse – of geographical names', *Cartographic Journal* 41: 85–7.

Kearns, Robin A., and Lawrence D. Berg (2002), 'Proclaiming Place: Towards a geography of place name pronunciation', *Social and Cultural Geography* 3 (3): 283–302.
Khalidi, Rashid (1997), *Palestinian Identity: The Construction of Modern National Consciousness*, New York: Columbia University Press.
Khalidi, Walid (ed.) (1992), *All That Remains: The Palestinian Villages Occupied and Depopulated by Israel in 1948*, Washington, DC: Institute for Palestine Studies.
Kletter, Raz (2003), 'A Very General Archaeologist: Moshe Dayan and Israeli Archaeology', *The Journal of Hebrew Scriptures* 4. Available at: www.arts.ualberta.ca/JHS/abstracts-articles.html#A27.
Levy, Gideon (2000), 'Exposing Israel's Original Sins', *Haaretz*, book review, 11 March. Available at: www3.haaretz.co.il/eng/scripts/article.asp?mador=8&ate=11/03/00&id=99286.
Levy, Gideon (2004), 'Twilight Zone/Social Studies Lesson', *Haaretz* 31 March. Available at: www.haaretz.com/hasen/spages/410906.html.
Long, Burke O. (1997), *Planting and Reaping Albright: Politics, Ideology, and Interpreting the Bible*, Philadelphia: Penn State University Press.
Long, Burke O. (2003), *Imagining the Holy Land: Maps, Models and Fantasy Travels*, Bloomington, IN: Indiana University Press.
Massad, Joseph A. (2006), *The Persistence of the Palestine Question: Essays on Zionism and the Palestinians*, London: Routledge.
Masalha, Nur (1992), *Expulsion of the Palestinians: The Concept of 'Transfer' in Zionist Political Thought, 1882–1948*, Washington, DC: Institute for Palestine Studies.
Masalha, Nur (1997), *A Land Without a People*, London: Faber & Faber.
Masalha, Nur (ed.) (2005), *Catastrophe Remembered: Palestine, Israel and the Internal Refugees*, London: Zed Books.
Masalha, Nur (2007), *The Bible and Zionism: Invented Traditions, Archaeology and Post-Colonialism in Palestine-Israel*, London: Zed Books.
Masalha, Nur (2008), 'Remembering the Palestinian Nakba: Commemoration, Oral History and Narratives of Memory', *Holy Land Studies* 7 (2): 123–56.
Masalha, Nur (2012), *The Palestine Nakba: Decolonising History, Narrating the Subaltern, Reclaiming Memory*, London: Zed Books.
Masalha, Nur (2014), *The Zionist Bible: Biblical Precedent, Colonialism and Erasure of Memory*, London: Routledge.
Masalha, Nur (2018), *Palestine: A Four Thousand Year History*, London: Zed Books.
Myers, David (1995), *Reinventing the Jewish Past: European Jewish Intellectuals and the Zionist Return to History*, New York: Oxford University Press.
Nash, Catherine (1999), 'Irish placenames: post-colonial locations', *Transactions of the Institute of British Geographers* 24 (4): 457–80.
Nebel, Almut, and Ariella Oppenheim (2000), 'High-resolution Y Chromosome Haplotypes of Israeli and Palestinian Arabs Reveal Geographic Substructure and Substantial Overlap with Haplotypes of Jews', *Human Genetics* 107 (6): 630–41.
North, Robert (1979), *A History of Biblical Map Making*, Wiesbaden: Reichert.
Nyangoni, Wellington (1978), *African Nationalism in Zimbabwe*, Washington, DC: University Press of America.
Pappe, Ilan (2004), *A History of Modern Palestine: One Land, Two Peoples*, Cambridge: Cambridge University Press.
Pappe, Ilan (2006), *The Ethnic Cleansing of Palestine*, Oxford: Oneworld Publications.
Pappe, Ilan (2021), 'Indigeneity as Resistance', in Leila H. Farsakh (ed.), *Rethinking Statehood in Palestine: Self-Determination and Decolonization Beyond Partition*, 271–94, Berkeley: University of California Press.

Peled-Elhanan, Nurit (2012), *Palestine in Israeli School Books: Ideology and Propaganda in Education*, London: I. B Tauris.
Piterberg, Gabriel (2001), 'Erasures', *New Left Review* 10: 31–46.
Piterberg, Gabriel, (2008), *The Returns of Zionism: Myths, Politics and Scholarship in Israel*, London: Verso.
Prior, Michael (1997), *The Bible and Colonialism: A Moral Critique*, Sheffield: Sheffield Academic Press.
Prior, Michael (1999), 'The Bible and the Redeeming Idea of Colonialism', *Studies in World Christianity* 5 (2): 129–55.
Qumsiyeh, Mazin B. (2004), *Sharing the Land of Canaan: Human Rights and the Israeli-Palestinian Struggle*, London: Pluto Press.
Ra'ad, L. Basem (2010), *Hidden Histories: Palestine and the Eastern Mediterranean*, London: Pluto Press.
Rabkin, Yakov M. (2010), 'Language in Nationalism: Modern Hebrew in the Zionist Project', *Holy Land Studies* 9 (2): 129–45.
Ram, Uri (1995), *Changing Agenda of Israeli Sociology: Theory, Ideology and Identity*, New York: SUNY Press.
Rainey, Anson F. (2001), 'Herodotus' Description of the East Mediterranean Coast', *Bulletin of the American Schools of Oriental Research* 321: 57–63.
Raz-Krakotzkin, Amnon (1993, 1994), 'Galut Betoch Ribonut: Lebikoret Shlilat Hagalut Batarbut Hayisraelit' [Exile Within Sovereignty: Toward a Critique of The 'Negation of Exile' in Israeli Culture], *Teurya Vi-Bikoret* [Theory and Criticism] 4: 23–56 and 5: 113–32. [Hebrew]
Robinson, Edward (1841), *Biblical Researches in Palestine, Mount Sinai and Arabia Petraea: A Journal of Travels in the Year 1838*, London: John Murray.
Robinson, Edward (1865), *Physical Geography of the Holy Land*, Boston: Crocker & Brewster.
Robinson, Edward, Eli Smith et al. (1860), *Biblical Researches in Palestine and Adjacent Regions: A Journal of Travel in the Years 1838 & 1852*. Boston: Crocker and Brewster.
Rose, John (2010), 'In Praise of the Sun: Zodiac Sun-Gods in Galilee Synagogues and the Palestinian Heritage', *Holy Land Studies* 9 (1): 25–49.
Said, Edward W. (1980), *The Question of Palestine*, London: Routledge & Kegan Paul.
Said, Edward W. (2004) *Freud and the Non-European*, London: Verso (in association with the Freud Museum).
Sand, Shlomo (2009), *The Invention of the Jewish People*, London: Verso.
Sand, Shlomo (2011), *The Words and the Land: Israeli Intellectuals and the Nationalist Myth*. Los Angeles: Semiotext(e).
Schrader, Eberhard (1878, 2012), *Keilinschriften Und Geschichtsforschung* [Cuneiform inscriptions and Historical Research], Charleston, SC: Nabu Press.
Segal, Rafi, and Eyal Weizman (2003), 'The Mountain', in Rafi Segal, David Tartakover, and Eyal Weizman (eds), *A Civilian Occupation: The Politics of Israeli Architecture*, 79–96, London: Verso.
Shaban, M. A. (1971), *Islamic History: A New Interpretation, A.D. 600–750 (A.H. 132)*, London: Cambridge University Press.
Shohat, Ella (2010), *Israeli Cinema: East/West and the Politics of Representation*, London: I. B. Tauris.
Slyomovics, Susan (1998), *The Object of Memory: Arab and Jew Narrate the Palestinian Village*, Philadelphia: University of Pennsylvania Press.

Slyomovics, Susan (2002), 'The Gender of Transposed Space'. *Palestine-Israel Journal of Politics, Economics and Culture* 9 (4). Available at: www.pij.org/details.php?id=114.

Smith, Linda Tuhiwai (1999), *Decolonizing Methodologies: Research and Indigenous Peoples*, London: Zed Books.

Thompson, Thomas L. (1975), *The Settlement of Sinai and the Negev in the Bronze Age*, Wiesbaden: Reichert.

Thompson, Thomas L. (1992), *The Early History of the Israelite People*, Leiden: Brill.

Thompson, Thomas L. (1999), *The Bible in History: How Writers Create a Past*, London: Jonathan Cape.

Thompson, Thomas L. (2003), 'Is the Bible Historical? The Challenge of "Minimalism" for Biblical Scholars and Historians', *Holy Land Studies* 3 (1): 1–27.

Thompson, Thomas, Francolino Goncalves and Jean-Marievan Cangh (1988), *Toponymie Palestinienne: plaine de St Jean d'Acre et corridor de Jérusalem,* Louvain: Institut orientaliste, Université catholique de Louvain.

Tübingen Bible Atlas [Tüebinger Bibelatlas] (2001), Wiesbaden: Reichert.

Wakim, Wakim (2001a), *The Internally Displaced: Refugees in Their Homeland*, Cairo: Centre of Human Rights Studies. [Arabic.]

Wakim, Wakim (2001b), 'Internally Displaced in their Homeland and the Main Stations', *Al-Ittihad* (special supplement for Land Day (March). [Arabic.]

Whitelam, Keith (1996), *The Invention of Ancient Israel: The Silencing of Palestinian History*, London: Routledge.

Yacobi, Haim (2009), *The Jewish-Arab City: Spacio-politics in a Mixed Community*, London and New York: Routledge.

Yiftachel, Oren (2006), *Ethnocracy: Land and Identity Politics in Israel/Palestine*, Philadelphia: University of Pennsylvania Press.

Zerubavel, Yael (1995), *Recovered Roots: Collective Memory and the Making of Israeli National Tradition*, Chicago: University of Chicago Press.

Zerubavel, Yael (1996), 'The Forest as a National Icon: Literature, Politics and the Archaeology of Memory', *Israel Studies* 1 (1): 60–99.

3

What's the Problem with the Jewish State?

Raef Zreik

This paper is about an old theme: the Israeli definition of the nature and character of the State of Israel as 'Jewish and Democratic'. I feel that many times the debate regarding whether the terms are contradictory goes off track and misses some crucial points. Something is lost in the discussion. In this paper I want to try to put the debate back on track. I will do this, in part, by drawing from some of the work that Zureik (1979) offered us. By invoking the terminology of 'internal colonialism', I intend to put politics, power, land, territory and resources back at the heart of the debate, in lieu of the discourse of culture, identity and difference that has dominated the debate in recent years.¹

Now, the concept of 'internal colonialism' has a long – and in many ways contested – history.² Within American academia, the term has been used to describe the nature of race relations *within* the US itself. Early on, African American scholars and activists used the concept in different variations; while Delaney spoke already in the nineteenth century of the status of African Americans as being one of a 'nation within a nation', Du Bois spoke of the colonial status of the Negroes, and Cruse spoke of 'domestic colonialism'.³ One of the most basic ideas is that relations of domination, exploitation and dispossession do not only prevail between different nations and countries, but in fact can exist within the same country between different groups, races and communities (Allen 2005). In another sense, the term has been widely used in economics to describe situations in the economy of a state whereby unequal exchange allows parts of a region to economically dominate other parts of the region (Love 2005; 5–6; Gramsci 1957). The way I want to deploy the concept of 'internal colonialism' in this paper goes beyond the more structural or static image of one group dominating and oppressing other groups or races. Rather, I want to emphasize the ongoing nature of colonization, or rather settler colonization, as an ongoing process that does not recognize a stopping point, and where the establishment of the new state – Israel in our case – is only a landmark within the wider process of a settlement project that continues to expand even after the establishment of the state. In this regard, the way I will be using the concept is rather more appropriate for describing relations between the White American and Native Americans in the nineteenth century.

My paper opens in the first section with what I consider a misplaced emphasis of the debate. It seems to me that at many times the question of the State of Israel as

'Jewish and Democratic' turns out to be a more philosophical debate rather than a political one, and that often the debate becomes more cultural than political. My aim is to forefront politics and questions of power at the expense of questions of philosophy and culture. Then I return for a moment to what seems to me the crucial problem that lies at the heart of Zionism's built-in violence; I do this by referencing the writings of Herzl, who is considered the source of inspiration of many Jewish Zionist liberal intellectuals. The importance of going back to Herzl in particular is that he was not obsessed with religion nor with Jewish culture, and though he might seem to be the paradigm of a secular liberal Zionist, his Zionism encapsulates the whole problem. Zionism was violent before its return to the ethno-religious discourse in the last fifty years, following the occupation of the religious sites in the 1967 war. I then revive the debate on the Jewish-Democratic nature of the State of Israel and offer – as a way to illuminate the debate – another dichotomy: that of the settler and liberal movement. Thus, instead of asking whether a Jewish and democratic state is possible, I suggest one should ask whether a settler colonial movement can conduct itself as a liberal state. My aim is not to try to answer the question but rather to pose the problem in such a way that it sheds some light on the question.

The political: beyond philosophy and logic

As a participant in many debates on Israel as a Jewish and democratic state, I often feel that the debate is a little misguided. In particular, I find the debate sometimes takes a philosophical twist and at other times a cultural twist, and both work together to disguise more basic and essential things: territory, land, power and politics.

What I mean by a philosophical twist in these debates is the focus on the question of whether there is a logical contradiction between the state being Jewish and democratic.[4] Of course, those who are anti-Zionist want to stress the argument that there is a contradiction between the state being Jewish and democratic. Zionists (mainly liberal Zionists) want to argue that there is no such inherent contradiction. I think that the language of 'contradiction' takes the discussion away from the political domain to the philosophical, and from history to logic. It might indeed be the case that there is no logical contradiction in arguing that Israel is a Jewish and democratic state akin to the contradiction of finding a triangle with four lines, or a father who does not have children. To think of parenthood without children is simply a contradiction in terms, but that is not the case with a state being Jewish and democratic. There is a difference between theoretical possibility and real possibility.[5] Something might be possible in theory but lacks the historical and factual elements that make this logical possibility a historical reality. The Jewish and democratic state is not a logical im/possibility: it is rather historically and politically impossible. This impossibility stems mainly from the ethno-national-colonial nature of the state and of Zionism as an ongoing process of negation of exile and of settlement.

At times it seems that liberal Zionists think that by proving a theoretical possibility they have proven the real historical possibility, and those who stress the contradiction in concrete historical-political terms think that that they have proved its theoretical impossibility. I think that the distinction between analytical-logical possibility and real possibility is helpful to set the discussion straight and put politics back into the picture. What I suggest is that we focus and stick to the level of reality, politics and history and on the praxis of Zionism. I do not think that much can be gained from focusing on the analytical-logical level.

Philosophically one can describe the relation between the democratic side of the formula and the Jewish side not as one of contradiction but one of tension, in the same manner that a state can commit to simultaneously respecting principles of equality and freedom. It is clear that there is a tension between freedom and equality and one can come at the expense of the other, and that there is no way that one of these principles can come to full implementation. But that is the nature of principles, as opposed to the nature of rules. Rules are not applied in the manner of either/or, whereas principles are always a matter of degree and gravity, a matter of quantity and not quality, and are never applicable as either/or.[6]

But one can raise the valid argument that there is a difference between the principle of the Jewish nature of the state compared to the principle of freedom. Freedom, as a principle, does put limits on the principle of equality but by its nature the kind of limits that it puts are different from those put by the principle of Jewish state. While the first principle is universal by its nature, the second is particular; there is a difference between competition between two universal principles (freedom and equality) and competition between a universal principle and a particular principle, which demands preference for one group over another. But we should notice that those who raise such an argument are not making a global-logical argument regarding the logical contradiction between Jewish and Democratic as guiding principles, rather they are making a more modest argument by drawing a distinction between different kinds of principles: universal principles (equality, freedom) and particular principles (Jewish nature). This argument posits that while we are allowed to put limits on freedom in the name of equality, we are not allowed to put limits on equality (or freedom) in the name of Jewish nature. But still, the argument concedes the fact that we can restrain one principle by another and does not conceive that there is a logical contradiction with this, or with the fact that several principles can put limits on each other. Acting on principle does not mean acting on *one* principle, but on a combination of principles. Still, can the state (any state) be that universal? Is it not the case that all self-proclaimed universal states are committed to particular principles? In what sense is Israel unique?

The critique of universal ethics and the celebration of the particular

In this sense the challenge to Israel still exists but it is not a conceptual challenge about the fact that principles should not limit each other but a more modest one arguing that only universal principles can put limits on universal principles. Acknowledging that there are certain universal principles that are allowed to limit other universal principles – and accepting the fact that principles or values might limit each other – the argument here is that there is no reason to put universal values like democracy, liberty or equality at the same level of particular values or principles like the Jewishness of the state or ethnic or religious affiliation. The posture that the Palestinian takes in this debate is a liberal, cosmopolitan, universal one against the Zionist attitude that insists on the value of particular attachment. This is a position that I am reluctant to adopt, at least for the sake of this paper, or for the sake of arguing against Zionism. I want to assume that there is a value – moral value – for particular attachments and for cultural belonging, and yet challenge the idea and practice of Jewish state within such a conceptual scheme. In other words, in order to challenge Zionism, I do not need to commit myself to a universal, cosmopolitan, philosophical view nor expand the terrain of the debate. Rather, I want to win the debate on their – nationalist-communitarian – terrain. In this respect, I am willing to accept *for the sake of the debate* most of the insights and arguments advocated by communitarians about the value of particular attachments. The mission Liberal Zionists assign themselves to prove the importance of attachment, culture and particular ethics is misplaced, but so is the counter literature of anti-Zionists who want to prove a liberal universalist point of view.

Advocates of ethics of attachment and ethics of the particular have been around since the rise of Kantian universal ethics during the Enlightenment and since the French Revolution. These include early critics (taking different approaches) like Burke,[7] Hegel,[8] Arnold (1869) and Stirner ([1844] 1955).[9] These nineteenth century figures critiqued universal ethics, praised culture, attachments and the ethics of the particular and had their descendants in the twentieth century. Following the rise of the individual rights discourse, and mainly after Rawls' (1971) publication of *A Theory of Justice* (which revived the Kantian universal tradition on rights) came a massive wave of literature that praised communitarian ethics, celebrating culture and group attachment. Notwithstanding, a whole tradition questioning universal Kantian ethics grew after the Second World War, stressing all kinds of existential ethics and arguing that existence precedes essence. Amongst those emphasizing culture and attachment is the clear committed liberal Kymlicka (1996);[10] but there were many other less liberal scholars who also fit in this strain, in the sense that they were ready to assign to groups, nations, tribes, communities and other modes of attachments a high degree of moral and ethical value. Amongst these one finds authors and philosophers like Sandel (1982), Taylor,[11] Parekh,[12] MacIntyre[13] and Galston (1995). Another mode of critique of universal ethics and liberal rights came from feminist writers like Young (1989) and Gilligan (1982).

Now, I must admit that I find these writers' critiques convincing on many levels, but only to a certain point. The most important kind of critique is the one that stresses the situatedness of citizens and their attachments, which makes them what they are. We are not abstract free-floating citizens connected to the state through a legal web of rights and duties. We are, rather, expressive selves who belong to certain cultural and linguistic groups; these attachments do matter in one way or another. Besides, the claim of the liberal state being neutral and universal is always problematic. The state can never be fully neutral, mainly in terms of culture and language: the state must have a language that is recognized in the public sphere and through which the public legal and political life is conducted; it must have holidays, days of rest, symbols and rituals. All of these are by definition cultural and cannot be neutral. The state (any state) speaks in its official document a particular language, not a universal one. In this sense, there is something to the argument that all liberal states (or states claiming to be liberal and neutral) are limited in being neutral, and that this neutrality is partly an illusion: it is a particular culture masquerading as being universal. The universal does not appear; it is always mediated through the particular. In many ways, this is a critique of formalism that was famously launched in the writings of Hegel but most incisively by Marx.[14] For Marx, the language of equal universal rights was simply a universal cover up: it aimed to hide the fact that as particular citizens (not as abstracts formal ones) we live in different conditions, we are still poor or rich, bourgeois or proletariat and diverge in terms of religion (Jews and Christians). The modern liberal state does not abolish difference and inequality, but relocates them.

A similar mode of critique has been launched against the whole secular discourse. In the last thirty years or so, the secular, secularization and secularism thesis has been under heavy attack from all sides.[15] Here again, one major strand of critique is that what seems or pretends to be an empty and neutral public sphere that allows all conceptions of the good to compete, has in itself a certain structure and includes – or presumes – a certain conception of the good. The secular position is not simply a universal neutral position above all other particular positions; it is rather in and of itself a position among many conceptions of the good and as such it is a particular that is pretending to be universal and feigning to represent the overall good of society. Ask any religious person and they will say that the secular public sphere is in many ways not neutral but hostile to their religious convictions. But how is this debate related to Israel and the Jewish state?

Beyond cultural discourse

Where do we stand as Palestinians – as victims of the Zionist settler project – in these theoretical philosophical debates? Does our stand in resisting Zionism commit us to take this or that side in these debates? In words, does the critique of Zionism oblige us to adopt the global critique of nationalism, or the ethics of belonging writ large? Is this the right locus of the debate?

The reason I raise this question is because (many liberal) Zionists do appropriate and further develop this kind of critical literature in order to justify the Jewish state and in order to offer a more liberal and humane face to Zionism. Often, in order to justify the Jewish ethno-cultural nature of the state, they do find recourse in this kind of literature. The writings of Gans (2008), Tamir (2020) and Rubinstein (2010) are just a few examples of this kind of appropriation of cultural discourse. They seek to normalize Israel's right to adhere to a certain language, symbols and culture and to even conduct immigration policy that somehow takes ethno-religious origins into account, trying (and managing) to find other cases and places in the world that consider similar considerations of ethnic and cultural identity.[16]

Here, Palestinians or anti-Zionists might be tempted to dismiss the critique of universal liberalism given that it is associated with the justification of the Jewish state and the establishment of the state of Israel – including what came with it: the Nakba, expulsion, occupation and dispossession. But it is exactly at this point that I suggest we should 'bracket' this philosophical theoretical debate about universalism and particular attachment. I myself do find that some of the critiques of liberal universalism are appropriate and convincing. But my aim here is not to address the communitarian argument or existential ethics. My point, rather, is that we can and should offer our opposition to Zionism regardless of our position on these theoretical-philosophical debates, and here the discourse of colonialism in general and the work of Zureik on internal colonialism in particular is most relevant, especially given the fact that it deploys the colonial frame in order to study the internal relation within Israel itself after the establishment of the state of Israel.

Focusing the debate on the definition of Israel as Jewish and democratic and the tension between the claim to equality and the claims to culture is misguided and hides questions of power, land and violence – particularly the founding violence. The debate about the state of Israel being 'Jewish and Democratic' is not merely an abstract philosophical debate between the universal commitment of democracy and the particular Jewish nature and culture. I have some sympathy towards the argument that for something to be real it must take a particular shape, and that there is no universal person: there is German, Jewish, Arab, poor, rich, man, woman, singer, carpenter (or a mix of these and other identities). The problem with Zionism does not lie in the abstract attempt to combine Jewish culture and democratic values, but in the specific historical and geographical context within which it has acted. It is exactly the latter that renders the achievement of its goals for the self-determination of Jews dependent on ongoing violence and the dispossession of Palestinians. Thus, I suggest focusing on Zionism as a practice – on its actions and the outcomes of these actions – and less on the philosophical aspects of the debate, or even on the intentions of Zionists. The crucial thing here is understanding what Zionism requires to achieve its goals, and not the intentions per se of Zionists.[17] Had Zionists decided to establish their homeland in the unpopulated territory of Greenland, then the problem of the Jewish and democratic nature of the state of Israel could not have arisen and the combination of these two values could have coexisted as it does exist in Palestine (at least for a while, not for ever).

Herzl: settler-national-colonial

The issue with Israel – and Zionism before that – is that its settler-colonial nature is of a specific type. It is a settler colonial project that is intimately tied to a certain ethno-religious group. Many other settler colonial projects did create certain forms of nationalism following settler projects, as in Australia and the Americas. But in Zionism the identity of the settler was decided beforehand and it was limited to Jews only and thus was exclusive from the start. This combination will end up to be crucial for the nature of the project, and for the violence it implies.

Settler-colonial projects – and ethno-religious ones in particular – have certain key characteristics. The settler is someone who moves between spaces, who comes to the new space but not as an immigrant. The immigrant arrives in the new land willing to accept the law of the land and to be subject to its nomos. The settler comes with their own law, their own nomos, to be imposed on the native. That is why the doctrine of *terra nullius* is built into the settler mindset, because it denies the native any collective agency as a people entitled to be sovereign.

When early Zionists started their project of settling Palestine with the aim of establishing a Jewish state in the midst of another people, the violence could be read between the lines of the project. There is almost[18] no possible way of establishing a Jewish majority in a land populated by Palestinians without violence. Masalha (2017), more than any other author, has spent much time showing and proving that Zionist leaders openly expressed the idea of transfer in their texts. But my point is that violence and transfer is the subtext of the whole project, and are inferred within the project.

I stress this point because if we go back to one of the founding fathers of Zionism – Herzl, who is often considered *the* founding father – we may not find any obsession with ethno-religious purity on the surface of the text. This entices many Zionist commentators to take him as the father of liberal secular Zionism.[19] But this brings me to the heart of the matter: diving into Herzl's text reveals the inherent violence in the project, a violence that lurks beneath the liberal pseudo universal language and is implied in the mix of the settler colonial project and the national aspiration.

The text that I want to focus on is not *The Jews' State*, but *Altnueland* [the old new land] (Herzl [1903] 1960), in which Herzl writes in the form of a novel and outlines the new society that he envisions Jews establishing in Palestine. In several places in the text, Herzl (through his main hero David) confronts what we might describe today as a right wing-ethno-religious Zionist, Guyer. In these encounters, Guyer argues time and again that this state is exclusively Jewish and made for the Jews, given that it was established by the Jews.[20] Herzl (still through his hero David) seems to take a universal stand in this debate, claiming that in the new society there will be no difference between Jews and non-Jews.[21] Furthermore, in several places in the novel Herzl describes the new state as one full of different European opera houses (German, Italian Spanish etc.).[22] The image that Herzl wants to portray is definitely one of a colorful and multicultural society without (almost) any reference to Jewish tradition, religion or values.

The problem with Herzl's text is his subtext. The protagonist in the novel, a European Jew, visits Palestine two times. During his first visit in 1903, he describes the place in utterly miserable and unpleasant terms, as poor, neglected and underdeveloped.[23] During his second visit twenty years later, the protagonist describes Palestine as his dream come true: the country is flourishing in every possible way, and it is here that he introduces the image of different opera houses and a culturally vibrant society; the Arabs are hardly mentioned at all – they are completely invisible. But as Khalidi points out,[24] there is no mention or explanation as to how this demographic change has taken place – how Jews have all of a sudden become the majority and how Arabs have almost disappeared from the scene or become a harmless ornament like the figure of Rasheed Bey.[25]

It is this demographic change that constitutes the subtext of Herzl's book, of his dream and of the Zionist project. Creating a majority in Palestine, which is already populated by Palestinians, requires a demographic change that can't be simply achieved through discussion or persuasion but through ongoing structural violence and dispossession. On this point, the relative openness of Herzl and his multiculturalism and claims to equality of human beings is built on a very particular ethnic footing and assumes that the demographic change had already taken place. Transfer is the base within which Herzl's humanism and pluralism can flourish. Now that the Jews are a majority in the country, they even can allow Palestinians who survived the transfer to become citizens and to have the right to vote. The dark side of the right to vote for Palestinian citizens in Israel is the statelessness of their sisters and brothers who became refugees. Transfer is the precondition for the limited liberalism Israel offers its citizens.

The Jewish democratic state – the Zionist liberal movement

One of the virtues of the model of internal colonialism is that it manages to understand and conceptualize the relation within the state as a very dynamic and an ongoing process. In this regard, one could rephrase Wolfe's (2006) famous dictum that settler colonialism is 'structure not an event' into something more dynamic – settler colonialism is 'structured dynamics not an event'. Thus, while Wolfe was right to insist that settler colonialism is not an event, he probably overemphasized that aspect by focusing on structure. The case of Israel and its relation to the Palestinian citizen as a case in an internal ongoing colonialism can be a productive frame to understand different processes within Israel in general. These processes, or stories of becoming, can be captured far better through the lenses of internal colonialism than by a mere focus on the Jewish nature of the state, though in the case of Israel the Jewish nature happens to be (through the idea of negation of exile) a settler nature of the state. Thus, we need both aspects to fully understand the dynamics that stand at the heart of an ethnoreligious settler colonial project.

It is almost impossible to understand the basic structures and dynamics of Israel without taking into account that this is a settler national state, and there is no way to comprehend its immigration policy, laws of citizenship, land regime, planning regime, housing policy and constitutional structure without acknowledging the basic fact that we are dealing with an ethnoreligious settler project.

Zureik already alluded to some of these aspects in his book more than forty years ago. Because I cannot go into detail explaining these dynamics and structures, I will discuss them only briefly in order to then suggest a slightly different dichotomy to understand the nature of these dynamics: instead of speaking about a Jewish democratic state I suggest speaking of a Zionist liberal movement. Instead of asking whether a Jewish democratic state is possible, one must ask if a liberal Zionist movement is possible.

One key dynamic relates to the nature of Israel's constitutional structure. I have dealt with this aspect elsewhere;[26] here I will only recount its major elements. Several factors combine to shape Israel's unique constitutional structure. First and foremost is the settler colonial nature linked to the idea of the negation of exile as the main organizing principle in Zionism. It is a settler project that combines colonial measures and tools with the politicization of an old Jewish idea related to the Jewish yearning to return to the land of Israel. Originally, this was a religious yearning, not a political or national one; but within Zionism this yearning has been turned into a national territorial project that aims to gather all Jews in Palestine, arguing that Jewish life in exile is deficient and that the Jewish existence outside the land of Israel is necessarily lacking.[27] This discourse has been complemented by another logic that claims that the land of Israel itself suffers a certain lack as long as the Jews are not settled in it. In other words, the land suffers from a certain lack without the people and the people suffer from a certain lack as long they are not living on the land. This creates a mutual destiny: the land is destined for the people and the people are destined for the land. According to this logic, the heart of the Zionist mission is not only establishing the state, but rather the gathering of Jews from all over the world on the land of Israel and to settle the land. Zionism must solve the problem of the Jewish people and the problem of the land at the same time. The establishment of the state of Israel is just one step in this journey. As such, Zionism is an ongoing, never-finished project that is always in the process of its establishment and always in the moment of its beginning – of its birth.[28]

Constitutional theory often distinguishes between two kinds of power related to constitution making.[29] One form of power is called the constitu*tive* power, while the other is the constitu*ted* power, which is a kind of derivative power. The constitutive power is the power that creates the states *ex nihilo*; it does not derive its authority from any former legal or constitutional norm, but is in and of itself the source of its own powers (and as such it is not derivative). The constitutive power on this matter connects the extra-legal order of history and politics to the legal structure: it is the moment of creation and birth. This is not a moment governed by rules but a moment that lies outside the norm – it is a moment of decision, a political decision, or a moment of exception , or norm-less moment that lies at the basis of norms.[30] If we were to ask where it gets its authority, the answer would be that it does not get its authority: it stands with its back to the wall and there is no legal norm or legal organ that authorizes its action.[31] By its very nature (and so it is assumed in the literature) the constituent power uses its power once and for all to establish the basic foundation of the new state, after which it sort of disappears. From that point (once the constitution is in place), things will follow from this basic structure. The constituent power is supposed to put the frame within which regular politics should take place.[32] In the case of Israel, given the fact that the state is an ongoing project where most of its potential citizens are still living outside the country – at least in 1948 – and can actualize their citizenship any minute, it is only natural that the state does not commit to constitution given that its potential citizens outnumber its actual ones. Those who declared the state were kind of trustees for all of Jewish people. But beyond that, and because the mission is not yet accomplished, such a constitutional commitment to fixed rules would put all kinds of limits on the sovereign that it can't accept. A state that perceives itself as always being in a transitory moment (to gather Jews, to settle and expand) can never perceive itself as fully established in this regard, but rather in the process of its establishment. This might explain the fact that in Israel the process of making constitutional laws is endlessly long and drawn out, and the recent Nationality Law[33] was enacted no less than seventy years after the establishment of the state. This also explains the fact that in Israel the Knesset holds so many powers within its hands: the derivative constituent power that has the power to make the constitution; the amending constitutional power that has the power to amend the constitution; and, at the same time, the legislative power that has the power to pass laws. This is a unique scenario in constitutional theory that conveys a sense in which the moment of birth, the revolutionary moment, is still with us and refuses to accept any strong legal frame within which it works. This kind of flexible unstructured structure conveys the image that the state is not in a static situation, but is rather always on the move. The energy of the exception is always with us, refusing to disappear.

This dynamic unsettled nature appears more clearly in issues of land and planning. At the time of the establishment of the state, the Jews in Palestine owned no more than seven per cent of the land. As such, it was abundantly clear that a Jewish state could not be established with this amount of land in Jewish hands and that the newly born state would not be able to achieve the mission it assigned itself in terms of the gathering of exiles and the redemption of the land and settling the country.[34] Thus, establishing the state was only one step in a far more ambitious and far reaching project. In this reality, taking over Palestinian land was almost a natural measure to be taken by the state. The issue goes beyond left and right political leanings: the existence of a Jewish state requires the takeover of Palestinian land and its transfer to Jewish hands (by transferring it to the state as a trustee for the Jewish people). Accordingly, the concept of internal colonialism is very much needed in order to describe the internal dynamics in the state, and the fact that the state was established by no means meant that the colonial dispossession within the state would come to an end. In the case of Israel, the transfer of sovereignty over the violent state apparatus preceded the transfer of property, and now it is the role of the state apparatus to transfer property and to distribute wealth. The colonial process does not end with the establishment of the state; it rather moves it onto a new scale.

The issue of land ownership is intimately tied to issues of zoning and planning that govern the whole issue of land use. The desire to take full control over the country in terms of land use stands at the heart, and the basis, of Israel's planning laws (Law of Planning and Construction 1965). Planning is entirely centralized, where the whole state constitutes one unit controlled tightly by the different ministries – the Ministry of Interior being the most central. A major and central goal of these planning bodies is clearly the establishment of Jewish settlement to solidify the stronghold of the State and Jewish communities over the land (on issues of planning and population settlement).[35] Part of this process is the policy of dispersal of the Jewish population from the center to the periphery in order to make sure that there is Jewish presence in all corners of the country. In this sense, the land has to be captured, concurred and occupied every day, time and again, even if we are talking about land *within* the country itself. Given that the state is not static, but in a constant movement of expansion, the difference between what is within and what is outside the state becomes secondary and both must be conquered. This aspect reflects the similarity between actions of the state when taking over lands in the Negev and taking over lands in the West Bank in order to build new Jewish settlements.

The objective of this very short survey is to show that the main problem is not merely the Jewish nature of the state: language, culture, symbols, holidays etc. The focus on this alone can miss the point and drive the debate into unproductive tracks. I suggest it is more adequate to speak of the tension of a Zionist liberal movement rather than a Jewish democratic state. The shift is not just semantic but aims to stress certain aspects that focus on politics and power instead of culture. The juxtaposition of state with movement aims to bring to attention that Israel is more of a movement, a process, than it is a static state. The substitution of 'Jewish' by 'Zionist' aims to bring to the fore the fact that what lies at the heart of the problem are not merely some cultural aspects of the Jewish state, culture, language, religion etc. I am myself willing to accept the argument that states always have some cultural inbuilt aspects, and that there is no universal identity to any state. But when the issue moves from being merely Jewish to the issue of Zionism, then the question goes beyond culture; it becomes a question of the political deployment of religion and ethnicity within a settler project that is taking place within a certain territory in a particular historical context. In my view, much of the literature deployed by liberal Zionists to prove the salience of cultural membership is beyond the point. The point is the structural violence built into such a project in the concrete circumstances of Palestine, and not in the general or in the abstract. Many Zionists wonder what is wrong with the idea of a Jewish state, given that many nations have their own national country that expresses their culture. The simple answer is that while there might be no problem in the abstract with such an idea, the problem is the concrete historical setting within which the implementation of the idea took place and the consequences that followed that implementation – of ongoing dispossession of another people.

Lastly, I suggest shifting the focus from the democratic discourse to the liberal one. Over the last few decades – mainly after the fall of the Eastern Bloc – it has become common to speak of democracy to mean liberal democracy. This is because other modes and alternative models for democracy seem to have lost the battle (such as socialist democracy and popular democracy models that were prevalent in Eastern Europe and many countries of the global South). But both conceptually and historically, democracy and liberalism descend from different intellectual traditions. Democracy in its literal meaning means the government of the people – of the demos, and the demos speaks through the majority. But liberalism that focuses on equal civil and human rights and a guaranteed sphere of autonomy immune from state intervention is only a recent concept that came to the surface in the last 200 years.[36] This sphere of autonomy/individual rights should be guaranteed by a constitution that puts limits on state power, on governments and on the majority itself, limiting their power pursuing policies and practices from invading the rights of the minority or the individual. In this regard, rights act as 'side constraints' (to use the term coined by Nozick 1988 to describe the concept of rights and their role) that place limits on the power of the majority, and as such may be viewed as being in tension with the democratic ideal that worships the rule of the majority. Thus, the constellation of liberal-democracy (as a hyphenated concept) is a particular combination of two ideals that in certain aspects complement each other but to a great extent are in tension.

In the last decade there has been a return to a kind of populist discourse that aims to separate the democratic aspect of the discourse from its liberal one, thus eviscerating democracy from a major component that guarantees equal rights, the separation of powers and constitutional structure that puts limits on the majority rule. But when democracy is being stripped of its liberal component and sticks to the idea of the majority rule, it can become another form of ethnic nationalism where the majority (a certain ethnic group) can decide for the minority without any safeguard to its rights. Thus, the populist discourse in Israel can appropriate the democratic discourse and argue that a commitment to democracy should mean a commitment to the majority rule, and given that the majority is Jewish, this logic pursues the line that commitment to democracy means commitment to the Jewish state. This way, instead of democracy being the concept that is in tension – if not in contradiction as others would say – with the Jewish nature of the state, it turns out to be its confirmation and instead of both being opposing ideals they turn out to be allies. This is the move that has been developed in recent years by many mainstream writers in Israel.[37] Putting liberalism – as a promise of equal respect, concern and rights for all – into the formula, can bring the debate back on proper track. Can there be a Zionist liberal movement? Is equal concern and respect possible within an ongoing ethnoreligious settler project?

Instead of a conclusion: The Abraham Accords and the persistence of Palestine

The recent accords signed with Arab Emirates and other Gulf States have been wrapped and justified by a quasi-religious cultural language that claims a certain affinity between Judaism and Islam both being Abrahamic religions, stressing the fact that Jews had always been part of the region and that we as Arabs and Muslims had no problem with Judaism.[38] To my ears this discourse sounds like an attempt to normalize Zionism at the disguise of normalizing Jews and accepting them. This discourse replaces on older one that prevailed for years ago where anti-Zionism was a disguise of anti-Semitism on the part of some Arabs, and now they turn the table while some want to reconcile with Zionism, this reconciliation takes the shape of reconciliation with the Jews and accepting them as culture and religion. But this discourse as a whole conceives or rather portrays the conflicts as being between different cultures and religions; when viewed in this way, the way to resolve it is through dialogue that aims to remove certain misunderstandings in the mode of interreligious and interfaith dialogue. In many ways this has been the motto of the accords and to certain level the discourse of the South branch of the Islamic movement in Israel that had entered the coalition.[39] But what is missing from this discourse is Palestine as a geographical unit that has been subject to colonization. Sometimes cultural talk is a way to bypass the direct talk about land, territory and dispossession. While one should not hide or underestimate the connectedness of Palestine to Arabic and Islamic culture, the mere focus on culture can be misguided, for Palestine at the end of the day is the name of a specific place and territory. Israel can live with cultural talk about Arabic tradition and religious diversity but when the name of Palestine comes up, the settler aspect comes to the fore and turns the loss more visible.

Zureik's book had warned early on against 'culture talk'[40] and draws our attention to the colonial aspect of the question of Palestine. For that we should be thankful.

Notes

1. For an excellent critique of the discourse of multiculturalism in the domain of religious rights in Israel see Karayanni 2021.
2. On the history of the concept and its contested meanings see for example Love 1989.
3. Pinderhughes 2011.
4. For the deployment of the term 'contradiction' see for example Jamal (2009) and Kahser (2005).
5. One way to describe this distinction would be by reference to Kant. By the end of the third antinomy (between causality and radical freedom) Kant reaches the conclusion that reason is not able to prove the impossibility of freedom and that in fact 'the antinomy rests on sheer illusion, and that causality through freedom is at least not incompatible with nature'. But this is a sheer theoretical possibility and does not prove the reality of freedom. Kant is very much aware that by showing the fact that there is no contradiction between nature and freedom all he manages to do is show mere possibility in the negative, not the reality of freedom. Thus, he adds 'our intention has not been to establish the reality of freedom as one of the faculties which contains the cause of appearances of our sensible world . . . it has not even been our intention to prove the possibility of freedom' (Kant 1965: 479. Kant (1898) had to write another book, *The Critique of Practical Reason* in order to show the reality of freedom beyond its non-incompatibility, or mere theoretical possibility.
6. Dworkin 1977: 22–30.
7. See his brilliant critique of the language of universal rights: Burke ([1790] 1999).
8. Hegel occupies a unique status in the debates between the particular and the universal. See his praise of nationalism and the particular attachment (Hegel 1975: 44–95; mainly 54–5, 72–6, 80–3, 89, 94–5).
9. Stirner, an almost forgotten name in the history of philosophy, was a sharp critic of universalism compared to the immediacy of concrete attachment. He is clearly distinguished from all of the rest of this group and he is far from being communitarian or culturalist, but his writings have some of the basic insights of existentialism or anarchism.
10. Within Liberal circles, Kymlicka is the most famous and popular writer who takes cultural rights seriously, still within a liberal frame.
11. Taylor develops this theme of mutual recognition in several papers, the most well known being Taylor 1994.
12. See Parrekh 2002, mainly Chapter 5 where he discusses the value of culture and the importance of attachments.
13. Most of MacIntyre's life project has been dedicated to the critique of enlightenment universal ethics. See MacIntyre 2003, mainly the chapter on Kant and the enlightenment project. See also MacIntyre 2013, 1984.
14. Marx (1844) 1992.
15. See Casanova 2011, Asad 2003 and Milbank 2013.
16. Carmi 2008, Gavison 2011, Sapir 2017 and Kahser 2005. For a review of some of these discussions and my reply see Zreik 2008a.
17. The issue of putting aside the intention is repeated many times by Zuriek (1979) where he distinguishes between manifest and latent intentions. Much historical research made after the publication of the book shows that not only the latent but also the manifest intent has been very clear.
18. Zionism contemplated different ideas on how to create a Jewish majority.

19 See e.g. Avinery 2013. The general attitude here is one celebrating Herzl as a liberal thinker.
20 Herzl [1903] 1960: 109–10.
21 Ibid.: 112.
22 Ibid.: 38, 64.
23 Ibid.: 33.
24 Khalidi 2001. For further elaboration on Herzl in general and on a close reading of the novel see Zreik 2016.
25 Herzl draws an image of Rasheed Bey being educated in the West but lacking any kind of social, cultural or national context or attachment whatsoever (Herzl [1903] 1960: 90–2).
26 Zreik 2008b, has recently further developed by Masri 2017. See also Sultani 2016.
27 On the idea of the negation of exile in Zionism and its centrality see Karkoskin (1993).
28 Ben-Gurion 1944.
29 Ackerman 2014; Preuss 1994.
30 Agamben 2008.
31 Kelsen 1967: 198–205. Here Kelsen speaks about the basic norm or the Grundnorm – the norm that is presupposed to stand as the last chain in the chain of authorization.
32 Ackerman (2014) makes a distinction between two tracks of politics, and distinguishes between different moments: between those constitutional moments that set the frame and other regular moments of every day politics.
33 Sefer Hahokim 2018: 898.
34 On land appropriation during the first decade see Kedar & Forman 2004, Kedar 2000 and Kedar & Yiftachel 2006.
35 Falah 1998, Yiftachel 2006, Jabareen 2017.
36 One can think of Locke 2021; Mill 1859; Kant's political writings *Metaphysics of Morals* (([1797] 1996), *Perpetual Peace and Other Essays* ([1795] 1983) and 'Theory and Practice' ([1793] 1983).
37 Taub 1999, 2007. See also Gavison 1999, who tries to put limits on the definition of 'democratic' and to limit it to certain thin procedures.
38 See for example Strimpel 2022.
39 Zreik 2022.
40 I borrow the term 'culture talk' from Mamdani 2005. For Zureik's take on issues of culture and mentality to explain the Jewish Arab relation, see Zureik 1979: 84–8, 197.

References

Ackerman, B. (2014), *We the People*, Cambridge, MA: Harvard University Press
Agamben, G. (2008), *State of Exception*, University of Chicago Press.
Allen, R. L. (2005), 'Reassessing the Internal (Neo) Colonialism Theory', *The Black Scholar* 35 (1): 2–11.
Arnold, M. (1869), 'Culture and Anarchy', in *Conservatism*, 167–86, Princeton: Princeton University Press.
Asad, T. (2003), *The Formation of the Secular: Christianity, Islam, Modernity*, Stanford University Press.

Avineri, S. (2013), *Herzl: Theodor Herzl and the Foundation of the Jewish State*, London: Weidenfeld & Nicolson.

Ben-Gurion, D. (1944), 'The Imperatives of the Zionist Revolution', *Zionism and Israel Information Center Historical Documents and References*, available at: https://zionism-israel.com/hdoc/Ben-Gurion_Jewish_revolution.htm.

Burke, E. ([1790] 1999), 'Reflections on the French Revolution', in I. Kramnick (ed.), *The Portable Edmund Burke*, 416–73), London: Penguin Books.

Casanova, J. (2011), *Public Religions in the Modern World*, Berkeley: University of Chicago Press.

Carmi, N. (2008), 'Immigration Policy: Between Demographic Consideration and the Preservation of Culture', *Law and Ethics of Human Rights* 2 (1): 1–29.

Dworkin, D. (1977), *Taking Rights Seriously*, Cambridge, MA: Harvard University Press.

Falah, G. (1998), 'Israelization of Palestine Human Geography', *Progress in Human Geography* 13 (4): 535–50.

Galston, W. A. (1995), 'Two Concepts of Liberalism', *Ethics* 105 (3): 516–34.

Gans, C. (2008), *A Just Zionism: On the Morality of the Jewish State*, Oxford: Oxford University Press.

Gavison, R. (1999). *Can Israel be Jewish and Democratic?* Van Leer Institute Press and Hakibbutz Hameuchad (Hebrew), available at: https://ruthgavison.files.wordpress.com/2015/10/can-israel-be-both-jewish-and-democratic-full-book.pdf.

Gavison, R. (2011), 'The Law of Return at Sixty Years: History, Ideology, Justification', available at SSRN: https://ssrn.com/abstract=1951784 or http://dx.doi.org/10.2139/ssrn.1951784.

Gilligan, C. (1982), *In a Different Voice: Psychological Theory and Women's Development*, Cambridge, MA: Harvard University Press.

Gramsci, A. (1957), 'The Southern Question', in *The Modern Prince and Other Writings*, 28–54, International Publishers.

Hegel, G. W. F. (1975), *Lectures on the Philosophy of World History* (trans. H. B. Nisbet), Cambridge: Cambridge University Press.

Herzl, T. ([1903] 1960), *Altnueland*, Haifa Publishing Company.

Jabareen, Y. (2017), 'The Right to Space Production and the Right to Necessity: Insurgent versus Legal Rights of Palestinians in Jerusalem', *Planning Theory* 16 (1): 6–31.

Jamal, A. (2009), 'The Contradictions of State Minority Relations: The Search for Clarifications', *Constellations* 16 (3): 493.

Kahser, A. (2005), 'A Jewish and Democratic State: Present Navigation in the Map of Interpretations', *Israeli Affairs* 11 (100): 165–82.

Kant, I. ([1793] 1983), 'Theory and Practice' in *Perpetual Peace and Other Essays*, Hackett Publishing.

Kant, I. ([1795] 1983), *Perpetual Peace and Other Essays* trans. T. Humphrey, Hackett Publishing

Kant, I. ([1797] 1996), *Metaphysics of Morals* trans. M. Gregor, Cambridge: Cambridge University Press.

Kant, I. (1965), *Critique of Pure Reason*, St Martin's Press.

Kant, I. (2002), *The Critique of Practical Reason*, Hackett Publishing.

Karayanni, M. (2021), *Multicultural Entrapment: Religion and State among the Palestinian-Arabs in Israel*, Cambridge: Cambridge University Press.

Karkoskin, A. R. (1993), 'Exile Within Sovereignty: Toward a Critique of the "Negation of Exile"', *Theory and Criticism* 4;: 23–55.

Kedar, A. (2000), 'The Legal Transformation of Ethnic Geography 1947–1967', *NYUJ Int'l & Pol.* 33: 923.

Kedar, A., & J. Forman (2004), 'From Arab Lands to "Israel Lands": The Legal Dispossession of the Palestinias Displaced by Israel in the Wake of 1948', *Environment and Planning D: Society and Space*, 22 (6): 809–30.

Kedar, A., & O. Yiftachel (2006), 'Land Regimes and Social Relations in Israel', in H. de Soto and F. Cheneval (eds), *Swiss Human Rights Book* (Vol.1), Ruffer & Rub Publishing House.

Kelsen, H. (1967), *The Pure Theory of Law* (trans. M. Knight), Berkeley: University of California Press.

Khalidi, M.-A. (2001), 'Utopian Zionism or Zionist Proselytism? Readings in Herzl's Altnueland', *Journal of Palestine Studies* 30 (4), 55–67.

Kymlicka, W. (1996), *Multicultural Citizenship: A Liberal Theory of Minority Rights*, Oxford: Oxford University Press.

Locke, J. ([1689] 2021), *Second Treatise on Government*, W. W. Norton & Company.

Love, J. (1989), 'Modeling Internal Colonialism: History and Prospect', *World Development* 17 (6): 905–22.

MacIntyre, A. (1984). *Is Patriotism a Virtue?*, University of Kansas, available at: https://mirror.explodie.org/Is%20Patriotism%20a%20Virtue-1984.pdf

MacIntyre, A. (2003). *A Short History of Ethics: a History of Moral Philosophy from the Homeric Age to the 20th Century*. London: Routledge.

MacIntyre, A. (2013), *After Virtue: A Study in Moral Theory*, London: Bloomsbury Academic.

Mamdani, M. (2005), *Good Muslim, Bad Muslim: America, the Cold War, and the Roots of Terror*, New York: Pantheon Books

Marx, K. ([1844] 1992), 'On the Jewish Question', in *Early Writings* (trans. R. Levingston), 211–43, London: Penguin Books.

Masalha, N. (2017), *Expulsion of the Palestinians: The Concept of Transfer in Zionist Thought, 1882–1948*. Washington, DC: Institute for Palestinian Studies.

Masri, M. (2017), 'Colonial Imprints: Settler Colonialism as a Fundamental Feature of Israeli Constitutional Law', *International Journal of Law in Context* 13 (3): 388–407.

Milbank, J. (2013), *Theology and Social Theory: Beyond Secular Reason*, Blackwell.

Mill, J. S. ([1859] 2010), *On Liberty*. London: Penguin Books.

Nozick, R. (1988), 'Side Constraints', in S. Scheffler (ed.), *Consequentialism and its Critics*, 134–42, Oxford: Oxford University Press.

Parekh, B. (2002), *Rethinking Multiculturalism*, Caamvbridge, MA: Harvard University Press.

Pinderhughes, C. (2011), 'Toward a New Theory of Internal Colonialism', *Socialism and Democracy* 25 (1): 235–56.

Preuss, U. K. (1994), 'Constitutional Power Making for New Polity: Some Deliberations on the Relations between Constituent Power and the Constitution', in M. Rosenfeld (ed.), *Constitutionalism, Identity, Difference, and Legitimacy: Theoretical Perspectives*, Durham, NC: Duke University Press.

Rawls, J. (1971), *A Theory of Justice*, Cambridge, MA: Harvard University Press.

Rubinstein, A. (2010), *Israel and the Family of Nations: The Jewish Nation-state and Human Rights*, London: Routledge.

Sandel, M. (1982), *Liberalism and the Limits of Justice*, Cambridge: Cambridge University Press.

Sapir, G. (2017), 'Law, Religion and Immigration', *Emory International Law Review* 32 (2): 201.

Sefer Hahokim. Book of Laws, 2743 (2018), available at: https://main.knesset.gov.il/EN/activity/Documents/BasicLawsPDF/BasicLawNationState.pdf

Stirner, M. ([1844] 1955). *The Ego and Its Own*, Cambridge: Cambridge University Press.

Strimpel, Z. (2022), 'Dubai's New Tribe: What's It Like Being Jewish in the United Arab Emirates?' *The Jewish Chronicle* 14 April, available at: https://www.thejc.com/life-and-culture/all/dubais-new-tribe-whats-it-like-being-jewish-in-the-united-arab-emirates-5MkeNhKl5wEBuizcqmk5gl.

Sultani, N. (2016), 'The Legal Structures of Subordination: The Palestinian Minority and Israeli Law', in N. N. Rouhana (ed.), *Israel and Its Palestinian Citizens: Ethnic Privileges in the Jewish State*, 191–237, Cambridge: Cambridge University Press.

Tamir, Y. (2020), *Why Nationalism*, Princeton: Princeton University Press.

Taub, G. (1999), 'Ideas for the Jewish Nation in Azur', *Azureonline* 6 (Winter 5759), available at: https://azure.org.il/article.php?id=328.

Taub, G. (2007), 'Are Liberalism and Democracy Parting Ways? On the Question of Jewish State, *Chronicle of Higher Education* (10 August), available at: https://www.gaditaub.com/eblog/are-liberalism-and-democracy-parting-ways-the-question-of-the-jewish-state/.

Taylor, C. (1944), 'The Politics of Recognition', in A. Gutman (ed.), *Multiculturalism: Examining the Politics of Recognition*, expanded edition, 25–73), Princeton: Princeton University Press.

Wolfe, P. (2006), 'Settler Colonialism and the Elimination of the Native', *Journal of Genocide Research* 8 (4): 387–409.

Yiftachel, O. (2006), *Ethnocracy: Land and Identity Politics in Israel/Palestine*, University of Pennsylvania Press.

Young, I. M. (1989), 'Polity and Group Difference: A Critique of the Ideal of Universal Citizenship', *Ethics* 99 (2): 250.

Zreik, R. (2008a), 'Notes on the Value of Theory; Readings in the Law of Return – a Polemic', *Law & Ethics of Human Rights* 2 (1): 1–44.

Zreik, R. (2008b), 'The Persistence of the Exception: Some Remarks on the Story of Israeli Constitutionalism', in R. Lentin (ed.), *Thinking Palestine*, 131–47, London and New York: Zed Books.

Zreik, R. (2016), 'Herzl: Between Two Palestines', in J. Picard, J. M. Ravel, M. P. Steinberg and I. Zartal (eds), 46–60, *Makers of Jewish Modernity: Thinkers, artists, leaders, and the world they made*, Princeton: Princeton University Press.

Zreik, R. (2022), A New Era in Arab Jewish Relations? *Tel Aviv Review of Books*, available at: https://www.tarb.co.il/mw_writer/raef-zreik/.

Zureik, E. (1979), *The Palestinians in Israel: A Study in Internal Colonialism*, London: Routledge.

Part Two

Zionist Settler-Colonialism: Tenets and Practices

4

The Epistemology of Zionist Settler Colonialism and the Ontological Securitization of Palestinians

Amal Jamal

Introduction

While writing this article I was undergoing great emotional turmoil, a combination of resentment and rage directed at Israeli planning authorities. My feelings were a result of the treatment I had received after applying for permission to construct a rock terrace on a private piece of land I had bought near my village and sought to clear and prepare for planting olive trees. The need to clear the land, a costly process that I would have liked to have avoided, was due to the fact that it was too steep to be used without levelling it in preparation for the planting. This simple and natural process has become a long and annoying bureaucratic procedure that has necessitated a plethora of documents and the involvement of an engineer, a lawyer and a planning advisor. This would not have been an issue if the process had progressed logically and smoothly. My rage, which increased as time went on, has been rooted in two different sources.

The first is the reluctant and irrational responses of the regional planning committee, which sets the conditions for issuing a licence for such a basic measure. The committee demanded numerous certificates of approval from the Environmental Ministry, the Antiquities Authority, the Ministry of Agriculture and the Local Authority, which involved great personal effort and various payments for their issue. One of these authorities demanded to visit the land before granting permission, but kept postponing the appointment, and when its representatives finally came, they rejected the entire plan and demanded impossible changes before issuing their approval. The Ministry of Agriculture invited me to a public hearing together with one of the engineers representing my file. We were asked intrusive questions about the contractor I planned to employ and about transporting soil to level the land, but much less about the plan itself and its purpose. The questions I was asked made me feel as though I were at a police interrogation rather than meeting with an authority that seeks to facilitate the simple and normal process of meeting one of the central slogans of the Israeli state, namely 'making the desert bloom'.[1]

The second source of my rage is the vivid contrast between the ease of establishing Jewish settlements in the area where I live, namely, Western Galilee, irrespective of the cost to nature this entails, and the impossible official demands from inhabitants of Arab villages in my surrounding area, when seeking to introduce changes on their own private land. The excuses used by the authorities are tremendous, aiming to make it really hard to develop the area, in line with the natural needs or interests of the population. Whereas six new Jewish settlements were established around my village, occupying the hills surrounding it, as a belt aiming to slowly limit the village's natural development, several of my neighbors, who seem to know the authorities' practices, rushed to build their own terrace without filing a legal request to the planning committee, despite the fact that they rendered themselves liable to over-inflated fines and criminal charges.

In the meanwhile, because of my stubbornness to avoid granting the authorities the chance to tire me, I have been dragged down with endless bureaucratic preconditions and postponements of meetings to visit the property, in order to receive the documents necessary to initiate my project. The inflating number of preconditions requested by the authorities has led my engineer to admit that they are illogical and are seemingly introduced in order to prevent issuing the permit. He claimed that issuing such a permit would be a precedent that may lead others to follow and open the door for land usage that the planning authorities would like to slow down. I haven't been shocked by the general claim that the authorities intentionally make it difficult for Arab-Palestinians to develop their lands, but it is different when it is a result of first-hand experience. It is actually the same politics of de-development that has come to mind (Roy 2016), albeit with different sophisticated legal and bureaucratic procedures, but that actually aim to slow down the time of the native and simultaneously speed up the development of areas inhabited by settlers.[2]

This story has coincidentally occurred while I have been writing this article, but I think that it demonstrates a growing notion in the study of Israel, namely, that the state, through its ever-growing sophisticated surveillance technologies, is promoting an exclusivist and racist colonization of Palestinian territories and a calculated population management project that dehumanizes them. The main aim of this project is establishing Jewish superiority and Palestinian subjugation, not only in the Palestinian areas occupied in 1967, as most of the literature on occupation demonstrates, but in the entire territory between the Jordan River and the Mediterranean Sea. Although different legal and technological means are employed in different areas, the end goal is the same.

This leads me to make the argument that the growing conceptualization of Israel as a settler colonial entity is reinforced by increasing evidence, refuting the common Israeli claim that it is merely an ideological allegation.[3] The settler colonial conceptualization is supported by tracking the daily legal, territorial and demographic policies of the state, especially from the standpoint of their victims.[4] It is the epistemic tradition of standpoint theory[5] that allows us to best explicate Israeli policies if we look at them through Palestinian experience and their placement in Israeli ideological and security strategy. This means that Zionism is best understood from the standpoint of its victims.[6] Further, it also demonstrates that procedural democracy and modern bureaucratic institutionalism, which characterize Israel, actually seem to skilfully veil its racist forms of discrimination and its subjugation of Palestinians, no matter where they live.⁷ These seem to be the tools to enhance the creeping colonization of Palestinian spaces of habitation, dispossessing the latter, physically and ontologically de-securitizing them and subordinating them to Jewish supremacy.⁸

This long introduction may not surprise many, since Israel's brutal colonial pursuit has been traced, tracked and documented in detail by many scholars. However, most of this scholarship focuses on the Palestinian territories occupied in 1967. Not many have addressed the commonalities in Israeli policies between what happen in these areas and those quietly taking place in Arab areas inside Israel, namely, in the Galilee, the Triangle and the Naqab regions. One of the pioneering scholars is Elia Zureik, who has asserted since the late 1970s that understanding Israel and its policies towards Palestinian territory and demography cannot be fully understood without considering its colonial surveillance across the entire area between the Jordan River and the Mediterranean Sea.⁹ This specific claim by Zureik combines epistemological, ontological and ethical dimensions that deserve to become a model for enhancing our study of the material and ideational dimensions of settler colonialism in general and in Israel/Palestine in particular.

In the following pages, I seek to elaborate the importance of combining these three dimensions in seeking to understand how settler colonial projects veil and disclose, differentiate and synergize, subjugate and objectify their native others in order to enable their multi-dimensional effort to realize their goals. Zureik's work introduces a model worth explicating since it presents an illuminating comprehensive theoretical framing and detailed sociological tracking of the interaction between Zionism, the Palestinians and Palestine, utilizing biopolitical analytical tools to shed light on the sophisticated technological surveillance of the latter, submitting them to Zionist strategy.¹⁰ It is a model based on a well-researched and theoretically and empirically founded study of the control mechanisms facilitating the expansionist nature of Zionism and its dehumanizing effect on Palestinians. It also makes a substantial contribution to the understanding of the epistemology of the unique settler colonial project in Israel/Palestine. This model is rooted in a social ontology of control and surveillance that challenges the hegemonic Israeli academic discourse on the Israeli entity, and the sociology of the Palestinians and their resistance in complying with the Zionist project.

The focus on the sophisticated technological mechanisms of surveillance provides us with a convincing explanation of Israel's ability to carry on with its colonial project despite active Palestinian resistance. This focus enables us to demonstrate how Zionist ideals are translated into practices by state agencies in the entire land of Palestine, irrespective of the official and academic Israeli differentiation between the internationally recognized Israeli territories and the Palestinian areas occupied in 1967. It demonstrates how the differentiation between Palestinian citizens of Israel and other Palestinians, which is pursued via administrative, legal and technological means, forms a sophisticated policy of control. This means that the focus on occupation, despite its merits, should not become a conceptual and ideological tool to mask the comprehensive Zionist endeavour in the entire area between the Jordan river and the Mediterranean Sea. Following the Israeli racist and securitizing colonial policies provides the best evidence for the unity of Palestine and the Palestinians and that conceiving them as such could easily be deduced from Israeli practices rather than being based on ideological or nostalgic lamentations of Palestinians, despite the importance of the latter's subjectivity. The fact that Palestinians, who have been forced to live in different locations and utilize different means to resist Zionist endeavors should not disguise their shared experience as victims of the same strategy of displacement and dispossession.

The aim of the following analysis is to use Zureik's scholarship of Israel/Palestine in order to reflect on the epistemological and ontological shift necessary in order to demonstrate the ethical ramifications of the one-state condition/reality[11] and the creeping apartheid in Israel/Palestine.[12] It also aims to deduce few conclusions concerning the possibilities to reconcile Jewish and Palestinian presence in Israel/Palestine. To that end, I shall limit myself to addressing the epistemological framework, the social ontology and ethical underpinning of Zureik's research model. This is a very limited mission and neither seeks to reintroduce his extensive work, nor to enter into a comprehensive engagement with all his arguments.

The epistemological paradigmatic shift in explicating the reality in Israel/Palestine

Colonialism has always been a disputed theoretical framework, employed by some and rejected by others when it comes to exploring the Zionist movement and Israeli policies in Palestine.[13] Some scholars have addressed the Israeli occupation of Palestinian territories and viewed Israeli policies in these areas as colonial.[14] Several others have adopted the colonial framework in order to explore Zionist policies in Palestine before the establishment of the State of Israel.[15] However, not many have applied the colonial epistemology to Israeli policies in the period between 1948 and 1967, and later in the entire sphere of control by the Israeli state after 1967. The main reason is that Israeli scholarship has managed to establish the modernization epistemology, laid down by Zionist leaders, such as Theodor Herzl, and analyze the Israeli regime and politics from within the Western democratic tradition.[16] As a result, the colonial epistemology has been silenced for a long period and only recently has been reinstituted as legitimate by some Israeli scholars, especially concerning the Palestinian areas occupied in 1967.

In contrast, Palestinian scholars have insisted on using the colonial epistemology in order to explicate Israeli policies in Palestine. Edward Said has been the inspiration for many and his theoretical contribution to the development of the postcolonial epistemology has empowered many to translate his concepts into empirical research projects.[17] Notwithstanding, since only a few Palestinian scholars have been closely exposed to Israeli reality after 1948, and only those living in Israel can bear witness to developments taking place on the ground, the use of colonial conceptual terms to relate to Israeli territorial and demographic policies has become rare. Several Palestinian scholars have addressed Israeli discriminatory policies against Palestinian citizens, but remained shy of utilizing colonial epistemology or depicting the entire Zionist project as colonial.[18]

This scholarly scene turns Zureik's first (1979) major study of Israeli politics towards Palestinian citizens and their systematic dispossession and subjugation into a pioneering study. He was already insisting on using colonial theoretical tools introduced by Frantz Fanon (1961) and Albert Memmi (2003) in order to explore Israeli policies in Palestine. Despite his modest claim that his study is limited to the sociology of the Arabs in Israel, he ends up introducing a very comprehensive analysis not only of the available Israeli studies on the Arab population at the time, or providing first-hand data on the economic, sociological and political reality of this population, but also an epistemological and theoretical challenge to most scholarship on the topic by introducing colonial analytical tools and an alternative interpretation of the social ontology of settler societies, which was not prevalent in most scholarship of his time.

This use of colonial epistemology, which starts with his study of internal colonialism in the late 1970s, continues into the settler colonial conceptual framework, as a tangible analytical system for enhancing a better understanding of the displacement, uprooting, dispossessing and subjugating policies of Israel towards Palestinians.[19] This scholarly endeavour explains the mechanisms by which Israel has managed to control millions of oppressed Palestinians for such a long time. What makes Zureik's settler colonial exploration of Israel/Palestine unique is his translation of the Foucauldian nexus of power and knowledge, which ignored colonialism, into a central dimension of explicating the Israeli colonial endeavour in Palestine. Choosing to draw attention to the knowledge/power dynamics forms an important epistemological shift that allow us to follow the particularities of Israeli colonization of Palestine, especially its detailed mechanisms of biopolitics and population management that aim to appropriate Palestinian land, while spatially relegating the Palestinians and restricting their presence to small and marginal parts of their original homeland. The focus of the nexus of power/knowledge allows Zureik to translate the epistemological framework developed by Said (1978, 1980, 1993) from an idealistic epistemic conceptualization into a detailed material tool kit to be used in order to explicate Israeli settler-colonial policies and thereby provide an overview of the brutality of the Israeli colonial project. It is also an epistemological shift that allows us to better understand the roots of Palestinian resentment of Israel and their resistance to its continuous appropriation of their homeland, something we shall separately address later.

The knowledge/power binary allows Zureik to reveal the unique nature of the Israeli knowledge of the Palestinian population and its deep affinity with the Israeli capacity to govern millions of Palestinians for a long period of time. Thereby, he provides us with a comprehensive explanation of Israeli exclusivist hegemony, despite the continuous resistance of the Palestinians. For that purpose, he explicates the huge investment in mapping, recording and analysing every detail of Palestinian lives, starting with the basic individual, such as his/her place in the economic, social and political structure, and reaching the most sophisticated ability to monitor all physical and communication activities conducted by individuals and groups.

The colonial epistemological framework is justified by Zureik in various ways. He addresses questions of epistemology in several places but one of the major ones is when he argues, 'I subscribe to what I call "multicultural epistemology," by which I mean the need to bring to bear points of view from the margin, views that are excluded in a system of domination and hegemony'.[20] He continues to clarify that he is close to Sandra Harding's (2004) conceptualization of 'standpoint epistemology' and adds that his approach 'resonates with Edward Said's (1993) "resistance culture" on the part of the marginalized',[21] but without falling into the traps of relativist or essentialist conceptualization of the marginalized Other. Like Said,[22] he avoids "ascribing superiority to any one experience or system of thought over another" and seeks to incorporate his liminal position into his intellectual endeavor of exploring the complexities of the conflictual reality in Israel/Palestine. That is why he chooses to speak of liminality, which

> is crucial to the borderline intellectual because, as Homi Bhabha (1994) points out, it fosters reflexive thought, which enables intellectuals to transfer their individual subjectivity to collective objectivity, although this occurs in varying degrees, depending on political circumstances and the intellectuals in question. Liminality allows individuals to move between spaces and time periods, testing the threshold of survival.[23]

Another argument Zureik makes for his use of settler colonialism as the main theoretical framework to understand the reality in Israel/Palestine is that it enables us to bridge the gap in the literature between scholarship that explores Palestinians living under occupation and in the diaspora, and those living as citizens in Israel. This theoretical standpoint enables us to demonstrate that the differentiation between these sectors of the Palestinian people isn't only empirically invalid, but also epistemologically and ethically misleading. When looking at Palestinians from the standpoint of Israeli policies, one notices that there is not much difference between them. The difference in the means of colonization and their discursive justifications should not blind us from seeing the coherent logic of displacing Palestinians for the sake of settling Jews. This logic brings him to argue that '[s]ince its early days, the main focus of Israel has been to depopulate Palestine of its original inhabitants, denationalize its refugees, and seize Palestinian land and property in order to accommodate Jewish settlers and actualize the Zionist project'.[24] That is why he reflexively argues, when speaking of his pioneering study from the late 1970s, 'my study remains a testimony to the fact that the colonialism framework once shunned by academic researchers is now being acknowledged by a wider segment of mainstream academic writers as an important contribution to the sociological study of the Palestinian population'.[25]

Accordingly, the three foundational concerns of colonialism – violence, territory, and population control – are manifested in the study of Israel. They rest on racialist discourse and practice that aim to transform the life of the indigenous population of Palestine 'beyond their choosing and control'.[26] To establish this argument, he manages to demonstrate how settler colonial policies in Israel are intrinsically associated with dispossessing Palestinians 'through violence, repressive state laws and practices, and racialized forms of monitoring (currently referred to as racial profiling)'.[27] He also addresses how these essential tools of governance extend from informal to technologically sophisticated formal means of monitoring and control. Therefore, surveillance in its material, corporeal, and discursive forms becomes not only an indispensable tool of governance, but also a social ontology worth explicating in order to provide the best analysis possible of settler colonial power.[28]

By observing these policies, Zureik provides us with the necessary evidence to dismantle the Israeli ideological assumption of a generic separation and differentiation between Israel within the green line and the occupation areas.[29] In this regard, Zureik's work shows that one cannot and should not take for granted the Israeli ontological assumption that Israel is a democratic country engaged in a national conflict with an equal rival, namely the Palestinians. This claim preceded the works of several Israeli scholars that came to the same conclusion years later. Later studies echo Zureik's initial claim.[30] They reiterate the spirit of his study from the late 1970s and provide comprehensive evidence of his argument that it is the colonial epistemology that best explains Israel's behaviour since its establishment.

Zureik's scholarship isn't inspiring since it is only pioneering. It is also refreshing since is provides the most tangible evidence needed for the importance of standpoint epistemology. He lays the epistemological groundwork for the study of Israel from a humanitarian perspective, namely, that of an exiled Palestinian who, as a result of his liminal positioning, provides us with a reflexive, historical, interactive and contextualized perspective. Thereby, he observes the intractability of the Jewish–Palestinian encounter, seeking to explicate the causes behind the Zionist success in subjugating his people and materializing one of the most brutal colonial projects in modern history. He invests much energy in deconstructing the 'Zionist mind' with the ontological underpinning necessary in order to empirically demonstrate how and for what purpose Israel securitizes the Palestinians. His accessibility to Hebrew sources, as a former Israeli citizen, has enabled him to delve deeply into the political reality in Israel and provide a well-founded understanding of social and economic processes that stand behind policies. Analysing many Hebrew sources has allowed him to show how the disciplinary system of biopower works and how mechanisms of surveillance promote the colonization process, while maintaining a democratic façade.

Another important dimension of Zureik's application of the colonial epistemological framework to Israel/Palestine is that it forms a very important academic strategy to counter the traditional and prevalent Zionist narrative that introduces Israel as a modern democratic and liberal state that, as a result of being engaged in a conflict of survival, has to wage wars and sometimes take exceptional security measures to guarantee the security of its inhabitants.[31] His contribution to the deconstruction of this discourse is not only tremendous, but also subversive, especially for a Palestinian who grew up in Israel, has access to Israeli discourse and documentation in Hebrew, but lives outside of Palestine, where he not only can experience academic freedom without fear, but also be exposed to theoretical and empirical academic traditions, deeply related to his home country – Canada – as well as other North and South American experiences.

Zureik's determination regarding the relevancy of the settler colonial epistemology is also rooted in his empirical data regarding the efforts made by the colonial power to replace the natives and the way this takes place.[32] This endeavour leads us to deal with his ontological assumptions. Treating the major ontological underpinnings of his research project could help us not only to complement the epistemological dimension of his contribution, but also to see how he frames the colonial reality in Israel/Palestine and the empirical evidence he provides in order to support his own claims.

Zureik manages to demonstrate the deep affinity between orientalism, as a discursive power system, and the practicalities of population management. Already in the late 1970s, he had argued that settler regimes 'create justificatory ideology based on the dehumanization of the culture and way of life of the indigenous population'.[33] This ideology is turned into a very sophisticated and complex control system, facilitated by new technologies that grant bureaucratic organizations new capacities to monitor, follow and control human behaviour. This system is translated into expectations of self-discipline, shored up with incentives or legally based negative sanctions, entailing the use of databases and networked communications to categorize populations based on their security risk. Therefore, securitization has become the main demarcating mechanism between different social groups, especially differentiating between Jews and Palestinians, on the one hand, and between various Palestinians, on the other.

The social ontology of colonial surveillance

When it comes to social ontology, colonial surveillance has become a central dimension of Zureik's academic voyage. His recent books and articles are focused on deconstructing the sophisticated Israeli surveillance policies, which explain the ability of Israel to control and sustain relative calm among a population of over six million Palestinians and, in spite of their resistance, still manages to maintain the status quo in its favour. Since colonialism plays a leading role in the development and adoption of surveillance and control technologies, as essential tools of governance, it becomes necessary to explore them in detail in order to understand Israel's biopolitics and population management.[34] In order to explicate how Israel manages to control millions of Palestinians against their will, it is not sufficient to analyse the Israeli official or academic discourse, for this already entails the justification of and for the hegemonic reality. The social ontology of what occurs on the ground is what determines the conceptual system to be used in order to provide the best analysis and understanding of the colonial regime. Zureik's social ontology brings together three major interrelated concepts, namely, racialization, securitization and surveillance. The following pages relate to these three concepts and how they interact with each other, forming a sophisticated explanatory mechanism, meeting the conditions set by scholars of causal mechanisms and discursive institutionalism.[35] 'Credible causal social scientific explanation can occur if and only if researchers are attentive to the interaction between causal mechanisms and the context in which they operate.'[36] Mechanisms are not observable attributes of the units of analysis, which have values – nominal, ordinal or numerical – or sample of population distribution; mechanisms 'reside above and outside the units in question and explain the link between inputs and outputs'.[37] Mechanisms tell us how things happen, especially 'how policies and institutions endure'.[38] This understanding is entailed in Zureik's unique model that explains how the structure of colonial power works. This model is deeply related to Vivien Schmidt's (2008) conceptualization of discursive institutionalism, which locates ideas and discourse in their institutional context, seeking to better understand the way they lead to change. This approach to discourse is dynamic and enables us show why certain ideas succeed in reinforcing the prevalent reality and convey it in ways that fit the colonial endeavour.

Racialization

Zureik argues that '[a] key feature of surveillance in colonized regions is its racialization of the "native".'[39] He follows Yasmeen Abu-Laban in arguing that 'what distinguishes surveillance in Israel/Palestine is its racialzed context'.[40] He cites Alex Lubin, arguing that '[r]acialization is always relational and comparative, establishing a clear order of right and wrong, strong and weak, civilized and savage'.[41] By applying Michel Foucault's work on biopolitics to colonialism, he reveals the way racism is central to the interrelationship between biopolitical policies and colonization projects. Following Foucault, Zureik clarifies that state racism in the colonial context is 'anchored in cultural and ethnic differences, not in any essentialist, biological considerations'.[42] In this context and in order to clarify the unique nature of Israeli racism towards Palestinians, he refers to Etienne Balibar's concept of 'neo-racism', which is a form of 'racism without races … whose dominant theme is not biological heredity but the insurmountability of cultural differences'.[43] In order to reiterate the unique nature of racism in the colonial context and its extreme ramifications on the life of the colonized, he cites Patrick Wolf, who argues that 'racism is colonialism speaking' and that settler colonialism is 'inherently eliminatory'.[44]

This understanding leads him to David Theo Goldberg (2008) and Nadia Abu El-Haj (2010), who speak of 'racial Palestinianization', which 'is today among the most repressive, the most subjugating and degrading, the most deadly forms of racial targeting, branding and rationalization' (Goldberg 2008: 39). Racialization is deeply engraved in state practices and Goldberg builds on studies conducted by Sa'di (2014), Shenhav (2012), Berda (2013) and others, showing the active role of the state bureaucracy in racializing the native Palestinians. He asserts that the Israeli bureaucracy does this 'with its depiction of the colonized as inferior, irrational and lacking civilization'.[45] Thus, the dehumanization of Palestinians becomes 'a frequent practice among members of the ruling establishment and, to a very large extent, among the public at large'.[46] 'The Palestinians are frequently presented as the bad guys: they are immoral evil beings who do not really care about the value of human life; they are the provokers, aggressors, assailants and terrorists, who are driven by emotions, irrational and fanatic aspirations'.[47]

Having established this point, Zureik devotes much attention to demonstrating the convergence in the levels of Israeli-Jewish racism among the public, governmental and private spheres. He refers to Nurit Peled's observation that 'Israel's children are educated within an uncompromisingly racist discourse, [a] racist discourse that does not stop at checkpoints, but governs all human relations in this country'.[48] He also refers to Ronit Lentin (2008), who characterizes Israel as 'racial state', by introducing the common attitudes toward Palestinians, not only among Jewish youth, but also permeating the institutional structure of the state, such as the Knesset and government officials.

Securitization

Zureik explicates securitization as another basic mechanism of the Israeli colonial surveillance of the Palestinians. According to him, it is the settler colonial nature of the Zionist endeavour that leads to the securitization of all aspects of life within the sphere of control of the Israeli state and not only under occupation. Palestinian physical presence is framed as a security challenge and in order to justify its surveillance policies the Israeli state invites ontological securitization as a complementary mechanism. Zureik's claims are supported by addressing the unique nature of Israeli securitization, which is achieved through a combination of establishing new Jewish settlements to keep watch, establishing security posts and surveillance mechanisms on the one hand and narrating, legalizing, publicizing and building consciousness on the other.

Zureik manages to demonstrate how normal social behaviour by Palestinians, who naturally seek to preserve their way of life in the material and cultural sense, and protect their ownership of their land and their social institutions, is transformed by the Israeli state into justifications for implementing the most brutal and sophisticated tools of repression and exclusion against them. Accordingly, he turns to Giorgio Agamben's (1998) conceptualization of the state of exception and the constitution of *homo sacer*. He mentions Ilan Pappe's (2008) critique of Agamben's conceptualization, especially the claim that 'three conditions characterize a state of exception: 'changes in sovereignty, amendments of constitutions and transformations on the ground, based on legislation or delegislation'... none of these prevail in the case of Israel'.[49] Following Pappe (2008), he warns that 'to say that Israel is in a state of exception is to subscribe to the notion that it was once a democracy for all of its citizens but has gradually become undemocratic'.[50] Therefore, he agrees with Pappe that Israel has always been a 'state of oppression', but this understanding does not mantle the beneficial use of Agamben's conceptualization in order to enhance understanding of Israel's securitization policies. According to Zureik, the racialization and dehumanization of Palestinians leads to a reality in which 'the universal laws of humanity do not apply to them'.[51] As a result, Palestinians are conceived by Israelis as deserving 'to exist in conditions of "bare life", as "homo sacer"', whose 'minimal existence is tolerated but not enhanced' and 'the law is suspended when it comes to rectifying [their] grievances'.[52] This treatment is justified by a thick discourse of 'national security', justifying lethal actions that, following Achille Mbembe (2003), are depicted as 'necropolitics'. 'Late-modern colonial occupation differs in many ways from early-modern occupation, particularly in its combining of the disciplinary, the biopolitical and the necropolitical. The most accomplished form of necropower is the contemporary colonial occupation of Palestine.'[53] This means that the most dangerous dimension of Israeli treatment of Palestinians is manifested in dismantling what Hannah Arendt has identified as being human, namely, the 'right to have rights' (Arendt 1951). This treatment does not only turn them into aliens in their own homeland, but also justifies the destruction of their social fabric by neglecting their ontological security. This is true not only for the Palestinians living under Israeli occupation and are target to daily military raids and administrative docility, but also to Palestinian citizens, who are subject to daily criminal violence without being protected by the police.

Surveillance

Zureik's basic argument is that surveillance, in all its forms, has become an indispensable tool of governance in the Israeli colonial system and it forms the main mechanism that explicates Israel's ability to subjugate and submit Palestinians to its power. When it comes to his treatment of surveillance, he follows David Lyon, who refers to 'the focused systematic and routine attention to personal details for purposes of influence, management, production or direction'.[54] He establishes this understanding on the centrality of everyday life and the continuation of subjectivities at the level of desire, fear, security, trust and risk which, in his view, influence and determine human dignity and individual autonomy. But he doesn't limit his treatment of surveillance to the dialectics between feelings and consciousness. He extends it to exploring experience and resistance. This combination allows him to overcome mystifying surveillance and simultaneously, to address the double meaning of subjectivity, that is, as a form of subjugation to external power, and as agency building that is capable of resistance and struggle. This treatment demonstrates Zureik's awareness of the importance of not turning the Palestinians into an object of history, which isn't only theoretically problematic, but also empirically inaccurate.

> Surveillance of individuals, groups and populations is accomplished through soft and hard technologies that involve information gathering by means of bureaucrats, informants, collaborators, direct observation, census taking, territorial mapping, categorical sorting, cross-referencing of identities in databases for the sake of profiling individuals, wiretapping and, more recently, the deployment of sophisticated electronic identification systems, from internet filtering, closed-circuit television, geopositioning systems, biometric profiling, and iris scanning to radio frequency identification and behavioral profiling.[55]

These tools are translated into empirical data, utilizing different methodologies and providing different examples in order to provide sufficient evidence as to the argument that Israel manifests its core identity, at best, as a settler colonial project seeking the subjugation of the native population of Palestine. Zureik's conclusions could be easily summed up in the following confession of Vladimir Jabotinsky:

> There can be no voluntary agreement between ourselves and the Palestine Arabs. Not now, nor in the prospective future. I say this with such conviction, not because I want to hurt the moderate Zionists. I do not believe that they will be hurt. Except for those who were born blind, they realised long ago that it is utterly impossible to obtain the voluntary consent of the Palestine Arabs for converting 'Palestine' from an Arab country into a country with a Jewish majority... *Zionist colonisation must either stop, or else proceed regardless of the native population.* Which means that it can proceed and develop only under the protection of a power that is independent of the native population – behind an iron wall, which the native population cannot breach.[56]

This statement does not deny Zureik's analysis of Herzl's vision. On the contrary, their combination more strongly validates Zureik's critique of many mainstream Israeli scholars who criticize the colonialism thesis. Zureik introduces the main arguments made by scholars such as Shlomo Avineri (2002), Ruth Gavison (2011), and to some extent Zeev Sternhell (2008) against the colonialism thesis. He also criticizes the continuous idealization of Zionism, as in the works of Eyal Chowers (2012) and Boaz Neuman (2011). Against this view of Zionism, Zureik introduces an extensive and thorough analysis of many Israeli scholars that provides sufficient evidence to support the colonialism thesis and even goes beyond it. By tracing Zionist perceptions of the Palestinians and their land, Zureik demonstrates that

> although there have been diversions and nuanced interpretations of Zionism on the part of Zionist spokespersons and their supporters, a constant core has remained, which continues to typify attitudes toward the Palestinians, whether they are citizens of Israel or reside in the occupied territories: a focus on affecting population management and territorial control so as to ensure perpetual Jewish dominance in historical Palestine.[57]

In the face of mainstream Zionist discourse, Zureik introduces sufficient evidence regarding territorial exchange, land confiscation, population displacement and expulsion; all promoted by state institutions under the combined banner of exclusive sacred ownership of the land and the holy needs of security.

Zureik's analysis demonstrates that a conceptual framework needed for explicating and understanding a certain reality, especially a colonial one, cannot be based on or deduced from the self-understanding or justifications provided by the hegemonic power. The examination of mainstream Zionist discourse, via Herzl and his followers demonstrate that their self-definition reflects not the reality on the ground, as much as the aspirations of Zionist leaders and academics, who seek to justify their policies and normalize the power structure that makes their wished-for reality possible. In other words, hegemonic concepts are the ideological justification of the reality rather than its explanation. The victimhood of the Israeli side, and the language of self-defence it employs, are two basic assumptions; when these are accepted, one becomes enmeshed in the machine of justifying the status quo, which means also accepting the argument that there is a fundamental difference between the areas west of the green line and those east of it. The mere acceptance of such a differentiation entails the normalization of Israel as a democratic state, the assumed dismantling of the colonial policies across the line, and accepting the fragmentation of the Palestinians according to the Israeli strategy of viewing them as different minorities that have to be treated differently.

Hybridity and Palestinian agentic power in resisting colonial surveillance

This is certainly not the place to enter into a discussion about the nature of agency and the debate over it in the sociological literature. Nonetheless, it is important to note that while one cannot take for granted the ability of individuals and groups to willfully and purposefully act, one cannot ignore the limits and constraints they have over their ability to act and lead to a change. Colin Campbell (2009) suggests differentiating between two dimensions of agency, in order to overcome the increasingly 'slippery' and puzzling treatment of the concept in social and political thought. According to him, the first type of agency is concerned with the individuals having the ability to implement a willful, volitional and purposive act, seeking to realize a chosen goal. The second type focuses on the capacity of individuals to operate independently of the determining limitations of structural constraints, such as the social structure of cultural norms. This differentiation is analytically important, since it contributes to enhancing our understanding of the power of agency to act and its ability to bring about change or to transform a structural reality. Furthermore, it contributes to the agency-structure debate that leads Anthony Giddens (1984) to introduce his theory of structuration and Pierre Bourdieu to speak of overcoming the dualism of social ontology, as manifested in the objectivism-subjectivism debate.[58]

Campbell's differentiation is very relevant to the understanding of the need for a reflexive treatment of Palestinian society and its daily struggle with the challenges its different components face, as a result of its displacement, dispersal and continuous dispossession. Having explicated the settler colonial nature of Israeli politics and the overwhelming power of the Zionist project that led to the displacement of hundreds of thousands of Palestinians from their homeland and continues to dispossess and repress those who remained, it is important to maintain the necessity not to strip Palestinians of their power of agency and especially their agentic power. Palestinians undertake willful action as subjects, to resist the colonization of their homeland.[59] The fact that they have lost in the combat with the Zionist movement and are subject to a brutal pursuit of a grand colonial project does not and should not mean that they are not engaged in intentional and willful action, seeking to maintain their autonomy vis-à-vis the constraining circumstances of their own social structure as well as against the iron fist of Israeli militarism and its technologically sophisticated surveillance system.

Zureik's sociological studies of the Palestinians, which partially rely on the agent-structure theorization introduced by Anthony Giddens (1984), form an important contribution to the agency-centred epistemological theorical tradition and to its sociological ontology. He justifies his choice by making clear that 'Structuration theory portrays human beings as knowledgeable agents who are capable of acting upon and reproducing social systems across space and time through the deployment of an array of material and non-material resources'.[60] This means that it is important to premise the conception of agency on 'the ability of human agents to make choices and intervene in the course of event by making a difference'.[61] This ability to act takes place within social structures, which are conceptualized as a set of rules and material, symbolic and legal resources that can be either enabling or disabling in the reproduction of social systems. The Palestinians, according to Zureik, are agents by being aware of the context of their actions and those of the Israelis, relying upon a reservoir of knowledge, tacit as well as explicit (discursive), in the production and reproduction of structures and in seeking to act independently of their constraints. This analysis illustrates the importance of the combination we alluded to earlier between Schmidt's (2008) discursive institutionalism and Falleti and Lynch's (2009) causal mechanisms, as explanatory model for complex social processes.

He again draws on Foucault, arguing that '[R]esistance is integral to power. The existence of power relationships depends on a multiplicity of points of resistance which are present everywhere in the power network. Resistances are the old terms in relations of power: they are inscribed in the latter as irreducible opposites.'[62] But this does not limit him to a Foucauldian understanding of resistance, seeking to avoid falling into the traps of elitist sociological theories. Therefore, he also draws on James Scott (1987), arguing that 'understanding resistance and counterhegemonic is not only a function of decoding and deconstructing the discourse of the powerful; it is also linked to revealing "unrecorded" histories as experienced by the less powerful, those in whose name intellectuals and governments speak'.[63]

This approach allows us to open an ontological space to explore Palestinian society through ethnographic methodologies. The focus on the everyday experiences of actors allows Zureik to draw attention to 'the way human agency resists, copes with, and constructs social order in the midst of adverse circumstances'.[64] That is why, according to him, ethnographic studies have "assumed special significance when describing the world of Palestinian refugees and those living in exile and under Israeli occupation" (Ibid, p. 154). This focus allows for revelation of the effects of power relations, without belittling the centrality of resistance. It also enables the capture of subjectivity, as the way the less powerful manage resources in such a way as to exert control over the more powerful in established power relations. The dialectical nature of power demonstrates that although Israeli violence is inscribed on the bodies of the Palestinians, this violence triggers resistance that is manifested in the success of the Palestinians in keeping their struggle alive, despite the brutal and sophisticated Israeli colonial project in their homeland. Approaching the dialectics of power allows Zureik to demonstrate the need for counter-differentiation and counter-submission epistemology and social ontology in order to better reflect and better understand the socio-political dynamics in Israel/Palestine. This type of analysis empowers the colonized subject by ontologically referencing her ability to constitute herself as an autonomous counter-agent, able to disrupt the colonial plans.

Consequently, he follows Arjun Appadurai (1996) in clarifying the way new electronic forms of communication give rise to 'solidalities', meaning 'communities that exist transnationally yet share with each other a field of imagination that fuels collective action. This is true for the various Palestinian communities, who despite that fact of not living under similar conditions seek to transform from "communities in themselves" to "communities for themselves".'[65] The electronic media facilitate collective forms of imagination as 'a staging ground for action, and not only for escape'.[66] They also 'creates idea of neighborhood and nationhood, of moral economies and unjust rule, of higher wages and foreign labour prospects'.[67] By shedding light on this form of Palestinian engagement with reality, Zureik demonstrates how Palestinians are able to develop 'subversive micronarratives and gives rise to subaltern oppositionary groups of various kinds'.[68] This is made possible by technology-people networks, as a hybrid configuration of subjectivity in confronting the brutal Israeli pursuits.

Conclusions

The above analysis of Zureik's contribution to the literature on Israel/Palestine enables us to refer to several conclusions, the first of which is that racialization has become not only a justifying ideology of superiority, but also practices that seek to chain Palestinians into a reality of inferiority. The settler colonial manifestations of Zionism entail intentions, policies and justifications that have led to displacement, subordination of the indigenous inhabitants of Palestine and institutionalized and legalized privileges to the settler society. The analytical and conceptual framework introduced by Zureik allows us to better understand the encounter between Palestinians and the Zionist movement, fleshing out the ideological justification provided by the latter and the practical means utilized in order to promote this mission. This means that the Zionist movement and the state of Israel have been fighting not only against the Palestinian presence in their homeland, but also against the natural human reaction to such efforts, namely, resistance.

Another important conclusion is the notion that it is mistaken to separate between Israel as a historical fact and its colonial character. It is only by looking at the comprehensive Zionist project that we are able to really appreciate the ramifications of its biopolitics and population management. In other words, the normalization of Jewish life wouldn't have been possible without the ethnic separation, exploitation, dispossession and cleansing of the Palestinians. The dialectics of power are manifested in the gap between how the Israelis frame reality based on discourses of offence and violence on the Palestinian side versus the discourses of defence and security on the Israeli side. The Israeli discourses are framed as defensive and are legitimized by the basic human right for security, as if Palestinians have the overhand, pose an existential threat to Israel's existence and therefore have to be controlled. This prevalent perception in the Israeli collective consciousness justify the development of one of the most sophisticated military-industrial and multidimensional surveillance systems that aims to guarantee Jewish superiority and Palestinian submission. This effort is nicely explicated by Zureik, providing us with a conceptual toolkit that reflects the unique interface between land, population, colonization, surveillance, racialization and resistance.

The focus on colonization and surveillance represents an epistemological paradigmatic shift from a positivist perspective to a more sophisticated post-positivist one. This shift is achieved by inviting the conceptual framework provided by post-structural philosophers, such as Michel Foucault and Giorgio Agamben, in order to reveal the disciplining and population management policies of the Israeli state. The combination of post-structural concepts with the structuration theory introduced by Anthony Giddens allows Zureik to draw attention to structural factors that play a central role in the construction of the colonial power system in Israel/Palestine, without ignoring the importance of agency, especially Palestinian agency in resisting it.

By focusing on the practical dimensions of Zionism with some support from discursive pronouncements made by Zionist leaders, Zureik manages to demonstrate that Israeli policies and goals implemented in the entire area of historic Palestine do not differ in nature, despite the differences in the means utilized to achieve them. The continuous experience of expulsion, uprooting, oppression and dispossession is common to all those living under the Israeli colonial project, albeit with the use of various means. Utilizing different means is part and parcel of the fragmentation and divide and rule strategy of the colonial endeavour. This analysis allows us to better understand the different means of resistance utilized by different Palestinians to cope with the multifaceted manifestations of settler colonialism. The diversity in Palestinian resistance emerges as an accommodative and unintentional division of labour that utilizes the opportunities available in the system of colonial power in order to disrupt its ability to sustain its own stability.

This leads us to the concluding argument that Zureik has been pioneering in promoting a paradigmatic shift when dealing with the reality in Israel/Palestine. His epistemological and ontological perspective of a one state reality is conditioned not only by the analytical, but also by the ethical approach necessary for a humanist solution to the protracted conflict between Jews and Palestinians. To that end, we must add that it is indispensable to differentiate between Zionism as an institutionalized colonial endeavor and the Jewish right to security and self-determination, as much as to deconstructing the prevalent differentiation between various Palestinian communities imposed by Zionism. Despite the fact that Zureik does not engage with the way Fanon and Memmi recommend dealing with the anti-human consequences of colonialism, his analysis lays the ground for an ethical approach to achieve this goal. According to what can be deduced from his approach, realizing justice in Israel/Palestine necessitates agentic power that leads to the decolonization of the mind and of the practices that have been instigating the continuous tension between Jews and Palestinians in the holy land in the first place. Decolonization is not a deterministic process and seems impossible to achieve by unethical means. This implicit understanding places part of the responsibility – not the blame – on the colonized, despite the fact that the colonizer is to blame. Given the asymmetric power relations in the colonial reality in Israel/Palestine and given that the decolonization process isn't deterministic, it seems that what Zureik is hinting is that for this process to be ethical, we should not wait until this reality gradually leads to its own negation. When looking at the impossibility of separating between Jews and Palestinians in the entire area between the Jordan River and the Mediterranean Sea, it seems that only cooperation between them can turn the inherent contradictions of Zionism to approach the point of no return, its own self-defeat.

Notes

1   George 1979.
2   Jamal 2011.
3   Veracini 2016.
4   Yacobi 2015.
5   Harding 2004.
6   Said 1980; Shohat 2003.
7   Shenhav and Yona 2008.
8   Jamal 2019.

9   Zureik 1979; 2016.
10 Zureik 2001.
11 Azoulay and Ophir 2012; Lustick 2019.
12 Yiftachel 2009.
13 Said 1980; Gorny 1987; Pappe 2006; Morris 1989; Masalha 2000; Shafir and Peled 2002.
14 Gordon 2008; Weizman 2007; Yiftachel 2006.
15 Shafir 1989.
16 Eisenstadt 1967; Talmon 1970; Avineri 1981; Medding 1990; Arian 2005.
17 Said 1978; Zureik 1979.
18 Giryis 1976; El-Asmar 1978.
19 Zureik 2016.
20 Ibid.: xiii.
21 Ibid.
22 Said 1996: 217.
23 Zureik 2016: xiv.
24 Ibid.: 1–2.
25 Ibid.: 2.
26 Ibid.: 3.
27 Ibid.
28 Zureik and Hindle 2004.
29 Jamal 2018.
30 See Kimmerling 1983; Shafir 1989; Azoulay and Ophir 2012; Yiftachel 2006; Shenhav 2012; and Pappe 2014.
31 Hazoni 2001; Gavison 2003.
32 Wolf 2006.
33 Zureik 1979: 29.
34 Zureik, Lyon and Abu-Laban (eds) 2011: 3.
35 Falleti and Lynch 2009, Schmidt 2008.
36 Falletti and Lynch 2009: 44.
37 Ibid.: 1147.
38 Ibid.
39 Zureik 2016: 95.
40 Ibid.
41 Ibid.
42 Ibid.: 4.
43 Ibid.: 5.
44 Ibid.
45 Zureik 2016: 120.
46 Ibid.: 87.
47 Gordon 2004: 319 cited in Zureik 2016: 87.
48 Zureik 2016: 53, citing Peled 2006: 1.
49 Zureik 2016: 85.
50 Ibid.
51 Ibi.: 88.
52 Ibid.: 89.
53 Mbembe 2013: 27.
54 Zureik 2011: 10; Lyon 2007: 14.
55 Zureik 2016: 5.

56 Jabotinsky 1923.
57 Zureik 2016: 89.
58 Bourdieu 1977; Evens 1999.
59 Johansson and Vinthagen 2014.
60 Zureik 2016: 31.
61 Ibid.: 155.
62 Foucault 1978: 30, 95–6.
63 Zureik 2016: 154.
64 Ibid.: 29.
65 Ibid.: 42.
66 Ibid.
67 Ibid.
68 Ibid.: 44; Appadurai 1996: 10.

References

Abu El-Haj, N. (2010), 'Racial Palestinianization and the Janus-Faced Nature of the Israeli State', *Patterns of Prejudice* 44 (1): 27–41.
Agamben, G. (1998), *Homo Sacer: Sovereign Power and Bare Life*, Stanford, CA: Stanford University Press.
Appadurai, A. (1996), *Modernity at Large: Cultural Dimensions of Globalization*, Minneapolis: University of Minnesota Press.
Arendt, H. (1951), *The Origins of Totalitarianism*. Berlin: Schocken Books.
Arian, A. (2005), *Politics in Israel: The Second Republic,* 2nd ed., Washington, DC: CQ Press.
Avineri, Sh. (1981), *The Making of Modern Zionism: The Intellectual Origins of the Jewish State,* New York: Basic Books.
Avineri, Sh. (2002), 'Zionism According to Theodore Herzl', *Haaretz.com*, 20 December. http://www.haaretz.com/culture/books/zionism-according-to-theodor-herzl-1.24821
Azoulay, A., and A. Ophir (2012), *The One State Condition: Occupation and Democracy in Israel/Palestine,* Stanford: Stanford University Press.
Berda, Y. (2013), 'Managing Dangerous Populations: Colonial Legacies of Security and Surveillance', *Sociological Forum* 28 (3): 627–30.
Bhabha, H., (1994), *The Location of Culture*, New York: Routledge.
Bourdieu, P. (1977), *Outline of a Theory of Practice*, trans. Richard Nice. Cambridge: Cambridge University Press.
Campbell, C. (2009), 'Distinguishing the Power of Agency from Agentic Power: A Note on Weber and the "Black Box" of Personal Agency', *Sociological Theory* 27 (4): 407–18.
Chowers, E. (2012), *The Political Philosophy of Zionism: Trading Jewish Words for a Hebraic Land,* Cambridge: Cambridge University Press.
Eisenstadt, Samuel Noah (1967), *Israeli Society,* London: Weidenfeld and Nicolson.
El-Asmar, F. (1978), *To Be an Arab in Israel,* Washington, DC: Institute for Palestine Studies.
Evens, T. M. S. (1999), 'Bourdieu and the Logic of Practice: Is All Giving Indian-Giving or is "Generalized Materialism" Not Enough?' *Sociological Theory* 17 (1): 1–33.
Falleti, T., and J. Lynch (2009), 'Context and Causal Mechanisms in Political analysis', *Comparative Political Studies* 42 (9): 1143–66.

Fanon, F. (1961), *The Wretched of the Earth*, trans. R. Philcox, New York: Grove Press.
Foucault, M. (1978), *The History of Sexuality.* Vol. 1, *An Introduction,* trans. R. Hurley, New York: Vintage.
Foucault, M. (2007), *Security, Territory, Population: Lectures at the College de France, 1977–1978,* trans. G. Burchell, Basingstoke and New York: Palgrave.
Gavison, R. (2003), 'The Jews' Right to Statehood: A defense', *Azure* 15: 70–108.
Gavison, R. (2011), 'Partition – for Zionism's Sake', *Haaretz.com*, 10 June. http://www.haaretz.com/print-edition/opinion/partition-for-zionism-s-sake-1.366891
George, A. (1979), '"Making the Desert Bloom": A Myth Examined', *Journal of Palestine Studies* 8 (2): 88–100.
Giddens, A. (1984), *The Constitution of Society: Outline of the Theory of Structuration,* Berkeley: University of California Press.
Giryis, S. (1976), *The Arabs in Israel,* New York: Monthly Review Press.
Goldberg, D. T. (2008), 'Racial Palestinianization', in R. Lentin (ed.), *Thinking Palestine* 25–45, London and New York: Zed Books.
Gordon, N. (2008), *Israel's Occupation,* Berkeley: University of California Press.
Gorny, Y. (1987), *Zionism and the Arabs, 1882–1948: A Study in Ideology,* Oxford: Clarendon Press.
Harding, S. (2004), *The Feminist Standpoint Theory Reader: Intellectual and Political Controversies,* New York: Routledge.
Hazoni, Y. (2001), *The Jewish State: The Struggle for Israel's Soul,* New York: Ingram Publisher Services.
Jabotinsky, V. Z. (1923), *The Iron Wall.* http://en.jabotinsky.org/media/9747/the-iron-wall.pdf
Jamal, A. (2011) 'Racialized Time and the Principles of Colonial Rule in the Israeli-Palestinian Context', in Y. Auron and I. Lubelsky (eds), *Genocide: Between Racism and Genocide in the Modern Era,* 185–219, Raanana: Open University. [Hebrew.]
Jamal, A. (2018), 'In the Shadow of the 1967 War: Israel and the Palestinians', *British Journal of Middle Eastern Studies* 44 (4): 529–44.
Jamal, A. (2019), 'Ontological Counter-Securitizations in Asymmetric Power Relations: Lessons from Israel', *International Studies Review* 22: 932–65.
Johansson, A. and S. Vinthagen (2014), 'Dimensions of Everyday Resistance: An Analytical Framework', *Critical Sociology* 42 (3): 417–35.
Kimmerling, B. (1983), *Zionism and Territory: The Socio-Territorial Dimension of Zionist Politics.* Los Angles: Institute for International Studies – University of California.
Lentin, R. (ed.) (2008), *Thinking Palestine,* London: Zed Books.
Lustick, I. (2019), *Paradigm Lost: From the Two-State Solution to One-State Reality,* Philadelphia: University of Pennsylvania Press.
Lyon, D. (2007), *Surveillance Studies: An Overview.* Cambridge: Polity.
Masalha, N. (2000), *Imperial Israel and the Palestinians: The Politics of Expansion,* London: Pluto Press.
Mbembe, A. (2003), 'Necropolitics', *Public Culture* 15 (1): 11–40.
Medding, P. (1990), *The Founding of Israeli Democracy, 1948–1967,* Oxford: Oxford University Press.
Memmi, A. (2003), *The Colonizer and the Colonized,* London: Earthsacn Publications.
Morris, B. (1989), *The Birth of the Palestinian Refugee Problem, 1947–1949,* Cambridge: Cambridge University Press.
Neumann, B. (2011), *Land and Desire in Early Zionism,* trans. H. Watzman, Waltham, MA: Brandeis University Press.

Pappe, I. (2006), *The Ethnic Cleansing of Palestine*. Oxford: Oneworld.
Pappe, I. (2008), 'The Mukhabarat State of Israel: A State of Oppression Is Not a State of Exception', in R. Lentin, (ed.), *Thinking Palestine*, 148–69. London and New York: Zed Books.
Pappe, I. (2014), *The Idea of Israel: A History of Power and Knowledge*, London: Verso.
Peled, N. (2006), 'About Educating towards Racism and the Murder of Children', *Mahsanmilim.com: Reports from the West Bank*, http://www.mahsanmilim.com/NuritPeledElhanan.htm (accessed 16 December 2009). [Hebrew.]
Roy, S. (2016), *The Gaza Strip: The Political Economy of De-Development*, 3rd ed., Washington, DC: Institute for Palestine Studies.
Sa'di, A. (2014), *Thorough Surveillance: The Genesis of Israeli Policies of Population Management, Surveillance and Political Control towards the Palestinian Minority*, Manchester: Manchester University Press.
Said, E. (1978), *Orientalism*, New York: Pantheon.
Said, E. (1980), *The Question of Palestine*, New York: Vintage Books.
Said, E. (1993), *Culture and Imperialism*, New York: Alfred A. Knopf.
Said E. (1996), *Representation of the Intellectual*, New York: Vintage.
Schmidt, V. (2008), 'Discursive Institutionalism: The Explanatory Power of Ideas and Discourse', *Annual Review of Political Science* 11: 303–26.
Scott, J. (1987), *Weapons of the Weak: Everyday Forms of Peasant Resistance*, New Haven, CT: Yale University Press.
Shafir, G. (1989), *Land, Labour and the Origins of the Israeli-Palestinian Conflict, 1882–1914*, Cambridge: Cambridge University Press.
Shafir, G., and Y. Peled (2002), *Being Israeli: The Dynamics of Multiple Citizenship*, Cambridge: Cambridge University Press.
Shenhav, Y. (2012), *Beyond the Two State Solution: A Jewish Political Essay*, Cambridge: Polity Press.
Shenhav, Y. and Y. Yona (2008), *Racism in Israel*, Jerusalem and Tel Aviv: The Van Leer Institute and Hakibbutz Hameuchad.
Shohat, E. (2003), 'Rupture and Return: Zionist Discourse and the Study of Arab Jews', *Social Text* 21 (2): 49–74.
Sternhell, Z. (2008), 'Colonial Zionism', *Haaretz.com*, 17 October. http://www.haaretz.com/print-edition/opinion/colonial-zionism-1.255642
Talmon, J. (1970), *Israel Among the Nations*, London: Weidenfeld and Nicolson.
Veracini, L. (2016), *Israel and Settler Society*, Ann Arbor, MI and London: Pluto Press.
Weizman, E. (2007), *Hollow Land: Israel's Architecture of Occupation*, London: Verso.
Wolf, P. (2006), 'Settler Colonialism and the Elimination of the Native', *Journal of Genocide Research* 8 (4): 388–409.
Yacobi, H. (2015), *Constructing a Sense of Place: Architecture and the Zionist Discourse*, London: Routledge.
Yiftachel, O. (2006), *Ethnocracy*, Philadelphia: University of Pennsylvania Press.
Yiftachel, O. (2009), '"Creeping Apartheid" in Israel-Palestine', *Middle East Report* 253. https://merip.org/2009/12/creeping-apartheid-in-israel-palestine/.
Zureik, E. (1979), *The Palestinians in Israel: A Study in Internal Colonialism*, London: Routledge and Kegan Paul.
Zureik, E. (2001), 'Constructing Palestine through Surveillance Practices', *British Journal of Middle Eastern Studies* 28 (2): 205–27.

Zureik, E. (2016), *Israel's Colonial Project in Palestine: A Brutal Pursuit*, New York: Routledge.
Zureik, E., and K. Hindle (2004), 'Governance, Security and Technology: The Case of Biometrics', *Studies in Political Economy* 73: 113–37.
Zureik, E., D. Lyon and Y. Abu-Laban (eds) (2011), *Surveillance and Control in Israel/Palestine: Population, Territory and Power,* London: Routledge.

5

Al-Naqab*

The Unfinished Zionist Settler-colonial Conquest of its Elusive 'Last Frontier', and Indigenous Palestinian Bedouin Arab Resistance

Ismael Abu-Saad

Introduction

Aotearoa/New Zealand Maori scholar Linda Tuhiwai Smith (1999) noted that for indigenous peoples, the colonial era never actually ended. This is abundantly clear in Al-Naqab, the elusive 'last frontier' of the Zionist settler colonial project in Palestine. Zureik (1979) provided an important framework for understanding Zionism, the state of Israel, and the experience of the Palestinians who remained within that state. Although this subgroup of the fragmented Palestinian population formally became citizens of Israel, they were also internally colonized by state policies and practices that dispossessed and displaced them, repressed independent economic development and limited their access to resources (e.g., land, education, housing, jobs) and the full scope of citizenship rights. While many aspects of Israel's implementation of colonizing policies toward the Palestinian population have been documented, I will revisit the pre- and early-state periods to provide some examples of how these colonial policies had their most extreme expressions against the Palestinian population in the Naqab. And moving into the present, the Naqab represents the internal frontier (i.e. within the 1949 armistice lines) in which the settler colonial policies of indigenous land confiscation and population displacement are still being most actively pursued.

Zureik's more recent book (2016) uses the framework of settler colonialism which is highly applicable to the Zionist colonial movement, as it involved not only the occupation but also the permanent settlement of the territory, as occurred in places such as the Americas, Australia, New Zealand and South Africa. Settler colonial projects require the transformation of the indigenous populations from the majorities to marginalized minorities (preferably in actual numbers, but at least in terms of political and economic power), and have achieved this through displacement, dispossession, subordination and in some cases extermination. Settler colonialism is also concerned with biopolitics or managing populations as political problems. I will review contemporary efforts to realize the Zionist settler colonial project in the Naqab, and ongoing Palestinian resistance. I will further argue that even though Zionist forces were 'granted' the Naqab by European colonial powers, 'captured' the territory during the course of the 1948 war, and sent in their settlers; they do not yet possess it.

Historical context

Zionist leaders such as Israel Zangwill and David Ben-Gurion exhibited a blatantly colonial perspective:

> If Lord Shaftesbury was literally inexact in describing Palestine as a country without a people, he was essentially correct, for there is no Arab people living in intimate fusion with the country, utilising its resources and stamping it with characteristic impress; there is at best an Arab encampment.[1]

> We do not recognize the right of the Arabs to rule the country, since Palestine is still undeveloped and awaits its builders.[2]

As noted by Zangwill in his reference to 'an Arab encampment', the colonial disregard for the indigenous population was at its highest when considering the Naqab Palestinians, who lived a semi-nomadic Bedouin lifestyle in harmony with the seasonal cycles of the desert. From David Ben-Gurion's perspective, they did not even exist: 'the Arabs have no right to close the country to us. What right do they have to the Negev desert, which is uninhabited?'[3]

Thus, I use the settler colonial framework as the basis for understanding the historical and current relationship between the Zionist movement, the Israeli state and the Naqab Palestinians. This is based on the foundation established by the architects of the Zionist movement, and confirmed by the indigenous Palestinians who both experienced and analysed its implementation.[4]

Pre-1948 Zionist settlement in the 'empty, barren' Naqab desert

From the late 1800s, World Zionist organizations worked to purchase property in Palestine and establish Jewish settlements. However, very little of this activity occurred in the Naqab initially, because of its harsh environmental conditions and its low priority from the perspective of the Zionist leadership.[5] Major Zionist settlement efforts occurred in the Naqab only after Jewish land purchases there were forbidden, and the 1937 Peel Commission plan for the partition of Palestine included it in the Arab, rather than the Jewish, state; while a subsequent plan split the Naqab between a future Arab state and a neutral, British-controlled zone. To prevent this outcome, Zionist settlement organizations clandestinely set up eleven illegal Jewish outposts in the Naqab.[6] They were surrounded with two rings of barbed wire fencing (setting the tone for relations with the Naqab's indigenous Palestinian inhabitants) and populated by young Zionist settlers with little agricultural or farming experience. When the British discovered these 'facts on the ground', they reversed their official policy of opposition to Jewish settlement in the Naqab. Between 1939 and 1948, additional

Jewish settlements were established in the Naqab, the operation and sustenance of which was subsidized by international Zionist organizations, to the amount of £1 million. Despite these intensified settlement efforts, when the 1947 UN partition plan included the Naqab in the Jewish state, it was populated by only 510 Jews (United Nations Conciliation Commission for Palestine 1947), while its indigenous Palestinian Bedouin population was estimated to be 65,000–90,000.[7]

'Absent presentees' making the desert bloom

'Present absentees' is an oxymoronic legal category created by Israeli policymakers in the early years of the state, which will be discussed in more detail below. Here, a reversal of the phrase, to 'absent presentees', captures the way in which the indigenous Palestinian Arabs were characterized and hidden from view by the early Zionists and their Western (European and American) patrons. Palestine was heralded as 'a land without a people for a people without a land',[8] and the Naqab in particular was characterized as a desert in need of technologically advanced (Zionist) pioneers to make it bloom.

In actual fact, the estimated 65,000–90,000 Palestinian Arabs populating the Naqab Desert prior to the 1948 war were organized into 95 tribes, and engaged in animal husbandry and seasonal agriculture. Turkish records dating as far back as the sixteenth century show that Palestinian Bedouin owned, cultivated and paid taxes on land; and that cultivation was extensive, particularly in the more fertile, less arid northern and northwestern Naqab.[9] Palestinian Bedouin cultivation in the Naqab was documented by European traveller accounts from the mid- to late-1800s, as well as Zionist explorer accounts from the late 1800s and early 1900s.[10] Reports produced both by British Mandate authorities and the Zionist Movement's Palestine Land Development Company in the early to mid-1900s indicated that over 2 million dunams were owned and cultivated by Naqab Palestinians.[11]

The great majority of Naqab Palestinians held their land under customary Bedouin law.[12] Neither the Ottoman or British Mandate governments ever completed land surveys of the vast Naqab region; however, they both recognized the Naqab Palestinians' traditional land ownership system, at the collective tribal and individual levels.[13] The Assistant District Commissioner of Beersheba, Lord Oxford, explained:

> All the tribes knew their land naturally without registering it with the government as the Ottoman codes of land asked...We did not oppose Bedouin land ownership, nor did we force them to register their land. They were happy about the way they recognized their land, so we thought it better not to impose on them something they did not like and would resist. Only the Ottomans enacted land codes; we, the British, did not have any registration system for land in Beersheba.[14]

However, prior to the 1948 war, Zionist leaders such as Ben-Gurion denied Naqab Palestinian land ownership, and characterized the Naqab as 'No Man's Land. It has no legal owners and anyone who cultivates it with the permission of the government is entitled to become its owner, according to a Turkish law, which still prevails in Palestine'.[15] He rejected the idea of purchasing land in the Naqab, saying to his staff:

'In the Negev we will not buy land. We will conquer it. You are forgetting that we are at war.'[16]

The Nakba and Naqab Palestinian displacement and dispossession

The 1948 war/Palestinian Nakba (Catastrophe) resulted in large-scale expulsion of Palestinian population, and internal displacement of many who remained in the territory that became the State of Israel.[17] Studies of the internally displaced Palestinians have generally not included the Bedouin Palestinians in the Naqab; aside from noting that the official governmental numbers did not include them,[18] or that a much higher proportion of the population was displaced, as compared to other regions.[19] They, indeed, faced the most extensive displacement and dispossession,[20] with 12 of the 19 tribes that remained in the Israeli state forced to move from their fertile lands in the northwestern Naqab to the infertile, arid region of the Seig. This resulted in nearly two-thirds of the communities losing their land, property and possessions.[21]

Although Israeli authorities initially told them that the displacement was temporary, and they would be allowed to return to their lands, this never occurred. Instead, an arsenal of laws was enacted and applied throughout Israel to transfer Palestinian-owned land to the Israeli state.[22] This played out in the Naqab in a uniquely extreme form. In the 1950s, the Israeli state took formal possession of all of the Naqab lands that had been emptied of Palestinians who had become refugees outside of the state's borders. They also took over the lands of the internally displaced persons, categorized by the Absentee Properties Act as 'Present Absentees', who were present in the state, but not on their lands, even temporarily, during a specified timeframe. Many Naqab Palestinians fell into this category precisely because the Israeli military government had removed them from their land and confined them to the Seig region.[23]

Recently uncovered archives and declassified government documents confirm that the displacement and land acquisition was not coincidental, but occurred according to an orderly, large-scale state plan to expel Palestinian citizens from the northwestern Naqab, with the goal of severing their physical ties to the land, and transferring this land to the possession of the state. Moshe Dayan, who commanded the military operation, wrote: 'It's now possible to transfer most of the Bedouin in the vicinity of [Kibbutz] Shoval to areas south of the Hebron-Be'er Sheva road. Doing so will clear around 60,000 dunams in which we can farm and establish communities.'[24] Although security issues were given as a rationale for the transfer, Dayan also clearly stated: 'Transferring the Bedouin to new territories will annul their rights as landowners and they will become tenants on government lands.'[25] The military government carried out the operation using a mix of threats, violence, bribery and fraud; but were careful never to give the displaced Naqab Palestinians written transfer orders, because such an operation for the purpose of land acquisition was illegal. Oral Palestinian histories of threats, violence and arrests were confirmed by archival kibbutz and state records.[26]

Although the official government story was that Naqab Palestinians voluntarily left their lands, declassified government records from the time document the 'Bedouin resistance and protests, the stubbornness with which they tried to hold onto their land, even at the cost of hunger and thirst, not to mention the army's threats and violence'.[27]

Archival kibbutz records also documented the military government's use of many methods to force the Bedouin to leave their lands, including stopping their food supplies for months.[28]

The Prime Minister's Advisor on Arab affairs, Yehoshua Palmon, wrote that the military government also prevented the Bedouin from sowing their lands to pressure them into agreeing to move. Thus, ironically, although Israel has been widely praised for the unprecedented achievement of 'making the desert bloom', by preventing Naqab Palestinian agriculture it actually reduced the amount of land in the Naqab under cultivation.[29] British Mandate records indicated that 1,900,000 dunums of cultivable land was owned and under cultivation in 1945. The hostilities and removals during 1947–48 resulted in Naqab Palestinians losing about 1,800,000 dunums of their land. As a result, in 1949–50, Israeli government statistics reported that only 554,000 dunums of land in the Naqab were under cultivation. As of 1975–76, with 1,095,000 dunums under cultivation in the Beersheba district, the Zionist settler state still had not succeeded in reaching the levels of cultivation of the indigenous Naqab Palestinians prior to their dispossession in 1948.[30]

Zionist efforts to settle the Naqab

The Naqab continued to be a major Zionist frontier icon, and Zionist leaders passionately called for Jewish pioneers to come and settle it, as the government engaged in Judaizing the geography.[31] Actually populating the Naqab with Jewish immigrants proved to be a challenge. However, the European-origin Israeli leaders devised a solution as a large wave of Jewish immigration from the Middle East and North Africa (MENA) began in the 1950s. Israel's leaders viewed the immigrants from the Arab countries, who were generally of a low socioeconomic background, through a classical orientalist lens.[32] Although, from a demographic perspective, they were needed to ensure an overwhelming Jewish majority in Israel, they were also viewed as a threat to the European dominance over Israeli Jewish society. In 1949, a leading journalist wrote:

> We are witnessing the arrival of a people whose primitivism reaches record levels, their education level is rock bottom and worse than all, they lack any talent to absorb anything spiritual or cultural ... Have you given a thought what would happen to our country if these people would be its residents? ... In the end, the masses of illiterate, primitive and poor will absorb us into their culture and not the other way around.[33]

The European-origin leadership of Israel developed a number of policies in order to maintain their dominance, especially as the number of MENA immigrants neared or reached parity with that of the European immigrants. One of the most important, for the purposes of this discussion, was the settlement of MENA immigrants in less developed, less desirable, peripheral regions (e.g., Naqab, Galilee) of the country in order to distance them from the Israeli centers of power and influence.[34] The 'frontier settlement' also was also an effort to forge a new, unifying identity of valiant pioneers judaizing the land of Israel, even in the harshest of environments, and building the nation. Israeli's first prime minister, David Ben-Gurion, claimed that:

> The people of Israel will be tested by the Negev … only by settling and developing the Negev can Israel, as a modern, independent and freedom-seeking nation, rise to the challenge that history put before us … All of us – [Zionist] veterans and [new immigrants], young and old, men and women – should see the Negev as their place and their future and turn southwards.[35]

Several development towns and moshavim (agricultural villages) were established in the Naqab in the 1950s and 1960s, and populated primarily with MENA Jewish immigrants.[36] Substantial public resources were invested in these towns (e.g., development of regional infrastructure, tax breaks, subsidized housing and land, investment incentives). However, their development never reached the level of development in the social and geographical centre of the country where European-origin Jews were dominant.[37] Factors such as cheap, mass-produced public housing, substandard service provision (e.g., health, education), limited employment opportunities mainly in labour-intensive industries, and distance from the country's commercial hubs ensured that the development towns remained underdeveloped, low socioeconomic status, and undesirable population centres.[38]

Thus, the Naqab remained an unpopular region for Jewish settlement. Over the years, the need to settle this region that was, through Zionist eyes, empty, remained. As Ben-Gurion stated in 1963:

> The Negev is an enormous Zionist asset, and there is no substitute for it anywhere else in the Land of Israel. First of all, it is half of the Land of Israel … The Negev is barren and empty now, and that is why it is important. We can create there a densely populated Jewish area, perhaps with room for millions of people … [I]t would be possible for 2 million Jews to make a living from farming in the Negev …[and] an additional 3 million could make a living from industry.[39]

This was of particular concern as the Palestinian population increased in these 'empty' regions. As a Jewish Agency policy document stated in 1978:

> We must continue and bring Jews to the Galilee and the Negev. The rapid increase in the numbers of Arabs in these regions and their wide-spread practices of seizing state land illegally, presents us with two main options: let the situation evolve naturally so we lose these regions, or reinvigorate the tradition of Jewish settlement and save them from Arab hands.[40]

Another frontier settlement wave was initiated in the 1970s and 1980s, consisting of establishing small suburban or rural settlements populated primarily by ex-urbanite European-origin Jews. This settlement effort further syphoned resources away from the struggling development towns, while not appreciably increasing the Jewish population of the region.[41]

In the early 1990s, there was a large wave of immigration from the former Soviet Union, some of whom settled in the development towns. This did not improve the towns' low socioeconomic status, however, because those who moved there were primarily the least educated and least well off.[42]

Parallel urbanization and on-going displacement of Naqab Palestinians

Despite the failure to achieve massive Jewish settlement in the Naqab, the Zionist settler colonial mandate to 'redeem' (i.e., wrest from Palestinian possession) the land continued to be actively pursued. In the 1960s, the government developed plans to reduce the presence of Naqab Palestinians in the Seig region (which represented 10 per cent of Naqab lands) to an even smaller area.[43] Their dispersed settlement and continued land use within the Seig, not to mention land ownership claims (for the 8 tribes who were not displaced), represented an obstacle to the ongoing Zionist conquest and settlement of the land.[44] Thus, the government formulated a programme for a new wave of Naqab Palestinian displacement and resettlement into high-density, urban-style towns.[45]

The displacement and urbanization plan also served another purpose. By the 1960s, the rapidly developing Israeli Jewish economy required an increasing number of unskilled and low-skilled workers,[46] a need which the Naqab Palestinian workforce could fill, once they were moved into urban-style towns and deprived of the land resources needed for their traditional way of life. As Moshe Dayan stated in 1963 while he was the Minister of Agriculture:

> We should transform the Bedouins into an urban proletariat—in industry, services, construction, and agriculture. 88 per cent of the Israeli populations are not farmers, let the Bedouins be like them. Indeed, this will be a radical move which means that the Bedouin would not live on his land with his herds, but would become an urban person who comes home in the afternoon and puts his slippers on. His children would be accustomed to a father who wears trousers, does not carry a Shabaria [the traditional Bedouin knife] and does not search for head lice in public. The children would go to school with their hair properly combed. This would be a revolution, but it may be fixed within two generations. Without coercion but with governmental direction ... this phenomenon of the Bedouins will disappear.[47]

Despite the obvious settler colonial aims driving the urbanization plan, the government framed the policy as a benevolent initiative to 'modernize the Bedouin' and provide them with services more efficiently.[48] This rationale, however, was belied by the explicitly urban and highly concentrated settlement model that represented the complete destruction of the traditional Naqab Palestinian lifestyle. If the goal of the government was in actuality only to modernize and provide people with services more efficiently, which the Naqab Palestinians also wanted, this could have been achieved by planning small agricultural villages or cooperatives with a land base (such as the Jewish moshavim and kibbutzim), as requested by Naqab Palestinians.[49]

The common settler colonial practice of expropriating indigenous land and then gifting or selling back small pockets to the indigenous people who once possessed all of it[50] was taken to the extreme with this urbanization plan.[51] In the late 1960s, the Housing Ministry launched the first town, Tel A-Seba, with a small commercial area including a few shops, a school and a clinic.[52] The commercial area was surrounded by small houses (70 square metres) on 400-square-metre plots each.[53] Each family would receive a renewable 49-year lease for the plot, but in return were expected to sign away all claims to land owned in the past.[54]

The small houses were unsuitable for the typically large Naqab Palestinian families, with an average of eight or nine children, and the high density of the town itself stood in conflict with the their traditionally widely-dispersed settlement patterns.[55] As a result, Naqab Palestinians largely refused to move to Tel A-Seba,[56] engaging in social non-cooperation as a form of resistance.[57] Instead of complying with governmental urbanization plans, they continued to live on their own lands or the lands to which the government had displaced them, in 'illegal' wood, tin and cement-block structures.[58]

After this failed model, the Israeli government planners initiated a second settlement, Rahat, in the early 1970s, that made limited efforts to take the population's traditions and culture into account, while still maintaining an urban model and advancing the Zionist aim of reducing the amount of land Naqab Palestinians occupied.[59] In this second town, tribes were placed in separate neighbourhoods according to their extended family groups, territorial distribution and willingness to move. Each street and lane was identified with an extended family, and its households were concentrated on adjacent plots.[60] Instead of providing small lots with small two-room houses, the Ministry of Housing allowed people to lease a larger vacant plot (800 square metres) for each household within an extended family. Residents were then free to build their houses according to their own budgetary resources, and household and social needs.[61] The planning model used in Rahat was extended to new neighbourhoods that were added to Tel A-Seba, as well as to the additional five planned Bedouin towns that were established during the 1980s and 1990s (Arara, Kseiffa, Shgeib a-Salam, Hura and Laqiya). These towns provided the only sites on which Naqab Palestinians could legally build houses. However, in all of them, even if they were established on the lands historically owned by some of the town's inhabitants, every family had to move to a plot assigned by the government, and legally considered state land, that they had the right only to lease.[62]

Along with these developments, increasingly coercive measures were applied to force Naqab Palestinians to move to the towns. In 1976, Agriculture Minister Ariel Sharon formed a new police unit, called the Green Patrol, whose mandate was to protect state land from the Bedouin.[63] It confiscated flocks; destroyed crops, tents and houses; and fined and arrested those resisting their forced urbanization.[64]

Over time, the Naqab Palestinian families who had been rendered landless by being removed from their traditional lands and relocated to the Seig, as well as those who had been landless before 1948, or were affected by a new wave of displacements in the 1980s (to build a new military airport), moved to the planned urban settlements.[65] For them, this was preferable to their ambiguous, 'illegal' status on lands classified as state land or, according to Bedouin law, land belonging to another family or tribe.[66] The requirement to sign away all land claims remained a huge disincentive, which people dealt with in different ways. For example, one household head who owned and claimed land in the northwestern Naqab purchased a plot of land in one of the towns, but put it in the name of his 18-year old son, who was not a direct land claimant.[67] In other cases, families pushed for the resolution of their land ownership claims before agreeing to move to a government-planned town.[68]

The urbanization process moved slowly. Jewish Israeli academics, who wittingly or unwittingly overlooked the context of indigenous resistance to dispossession and settler colonialism, focused on other disincentives for Naqab Palestinians to urbanize:

> Whereas the planning model adopted in Rahat and replicated in subsequent towns succeeded in reducing some of the socio-cultural barriers related to allocation of space that had caused the first model to fail, it did not address the employment needs of the population. With no local industry, local employment was non-existent beyond small grocery shops and work for the local government councils. The planned Bedouin towns never became more than dormitory communities with large numbers of men leaving very early in the morning for their places of employment and returning late at night. A survey commissioned by the Rahat Municipality in 1997 found that of the 66% of men over 18 who were employed, fully 64% worked outside Rahat in construction, trucking, industry, agriculture, and services.[69]

Furthermore, aside from the provision of basic services (water, electricity, telephone hook-up, schools and clinics), in 2002, nearly forty years after the urbanization programme began, the Israeli State Comptroller reported that none of the towns had a completed sewage system, despite the fact that thousands of families had already paid for this essential system. In four of the seven towns the sewage system was not operational at all. Unlike neighbouring urban settlements in the Jewish sector, they also lacked intra- and inter-city public transport, banks, post offices, public libraries, public car parks, recreational and cultural centres. The only exception was the largest town, Rahat, which had nearly 40,000 residents by then, and had one bank, one post office and a cultural centre.[70]

By the early 2000s, an estimated 50 per cent of Naqab Palestinians still lived in officially 'unrecognized' villages. In some of these, people lived on their original lands, predating the State of Israel; others were established on the lands where the government had confined the people it displaced during the military government.[71] The unrecognized villages were denied basic services and infrastructure (e.g., connection to water and electricity grids, paved roads, community clinics, community schools aside from ones established before initiation of the urbanization programme).[72]

The plan to concentrate all Naqab Palestinians into the initial seven government-planned towns had clearly failed, so in 2000 the government began the process of recognizing another eleven villages. On the surface, it appeared that the government was complying with the requests of the community by recognizing existing villages. However, in reality, it again did the planning without consulting the villages' current inhabitants, arbitrarily selecting areas to be recognized and ignoring outstanding land ownership claims in the 'recognized' village areas.[73] This government 'recognition' of existing villages still required the displacement of the residents from their current locations to designated plots drawn by planning authorities in the recognized areas, and so the 'recognized villages' did not attract residents. Furthermore, since in most cases they were located on contested territory with unsettled land claims, they were not able to produce valid statutory outlines, or issue their residents permits to build legally.[74]

In 2003 a regional council, Abu-Basma, was established for the eleven newly recognized villages. It was run by a government-appointed (rather than elected) Jewish mayor and a slate of Naqab Palestinian representatives.

> unlike the Jewish regional councils, which provide a powerful spatial, economic, and political organizational framework for Jewish rural localities, the Abu Basma Regional Council has been denied any territorial continuity or appropriate budgets. As a consequence, it had great difficulty providing minimal services to its eleven localities and focused chiefly on the provision of educational facilities, with the construction of several large and modern schools.[75]

Funds for the development of the new villages were largely administered by preexisting organizations created to deal with Naqab Palestinians. The Bedouin Advancement Authority (later the Bedouin Authority) was mandated with managing all government development funds to the Naqab Palestinians, including those for the first seven government-planned towns. It received a large annual budget for settling land claims at a very low rate of compensation, most of which was consistently unused.[76] It also controlled water allotments and distribution to all unrecognized villages, and all development and urban planning for employment, education and welfare services for both recognized and unrecognized towns.[77] In addition, during this period, high budgets were allocated to a number of policing and enforcement units for the purpose of prosecuting Naqab Palestinians living in unrecognized villages, and advancing their forced urbanization.[78] The Bedouin Authority continues to work in close collaboration with law enforcement and the police, including the special divisions responsible for carrying out house demolitions.[79]

In contrast to all other communities in Israel, the relationship between national government offices and services and recognized and unrecognized Naqab Palestinian towns and villages is not direct, but is mediated through the Bedouin Authority, whose top priority is settling land claims and overseeing the coercive transfer of residents of the unrecognized villages to the government-planned towns.[80] While generous plans and budgets have been allocated for the socioeconomic development of Naqab Palestinian communities, they are conditional on carrying out the evictions and home demolitions to empty the unrecognized villages of their inhabitants.[81] From its inception to present day, all high-level Bedouin Authority officials have been Jewish; the local Naqab Palestinian employees have no policy- or decision-making powers.[82]

Under these conditions, the Naqab Palestinians in the unrecognized villages have continued to resist moving into the government-planned towns and villages. The government-appointed regional council for the eleven newly-recognized villages, Abu-

Basma, was subsequently split into two government-appointed, Jewish-run regional councils (Wahat A-Sahra and Al-Qasum). Little to no development occurred in these villages – as with the residents of unrecognized villages, they are not authorized to build legally and remain disconnected from national service infrastructure.[83]

Between 1997 and 2007, a number of NGOs supporting the civil and land rights of Naqab Palestinians were formed. These NGOs strengthened community resistance, raised national and international awareness of denial of services to and on-going dispossession of Naqab Palestinians in unrecognized villages, and created their own regional plan for the recognition and development of Naqab Bedouin villages.[84] In addition, they had some success with altering government development plans for the Naqab, including canceling expansion plans of Jewish towns that annexed the lands of Naqab Palestinian villages, and requiring the National Master Plan for the Naqab to take into account the existence of Naqab Palestinian villages in its future planning.[85]

Fulfilment of the Zionist vision to bring all Naqab land under Jewish control remained elusive, which generated increasingly urgent right-wing demands to halt 'Bedouin trespassing' and protect state lands. In 2008 the government appointed the Goldberg Committee to recommend policies for completing the transfer of Naqab Palestinian residents from the unrecognized villages to the towns and settling their land claims. All committee members (including the two Naqab Palestinians) represented government interests; none came from the community's NGOs or civil rights groups.[86] The Goldberg Committee heard testimony from Naqab Palestinian community members, and its report acknowledged some of the historic injustices committed by the government against the Naqab Palestinians. Although it encouraged recognizing more of the unrecognized villages, it did not recognize their land rights.[87] Rather, it recycled the same mechanisms that had been used in the past to try to bring the land under full government control and concentrate the Naqab Palestinians in selected areas that did not conflict with other (i.e. Jewish settlement and development) plans.[88] Another committee (the Prawer Committee, later modified to the Prawer-Begin Committee), which did not have any Naqab Palestinian members or community input, was then formed to develop a plan for implementing the Goldberg Committee recommendations. It recommended that people with land claims who were not in possession of their land (i.e. the vast majority of land claimants, since the government had removed them from their lands) receive only some monetary compensation; while the minority who originally lived in the Seig region could receive *up to* 50 per cent (with caveats that meant they would probably receive only 13 to 20 per cent) of their claims in alternative land determined by the government, on the condition of giving up all land claims.[89] The government would unilaterally decide upon the amount of land and monetary compensation (which, where detailed, was far below the market rate), and would not allow judicial review of its land settlement or planning decisions.[90] In addition, the Prawer-Begin plan required that all Naqab Palestinian residents of unrecognized villages be transferred to existing recognized towns and villages, allowing only possibly for recognition of a few additional villages, meeting stringent conditions (e.g., of adequate scale, not infringing on any other Naqab [Jewish] development plans). Consequently, the plan called for at least two-thirds of the residents of unrecognized villages to be uprooted, and also included budgetary provisions for the

Israel Land Authority, police and other special enforcement units to carry out evictions and house demolitions.[91]

The Israeli govenment has continuously claimed that it cannot efficiently supply services to small, scattered Naqab Palestinian villages (which range in size from 300 to 10,000 inhabitants).[92] However, the fallacy of this rationale becomes apparent when considering Jewish settlement in the Naqab. The government financially supports and delivers services to over 100 Jewish rural Naqab towns, with an average of less than 300 residents each. In addition, there are 59 individual Jewish family farms in the Naqab, all of which receive services, and 35 of these were established illegally (without official building permits) and retroactively recognized by the government.[93]

The Prawer-Begin plan conducted a token process to respond to community feedback after the plan had been completed, but this did not result in substantive modifications.[94] The Naqab Palestinians opposed the plan, and again called for the implementation of the regional plan they had developed for the Naqab Palestinian villages (1999, 2006, 2014), which was consistently rejected or ignored by the government.[95] Extensive local, national and international efforts were mobilized to oppose the Prawer-Begin plan.[96] In the end, it was tabled, both because of local and international opposition on behalf of Naqab Palestinians, and because right-wing members of the government thought the settlement was too generous, and the enforcement not severe enough.[97] No clear government plan has replaced it, but the policy of uprooting and concentrating the Naqab Palestinians has remained the same, with numerous government agencies carrying out evictions, demolitions and crop destruction in the unrecognized villages.[98]

It is important to note that the governmental efforts to 'modernize' the Naqab Palestinians through urbanization have resulted in the most entrenched poverty in Israel (Figure 5.1). All of the original seven planned towns, and two regional councils with the eleven semi-recognized villages, consistently rank lowest in the socioeconomic ranking of towns and regional councils in Israel.[99] They remain lower than the Naqab Jewish development towns (populated mainly by low-SES MENA-origin Jews and other low-SES Jewish immigrants), and markedly lower than the suburban Naqab Jewish towns and regional councils (populated mainly by high-SES European-origin Jews).[100] According to the Israeli National Insurance Institute, 79.6 per cent of Naqab Palestinian children live below the poverty line.[101]

Naqab Palestinian legal efforts to restore their land holdings

Naqab Palestinian efforts to restore their land holdings through the Israeli courts have been extensively documented.[102] Here I will provide a brief summary. In the 1960s, Naqab Palestinians began to appeal to Israeli courts for recognition and protection of their land ownership rights, but they have not won a single case.[103] This legal saga must be viewed within the framework of Zionist settler colonialism, which removed most Naqab Palestinians from their lands for the explicit purpose of severing their connection and claims to the land, and acquiring it for Jewish settlement.[104] Israeli courts have functioned as an integral component of the settler colonial apparatus, the aims of which they furthered by excluding the extensively-developed system of

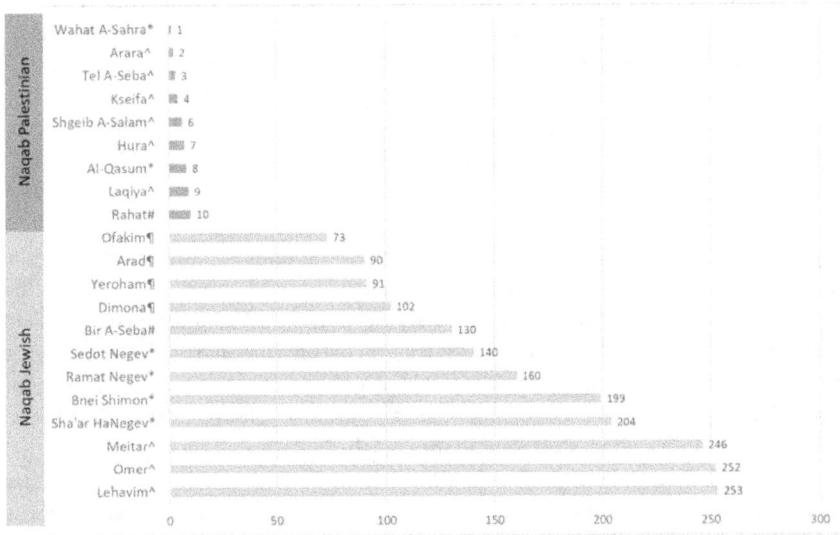

Figure 5.1 Socioeconomic ranking of Naqab Palestinian and Jewish localities, 2017.
Source: Central Bureau of Statistics 2022

Ranking includes all localities in Israel (except for the unrecognized villages) and ranges from 1 (lowest) to 255 (highest).

\# – City
∧ – Town
¶ – Development town
* – Regional council

Bedouin law, thus making it irrelevant to determining land rights. 'Bedouin presence, culture, and land possession were brutally and *strategically* ignored.'[105] In addition, the Israeli courts employed 'formalistic and questionable interpretations of carefully selected Ottoman and British statutes' to deny Naqab Palestinian land ownership claims, and to classify the people as illegal trespassers.[106] For example, the Israeli legal precedents created by a highly Eurocentric interpretation of Ottoman law basically invalidated all of the land claims of Palestinians who had maintained semi-nomadic lifestyles, because if land claims were not within a specified distance from a permanent town or village, they were considered 'dead' lands that could automatically be registered as state lands. Though the Israeli legal system used principles drawn from Ottoman law, they did not follow the more flexible Ottoman definition of a settlement to include the temporary settlements and tribal areas of the semi-nomadic Bedouin.[107] The Israeli state's legal experts also relied upon carefully selected nineteenth-century travel literature and maps, coloured by Christian/orientalist and colonial outlooks, while disdaining accounts of the indigenous Naqab Palestinians.

All legal challenges to the confiscation of Naqab Palestinians' land were shut down by an Israeli Supreme Court decision in May 2015:

We call this official position the Dead Negev Doctrine (DND), a concept strongly evocative of the terra nullius colonial doctrine. To be sure, just as terra nullius relied on a settlers' imagined and distorted historical geography, which legally emptied the land from its previously existing indigenous population, so Israel treated the Negev as 'dead,' though it was neither 'dead' nor empty. It was inhabited, demarcated, allocated, used, and cultivated for generations by its indigenous Bedouin population.[108]

Flying in the face of the Naqab Palestinians' multigenerational historic land ties, the Israeli courts have created a completely unassailable legal bulwark in service of the Zionist settler colonial project. Israeli Jewish law professor Alexandre Kedar asserted that the courts have engaged in 'judicial activism' through their self-serving interpretations of Ottoman law, and the evidence they refuse to consider; the goal of which has been to protect Jewish and State land against Palestinian land claims; and nowhere to more extreme effect than in the Naqab.[109]

Few Naqab Palestinians view the Israeli courts as a source of salvation or a process in which they have a real chance to prove their rights. Most, and particularly those living in unrecognized villages, do not consider the court rulings legitimate and continue to manage their land affairs according to their customary law.[110]

The settler colonial displacement and dispossession of the Naqab Palestinians was not limited to the early period of Israel's statehood. It is an ongoing, unfinished process that frames their current relationship to and resistance against the State. Scholars writing about the dispossession of internally displaced Palestinians in Israel note that:

> The story of dispossession is incomplete without the denial of Bedouin land rights in the Naqab in southern Israel. Ronen Shamir, who reviewed the Court's rulings on Bedouin land rights, argues that the question cannot be reduced to a binary between 'nomads' and Western conceptions of property. Rather, this binary – as the Court constructs it – is itself part and parcel of the Bedouins' dispossession (Shamir 1996). On the one hand, the Court constructs the Naqab as an empty space waiting for (Zionist) redemption, and perceives the Bedouin as nomads even when they reside in permanent communities (ibid.). On the other hand, the law facilitates their concentration in specific townships. Bedouin are allowed to reside and build only in designated places; all the other places are considered state lands. Thus, the law transforms them from citizens with claims over disputed lands into lawbreakers of the Planning and Construction Law – 1967, which the state enacted long after many of their communities have existed. In light of this, state law transforms the conflict between the Palestinian Bedouin and the state from a collective question into individual criminal cases (ibid.).[111]

Current context

The current conditions of the Naqab Palestinians represent nothing new, except in the level of their intensity. They reflect, perhaps, a desperately increased effort to achieve the elusive Zionist settler colonial vision of the Naqab. This is evidenced by: 1) the increase of coercive measures to destroy the unrecognized villages and transfer their residents to the impoverished government-planned towns; 2) increased struggle for physical control of the land and Jewish demographic dominance; and, 3) blatant legislative erosion of the citizenship rights and equality of Palestinian Arabs in Israel.

House and village demolitions

In the on-going Nakba, Israeli government policymakers and forces continue to destroy homes and even entire villages. During the period 2013–20, some 13,265 structures were demolished in Naqab Palestinian communities (Figure 5.2). The rate of destruction has increased over the years, including in the COVID-19 pandemic year of 2020, during which 2,568 structures were demolished. This represents an increase in annual demolitions of 268 per cent since 2013. In addition, the Israeli governmental and non-governmental forces (e.g., the Jewish National Fund [JNF]), continue to oppose Naqab Palestinians' making the desert bloom. The NGO, Negev Coexistence Foundation (NCF) documented the destruction of approximately 14,500 dunams of crops planted by Naqab Palestinians in 2021.[112]

The government has also restarted its pre- and early-state practice of demolishing entire Palestinian villages. One such village, Al-Araqib, represents a particular threat because it is a story of displaced Naqab Palestinians moving *back* to their ancestral lands and re-establishing their village. This village, established in the early 1900s, was depopulated by the Israeli military government in 1953, when all inhabitants were

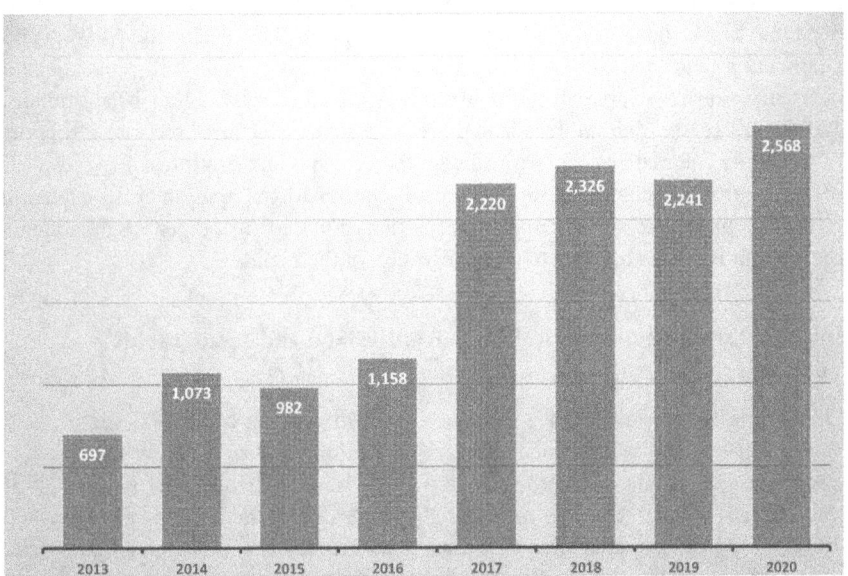

Figure 5.2 Number of structures demolished in Naqab Palestinian towns and unrecognized villages 2013–20. *Source:* Kremer 2022.

evacuated, ostensibly for six months in order to use the land for military training.[113] The Israeli authorities, however, never allowed the Al-Araqib villagers to return, and eventually they resettled in Rahat, while continuing to register claims for their land, to use it for grazing and agriculture (though crops were repeatedly destroyed by the authorities), and bury their dead in the village cemetery.[114] In 1998, around fifty Bedouin families decided to return to al-Araqib to live on their land, when an operation by the JNF to plant trees on their land was initiated.[115] Like other unrecognized villages, Al-Araqib has no modern services or infrastructure, and has been repeatedly subjected to demolitions, threats and arrests by Israeli authorities. On 27 July 2010, the entire village was demolished by the state, including olive trees and livestock. When the UN Human Rights Council questioned the Israeli government about the demolition of this village in 2011, it maintained a staunchly settler-colonial denial of indigenous land rights, stating that 'the so-called El-Arkib village was simply an act of squatting on state owned land. The individuals never had ownership over this land.'[116] The people of Al-Araqib rebuilt their village and have staunchly refused to leave. Since then, as of 25 January 2022, the village has been demolished another 197 times,[117] often with the Israeli forces also destroying, burying or confiscating the wood and tin building materials to try to prevent the residents from using them to rebuild Al-Araqib again. These serial demolitions have also resulted in many injuries and arrests, and state authorities have sued the families for over a million shekels (~US$330,000) to cover the costs of the demolitions.[118]

Some Al-Araqib villagers are continuing to pursue a legal battle for their land, using the recently uncovered evidence from government documents, discussed above, of an orderly state plan to expel the Naqab Palestinians in order to dispossess them and acquire their land.[119] This evidence from government sources provides a slim ray of hope that Israeli courts might acknowledge the illegality of displacing the villagers and confiscating their land, and so finally recognize and restore their land rights. Such a decision would have ripple effects for all dispossessed and displaced Naqab Palestinians, and would represent an unprecedented break in the Israeli courts' consistent support of the settler colonial project. Nevertheless, the evidence and continued struggle itself provides further documentation to the court of international opinion of the explicitly settler-colonial nature of the Zionist policies that displaced the indigenous inhabitants throughout Palestine in order to take possession of their land.

Increased struggle for physical control of the land and demographic dominance

Despite the Israeli state's legal successes to date in denying Naqab Palestinian land rights, it has failed to implement David Ben-Gurion's vision of taking indisputable control of the land and filling the Naqab with Jewish inhabitants. Only 10 per cent of the residents of the state live in the Naqab,[120] 35 per cent of them being Palestinians.[121] The Zionist project is threatened by the fact that the traditional Palestinian inhabitants, rather than Jewish pioneers, are spreading out to fill the Naqab. For example, a veteran Israeli Jewish journalist (and West Bank settler) wrote an alarmist op-ed in the liberal mainstream *HaAretz* newspaper[122] in response to a new law that he erroneously claimed approved connecting the unrecognized Naqab Palestinian villages to the national electricity grid.[123] In his view, Israel was clearly not the state of all of its citizens, but rather a passive Jewish state being actively conquered by the lawless presence, natural growth and land claims of its colonized subjects:

> With perseverance, openly and without resistance, the Bedouin have advanced to the point that the state of the Jews recognized their state: Bedouiland. Last week in a historic Knesset vote, this state, which effectively subtracts the heart of the central Negev from the state founded by David Ben-Gurion ('If we do not hold on to the Negev, we will eventually lose Tel Aviv'), received de facto recognition. Some are burying their heads in the Negev's sands. What's the big deal? All they did was whitewash the (intolerable) status quo, in which thousands of illegal buildings are connected illegally to utilities … [I]n so doing we determine, in both theory and practice, that the piratical construction that extends over hundreds of thousands of acres will become permanent.[124]

Similarly, government officials from the far-right[125] to the centre of the political spectrum,[126] media[127] and academia[128] decry 'illegal Bedouin settlement' and 'the Bedouin taking over the Negev'. However, as a result of the semi-successful settler colonial project to concentrate the Naqab Palestinian, in actuality, the territory they live on represents only 3 per cent of Naqab land.[129] Figure 5.3 graphically depicts the extreme disparity between the populations of and land area allocated to Naqab Jewish communities, as compared to Naqab Palestinian communities.[130]

Approximately two-thirds of the Naqab Palestinians have been concentrated into 18 recognized localities that take up only 1 per cent of the Bir A-Seba sub-district's land area. In contrast, there are 127 recognized Jewish localities in the district.[131]

Ongoing efforts to assert Jewish sovereignty over the remaining 2 per cent of Naqab land take several forms. One, in lieu of succeeding to achieve massive Jewish settlement, is to impose control on the land by planting trees, particularly in disputed areas for which Naqab Palestinian have registered ownership claims.[132] These projects are explicitly aimed at wresting control of the land from its Palestinian inhabitants, although they are simultaneously 'green-washed' as combating desertification or greening the desert. This claim has been challenged, however, by the Israeli Society for the Protection of Nature which sued the JNF to stop the afforestation projects, claiming that they are actually harmful to the desert ecosystem.[133]

The most recent JNF afforestation effort exploded into violence in January 2022 when it started preparing the land for planting near two unrecognized villages, for which the Palestinian owners have unresolved claims that were submitted in 1973. The JNF uprooted at least twenty-five olive and fig trees, as well as annual wheat and barley crops.[134] Several rightwing Israeli parliament members joined in the tree-planting operation, while large numbers of Palestinians from within and beyond the Naqab gathered to protest against it.[135] Hundreds of police officers were brought in to support the JNF operation, setting up checkpoints and meeting Palestinian protesters with riot gear, mounted police, helicopters, tear gas launching drones, shock grenades, water cannons and rubber-coated metal bullets.[136] A number of protesters were shot,

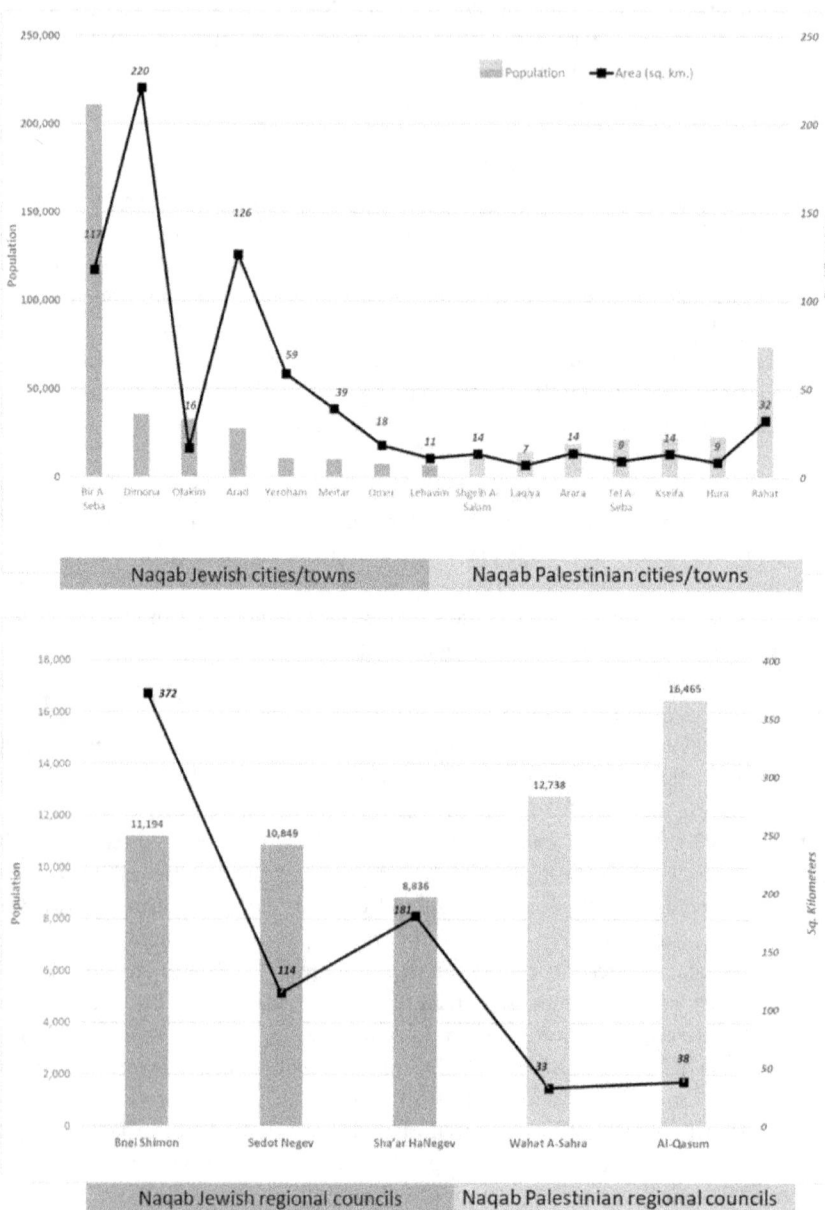

Figure 5.3 Population and area of Naqab Jewish and Palestinian cities, towns and regional councils. *Source:* Central Bureau of Statistics 2022.

including three in the upper body and four in the face, resulting in one person with a shattered skull and two with shattered jaws; and in all cases, the Israeli police claimed the shootings complied with proper procedure.[137] Over 150 Palestinians were arrested, including 60 minors, some of whom were as young as 12 and were taken from home in pre-dawn raids.[138] Police repeatedly asked for extensions on the arrestees' detention while they investigated, and eventually 16 protestors were indicted, including three minors.[139] Such ostensibly 'green' efforts to physically establish Zionist sovereignty over the Naqab demonstrated both how quickly the Israeli establishment's distinction between Palestinian 'citizens' and 'occupied subjects' disintegrated; and how determined Palestinians within, as well as beyond, the Green Line were to resist further erasure, displacement and colonial conquest.

Although Israeli state efforts to establish its sovereignty over the Naqab by filling it with Jewish pioneers have not been widely successful, it also continues to pursue this goal. Government officials have announced plans to establish three or four new Jewish towns in the Naqab that will bring in 3,000 families.[140] The JNF's blueprint for the Naqab includes bringing in 500,000 new residents, with multiple levels of development, including an Israel Technology and Education Campus that will 'revolutionize Zionist and Jewish educational engagement for the decades ahead', and creating 'waterfront parks' and new places of employment in cities like Bir A-Seba and Yeroham.[141] Similarly, spokespersons of the region's Ben-Gurion University of the Negev (BGU) propose Zionist visions of developing the Naqab, imbued with the 'pioneering', settler colonial vision of David Ben-Gurion:

> David Ben-Gurion ... famously said that 'Israel's future lies in the Negev'... 'it is in the Negev where the creativity and pioneering vigor of Israel shall be tested' ...
>
> This region, once a vast desert, today represents a Zionist rebirth of Israeli pioneering – university scientists, farmers, entrepreneurs, new immigrants and an ever-growing presence of the Israel Defense Forces (IDF), all of whom are working to secure Israel's future. This is Ben-Gurion's Zionism transplanted and reinvigorated in the 21st century.[142]

Additional military units and installations are being moved or established in the Naqab to increase employment opportunities for Jews (as Palestinians will not receive security clearance to work in such facilities), and hopefully attract more of them to settle there:

> The IDF is moving its elite intelligence groups, including the prestigious 8200 Intelligence Unit [a.n. incubator for the notorious cyber spyware Pegasus and companies such as the NSO group], to a high-tech campus adjacent to the university that was once an arid field of dirt and sand. It's part of an innovation ecosystem that involves a unique collaboration between academia, industry, government and the IDF.[143]

While the Israeli government is displacing Naqab Palestinians from their traditional lands and forcing them to urbanize, BGU advocates proudly state that 'Israeli environmental research students work in African villages to provide low-tech solutions for farming, irrigation, soil management, and safe drinking water without electricity'.[144] The irony of this could not be greater, as the Israeli government, police forces and JNF destroy the crops, homes and villages of the country's own citizens; prevent Naqab Palestinian farmers from managing the soil by leasing them different plots every year; and deny Naqab Palestinian villages recognition, thus keeping them without safe drinking water and electricity.

The juxtaposition of Israel's treatment of the indigenous Palestinians in the Naqab and throughout historic Palestine with flowery expressions of Ben-Gurion's vision creates a jarring dissonance:

> Ben-Gurion's vision of Zionism highlights how crucial science, education and a moral compass are for the Jewish State, not just for its survival but to be a light among nations. 'The State of Israel will prove itself not by material wealth, not by military might or technical achievement, but by its moral character and human values,' Ben-Gurion said.[145]

The efforts to increase the Jewish population in the Naqab have also recently come to involve new actors, including nationalist religious settlers from the West Bank. On the heels of volatile JNF afforestation efforts in January 2022, in early February a group of West Bank Jewish settlers came under the cover of night to establish an illegal settlement near the Naqab Palestinian city of Rahat, just as they have done across the Israeli-occupied West Bank in violation of international law. The settlers named the outpost after Ben-Gurion's wife, and claimed that it was the first of many they planned to establish in order to create 'facts on the ground'.[146] The organizers stated:

> This is a Zionist response to the lack of governance and sovereignty in the Negev vis-à-vis the Bedouin and the laundering of illegal [Bedouin] buildings in the region by the government.[147]

This operation also received the personal support of Israeli Parliament members from rightwing religious nationalist parties and the Likud party. The head of the Jewish Power party, MK Itamar Ben Gvir, confronted Naqab Palestinian protestors, shouting: 'We are the landlords here. It's ours. Whoever wants to come and live here, fine, but we are the landlords.'[148] Israeli police arrived and asked the settlers to leave of their own accord, and eventually removed those who did not, arresting two, one of whom was from a West Bank settlement. However, the police did not open a criminal investigation into who funded or established the outpost.[149] The Israeli-establishment distinction between Palestinian 'citizen' and 'occupied subject' was again erased, this time by West Bank Jewish settlers who actively pursue illegal Zionist settlement on both sides of the Green Line, largely with impunity, if not outright support, from the government.

Legislative erosion of the citizenship rights and equality

The citizenship of Palestinians in Israel came with many caveats, from the founding moment of the Israeli state.[150] Two of the most glaring included providing a 'right of return' and immediate citizenship to all Jews from anywhere in the world, while denying the Palestinian refugees displaced during the 1948 war the right to return; and then subjugating Palestinian citizens under a military government until 1966.[151] While claiming to be a democracy (and indeed, 'the only democracy in the Middle East') based on principles of equality, the Israeli state has continued to introduce laws and provisions that discriminate against Palestinian citizens, in an increasingly blatant manner. Although there is a large body of scholarship covering these issues,[152] I will briefly describe two recent laws that demonstrate how the Zionist project continues to actively roll out its settler colonial aims.

The Basic Law on Israel as The Nation-State of the Jewish People

In 2018, the Israeli parliament enacted the 'Nation-State' law as part of the Basic Law, which has the status of a constitutional law in Israel. The Nation-State law officially defined Israel as 'the national homeland of the Jewish people', and stipulated that 'the right to exercise self-determination in the State of Israel' belonged exclusively to Jews.[153] The law enshrined the annexation of occupied East Jerusalem in constitutional law, designating Jerusalem as Israel's 'united' capital, and it demoted Arabic from an official language to a language with 'special status'.[154] In addition, the Nation-State law enshrined 'the development of Jewish settlement as a national value' and directed the state to 'act to encourage and promote its establishment and consolidation'.[155] Critics and advocates of the law understood it to promote the establishment of Jewish-only settlements, and further entrench discrimination against Palestinian citizens in planning and building.[156] Law professor Mordechai Kremnitzer characterized this development as the extension of the settlers' apartheid policies in the Occupied Territories into Israel proper,[157] with complete disregard for the principles of democracy and equality, terms which were not once mentioned in the text.[158] The law has since buttressed the planning and establishment of exclusively Jewish towns in areas where Palestinian citizens are most heavily concentrated, including in the Naqab.[159] It has also provided constitutional support for discriminatory budgeting policies that channel public funds to Jewish communities and individuals as incentives to relocate to the Naqab, in order to secure a Jewish demographic majority there.[160]

A number of petitioners, including Adalah – The Legal Center for Arab Minority Rights in Israel (Adalah), the Association for Civil Rights in Israel, a left-leaning Zionist party (Meretz), and the Joint List of non-Zionist Palestinian parties, brought suit against the law in the Israeli Supreme Court. They argued, in particular, that the section of the law promoting Jewish settlement violated a previous Supreme Court precedent that declared the leasing of state land for exclusive Jewish use an illegal and discriminatory practice. In July of 2021, the Supreme Court ruled against all of the claims of the petitioners, and upheld the Nation-State law, concluding that while it 'further consolidate[d] Israel's Jewish character', it did not 'contravene the state's democratic character.'[161] As Adalah asserted, the law enshrined Jewish supremacy in the constitutional principles of the state, reaffirming the relevance of its settler colonial Zionist roots to its present-day character. However, as long as the state maintains Jewish demographic superiority, it can also maintain the façade of being a democracy, whose discriminatory policies and practices were enacted by democratically elected majorities.

Family reunification amendment to the Citizenship Law

In 2002, during the Second Intifada, the Israeli cabinet suspended naturalization for Palestinians from the Occupied Territories who married Israelis (primarily Palestinian citizens of Israel), for security reasons. This provision was renewed on a yearly basis, and was later expanded to include residents or nationals of 'hostile nations' (specifically Iran, Iraq, Lebanon and Syria).[162] After a short lapse in 2021, the provision was again renewed in March 2022, and stipulated that only applicants aged 50 or older, who had legally resided in Israel (on temporary permits) for at least ten years, could apply to receive permanent residence. However, even if accepted, they would not receive the social rights (e.g., national health insurance, social security benefits) that all other citizens and temporary and permanent residents in Israel receive. Men under 35 and women under 25 were barred from receiving residency.[163]

Over the years, Jewish Israeli lawmakers have become increasingly open about admitting that this 'security' provision also serves the aim of bolstering the Jewish demographic majority in Israel. In February 2022, Interior Minister Ayelet Shaked, of the right-wing Yamina party, said:

> we don't need to mince words, the law also has demographic reasons ... The law wants to reduce the motivation for immigration to Israel. Primarily for security reasons, and then also for demographic reasons. It is meant to prevent a 'creeping right of return'.[164]

Foreign Minister Yair Lapid, from the centrist 'Yesh Atid' party, also clearly affirmed the provision's demographic aims, saying: 'We don't need to hide from the substance of the Citizenship Law. It's one of the tools aimed at ensuring a Jewish majority in Israel.'[165] The right-wing and centrist Zionist parties that united to support adding this provision to the Citizenship Law drew upon the 2018 Nation-State law to justify it.[166] Only two Palestinian parties, and the leftist Zionist party, Meretz, voted against it, while the centrist Labor party abstained. After the law's passage, Interior Minister Shaked flippantly tweeted: 'Jewish and democratic state: 1. State of all its citizens: 0',[167] and reaffirmed the distain of the Zionist settler colonial establishment for the idea that all citizens of the State of Israel should have equal standing and rights.

Adalah filed a petition to the Israeli Supreme Court demanding that the law be revoked due to its explicit discrimination and violation of fundamental rights enshrined in Israel's basic law. They claimed a law prohibiting people from living with spouses from among their own people was unheard of, even in apartheid South Africa:

> The [Law] is not only the most racist Law in the Israeli law books, but there is no country in the world that harms the status of citizenship or residency of its own citizens or residents, the core of which is family life, based on ethnic or national affiliation. There is no country in the world that restricts the right of its citizens or

residents to family life with spouses from their own people. Even the Supreme Court in South Africa in 1980 during Apartheid, in a precedent-setting judgment, struck down a similar law which prohibited the unification of Black families in areas where whites lived, arguing, among other things, that Apartheid was never intended to harm family life.[168]

To prevent what Zionists fear would be 'a creeping Palestinian return' via family unification, they use the legal system to fuel 'a creeping self-initiated displacement' of Palestinian citizens who want to live with non-citizen Palestinian spouses *out* of Israeli jurisdiction. As the human rights organization Al-Haq stated: 'Palestinians are forced to make life choices – ranging from their personal relationships to the location of their residence – based on the constraints of Israeli policies and practices that not only target them, but are ultimately aimed at their transfer'.[169]

Conclusion: Sumood – Indigenous resistance

On one level, it seems that the Zionist settler colonial project in the Naqab has succeeded. For the majority of the Israeli Jewish public, the Naqab Palestinians (like all other Palestinians) have regressed to being 'absent presentees', rarely penetrating their awareness, or garnering their concern. For others, with more proactive Zionist settler colonial sentiments, Naqab Palestinians are trespassers and invaders on 'state lands'. The courts and national legislative bodies have solidly affirmed these positions, and have rejected all Naqab Palestinian claims for land ownership or reparations.

> [T]he Beersheba region has been thoroughly Judaized during the last seven decades. It is characterized by a stark contrast between the recognized, planned, and developed Jewish spaces, the recognized but deprived Bedouin towns, the partly recognized Bedouin localities, and the unrecognized Bedouin indigenous localities in which more than 100,000 citizens and vast tracts of land exist under conditions of distress and existential insecurity.[170]

However, it has in fact been less than thoroughly Judaized. The same authors acknowledged that while virtually all legal doors may have been slammed shut, there were other means of resisting Zionist settler colonialism and the erasure of the indigenous presence:

> One such course of action ... is sumood. It consists of maintaining the sheer magnitude of the problem on the ground. Although Israel attempts to displace the Bedouins, they cling stubbornly to the land, and notwithstanding the state efforts and investments, Bedouin presence and demographic expansion change the region's geography.[171]

As one of the leading plantiffs in the Al-Araqib case stated:

> Even if we don't win, heaven forbid, I've achieved my goal...The history has been told, and also written. My story, that of my father and my grandfather, won. This isn't just another case, just another name. This is Al-Arakib, which has insisted on continuing to live and refused to die, even if they buried us alive.[172]

The accumulation of evidence supporting Naqab Palestinian land claims and confirming their illegal expulsions for the purpose of land acquisition, push the courts to take increasingly absurd and transparently self-serving positions to deny these claims. The progressively more racist laws that deny Palestinian citizens of the state the right to self-determination in Israel, while making Jewish settlement a 'national value', make a mockery of Israel's claim to be a democracy. They also make it more and more difficult to refute the local and international accusations that Israel is an apartheid state.[173] Furthermore, national Zionist settler movements and right-wing political parties, as well as institutions such as the JNF and Israel Land Authority, are panicking over their lack of control over the land of the Naqab, and their failure to fill it with millions of Jewish settlers, or at the very least JNF trees.

> [I]n the end, no matter how many legislative bills are passed, no matter how many Bedouin homes are demolished, and no matter how many discriminatory policies the Israeli government pursues, Moshe Dayan's vision will not be achieved. The 'phenomenon of the Bedouin' will never disappear.[174]

Indigenous peoples in settler colonial states around the world have survived concerted efforts to exterminate, isolate, and assimilate them out of existence. They have faced many coercive pressures and attacks on the cultural, social, economic, and political foundations of their societies, and yet have survived. If the story of indigenous survival worldwide is any indication, Palestinians in the Naqab and beyond will also survive the settler colonial project, with their connections to their history, heritage, and land intact.

Notes

*   A note about the terminology used in this chapter: I will use the term Al-Naqab, which is the Arabic name for the southern Palestinian desert (or 'Negev' desert in Hebrew), except for direct quotes in which the different terminology is used. The Palestinians who traditionally inhabited this region were known as Bedouin because of the semi-nomadic lifestyle and seasonal migrations they followed in order to survive and thrive in the harsh desert environment. After the establishment of the state of Israel, the authorities greatly restricted the mobility of Naqab Palestinians, and imposed sedentarization and later urbanization processes on the population. As a result, the term 'Bedouin', which refers to a semi-nomadic/nomadic lifestyle, is no longer an accurate descriptor or identifier of Naqab Palestinians. I therefore avoid using the term Bedouin, particularly post-1948, except for where it appears in direct quotations.

1   Zangwill, quoted in Masalha 1997: 62.
2   Ben-Gurion, quoted in Teveth 1985: 38.
3   Quoted in Teveth 1985: 38.

4   Zureik 1979, 2016; Abu-Saad 2008; Elsana 2021; Nasasra 2017; Sa'di 2014.
5   Kark 1981.
6   Ibid.
7   Falah, 1989; United Nations, 2022; Yiftachel, 2003).
8   Masalha 1997.
9   Falah, 1989; Kedar, Amara & Yiftachel 2018; Nasasra 2017.
10 Kedar, Amara & Yiftachel 2018.
11 Falah, 1989; Kedar, Amara & Yiftachel 2018; Nasasra 2017.
12 Abu-Saad & Creamer 2013; Elsana 2021; Falah 1989; Kram 2013.
13 Elsana 2021; Kedar, Amara & Yiftachel 2018; Kram 2013; Nasasra 2017.
14 Quoted in Nasasra 2017: Kindle edition location 2948–51.
15 Quoted in Kark 1981: 344.
16 Kedar 2021: 202.
17 Abu-Saad 2008; Falah 1989.
18 Cohen 2003; Ghnadre-Naser 2016.
19 Saabneh 2019.
20 Elsana 2021.
21 Sa'di 2014.
22 Jiryis 1976; Elsana 2021; Nasasra 2017; Kedar, Amara & Yiftachel 2018.
23 Abu-Saad 2008; Falah 1989; Jiryis 1976; Kedar, Amara & Yiftachel 2018.
24 Quoted in Bandel 2022.
25 Ibid.
26 Jiryis 1976; Nasasra 2017; Bandel 2022.
27 Bandel 2022.
28 Ibid.
29 George 1979.
30 Ibid.
31 See Chapter 2 above.
32 Said 1978.
33 Quoted in Yiftachel 1998: 40
34 Yiftachel 1998.
35 Quoted in Yiftachel, 2003: 28–9.
36 Swirski 1989; Yiftachel 1998.
37 Ibid.
38 Ibid.
39 Report to the Provisional Government by Prime Minister and Minister of Defence David Ben-Gurion, 17 June 1948, https://www.gov.il/en/Departments/General/12-report-to-the-provisional-government-by-pm-ben-gurion (accessed 17 December 2022)
40 Quoted in Yiftachel 1998: 46.
41 Yiftachel 1998.
42 Ibid.
43 Abu-Saad 2008; Nasasra 2017; Zureik 1979.
44 Abu-Saad 2008; Marx 2000; Yiftachel 2003.
45 Abu-Saad 2008; Falah, 1989; Marx 2000; Nasasra 2017; Shamir 1996; Yiftachel 2003).
46 Marx 2000.
47 Quoted in Shamir 1996: 231.
48 Abu-Saad 2008; Falah, 1989; Nasasra 2017.
49 Ibid.

50 Smith 1999.
51 Abu-Saad 2008.
52 Falah 1983, 1985; Marx 2000.
53 Lewando-Hundt 1979.
54 Abu-Saad 2008; Falah, 1989.
55 Nasasra 2017.
56 Abu-Saad 2008.
57 Nasasra 2017.
58 Ibid.
59 Abu-Saad 2008; Nasasra 2017.
60 Falah 1983, 1985; Marx 2000.
61 Nasasra 2017.
62 Falah, 1989; Kedar, Amara & Yiftachel 2018; Nasasra 2017.
63 Abu-Saad 2008; Nasasra 2017.
64 Ibid.
65 Abu-Saad 2008; Falah, 1989; Nasasra 2017.
66 Abu-Saad 2008; Falah, 1989; Marx 2000.
67 Personal communication 2021.
68 Nasara 2017.
69 Marx 2000: 113.
70 Abu-Saad 2008; Swirski & Hasson, 2006.
71 Nasasra 2017.
72 Abu-Saad 2008, 2014; Nasasra 2017.
73 Abu-Saad & Creamer 2013.
74 Abu-Saad & Creamer 2013; Kedar, Amara & Yiftachel 2018.
75 Kedar, Amara and Yiftachel 2018: 224.
76 Abu-Saad & Creamer 2013.
77 NCF 2022c.
78 Abu-Saad & Creamer 2013.
79 NCF 2022c.
80 Abu-Saad & Creamer 2013; NCF 2022c; Kremer 2021; Abu-Saad 2014.
81 NCF 2022c; Kremer, 2021; Abu-Saad 2014.
82 NCF 2022c; Kremer 2021; Abu-Saad 2014.
83 Ibid.
84 Elsana 2021; Nasasra 2017; Kedar, Amara & Yiftachel 2018.
85 Elsana 2021; Kedar, Amara & Yiftachel 2018.
86 Elsana 2021.
87 Elsana 2021; Kedar, Amara & Yiftachel 2018.
88 Ibid.
89 Elsana 2021; Adalah 2012; Kedar, Amara & Yiftachel 2018.
90 Adalah 2012; Kedar, Amara & Yiftachel 2018.
91 Elsana 2021; Kedar, Amara & Yiftachel 2018.
92 Adalah 2012.
93 Adalah 2012; Elsana 2021.
94 Elsana 2021; Kedar, Amara & Yiftachel 2018.
95 Elsana 2021; Adalah 2012; Kedar, Amara & Yiftachel 2018.
96 Elsana 2021; Nasasra 2017.
97 Kedar, Amara & Yiftachel 2018.
98 NCF 2022b; Kedar, Amara & Yiftachel 2018.

99 Central Bureau of Statistics 2022.
100 Ibid.
101 Endeweld *et al.* 2018.
102 Elsana 2021; Kedar, Amara & Yiftachel 2018; Kram 2013; Nasasra 2017.
103 Bandel 2022; Elsana 2021.
104 Bandel 2022.
105 Kram 2013: 143 (emphasis added).
106 Kedar, Amara & Yiftachel 2018: 246; Elsana 2021; Kram 2013; Nasasra 2017.
107 Kedar, Amara & Yiftachel 2018.
108 Kedar, Amara & Yiftachel 2018: 264.
109 Elsana 2021.
110 Kedar, Amara & Yiftachel 2018.
111 Sultany 2017: 204.
112 Kremer 2022.
113 Bandel 2022.
114 NCF 2022a.
115 Institute for Palestine Studies 2022.
116 UN Human Rights Council 2011.
117 NCF 2022b.
118 Institute for Palestine Studies 2022.
119 Bandel 2022.
120 Seserman 2019.
121 Central Bureau of Statistics 2021; Adalah 2019.
122 Harel 2022a.
123 Aburabia & Yiftachel 2022.
124 Harel 2022a.
125 Yefet & Khoury 2022.
126 Swirski & Hasson 2006.
127 Ben Zikri 2018; Curiel & Somfalvi 2013; Frantzman 2021.
128 Yahel 2006.
129 Aburabia & Yiftachel 2022.
130 Central Bureau of Statistics 2022.
131 Adalah 2019.
132 NCF 2022c.
133 Pfeffer 2022.
134 NCF 2022c.
135 NCF 2022c; Pfeffer 2022.
136 Ibid.
137 Yefet 2022a.
138 NCF 2022a; Yefet 2022b.
139 Yefet 2022c.
140 Melhem 2022; Harel 2022b.
141 Jewish National Fund 2022.
142 Seserman 2019.
143 Ibid.
144 Ibid.
145 Ibid.
146 Marsden 2022.
147 Quoted in Yefet & Khoury 2022.

148 Quoted in Marsden 2022.
149 Yefet & Khoury 2022.
150 Zureik 2016.
151 Abu-Saad 2014.
152 Adalah 2019, 2022; Jabareen & Bishara, 2019; Sa'di 2019; Pinto 2021.
153 Murphy 2022; Lis & Landau 2018.
154 Pinto, 2021.
155 Quoted in Lis & Landau 2018.
156 Kremnitzer 2018; Lis & Landau 2018.
157 Kremnitzer 2018.
158 Bandel 2021.
159 Melhem 2022; Harel 2022b; Jewish National Fund 2022.
160 NCF 2022c.
161 Bandel 2021.
162 Shpigel 2022.
163 Ibid.
164 Ibid.
165 Ibid.
166 Adalah 2022.
167 Murphy 2022.
168 Adalah 2022.
169 Al-Haq, 2019: 25.
170 Kedar, Amara & Yiftachel 2018: 265.
171 Ibid.: 275.
172 Quoted in Bandel 2022.
173 B'Tselem 2021; Human Rights Watch 2021; Amnesty International 2022; UN Human Rights Council 2022.
174 Kestler-D'Amours 2013.

References

Aburabia, R., and O. Yiftachel (2022), 'Israel Harel's Racist Diatribe Against Bedouins Reveals the Depths of Apartheid', *HaAretz*, 18 January. https://www.haaretz.com/opinion/.premium-israel-harel-s-racist-diatribe-against-bedouins-reveals-the-depths-of-apartheid-1.10545530 (accessed 28 March 2022).

Abu-Saad, I. (2008), 'Spatial Transformation and Indigenous Resistance: The Urbanization of the Palestinian Bedouin in Southern Israel', *American Behavioral Scientist* 51 (12): 1713–54.

Abu-Saad, I. (2014), 'State-Directed "Development" as a Tool for Dispossessing the Indigenous Palestinian Bedouin Arabs in the Naqab', in M. Turner and O. Shweiki, *Decolonizing Palestinian Political Economy: De-development and Beyond*, 138–57, London: Palgrave Macmillan.

Abu-Saad, I., and C. Creamer (2013), 'Socio-Political Upheaval and Current Conditions of the Naqab Bedouin' in A. Amara, I. Abu-Saad & O. Yiftachel (eds), *Indigenous (In) Justice: Human Rights Law and Bedouin Arabs in the Naqab/Negev*, 18–67, Cambridge, MA: Harvard University Press.

Adalah (2012), *The Arab Bedouin and the Prawer Plan: Ongoing Displacement in the Naqab*. https://www.globalgiving.org/pfil/14629/projdoc.pdf (accessed 28 March 2022).

Adalah (2019), *The Illegality of Article 7 of the Jewish Nation-State Law: Promoting Jewish Settlement as a National Value,* Adalah Position Paper, Shafa'amr, Israel: Adalah-the Legal Center for Arab Minority Rights in Israel.

Adalah (2022), 'Adalah petitions Israeli Supreme Court against New Citizenship Law Banning Palestinian Family Unification', Shafa'amr, Israel: Adalah-the Legal Center for Arab Minority Rights in Israel. https://www.adalah.org/en/content/view/10581#:~:text=Adalah%20petitions%20Israeli%20Supreme%20Court%20against%20New%20Citizenship%20Law%20banning%20Palestinian%20Family%20Unification,-13%2F03%2F2022&text=The%20Law%20explicitly%20states%20that,solely%20on%20unsubstantiated%20security%20arguments. (accessed 28 March 2022).

Al-Haq (2019), 'Engineering Community: Family Unification, Entry Restrictions and other Israeli Policies of Fragmenting Palestinians', Ramallah: Al-Haq. https://www.alhaq.org/cached_uploads/download/alhaq_files/images/stories/PDF/Family_Unification_14%20February%20(1).pdf (accessed 28 March 2022).

Amnesty International (2022), 'Israel's Apartheid against Palestinians: Cruel System of Domination and Crime against Humanity', February. https://www.amnesty.org/en/wp-content/uploads/2022/02/MDE1551412022ENGLISH.pdf (accessed 28 March 2022).

Bandel, N. (2021), 'Israel's Top Court Rules the Nation-state Law Is Constitutional, Denies Petitions Against It', *HaAretz* 8 July. https://www.haaretz.com/israel-news/.premium-high-court-rules-nation-state-law-is-constitutional-denies-petitions-against-it-1.9982856 (accessed 28 March 2022).

Bandel, N. (2022), 'Documents Reveal Israel's Intent to Forcibly Expel the Bedouin from Their Lands', *Ha-Aretz* 31 Jan. https://www.haaretz.com/israel-news/.premium.MAGAZINE-documents-reveal-israel-s-intent-to-forcibly-expel-bedouin-from-their-lands-1.10579891 (accessed 28 March 2022).

Ben Zikri, A. (2018), 'Israeli Plan against "Illegal and Hostile Bedouin Construction" Falsifies Data', *HaAretz* 6 June. https://www.haaretz.com/israel-news/.premium--1.6153617 (accessed 28 March 2022).

B'Tselem (2021), 'This is apartheid: The Israeli regime promotes and perpetuates Jewish supremacy between the Mediterranean Sea and the Jordan River', 1 Jan. https://www.btselem.org/sites/default/files/publications/202101_this_is_apartheid_eng.pdf (accessed on 28 March 2022).

Central Bureau of Statistics (2021), *Statistical Abstract of Israel 2021, No. 72. Table 2.19 Population, by population group, religion, age and sex, district and sub-district.*

Central Bureau of Statistics (2022), 'Local authorities in Israel – data files for processing 1999 – 2020'. https://www.cbs.gov.il/he/publications/Pages/2019/%D7%94%D7%A8%D7%A9%D7%95%D7%99%D7%95%D7%AA-%D7%94%D7%9E%D7%A7%D7%95%D7%9E%D7%99%D7%95%D7%AA-%D7%91%D7%99%D7%A9%D7%A8%D7%90%D7%9C-%D7%A7%D7%95%D7%91%D7%A6%D7%99-%D7%A0%D7%AA%D7%95%D7%A0%D7%99%D7%9D-%D7%9C%D7%A2%D7%99%D7%91%D7%95%D7%93-1999-2017.aspx (accessed 28 March 2022).

Cohen, H. (2003), 'Land, Memory, and Identity: The Palestinian Internal Refugees in Israel', *Refuge: Canada's Journal on Refugees* 21: 6–13.

Curiel, I., and A. Somfalvi (2013), 'Gov't to Recognize Illegal Bedouin Villages', *Ynet News* 27 January. https://www.ynetnews.com/articles/0,7340,L-4337613,00.html (accessed 28 March 2022).

Elsana, M. (2021), *Indigenous Land Rights in Israel: A Comparative Study of the Bedouin,* New York: Routledge.

Endeweld, M., D. Gottlieb, O. Heller and L. Karady (2018), *Poverty and Social Gaps Annual Report 2017,* Jerusalem: National Insurance Institute. https://www.btl.gov.il/Publications/oni_report/Documents/oni2017.pdf [Hebrew] (accessed 0n March 28 2022).

Falah, G. (1983), 'The Development of the "Planned Bedouin Settlements" in Israel 1964–1982: Evaluation and Characteristics', *GeoForum* 14: 311–23.

Falah, G. (1985), 'The Spatial Pattern of Bedouin Sendentarization in Israel', *GeoJournal* 11: 361–8.

Falah, G. (1989), 'Israel State Policy towards Bedouin Sedentarization in the Negev', *Journal of Palestine Studies* 18: 71–90.

Frantzman, S. J. (2021), 'Can the Incoming Gov't Change Israel's Approach to the Negev Bedouin?' *Jerusalem Post* 10 June. https://www.jpost.com/israel-news/can-the-incoming-govt-change-israels-approach-to-the-negev-bedouin-670714 (accessed 28 March 2022).

George, A. (1979), '"Making the desert bloom": A Myth Examined', *Journal of Palestine Studies* 8 (2), 88–100. https://doi.org/10.2307/2536511 (accessed on 28 March 28 2022).

Ghnadre-Naser, S., and E. Somer (2016), '"The Wound is Still Open": the Nakba Experience among Iinternally Displaced Palestinians in Israel', *International Journal of Migration, Health and Social Care* 12: 238–51.

Harel, I. (2022a), 'With its Electricity Law, Israel is Recognizing Bedouin Conquests', *HaAretz*, Jan 12. https://www.haaretz.com/opinion/with-the-electricity-law-israel-recognizes-bedouin-conquests-1.10531631 (accessed 28 March 2022).

Harel, I. (2022b), 'Finally, the Israeli Government Adopts a Zionist Policy for the Negev', *HaAretz* 17 March. https://www.haaretz.com/opinion/.premium-finally-the-israeli-government-adpots-a-zionist-policy-for-the-negev-1.10682339?utm_source=App_Share&utm_medium=iOS_Native (accessed 28 March 2022).

Human Rights Watch (2021), 'A Threshold Crossed: Israeli Authorities and the Crimes of Apartheid and Persecution', https://www.hrw.org/sites/default/files/media_2021/04/israel_palestine0421_web_0.pdf (accessed 28 March 2022).

Institute for Palestine Studies (2022), 'The village of al-Araqib: rebuilding home for the hundredth time and beyond'. https://www.paljourneys.org/en/timeline/highlight/14372/village-al-araqib (accessed 28 March 2022).

Jabareen, H., and S. Bishara (2019), 'The Jewish Nation-State Law', *Journal of Palestine Studies* 48 (2): 43–57.

Jewish National Fund (2022), 'Community building – our blueprint Negev strategy. https://www.jnf.org/our-work/community-building/our-blueprint-negev-strategy' (accessed 28 March 2022).

Jiryis, S. (1976), *The Arabs in Israel*, New York: Monthly Review Press.

Kark, R. (1981), 'Jewish Frontier Settlement in the Negev, 1880–1948: Perception and Realization', *Middle Eastern Studies* 17 (3): 334–56.

Kedar, A., A. Amara and O. Yiftachel (2018), *Emptied Lands: A Legal Geography of Bedouin Rights in the Negev,* Redwood City: Stanford University Press.

Kedar, N. (2021), *David Ben-Gurion and the Foundation of Israeli Democracy*, Bloomington, IN: Indiana University Press.

Kestler-D'Amours, J. (2013), 'Peddling the Myth of the Bedouin "Take-over"', *HaAretz* 1 July. https://www.haaretz.com/opinion/.premium-jillian-kestler-myth-of-the-bedouin-take-over-1.5289626 (accessed 28 March 2022).

Kram, N. (2013), 'The Naqab Bedouins: Legal Struggles for Land Ownership Rights in Israel', in A. Amara, I. Abu-Saad & O. Yiftachel (eds), *Indigenous (In)Justice: Human*

Rights Law and Bedouin Arabs in the Naqab/Negev, 126–57, Cambridge, MA: Harvard University Press.

Kremer, E. (2021), *No Shelter in Place: State Demolitions in the Naqab Arab Bedouin Communities and its Impact on Children During the COVID-19 Pandemic,* Beer-Sheva: Negev Coexistence Forum for Civil Equality. https://www.dukium.org/wp-content/uploads/2021/07/HDR-2021-Data-on-2020-Eng-5.pdf (accessed 28 March 2022).

Kremer, E. (2022), *Violations of Human Rights of the Arab Bedouin Community in the Naqab/Negev during 2021,* Beer-Sheva: Negev Coexistence Forum for Civil Equality. https://www.dukium.org/wp-content/uploads/2022/01/HR-report-2021-online.pdf (accessed 28 March 2022).

Kremnitzer, M. (2018), 'Jewish Nation-state Law Makes Discrimination in Israel Constitutional', *HaAretz* 20 July. https://www.haaretz.com/israel-news/.premium-nation-state-law-makes-discrimination-in-israel-constitutional-1.6291906 (accessed 28 March 2022).

Lewando-Hundt, J. (1979), 'Tel-Sheva –a Planned Bedouin Village', in A. Shmueli & Y. Gradus (eds), *The Land of the Negev,* 662–72, Jerusalem: Defense Ministry Press. [Hebrew.]

Lis, J., and N. Landau, N. (2018), 'Israel Passes Controversial Jewish Nation-state Bill after Stormy Debate', *HaAretz* 19 July. https://www.haaretz.com/israel-news/israel-passes-controversial-nation-state-bill-1.6291048 (accessed 28 March 2022).

Marsden, A. (2022), 'Right-wing Activists Set up New Settlement in the Negev', *Jerusalem Post* 9 February. https://www.jpost.com/breaking-news/article-695929 (accessed 28 March 2022).

Marx, E. (2000), 'Land and work: Negev Bedouin Struggle with Israel Bureaucracies', *Nomadic Peoples* 4: 106–20.

Masalha, N. (1997), *A Land without a People: Israel, Transfer and the Palestinians,* London: Faber and Faber.

Melhem, A. (2022), 'Israeli Settlements Threaten Negev Once Again', *Al-Monitor* 8 January. https://www.al-monitor.com/originals/2022/01/israeli-settlements-threaten-negev-once-again (accessed 28 March 2022).

Murphy, M. C. (2022), 'Israel Doubles Down on Apartheid', *Electronic Intifada,* 11 March 11. https://electronicintifada.net/blogs/maureen-clare-murphy/israel-doubles-down-apartheid (accessed 28 March 2022).

Nasasra, M. (2017), *The Naqab Bedouins: A Century of Politics and Resistance,* New York: Columbia University Press.

NCF (Negev Coexistence Forum for Civil Equality) (NCF) (2022a), 'On the Map: the Arab Bedouin Villages in the Negev-Naqab: Al-Aragib'. https://www.dukium.org/village/al-arakib/ (accessed 0n March 28 2022).

NCF (Negev Coexistence Forum for Civil Equality) (2022b), 'House demolitions'. https://www.dukium.org/articles-reports/house-demolitions-and-destruction-of-crops/house-demolitions/?page_id=11916 (accessed 28 March 2022).

NCF (Negev Coexistence Forum for Civil Equality) (2022c), NGO Report to the UN Human Rights Committee in Advance of its review of the State of Israel, UN Treaty Body Database, 7 January. https://tbinternet.ohchr.org/_layouts/15/treatybodyexternal/Download.aspx?symbolno=INT%2fCCPR%2fCSS%2fISR%2f47663&Lang=en (accessed 0n March 28 2022).

Pfeffer, A. (2022), 'Clashes in Southern Israel Are a Ticking Time Bomb for Bennett Government', *HaAretz* 12 January. https://www.haaretz.com/israel-news/.premium.

HIGHLIGHT-clashes-in-southern-israel-are-a-ticking-time-bomb-for-bennett-government-1.10533954 (accessed 28 March 2022).

Pinto, M. (2021), 'The Impact of the Basic Law: Israel as the Nation State of the Jewish People on the Status of the Arabic Language in Israel', *Minnesota Journal of International Law* 30 (1): 1–41.

Saabneh, A. (2019), 'Displaced and Segregated: The Socio-economic Status of the Second Generation of Internally Displaced Palestinians in Israel', *Population Studies* 73 (1): 19–35.

Sa'di, A. (2014), *Thorough Surveillance: The Genesis of Israeli Policies of Population Management, Surveillance, and Political Control Towards the Palestinian Minority*, Manchester: Manchester University Press.

Sa'di, A. (2019), 'The Nation State of The Jewish People's Basic Law: A Threshold of Elimination?' *Journal of Holy Land and Palestine Studies* 18 (2): 163–77.

Said, E. (1978). *Orientalism*. New York: Vintage Books.

Seserman, B. (2019), 'Ben-Gurion University Shares Prime Minister's Name, Vision', *South Florida Sun Sentinel* 19 February. https://www.sun-sentinel.com/florida-jewish-journal/opinion/fl-jj-opinion-seserman-negev-lies-israel-future-20190227-story.html (accessed 28 March 2022).

Shamir, R. (1996), 'Suspended in Space: Bedouin under the Law of Israel', *Law & Society Review* 3: 231–57.

Shpigel, N. (2022), 'Israel Just Re-banned Palestinian Family Unification. What Does This Law Do, and How Can It Be Fought?' *HaAretz* 12 March 12. https://www.haaretz.com/israel-news/.premium-what-s-new-in-the-citizenship-law-what-s-the-next-step-in-fighting-it-1.10670464 (accessed 28 March 2022).

Smith, L. (1999), *Decolonizing Methodologies: Research and Indigenous Peoples*, London: Zed Books.

Sultany, N. (2017), 'The Legal Structures of Subordination: The Palestinian Minority and Israeli Law', in N. Rouhanna & S. Huneidi (eds), *Israel and its Palestinian Citizens: Ethnic Privileges in the Jewish State*, 191–237, Cambridge: Cambridge University Press.

Swirski, S. (1989), *Israel: The Oriental Majority*, London: Zed Books.

Swirski, S., and Y. Hasson (2006), *Invisible Citizens: Israel Government Policy toward the Negev Bedouin*, Be'er-Sheva, Israel: Negev Center for Regional Development, Ben-Gurion University of the Negev.

Teveth, S. (1985), *Ben-Gurion and the Palestinian Arabs: From Peace to War* Oxford: Oxford University Press.

United Nations (2022), *The Origins and Evolution of the Palestine Problem: Part II (1947–1977)*. https://www.un.org/unispal/history2/origins-and-evolution-of-the-palestine-problem/part-ii-1947-1977/ (accessed 28 March 2022).

United Nations Conciliation Commission for Palestine (1947), *Supplement to the Survey of Palestine*, https://www.un.org/unispal/document/auto-insert-210930/ (accessed 28 March 2022).

UN Human Rights Council (2011), 'Report by the Special Rapporteur on the rights of indigenous peoples, James Anaya', UN Human Rights Council (A/HRC/18/35/Add.1). https://www.ohchr.org/Documents/Issues/IPeoples/SR/A-HRC-18-35-Add-1_en.pdf (accessed on March 28 2022).

UN Human Rights Council (2022), 'Report of the Special Rapporteur on the situation of Human Rights in the Palestinian territories occupied since 1967', (A/HRC/49/87) 28 February – 1 April. https://www.ohchr.org/en/press-releases/2022/03/special-rapporteur-situation-human-rights-occupied-palestinian-territories (accessed 28 March 2022).

Yahel, H. (2006), 'Land Disputes between the Negev Bedouin and Israel', *Israel Studies* 11 (2): 1–22.

Yefet, N. (2022a), 'Ten Days, Five Israeli Bullets, Five Bedouin with Serious Head Injuries', *HaAretz* 10 March. https://www.haaretz.com/israel-news/.premium.MAGAZINE-five-israeli-bullets-five-bedouin-seriously-injured-in-the-head-in-just-ten-days-1.10596597 (accessed 28 March 2022).

Yefet, N. (2022b), 'Israeli Police Arrest 30 Bedouin, Days After Negev Protests Over JNF Tree-planting', *HaAretz* 18 January. https://www.haaretz.com/israel-news/.premium-israeli-police-arrest-30-bedouin-days-after-negev-protests-over-jnf-tree-planting-1.10547911 (accessed 28 March 2022).

Yefet, N. (2022c), 'Israel Indicts 16 Bedouin Over Negev Protests Against JNF Tree-planting', *HaAretz* 20 January. https://www.haaretz.com/israel-news/.premium-israel-indicts-16-bedouin-over-negev-protests-against-jnf-tree-planting-1.10554360 (accessed 28 March 2022).

Yefet, N., and J. Khoury (2022), 'Police Evict Right-wing Activists who Declared New 'Settlement' near Southern Bedouin City', *HaAretz* 9 February. https://www.haaretz.com/israel-news/.premium-right-wing-activists-declare-settlement-near-israeli-bedouin-city-sparking-row-1.10600994 (accessed 28 March 2022).

Yiftachel, O. (1998), 'Nation-building and the Division of Space: Ashkenazi Domination in the Israeli 'Ethnocracy', *Nationalism and Ethnic Politics* 4 (3): 33–58.

Yiftachel, O. (2003), 'Bedouin-Arabs and the Israeli Settler State: Land Policies and Indigenous Resistance', in D. Champagne & I. Abu-Saad (eds), *The Future of Indigenous Peoples: Strategies for Ssurvival and Development*, 21–47, Los Angeles: American Indian Studies Center, UCLA.

Zureik, E. (1979), *The Palestinians in Israel: A Study in Internal Colonialism*, London: Routledge and Kegan Paul.

Zureik, E. (2016), *Israel's Colonial Project in Palestine: Brutal Pursuit*, London: Taylor and Francis.

6

The Paradox of Settler Colonial Citizenship in Israel: The Dialectics of Dispossession and Palestinian Resistance[1]

Areej Sabbagh-Khoury

In his seminal book on the dynamics of 'internal colonialism' in Israel, Elia Zureik (1979) analyses the conflictual and unequal processes of social class transformation in an effort to depart from the cultural and pathological factors used to explain stratification among Jewish-Israeli and Palestinian citizens is Israel. Establishing a Marxian-inspired sociological analysis of the proletarianization of Palestinians in Israel, and of the amplifying economic dependency of Palestinians on the newly incepted Israeli state, Zureik instead offers a deeply historicized account of the relationship between indigenous social structure and settler developmental patterns. Therein, he tethers the political and economic to the social, to explain the institutional and ideological bases of asymmetry, especially with regard to the effects of territorial (e.g., expropriation) and demographic transformations. In the analytical argument that follows in this chapter, I develop a theory of citizenship as accumulation by dispossession to explain how settler colonial practices of encroachment and displacement relate to the political apparatus of classification. Settler social-institutional changes transformed the class formations of Palestinian social life in Israel, setting a form of path dependency in the early state years. I take up the case of the Palestinians in Israel, noting cites of dispossession in frontier zones such as the historic Palestinian cities of Haifa, Jaffa and Lydda, and that are called 'mixed-cities', and more specifically centre the case of the Internally Displaced Palestinians to understand how dispossession and accumulation are two sides of a singular process in settler colonial states. Zureik's 1979 work seemed to view internal colonialism as distinct from settler colonialism. Discussing systematic governance practices in which indigenous replacement undergirds the functioning of the settler colonial state, this chapter views settler colonialism not solely as an incipient moment of incursion and expropriation, but as an overarching social formation constituted by a set of processes and events that are durable, even and especially when institutionalized in a state that is dialectically formed through settler colonial domination and indigenous resistance and agency.

Citizenship and colonialism

From a sociological perspective, citizenship is a social process rather than a thing-in-itself, used to create and enforce the boundaries of the nation-state. Through categorizing membership, citizenship also serves as a symbol of social belonging; it is a relational mechanism that provides political agency and participation from below, and imposes rights and entitlements from above.[2] It thus anchors people to polities, most often strapping citizens to states to which they were assigned at birth.

Where citizenship defines nationalist boundaries,[3] in colonialism and empire citizenship practices are shifted to be used as a mode of colonial population management. In the settler colonization context, settler colonizers carry their sovereignty with them; they aim to settle and establish a new social order rather than preserve the existing sovereignty configuration. Using a 'logic of elimination',[4] a group of settler immigrants appropriates a space inhabited by an indigenous population, aspiring to shift the demographic balance in their favour and appropriate the land with the aim of permanent settlement. Under this logic, the settler colonizers enact mechanisms of dispossession and expulsion to ensure the 'elimination of the native as native'.[5]

Settler colonialism has been studied across varied spatial and temporal contexts. No case operates the same, and debates continue to raise what unites cases of settler colonization.[6] Citizenship in settler colonial societies, most agree, does not operate in homologous form; different settlers attribute different indigenous threats to their colony's territorial viability, and thereby utilize citizenship differently in response to indigenous counterinsurgency. To eradicate indigenous claims to sovereignty, the settler state may offer citizenship to the indigenous population – their 'acceptance' of which is recognized as acquiescence to the settler state. But this rendering is too simplistic. Settler colonial citizenship is defined by indigenous dispossession and subjugation – almost all settler colonial cases show that citizenship does not preclude historical violence merely through the extension of membership and liberal rights. But neither are indigenous subjects merely passive recipients of state power – settler colonial citizenship regimes also contain variable native strategies of acceptance, rejection, refusal, negotiation and preservation that redefine what citizenship means.

The Palestinians in Israel

With the onset of the Zionist movement, European Jews began to settle a territory populated by Palestinians. Initially based on the acquisition of land, the process accelerated with the British Empire's conquest of Palestine and new legal land-tenure configurations. Zionist settlers often forcibly expelled Palestinian cultivators from the land on which they lived and laboured, on their own or with the assistance of the British Governor. Palestinians, in turn, often resisted colonization, for example by burning fields, forcibly reclaiming possessions, or combatting settlers.[7]

Takeover was gradual, however, as under the late British Mandate consent had to be sought and compensation given to the indigenous who lived on the land prior to their evacuation, and by 1948 the Zionist movement had acquired less than 10 per cent of Mandatory Palestinian territory.[8] The 1948 war provided the opportunity for the ostensibly legal land expropriation of the territory to establish Jewish sovereignty and expel, en masse, its Palestinian population. After the Israeli state's inception, the Zionist movement and its different arms were capable of acting without interference or constraints from the British.[9]

The approximately 156,000 Palestinians who remained in what became the State of Israel seemingly "accepted" Israeli citizenship, but in a settler state this citizenship rendered them entrapped. However, the Palestinians' dynamic practices have contested and redrawn the contours of this citizenship from within. I will unpack this by turning to the case of the IDPs specifically, and by discussing the frontierization of Palestinian spaces as in the cases of al-Naqab and the historic Palestinian cities.

The case of the IDPs

The Palestinian Internally Displaced Persons (IDP) population, who made up approximately 46,000 people or 30 per cent among the 156,000 Palestinians who remained in Israel in 1948,[10] was comprised of two groups of Palestinians who were displaced from their original homes as a result of forced expulsion or fleeing: those who were driven from their homes by Zionist militia forces before the State of Israel was founded and after the Partition plan in November 1947, and those who were displaced through internal transfer operations or expulsions after the Israeli state was formed in May 1948.[11] The case of the IDPs, whose paradoxical citizenship rights alongside the prevention of return became constitutive features of their citizenship, instantiates the tethering in settler colonialism of citizenship to dispossession.

Despite being prohibited from returning, dispossessed of their land and means of production, and subjected to Israeli martial rule, most were granted Israeli citizenship. Their citizenship give them some protection from future expulsion[12] – despite the threat of transfer looming over Palestinians – as the absence of Israeli citizenship rendered a Palestinian subject to deportation.[13] Appropriation of the IDPs' land and property was implemented through legislative decisions as well as martial practices. The 1950 Absentees' Property Law of 1950 deemed the state to be the owner of 'absentee' properties and authorized the expulsion of individuals residing on property unless they could prove their status was not that of an absentee.[14]

This was a near impossible task.[15] Although most IDPs were entitled to Israeli citizenship, they were prevented from returning to their property via a system of pass permits that restricted their mobility. The state could then appropriate their land and properties. They were colloquially termed 'present-absentees' – that is as I argue, present for political purposes and absent for property purposes because they had vacated their villages in the 1948 War and hence had irreversibly lost their rights to these properties.

After 1948, the IDPs first sought safe refuge, often migrating between villages,[16] believing they would eventually be allowed to return to their villages. From 1957, the IDPs started to purchase land in the towns and villages they had taken refuge, with the Israeli government providing a budget to create employment opportunities in the Palestinian-populated cities and villages that were still standing.

For the IDPs and the Palestinian citizens in general, the 1948 rupture was experienced as a trauma that was distinct from the loss experienced by those Palestinians who were expelled from the new state. They remained in their homeland, but found themselves cast as internal enemies in their new status as subjects of a foreign sovereignty. Their properties stolen and their possessions redistributed to new Jewish citizen-settlers, the IDPs witnessed the destruction and subsequent Judaization of their villages and cities. Relations between the settler state and its dispossessed citizen-subjects was constitutively traumatic,[17] and multiple mechanisms shaped continued dispossession: citizenship, land law, martial rule, and practices of resistance.

Military rule, 1948–66: inscribing settler accumulation through population management

The population management of Palestinian IDPs after 1948 reveals the principal momentum of settler colonial power wielded by the Israeli government: to achieve the erasure of as many Palestinians as possible from desired space through the securing and normalizing of new methods of statist domination. During the period of military rule between 1948 and 1966, the majority of the remaining Palestinian population were placed under the jurisdiction of a military government. Laws of appropriation were enacted that combined direct violence, fines for violations of military rule orders, imprisonment, and the forceful prohibition of return for IDPs.[18] The military government unilaterally implemented regulations to control Palestinian mobility, which enabled the authority to restrict movement, to detain any person suspected of incitement, to deport and administratively detain people, to impose curfew and to declare certain areas closed or restricted for military purposes.[19]

Newly declassified sources reveal the extent to which Israeli officials conspired to prevent IDPs from returning to their homes.[20] This included forestation efforts, fencing land and further weaponizing the Absentee Property Laws, but also military enforcement of temporary ghettos in certain cities during the 1948 Nakba.[21] During military rule in Jaffa, Haifa, Lydda, Asqalan and Acre, Palestinian citizens were gathered, separated according to religious affiliation, and concentrated in specific areas (sometimes in refugees' homes) that were often surrounded by barbed-wire fences. Exit from the security zones (often referred to as 'ghettos' in the primary Israeli archival sources) without proper permits was prohibited; permits were generally offered only to those who labored in Jewish fields. These ghettoized Palestinians were prevented from returning to their original homes and, out of economic precarity, were often made to cultivate land newly transferred to Jewish-Israeli control.[22] This ghettoization of Palestinians in cities and villages endured through urban and economic planning.

The new settler state also intervened in Palestinian affairs economically in the aftermath of the 1948 War. Palestinian property and the surplus-value of Palestinian labor was co-opted by the state or by Jewish-Israeli citizens-settlers. In some places, Palestinians who became dispossessed from subsistence agriculture were forced into the labour market, where their wages would be the lowest among workers.[23]

Military rule and its policies toward the Palestinians, especially IDPs, came to define the new settler state in Israel,[24] creating the conditions for its governmentality over the remaining Palestinian community by stymieing Palestinian reclamation and repressing dissent, as well as by offering remaining indigenous individuals – as opposed to collective – qualified rights in the form of citizenship.[25]

Military rule was dismantled in 1966 because it had achieved, if only partially, the goals of territorial appropriation, settlement, and the prevention of return. New mechanisms of population management for the Palestinians in Israel were instituted in the form of police control, and in 1967, another Israeli military regime came to regulate the Occupied Palestinian Territories (OPT), which continues to this day. The legacies of military rule continued to shape the conditions of sociality for the Palestinians in Israel following 1966. Although generally understood as a permanent social fact, their fragile citizenship remains under threat, namely by border change plans that advance the revocation of citizenship (see, e.g., U.S. President Donald Trump's 'Peace to Prosperity' plan,[26] or efforts by Israeli politicians like Ephraim Sneh to 'transfer' Palestinian citizens out of Israeli jurisdiction[27]), a renewed Schmittian adversarial politics, and the collusion between settler colonial groups and the state that perpetuates colonization in the form of urban land-grab and extra-judicial violence in Palestinian urban localities.[28] Palestinian citizens, whether IDP-descended or not, still face the spectre of land confiscation and colonization. Violence by numerous national and municipal Israeli state arms *and by individual settlers* includes spatial encroachment, dispossession and the continued marginalization of Palestinians. The so-called 'mixed-cities', historically Palestinian towns that became inhabited with a majority of Jewish-Israelis following the expulsion of the bulk of their Palestinian inhabitants since 1948, have been a prime locus of continued colonization and urban land grab. This is why the 'Dignity Uprising' of May 2021, which responded to the triggering incursions of Jewish Israeli citizens-settlers, centred in the so-called mixed-cities of Jaffa, Lydda, Acre (Akka) and Haifa. Meanwhile, in January 2022 the Jewish National Fund attempted to plant forests in order to grab land from the Palestinian Bedouins of the Al-Araqib village in the Naqab region of what is now southern Israel. Like Jerusalem, al-Khalil (Hebron), and other areas of the West Bank, these areas within Israel have become the site of a process of internal frontierization, turning urban space into land available for 'Judaization' and nationalization. But settlement practices continue through different modes, now taking an increasingly privatized[29] and individualized form. While citizenship does not protect Palestinian citizens from these dispossessory practices, as we will see below it does prefigure certain types of social action agency.

Citizenship is not a fixed thing in itself, but an institutionalized historical process. Understanding the relation between Palestinian citizens and Israeli governmentality entails consideration of the settler colonial process that preceded the state's inception and continued through statecraft and bureaucratic population management.

Citizenship and sovereignty in the new Jewish State

In Israel, citizenship, I argue, is a political status based around territorial access. Palestinians with Israeli citizenship are largely excluded from territorial belonging, land acquisition rights, return and immigration and naturalization (the Law of Return of 1950 is a capacious mechanism that enables world Jewry Israeli naturalization, but not Palestinians). An 'internal frontier' has subjected them to continued spatial control, wherein municipal and infrastructural services are unevenly controlled by the Israeli government.[30] Dispossession is therefore the prerequisite for Palestinians' Israeli citizenship. Citizenship can be seen to be inherently imbricated in the process of settler colonization – both in the Palestinian case and other cases.

For Shafir and Peled (2002: 117), such divisions encapsulate the three concatenated dynamics – colonialism, ethno-nationalism and democracy – that define the Israeli citizenship regime. Their framework of citizenship is cognizant of colonialism, delving mainly into the settlement that prefigured the Israeli state before 1948, and delineates the colonial project's results on post-1948 Palestinian economic mobility. However, they do not further explain how colonial accumulation enduringly structures the post-1948 citizenship apparatus, as I seek to do here. Citizenship did not grant the Palestinian IDPs the right to return to their homes, which paradoxically engendered an enduring struggle against domination.

To theorize the case of Israeli settler colonial citizenship, one can turn to Hannah Arendt (1973), who extended her analysis of European totalitarianism to show the inextricable link between Europe and its colonies and the effect it had on political liberalism. Arendt theorized that the 'external' processes of imperialism were not separate from European democratic structures; in fact, the disconnect between forms of citizenship – legal citizens at home and 'subject races' abroad[31] – necessarily shaped the condition of statelessness. The imperial impulse and the gap between European citizens and colonial subjects thus threatened democratic structures.

Extending this thought to the case of Israeli settler colonial citizenship, one can assert that the gaps between Jewish-Israeli citizens and indigenous Palestinians citizens constitute governmentality writ large. However, compared to Arendt's vision of a prior 'democratic' European culture, in the Israeli settler colonial context citizenship has only ever taken a hierarchical form. Citizenship originally based around settler colonial territorial and population management therefore cannot be theorized as external to the state, but rather as constitutive of it. Rather than reflect a universal democratic structure of Israel, the granting of citizenship to Palestinians in the early years of the Jewish state contributed to the settler regime's geopolitical framing of the state as a democratic entity, that is, to its international legitimation and acknowledgement.

It is important to consider who were the beneficiaries of accumulation in this scenario. Focusing solely on Palestinian citizenship at the national level neglects the processes of 'internal colonialism' that Zureik (1979) expertly adumbrates: the economic and material impoverishment of the predominantly agrarian Palestinian society in which land was the primary means of production. Jewish-Israeli settlers were transformed into owners and land cultivators within a socialist (collectivist) framework, collective sovereignty as land was nationalized, and Palestinian land tenure (including *musha'a*, collective) was transformed into exclusive Jewish property.[32] Without access to their land, most remaining Palestinians in Israel turned into "unskilled workers" overnight.

As systematic as the Zionist collective accumulation and concomitant Palestinian dispossession were, it is crucial to complicate the universalizing trope of 'elimination of the native' that Wolfe (2006) characterized as a dominant feature of settler colonialism. From the 1950s, some Zionist settlers in the kibbutzim subleased land to Palestinians, even to some who had previously owned the same land.[33] Subleasing occurred mostly out of practical need: Zionist settlers simply could not manage property in the frontier, and the indigenous often knew how to care for the land. Palestinians' presence, resistance and embodied knowledge shaped the settler colonial frontier, despite the wider Zionist political project's attempt to replace Palestinians on as much land as possible.

The incidental membership IDPs had to the Israeli state became a means through which they could have dispossession enacted against them. As citizens but without the essential right to territorial belonging meant that to demand return or re-possession of property could have threatened their very right to remain, by exposing oneself to the 'arbitrary governance' and 'bureaucratic aloofness'[34] of the settler colonial state. For the indigenous, it was citizenship manqué, one that did not guarantee the full set of liberal and collective rights but still subjected Palestinians to being recognized and classified by the state.

Accumulation by dispossession

Citizenship within settler states operates not simply as a device for inclusion within the polity (or exclusion from it), but as the mechanism for a bifurcated process of accumulation/dispossession tethering legal and material realms. Drawing on the method of contrapuntal reading,[35] I attend to the accumulatory functions of settler colonizers alongside the dispossession and resistance practices of indigenous people through citizenship. Recentering the study of colonialism in sociology, I am interested in the state and non-state actors whose various tactics of plunder, subjugation, and hierarchization lie at the heart of the settler colonial state's constitution, and in the practices, negotiations, and indigenous co-production that together shape the state and citizenship.

Citizenship is not neutral. Political processes, often contentiously, classify group and territorial memberships and differentially distribute rights. Neither is citizenship solely imposed from above nor individually accepted from below; it is dialectically negotiated. In states formed by and operating under a logic of settler colonialism – that is, the accumulation of land and power for the benefit of settler colonial immigrants – citizenship of the indigenous populations is premised on a process of dispossession. In other words, settler citizenship derives its function from recursive accumulation by dispossession, this chapter poses. Largely neglected by sociological theory, settler colonialism as a *sui generis* social formation makes us rethink the nature of citizenship as it operates not solely to incorporate or exclude through the process of social closure. I pose that thinking of citizenship in settler colonial societies as a process of accumulation by dispossession (ABD) complicates the relationship between settler colonial sovereignty and citizenship.

In some accounts, primitive accumulation models the material conditions that generated the conditions for the implementation of wage labour.[36] ABD, however, describes the more contemporary crisis of the over-accumulation of capital,[37] with imperialism being a spatio-temporal fix for the need to garner additional land, resources, and markets. ABD is an extension of primitive accumulation, a temporal reconfiguring that deems accumulation not as 'primitive' but as reconstituted in different forms. ABD is said to be a product of the modern crisis of neoliberalism, that is how states continuously seek accumulation through global and unequal dispossessory processes. To appropriate land and resources for further capital accumulation and market access has become the primary function of modern imperialism. How does Harvey's (2004) generative concept of ABD fit into the constitution of settler colonial sovereignty? The particularities of capital are not the focus here, but I am concerned with the systems of hierarchy inherent in materialist processes, especially as they pertain to ownership over the means of production (land and resources). By attending to the materialist realm, I aim to show how ABD is a characteristic feature of citizenship that has specific dynamics and logics in settler colonial cases (See figure 6.1).

Zionist colonization was not a spatial fix for capitalism. Despite the Israeli state's purported socialist ideologies and practices, capitalism played a role in its development.[38] The dispossessed land in Palestine was instrumental in the construction of Israeli territorial sovereignty.[39] It is crucial to distinguish Zionism from other settler colonial cases; the reason for settlement cannot be regarded as solely economic, or national or religious, or as motivated by the actions of a single metropole. Moreover, the presence of empire is central; British imperial rule paved the way for Zionist accumulation, despite discordance between Zionists and the British (who, for instance, did not easily facilitate land transfer through mechanisms of force, but insisted on legal purchase).[40] My aim is to keep hold of the centrality of land, of the materiality of dis/possessions of resources, in identifying how settler colonial sovereignty and supremacy were constructed and are preserved through differentiated citizenship. In extending a materialist argument about the centrality of land, I pose that settler sovereignty in this case and others is constituted through ABD. Citizenship is upheld by two interdependent forms: one premised on accumulation and one premised on dispossession.

ABD in the Zionist case did not take the form of capitalist privatization, as in other settler colonial cases, but instead collectivist privatization that served the Jewish national body (often following an ethno-socialist ideology). Zionist accumulation exclusively prioritized Jewish (mainly European) populations over Palestinians. The earlier pre-Zionist process of land expropriation from Arab landowners had not generated a mass expulsion of the peasantry from the land. Transformations in ownership of Palestinian land were enabled by gradual privatization and legal reforms under the Ottoman and British regimes, particularly the privatization and concentration of Arab estate owners' land under the British Mandate.[41] This concentration produced the conditions for liquidity through which Zionists garnered territory.[42]

Such transformations continued at the turn of the twentieth century, when the expulsions began with Zionist land purchases. These land purchases prior to 1948 initiated the dispossession of Palestinians, generating loss of land and labor at a much smaller scale than what would come in 1948.[43] Post-1948, the Jewish state used the pretext of 'national need' for territorial confiscation. The accumulation of wealth, or the means of production, was a settler colonial mechanism of expansion, providing land,

The Paradox of Settler Colonial Citizenship in Israel: The Dialectics of Dispossession

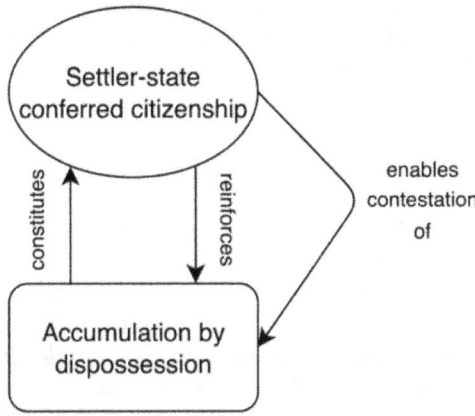

Figure 6.1 The relationship between ABD and citizenship.

resources, and labor to the Jewish population while dislocating the Palestinians. In the Zionist case, dispossession was not a means to an end of the creation of a new labor force, despite enduring needs for labor, but constituted Jewish territorial sovereignty. 'Accumulation' identifies how loss was a prerequisite for constituting exclusivist Jewish sovereignty in Palestine, not that it had to be such, but that historically the Zionist project rendered the process zero-sum. Displacement, encroachment, and expulsion allowed for the continuation of the accumulation process, encapsulated in the shift from British imperial and Zionist settler colonial semi-sovereignties to the Israeli sovereignty that now foments further accumulation or dispossession.

ABD entails the forceful expropriation and redistribution of land and resources to *capital*.[44] In the case of settler colonialism, redistribution flows to the racially defined settler group (even amid internal divisions) and is buttressed by the state, whose ability to exist in the colonial space depends on forceful accumulation and the classificatory apparatus of citizenship. This is why settler colonialism is 'a form of structured dispossession'.[45] ABD is a dyadic process in settler colonial cases, where land and resources are appropriated for the exclusive redistribution to the settler colonial group. This accounts for appropriation of land in obtaining the means of production, constituting the conditions of social relations (including citizenship), and inhibiting the capacities needed for indigenous sovereignty when faced with usurpation. If we reverse the aphorism to *dispossession as accumulation*, we can recentre what the production of settler supremacy and enduring loss entails for indigenous social reproduction.

In the case of Israel, it is not just that the state apparatus, through absentee property laws and martial rule, accumulated the capacity to claim ownership over the means of production, but that the processes of dispossession constituted exclusive settler sovereignty to rule over natives and dispossessing them of institutional and political capacities to rule themselves. ABD constitutes a settler colonial citizenship regime – a hierarchy determining who can remain, under what conditions of spatial and social mobility, and with what privileges – and the citizenship configuration facilitates further accumulation and dispossession as it also structures spaces of opportunity to resist it. 'Citizenship', as a bifurcated analytic concept, allows us to articulate agency alongside the state practice of classification, more precisely pinpointing a mechanism of population management and responses to it.

How Palestinians re-draw the contours of citizenship

Even so, in settler colonial states citizenship does not only entrench settler ABD processes, it can also open up spaces for the indigenous to challenge their domination. One approach subjugated indigenous populations have historically used is by 'refusal' to engage with the settler state.[46] Where the settler state confers liberal citizenship rights to the indigenous group, as in the case of the Kahnawà:ke in North America, the indigenous group then utilizes this legal status to entrench their acts of refusal – to recognize and be recognized by the settler state. As Audra Simpson finds, however, this aporia is the basis of the Kahnawà:ke's entrapment within the Canadian and U.S. state systems.

Refusal is not the only possible mode of indigenous relations to a settler state. In the Palestinian case generally and in the case of Internally Displaced Persons (IDPs) specifically offer a model of how indigenous 'acceptance' of citizenship can challenge settler attempts at replacement by being positioned both within and against structures of domination. Constituting approximately 46,000 of the 156,000 Palestinians who remained in Israel in 1948, IDPs occupy a kind of interim category among Palestinians in Israel. Fully dispossessed of their property but also granted citizenship rights, the IDPs resisted their dispossession with limited success. Occupying a liminal space within the dynamics of settler and settler colonial state practices of domination and indigenous resistance, IDPs can illuminate the relationship between citizenship and ABD in Israel, with scope to apply to other settler colonial cases. A double paradox lies at the heart of this case: settler colonial citizenship is constituted on accumulation; indigenous citizenship is constituted on being granted a certain amount of agency within the settler colonial state, but it is an agency that can lead to their further deprivation and dispossession.

Returning to Simpson's (2014) theory of indigenous refusal, in the case of the Palestinian citizens and the IDPs, citizenship is received divergently. Refusal describes a denial to recognize and to be recognizable. By only focusing on structural dispossession and dislocation, one omits the role of indigenous agency in settler colonial sovereignty configurations and citizenship. Palestinians in Israel have used citizenship within the ABD model of settler colonial politics in a myriad of ways to engage in anti-colonial struggle. I have explained how Palestinian resistance practices gradually constituted the 'return of history',[47] that is, the ascription and reinvigoration of new political meaning to 1948's foundational violence. So here I want to argue that Palestinians in Israel have enacted indigenous refusal through redrawing the boundaries of citizenship. I will present a few examples of the IDPs' processes of indigenous resistance.

The Paradox of Settler Colonial Citizenship in Israel: The Dialectics of Dispossession   159

In a unique case, after the inception of the Israeli state the Israeli military forcibly depopulated the two Palestinian villages of Iqrit and Bir'im. But the IDPs from these two villages used their citizenship as a means of contesting their dispossession.[48] They initiated their public legal defence immediately following their removal, when village committees mobilized to ask that government officials permit their return. They believed that they were entitled to return as they had been evacuated by the military *after* the state's inception. The committees sent numerous letters to the Minorities Ministry and the military governor on a range of everyday matters. They claimed property damage, requested permission to hold ceremonies and holiday celebrations in their displaced villages, and requested fair labour arrangements. They also protested against the improper treatment of their women and expressed concern regarding acts of violence committed on village lands.[49] Many legal battles ensued, often with contradictory rulings.[50]

A July 1951 ruling found Iqrit's original evacuation illegal and permitted return. Yet within months, the military demolished everything in the Christian village save the

Figure 6.2 Easter celebration at the church of displaced village Ma'alul, 18 April 2022. Photo by Sameh Damouni.

church and cemetery. The legal battles escalated and reached the Israeli Supreme Court. Village inhabitants were permitted only to pray in the church and bury the dead in the cemetery. In Bir'im, a 1953 Supreme Court ruling challenged the military's expulsion, yet the military further destroyed the village. In these cases, citizens mobilized to access return through various legal avenues and emphasized the legal exceptionalism of their cases vis-à-vis those of other IDPs. The bureaucratic and legal restrictions for the IDPs from Iqrit and Bir'im remain unresolved to this day. Inhabitants of these two villages use citizenship to practise symbolic return through holding celebrations and social, religious and political activities in the villages (See figure 6.2 above). Israeli governments continued to reject the IDPs' ability to return, citing 'security-factor justifications' such as the potential precedent any permission to return would bring and the unrest it would foment among other Palestinians.[51]

These are not the only examples. ADRID (the Association for the Defense of the Rights of the Internally Displaced), which beginning in 1998 organized return marches to depopulated villages, became central to the 'return of history'.[52] Memory practices perform an active refusal to forget the foundational violence in the Nakba and to assert the continuity of Palestinian *baqa'a* (remaining in the homeland). Palestinians have practised symbolic return to destroyed villages or, for younger generations, those of their ancestors (see Figure 6.3). In the first years of military rule, Palestinians visited or temporarily returned to depopulated villages on Israeli Independence Day, the only day they were permitted to move without permits. In the wake of the Kufr Qassem massacre in 1956, the Land Day commemoration in 1976 took off as a popular practice of social protest against domination, conspicuously refusing the erasure of the state's constitutive violence from Palestinian and Israeli consciousness.[53] Collective return to family villages to commemorate the Nakba continues, refusing a delinkage from dispossession by using the rights of citizenship (mobility and territorial presence) to preserve a demand for decolonization. Through such embodied practices, the demand for a return of land and the negation of exile (especially for IDPs) is sustained despite decades of governmental suppression of a history of constitutive violence. Returns in 2021 and 2022 to the displaced villages of al-Bassa', Iqrit, Suhmata, Mi'ar, Hitin, Saffouri, and al-Lajjun are another recent manifestation of the practice of collective contestation through memorialization (see Figure 6.2 for an Easter return to Ma'alul). So too, the efforts at mutual aid and protection during the Dignity Intifada of May 2021 in the 'mixed cities' exemplifies the connective threads of collective Palestinian resilience in the face of grave danger to indigenous national communal viability.

These practices present a few ways Palestinians redraw the boundaries of citizenship, even under conditions of domination. The classification the state ascribed to Palestinians (citizenship) has become the basis for their struggle against the legitimacy of settler colonization and the institutions erected to perpetuate it. Citizenship, in one sense, is held as a strategic asset for anticolonial social movements. I find most mobilization against state domination cultivates a habitus of *sumud* (steadfastness) – a cultivated set of dispositions, learned habits, embodied understandings, and a skill set for navigating the violence of domination – wherein Palestinians have phenomenologically encountered and learned ways of living amid frequent violence. Settler colonial citizenship seeks to strip the indigenous of their nativeness, rendering

Figure 6.3 Return March, May 20, 2022. Photo by Rana Awaisi.

them subjects of a settler state who enjoy no special political rights for redress from displacement and dispossession. Yet the legal, material, institutional and symbolic displays of indigenous objection to erasure demonstrate the paradox of citizenship. Citizenship, I argue, is both a social classificatory mechanism used from above to ascertain the conditions for continuous accumulation and an instrument of anticolonial dissent used by the indigenous from below.

Through their mobility, presence and petitioning, Palestinian citizens tried to use their citizenship classification to seek redress through legal means, even though they were not entirely successful. Yet, in their acts IDPs, as with Palestinian citizens write large, drew a great deal of attention to their dispossession at the hands of state bodies, and through their resistance demonstrate the fissured nature of the concatenated Israeli state, which does not operate coherently. Moreover, the Palestinian case in Israel delineates a form of indigenous agency that does not simply accept purely individual rights offered via settler colonial governmentality, but seeks cracks and opportunities to assert and, to an extent, effectively deploy self-sovereignty. This agency operates between the rejection and entrapment of citizenship and seeks to reconfigure the opportunities opened by citizenship's relative protection and qualified provision of rights.

The Israeli state is shaped and articulated by indigenous resistance practices and organizations. The Knesset's 2018 Basic Law: Israel as the Nation-State of the Jewish People and the 2011 Amendment No. 40 to the Budgets Foundations Law (known colloquially as Nakba Law) can be read as reactionary responses to Palestinian citizens' aggrandizement. State responses to indigenous resistance practices seeking to dismantle the colonial order underscore the strength of indigenous social action. Resistance reframes the state's perpetuation of settler colonial (Sabbagh-Khoury, 2012) against the Palestinians. This assertion that Palestinians' displays of agency engender reactionary and oppressive state responses risks being read as if the Palestinians are to blame for their own subjugation, but I am instead emphasizing the nature of settler colonial governance: it is responsive to indigenous agency.

Conclusion

Zureik (1976; 1979), Abdo (1991) and numerous other Palestinian scholars were among an early generation of social scientists to note that, following British conquest and Zionist incursion, numerous changes to Palestinian life had taken firm hold. The Palestinian village lost its traditional characters; the agricultural worker had become dispossessed and proletarianized, having to sell his/her labour on the racialized market; modernization lagged in Palestinian towns and villages; the Palestinian village was economically stagnant; per capita income was significantly higher among Jewish-Israelis than Palestinian citizens; and the labour market was largely ethno-racially split, with Palestinians predominantly employed in the construction and manual labour sector and Jewish-Israelis in more high-skilled occupations. These characteristics of exploitation and subjugation, among others, led Zureik to declare the Arab minority, or Palestinian citizens in Israel, as an internal colony. This chapter adds to such scholarship the notion that the legal-classificatory apparatus of citizenship as a tool of population management all but secured stratification by facilitating accumulation by dispossession, rather than securing 'full and equal citizenship and due representation in all its provisional and permanent institutions'.[54] However, if for these reasons the population of Palestinian citizens *became* an internal colony, I am more inclined to see the early state years as but the continuation of a durable process of accumulation by dispossession that Zionist settler colonizers had already began undertaking with British support in the early decades of the twentieth century. The Israeli state, its provisional and then established governments, its numerous civilian and martial arms, became the institutionalized forms of settler colonization.

This chapter set out to show how citizenship in settler colonies has been historically constituted. I have done this by examining the concept of ABD by way of the IDPs who remained within the new Israeli state and were granted citizenship, by depicting the continuity of colonization in the new frontiers in which indigenous citizens face dispossession, and by linking dispossession to state classification and enduring settler encroachments. First, settler colonial citizenship is prefigured by ABD, which entails a twin maneuver: settler accumulation and indigenous dispossession. The classification of citizenship in settler colonies operates within an appropriative apparatus in which the displacement or dispossession of indigenous citizens becomes a foremost concern for ascertaining settler territorial sovereignty *through accumulation*. Second, citizenship, a tool for the enduring exclusion of settler governmentality, enables further dispossession of material and symbolic assets and atomizes collective political indigeneity. And third, settler citizenship is necessarily articulated by (i.e. which is to say shaped, negotiated and contested through) indigenous practice and agency. Citizenship is not only a top-down process practised differently within a fissured state; it is also practised from below, enlivened by contradicting and often incohesive desires.

The dialectic of dispossession and accumulation is manifested in the political realm vis-à-vis citizenship, and thus citizenship becomes a form of property available to settler colonial groups at the expense of hollowing out indigenous material and symbolic claims. By tethering territorial dispossession typical to settler colonies to the legal configuration of citizenship as an institutionalized process, I highlight in the former political, and in the latter material, dimensions. It might be argued that focusing on the material realm – (dis)possession and access to territory – elides the cultural erasure of indigeneity central to settler colonialism. This has not been my intention. Rather, I am seeking to assess the ways in which the classificatory apparatus of citizenship operates to lock in stratified status based on settler–indigenous subject positions, and yet also enables indigenous challenges to settler domination.

My undergirding argument, that it is crucial to discern citizenship in settler colonies by dissecting its relation to the accumulation of territorial sovereignty, is also a historical assertion attentive to the interplay of context and contingency. Settler colonial citizenship does not redress foundational loss of sovereignty and land, fomented through accumulation. Citizenship is fragile; indigenous citizens have been and remain subject to the whims of settler colonial states (population transfer, repealed citizenship, displacement) that have seen and may still envision their erasure as configuring the realization of a viable new social order. But indigenous people also organize, mobilize and often reconfigure state priorities.

The existence and persistence of the Palestinians in Israel, alongside their continued political practices, signifies the incomplete nature of the settler colonial project's attempts at erasure *and* the agentic praxis of Palestinian citizens who, because they are partially incorporated into the polity, challenge erasure. Zionist epistemic violence may point to the unfinished remnants of an expansive project of replacement, but such pronouncement of the failure of settler colonialism to eliminate the natives is counterintuitively indicative of indigenous persistence. In this way, my analysis of the Palestinian citizens of Israel may centralize attention on structural erasure, leading to a conception of a totalizing settler colonial project. However, the case of Palestinians in Israel, and more specifically the IDPs, offers a more complex understanding of indigenous presence and agency. In other words, the existence of remaining indigenous, despite their deracination, challenges settler colonial path dependency. The case of the Palestinian citizens offers one way in which settler colonial sovereignty is constituted through contestation. It also challenges liberal conceptions of citizenship, pointing to the centrality of ABD in settler colonies.

The Palestinian question – what Israel is to do with the indigenous population – is fundamentally one of biopolitical and territorial control (Zureik 2016). Citizenship, a dialectical process like settler colonialism itself, is, perhaps, central to both biopolitical and territorial domination. It is at once premised on settler colonial territorial and politico-sovereign dispossession and accumulation, but also shaped iteratively by indigenous practices. It is not a unitary apparatus of domination nor simply a tool of indigenous resistance, which itself depends on resources, attribution of opportunity, endogenous and exogenous conditions, and the intended target and strategies. Rather, citizenship presents many confounding processes and structures that coalesce into a strategic apparatus. Citizenship embodies settler colonial state logics, but also the diversity, and disunity, of indigenous desire. Tracking this history of the constitution of settler colonial citizenship is to ask how the social order in settler colonies could be decolonized.

Notes

1. This chapter is adapted in part from Areej Sabbagh-Khoury, "Citizenship as Accumulation by Dispossession: The Paradox of Settler Colonial Citizenship," *Sociological Theory* (2022): 1–28. I thank the editors for providing me the opportunity to reflect on the legacy of Elia Zureik's scholarship. As a young undergraduate Palestinian student at an Israeli university, reading the work of Palestinian scholar and sociologist Elia Zureik was constitutive and inspiring. His was among the first rigorous sociologies of domination I read that provisioned an analytical approach to explaining state–society relations in Israel through an anti-hegemonic lens – the framework of internal colonialism. To experience the impact of Zureik's work on my own thinking was also to first realize that I too, as a Palestinian student, could make it my life's work to study the exigencies of Palestinian life carefully and methodically. Zureik has modelled for me the way to study socio-political life in Palestine, while also being dedicated to a broader nomothetic pursuit – the study of power, governance and patterned social action writ large in sociology. He has also modelled how one can communicate with the next generation, facilitating, in Edward Said's words, the 'permission to narrate' for a young female scholar. I thank Zureik for exemplifying what it means to be a Palestinian sociologist, for being an aspiration as I sought to follow in his footsteps, and for the knowledge he continues to share with the world in hopes of engendering a more just and decolonized future.
2. Bloemraad, Korteweg, and Yurdakul 2008.
3. Anderson 1983.
4. Wolfe 2006.
5. Kauanui 2016.
6. Sabbagh-Khoury 2022.
7. Sabbagh-Khoury 2023.
8. Yiftachel and Kedar 2000.
9. Sabbagh-Khoury 2023.
10. Complete demographic data on the IDPs is lacking. In 1950, the UN Relief and Works Agency for Palestinian Refugees (UNRWA) estimated the number of IDPs to be 46,000 people, 30 percent of the 156,000 Palestinians who remained in Israel during that period (Wakim 2001; see also Al-Haj 1986: 654). This estimation refers only to those who were displaced in 1948, and not to Palestinian citizens who were internally displaced after 1948.
11. Sabbagh-Khoury 2011.
12. Jiryis 1976.
13. IDPs were granted temporary identity cards that necessitated renewal every three months, conditional to the recommendations of the military ruler and police (Berda 2020:12).
14. For example, Israel declared 300,000 dunams of IDP land "absentee property" (Masalha 2003).
15. Jiryis 1976; Masalha 2003; Kabha and Barzilai 1996.

16 Al-Haj 1988.
17 Rouhana and Sabbagh-Khoury 2014.
18 Sa'di 2016; see also Kimmerling 1977.
19 Jiryis 1976; Nasasra 2020.
20 Cf. Berger 2019.
21 Raz 2020.
22 Algazi forthcoming.
23 Nuriely 2019.
24 Robinson 2013: 8.
25 The approximately 13,000 Bedouin Palestinians in the Naqab under military rule offer a further example of four interwoven processes: the incidental nature of citizenship (Bishara 2017) in the early years of the settler state, the capricious state classification practices that determine remaining in the homeland, the ways Palestinians utilized citizenship to resist, and the relation of entrapment. Many Bedouins returned to the territory within the 1949 Armistice boundaries after expulsion; their practices of resistance (e.g., skillfully traversing the geography and sneaking back in and then seeking restitution through legal means) shaped the military rule itself, according to Nasasra (2020).
26 White House 2020.
27 Zureik 2003.
28 Sabbagh-Khoury 2021.
29 See Clarno 2017; Yacobi and Milner 2022; see also, "How was Kohelet Forum born," *Haaretz* March 11, 2021: https://www.haaretz.co.il/news/politi/2021-03-11/ty-article-magazine/.highlight/0000017f-e82e-dea7-adff-f9ffb21d0000
30 Yiftachel 1996.
31 Shenhav 2012: 21.
32 Al-Hazmawi 1998; Hadawi 1988; Kedar 2000.
33 Algazi forthcoming.
34 Shenhav 2013.
35 Said 1993.
36 Marx & Engels 1978: 431–4.
37 Harvey 2004.
38 Silver 1990).
39 Yiftachel and Kedar 2000.
40 Sabbagh-Khoury 2023.
41 Al-Hazmawi 1998; Khalaf 1997; Yazbak 2000.
42 Khalidi 1997: 95.
43 Sabbagh-Khoury 2023.
44 Harvey 2004.
45 Coulthard 2014: 58.
46 Simpson 2014.
47 Rouhana and Sabbagh-Khoury 2019.
48 Kimmerling 1977.
49 Ozacky-Lazar 1993.
50 Ryan 1973.
51 Kimmerling 1977:163–4.
52 Rouhana and Sabbagh-Khoury 2019.
53 Ghanem and Mustafa 2018; Sorek 2015.
54 Provisional Government of Israel, "Declaration of Independence," *Reshumot* [Official Gazette] 1 (1948).

References

Abdo, N. (1991), 'Colonial Capitalism and Agrarian Social Structure: Palestine: A Case Study', *Economic and Political Weekly* 26 (30): 73–84.

Algazi, G. (forthcoming), 'Colonial Profits in the Shadow of Military Rule', in D. DeMalach and L. L. Grinberg (eds), *Colonization and Resistance*, Jerusalem: Van Leer Institute Press and Hakibbutz Hameuchad.

Al-Haj, M. (1986), 'Adjustment Patterns of the Arab Internal Refugees in Israel', *International Migration* 24 (3): 651–74.

Al-Haj, M. (1988), 'The Changing Arab Kinship Structure: The Effect of Modernization in an Urban Community', *Economic Development and Cultural Change* 36 (2): 237–58.

Al-Hazmawi, M. (1998), *Mulkīyat Al-Ārāḍī Fī Filasṭīn, 1918–1948 [Land Ownership in Palestine 1918–1948]*, Acre, IL: Aswar Foundation.

Anderson, B. (1983), *Imagined Communities: Reflections on the Origin and Spread of Nationalism*, London: Verso.

Arendt, H. (1973), *The Origins of Totalitarianism*, New York: Harcourt Brace Jovanovich.

Berda, Y. (2020), 'Citizenship as a Mobility Regime', Project on Middle East Political Science, https://pomeps.org/citizenship-as-a-mobility-regime (accessed 9 January 2023)

Berger, Y. (2019), 'Israel Made Sure Arabs Couldn't Return to Their Villages', *Declassified* 27 May.

Bishara, A. (2017). 'Zionism and Equal Citizenship: Essential and Incidental Citizenship in the Jewish State', in N. N. Rouhana (ed), Israel and Its Palestinian Citizens: Ethnic Privileges in the Jewish State, 137-156, Cambridge, UK: Cambridge University Press.

Bloemraad, I., A. Korteweg and G. Yurdakul (2008), 'Citizenship and Immigration: Multiculturalism, Assimilation, and Challenges to the Nation-State', *Annual Review of Sociology* 34 (1): 153–79.

Clarno, A. (2017), *Neoliberal Apartheid: Palestine/Israel and South Africa After 1994*, Chicago: University of Chicago Press.

Coulthard, G. S. (2014), *Red Skin, White Masks: Reflecting the Colonial Politics of Recognition*, Minneapolis: University of Minnesota Press.

Ghanem, A., and M. Mustafa (2018), *Palestinians in Israel: The Politics of Faith after Oslo*, Cambridge: Cambridge University Press.

Hadawi, S. (1988), *Palestinian Rights and Losses in 1948: A Comprehensive Study*, London: Saqi Books.

Harvey, D. (2004), 'The "New" Imperialism: Accumulation by Dispossession', *Socialist Register* 40: 63–87.

Jiryis, S. (1976), *The Arabs in Israel*, New York: Monthly Review Press.

Kabha, M., and R. Barzilai (1996), *Refugees in Their Land: The Internal Refugees in Israel 1948–1996*, Givat Haviva, IL: Institute for Peace Studies.

Kauanui, J. K. (2016), '"A Structure, Not an Event": Settler Colonialism and Enduring Indigeneity', *Lateral* 5 (1).

Kedar, A. (2000), 'The Legal Transformation of Ethnic Geography: Israeli Law and Palestinian Landholder 1948-1967', *New York University Journal of International Law and Politics* 33 (4): 923–1000.

Khalaf, I. (1997), 'The Effect of Socioeconomic Change on Arab Social Collapse in Mandate Palestine', *International Journal of Middle East Studies* 29 (1): 93–112.

Khalidi, R. (1997), *Palestinian Identity: The Construction of Modern National Consciousness*, New York: Columbia University Press.

Kimmerling, B. (1977), 'Sovereignty, Ownership, and "Presence" in the Jewish-Arab Territorial Conflict: The Case of Bir'im and Ikrit', *Comparative Political Studies* 10 (2): 155–76.

Marx, K., and F. Engels (1978), *The Marx-Engels Reader*, 2nd edn, ed. R. C. Tucker, New York: Norton.

Masalha, N. (2003), *The Politics of Denial: Israel and the Palestinian Refugee Problem*, London: Pluto Press.

Nasasra, M. (2020), 'Two Decades of Bedouin Resistance and Survival under Israeli Military Rule, 1948–1967', *Middle Eastern Studies* 56 (1): 64–83.

Nuriely, B. (2019), 'The Hunger Economy: The Military Government in Galilee, Ramle, and Lydda, 1948–1949', *Arab Studies Journal* 27 (2): 64–84.

Ozacky-Lazar, S. (1993), *Iqrit and Bir'am, Surveys on Arabs in Israel No. 10*, Givat Haviva, IL: Institute for Peace Research.

Raz, A. (2020), 'When Israel Placed Arabs in Ghettos Fenced by Barbed Wire', *Haaretz* 27 May.

Robinson, S. (2013), *Citizen Strangers: Palestinians and the Birth of Israel's Liberal Settler State*, Stanford: Stanford University Press.

Rouhana, N., and A. Sabbagh-Khoury (2014), 'Settler-Colonial Citizenship: Conceptualizing the Relationship between Israeli and Its Palestinian Citizens', *Settler Colonial Studies* 5 (3): 205–25.

Rouhana, N., and A. Sabbagh-Khoury (2019), 'Memory and the Return of History in a Settler-Colonial Context: The Case of the Palestinians in Israel', *Interventions* 21 (4): 527–50.

Ryan, J. L. (1973), 'Refugees within Israel: The Case of the Villagers of Kafr Bir'Im and Iqrit', *Journal of Palestine Studies* 2 (4): 55–81.

Sabbagh-Khoury, A. (2011), 'The Internally Displaced Palestinians in Israel', in N. N. Rouhana and A. Sabbagh-Khoury (eds), *The Palestinians in Israel: Readings in History, Politics and Society*, 26–46, Haifa: Mada al-Carmel: Arab Center for Applied Social Studies.

|Sabbagh-Khoury, A. (2012), 'War by Other Means Against the Palestinians in Israel', *Jadaliyya* 18 June.

Sabbagh-Khoury, A. (2021), 'Ha-Meḥa'ah Ha-'amimit v'alimut: Ha-Medina Ha-Ḳoloni'alit Ha-Hityashvutit [Popular Protest and Violence: The Settler Colonial State]', *Teoria u'Bikoret [Theory and Criticism]*, Special Issue: Fire in a Field of Thorns: Thoughts on Violence and Solidarity, 19–26.

Sabbagh-Khoury, A. (2022), 'Tracing Settler Colonialism: Genealogy of a Paradigm of Knowledge Production in Israel', *Politics and Society* 50 (1): 44–83.

Sabbagh-Khoury, A. (2023), Colonizing Palestine: The Zionist Left and the Making of The Palestinian Nakba Stanford: Stanford University Press.

Sa'di, A. H. (2016), *Thorough Surveillance: The Genesis of Israeli Policies of Population Management, Surveillance and Political Control Towards the Palestinian Minority*, Manchester: University of Manchester Press.

|Said, E. (1993), *Culture and Imperialism*, New York: Vintage.

Shafir, G. and Y. Peled (2002), *Being Israeli: The Dynamics of Multiple Citizenship*, Cambridge: Cambridge University Press.

Shenhav, Y. (2012), 'Imperialism, Exceptionalism and the Contemporary World', in M. Svirsky and S. Bignall (eds), *Agamben and Colonialism*, 17–31, Edinburgh University Press.

Shenhav, Y. (2013), 'Beyond "Instrumental Rationality": Lord Cromer and the Imperial Roots of Eichmann's Bureaucracy', *Journal of Genocide Research* 15 (4): 379–99.

Silver, B. J. (1990), 'The Contradictions of Semiperipheral "Success": The Case of Israel', in W. G. Martin (ed), *Semiperipheral States in the World-Economy*, 161–81, New York: Greenwood Press.

Simpson, A. (2014), *Mohawk Interruptus: Political Life Across the Borders of Settler States*, Durham, NC: Duke University Press.

Sorek, T. (2015), *Palestinian Commemoration in Israel: Calendars, Monuments, and Martyrs*, Stanford: Stanford University Press.

Wakim, W. (2001), 'Refugees in Their Homeland: The Present-Absentees in Israel', *Journal of Palestine Studies* 45/46: 90–104.

White House (2020), 'Peace to Prosperity: A Vision to Improve the Lives of the Palestinian and Israeli People', Washington, D.C.: White House.

Wolfe, P. (2006), 'Settler Colonialism and the Elimination of the Native', *Journal of Genocide Research* 8 (4): 387–409.

Yacobi, Haim, and Elya Milner (2022), 'Planning, Land Ownership, and Settler Colonialism in Israel/Palestine', *Journal of Palestine Studies* 51 (2): 43–56.

Yazbak, M. (2000), 'From Poverty to Revolt: Economic Factors in the Outbreak of the 1936 Rebellion in Palestine', *Middle Eastern Studies* 36 (3): 93–113.

Yiftachel, O. (1996), 'The Internal Frontier: Territorial Control and Ethnic Relations in Israel', *Regional Studies* 30 (5): 493–508.

Yiftachel, O., and A. Kedar (2000), 'On Power and Land: The Land Regime in Israel', *Teoria u'Bikoret [Theory and Criticism]* 16, 67–100.

Zureik, E. (1979), *The Palestinians in Israel: A Study in Internal Colonialism*, London: Routledge and Kegan Paul.

Zureik, E. (2003), 'Demography and Transfer: Israel's Road to Nowhere', *Third World Quarterly*, 24 (4): 619–30.

Zureik, E. (2016), *Israel's Colonial Project in Palestine: Brutal Pursuit*, London: Routledge.

Zureik, E. T. (1976), 'Transformation of Class Structure among the Arabs in Israel: From Peasantry to Proletariat', *Journal of Palestine Studies* 6 (1): 39–66.

7

Celebrating Survival

Palestinian Epistemes and Resisting Anti-Palestinian Racism

Yasmeen Abu-Laban

Palestinian-origin social scientists are a rare breed in Canada's institutions of higher education. This may stem from the fact that Canadian universities have exhibited patterns of exclusion when it comes to the representation of immigrants, racialized minorities and indigenous peoples in the academy.[1] Moreover, there are sustained examples of academic freedom being pummelled in Canada when Palestinian perspectives and experiences are given voice or the *status quo* of Israel's settler project is critiqued.[2] Combined, these make their presence in the social sciences and humanities in institutions of higher learning rather exceptional.

I first knew Elia Zureik not as a rare breed, but as a family friend well before I entered university because my father Baha Abu-Laban, a 1948 refugee from Jaffa, was also a Canadian-based sociologist. However, it was as a graduate student reading voraciously in the 1980s that I encountered Elia Zureik as the internationally respected and multidimensional scholar he is. I was a political science PhD student specializing in Comparative and Canadian politics, and Zureik's classic work on political socialization and values was required reading for the comprehensive field specialization exams forming part of training and accreditation.[3] But his work on Palestine, so critical to a more informed understanding Palestinians after 1948, stands apart.

One reason Zureik's work on Palestine was so important was personal. Today's 'Generation Z' students speak about 'safe spaces' for those experiencing marginalization to communicate their experiences. While not a concept in my graduate student days, in retrospect, I sought out a carefully curated selection of what might be called 'safe professors' who were knowledgeable about Palestine and Palestinians even if they were not Palestinian. They were small in number, and reserved for the times I wanted to simply be better understood in relation to the Palestinian component of my mixed identity, or perhaps even do a course paper on Palestine and feel I would be judged fairly and without navigating pre-existing ideological blinders. My litmus test of such professors became their having read and understood books that theorized and analysed Palestine and Palestinians in terms that would resonate with actual Palestinians. Two key authors for this litmus test of mine were Edward Said – for his works *The Question* of *Palestine* (1979a) and *Orientalism* (1979b) – and Elia Zureik for his book *The Palestinians in Israel: A Study in Internal Colonialism* (1979).

The second reason Zureik's work was so critical was epistemological: there were certain commonalities to the books published by Said and Zureik in the banner year of 1979. They challenged deeply-held conventional orthodoxies in North American, European and Israeli universities through evidence and logic; they made use of (settler) colonialism to understand Palestinians and their past, present and possible futures; and they were written by Palestinian authors who witnessed the Nakba (catastrophe) of 1948. These were, in short, deeply scholarly contributions to world ideas that were constituted through Palestinian knowledge including full awareness of the experience and consequences of utter social upheaval, dispossession and statelessness.

In what follows I wish to situate Elia Zureik's path-breaking work on Palestinians for illuminating key aspects of their oppression and experiences in Israel/Palestine and in the diaspora. Rich and varied, his oeuvre especially draws attention to the inequitable and violent nature of Israel's settler colonial project, as well as the extensive state and private forms of surveillance which accompanies it. His empirical insights have not only worked to broaden our collective historic and contemporary knowledge, but he has also contributed to our theoretical and comparative understanding of settler colonial states, as well as power and control in an era of rapidly expanding technological advances.

This chapter has three parts. First, I review Zureik's extensive work which has given a firm base to the sociological study of Palestinians, as well as the centrality of this population for understanding surveillance as a broader social and political phenomenon of the contemporary world. Second, I build from his foregrounding the systemic and sustained nature of racism directed towards Palestinians in Israel/Palestine a consideration of its local and global manifestations. At one level, a concern with racism is not inherently new, and has been voiced by Palestinian scholars and activists for decades. However, for a variety of reasons, including the uneven and devastating impact of the COVID-19 pandemic, we are living in a time when increased political attention is being paid to anti-racism both by governments and by civil society groups across states. It is argued that within this context, the need to centre anti-Palestinian racism as a specific form of racism is especially critical to the challenges to it. The third part of the chapter discusses the advances and potential of three key areas of mobilization that speak, either implicitly or explicitly, to resisting anti-Palestinian racism. These relate to 1) the 'boycott, divestment and sanctions' (BDS) movement; 2) efforts to characterize the Israeli state as practising apartheid; and 3) organizing to name and contest 'anti-Palestinian racism' in the aftermath of the murder of George Floyd by Minneapolis police in May 2020.

Situating key contributions of Zureik

The 1948 Nakba (catastrophe) has become a defining temporal marker in the narrative of Palestinians.[4] The Nakba is also a site of both increased scholarly and public awareness, as well as active attempts at suppressing acknowledgement.[5] As Abu-Lughod and Sa'di note of 1948:

A society disintegrated, a people dispersed, and a complex and historically changing but taken for granted communal life was ended violently. The Nakba has thus become, both in Palestinian memory and history, the demarcation line between two qualitatively opposing periods. After 1948, the lives of the Palestinians at the individual, community, and national level were dramatically and irreversibly changed.[6]

If the vocation of the sociologist is to study 'society' how is it done in such a distinct context of social disruption, destruction and dislocation? Indeed, this question is all the more pressing because the Nakba is effectively an ongoing continuity of trauma for Palestinians,[7] making the challenge also of ongoing relevance.

Zureik's response, first articulated nearly five decades ago, remains a scholarly standard: this was to have what he termed a 'sociology of the Palestinians'. He acknowledges the different eras of Palestinian social experience with pre- and post-1948 being important markers in relation to power, alongside post-1967. He reflects on the concept of minority as used in relation to social power:

While each period is characterized by a specific type of social experience, the post-1948 periods saw the transformation of the Palestinians from a majority to a minority in Palestine. In spite of differences in the regional locations of the Palestinians, this subordinate minority status produced a shared historical experience and eventually the crystallization of a Palestinian identity. For this reason the post-1948 sociology of the Palestinians has to draw largely upon the sociology of minorities. More specifically, as far as the larger segment of the Palestinians is concerned (particularly those living in Israel and the occupied territories, Jordan and, to a lesser extent and for different reasons – in Lebanon, Syria and the Gulf), theirs is the sociology of the colonized.[8]

Reflecting on these tenets of a 'sociology of the Palestinians', Zureik's research contributions have been wide-ranging, and attuned to findings and studies that might have originally been in English, along with Arabic or Hebrew. His work is always concerned with the human dimension of what people experience and what people think in light of the distinctive circumstances and structural conditions befalling the Palestinians as the colonized. For example, Zureik's early work on the attitudes of Palestinian youth in Israel, as well as Israeli Jews, expressly considers results in relation to how a settler state 'creates in the public eye a mythology which dehumanizes the culture and way of life of the native people'.[9] Likewise, findings on the abysmal socioeconomic conditions of Palestinians in refugee camps in Lebanon, Syria, Jordan, the West Bank and Gaza are considered in the dual light of how camps have been a locus of familial and communal solidarity as well as 'the most visible symbol of Palestinian suffering'.[10]

The 'sociology of the Palestinians' is by no means easy, and Zureik consistently points to the problematic gaps in knowledge. Hence, in reviewing diverging interpretations when it comes to the causes, responsibility, and numbers Palestinian refugees as well as the solution to their plight, Zureik underscores the lack of 'systematic studies of refugees' views regarding possible solutions'.[11] More broadly, he has observed the particular challenges that come from studying Palestinians since 'the majority of the society's members live in dispersion as refugees and members of exiled communities, whether in the Arab countries or the West', even as at the same time some still live in their homeland 'such as in Israel where they live as a minority, or as a majority in highly contested political environments such as the West Bank and Gaza'.[12] Indeed, due to their geographic dispersal, studying the Palestinians defies the hegemonic logic of 'methodological nationalism' underpinning work in much of the social sciences whereby scholars problematically embrace and naturalize their approach to their subject matter by confining it in relation to an extant state.[13]

If it is issues of 'identity, control, and resistance' that present unifying themes of inquiry into the experience of Palestinians as a dispersed people,[14] it is Zureik's innovative work on surveillance that cuts to the heart of these themes by identifying their linkages with territory, power and violent colonial conditions.[15] Of course surveillance studies as an area, in which Zureik is an acknowledged world expert, is concerned with understanding the technological and ideological shifts which have come to enable increasingly novel and globalized forms of identifying individuals and groups, watching, as well as policing within and at state borders.[16] Israel has been at the forefront of such trends because it is not only a military superpower in the context of the Middle East, but also a global leader in relation to cybertechnology and exports of cybersecurity equipment.[17] Zureik likens contemporary Israel to a late nineteenth-century colonial state: 'Israel's plans to secure and maintain dominance in the area of surveillance technology lie in its desire to remain in control of the colonized Palestinian population and the territory they inhabit'.[18] Israel (and Israel's occupation) are also distinct for the way in which state racism meshes with biopolitical governmentality in a settler-colonial context.[19]

> ... biopolitics and territoriality intersect at various levels to advance the state's racialised agenda, and they are framed by Western-based colonial law to facilitate the seizure of territory, privatisation of communal land, dispossession of indigenous people, and population transfer.... In the case of colonial regimes, however, identification systems are distinguished by their discriminatory practices and racialised targeting of the population, thus creating a rigid stratification of citizens, subjects, and noncitizen immigrants, displaced people being an example of the latter.[20]

Zureik and Lyon (2022) further illuminate the intersections between colonialism and racism in relation to Israel's mass surveillance, digital contact tracing and policing in responding to the COVID-19 pandemic.

In his distinct and sustained contributions to the sociological study of the Palestinians, Zureik's work has served to bolster and anchor the more multidisciplinary field of Palestine studies. His work on surveillance further contributes to the field, and helps to underscore how racialized and colonial logics stemming from the nineteenth century and political Zionism relate and contribute to surveillance studies as a global focus of study. Building from Zureik's underscoring of the centrality of racism to

Israel's colonial project, the centrality of resistance to the study of Palestinians, as well as the various geographic contexts these phenomena may play out, in the next section I consider anti-Palestinian racism as a phenomenon that has local and global manifestations. This is followed by a consideration of key contemporary sites of resistance to it.

Anti-Palestinian racism

There is a peculiar absence of discussions of both settler-colonialism and racism in much work and political commentary on Israel/Palestine that is not grounded in scholarly Palestinian knowledge of the sort Zureik has advanced in his published work. Indeed, one has only to look at maps of Palestine before and after Israel was proclaimed in 1948, and the mushrooming of Israeli settlements after 1967, to see how access to territory is 'the primary motive' for what Patrick Wolfe calls 'the elimination' of the native. As Wolfe also notes, however, racialization occurs in such targeting since 'where they are *is* who they are'.[21] For decades Palestinian leaders have also used available avenues, including the United Nations (UN), to contest the settler-colonization of historic Palestine and what they experienced as racialized targeting.[22] Yet, there has been resistance and suppression of these claims, and many scholarly and journalistic analyses persist in viewing the situation as one of a 'conflict' (ostensibly of equal sides) rooted in religion, nationalism or responding to 'terrorism'.

In marked contrast to the situation of Israel/Palestine, in other world regions, particularly Canada and the United States, considerations of race, racism and anti-racism have dramatically amplified in recent years. Of course since the 1980s the work of critical race theorists in the field of law, such as Kimberlé Crenshaw, have been of special importance to this outcome.[23] But it has also impacted other disciplines, such as political science, which have traditionally been neglectful in studying race.[24]

Moreover, in North America and other regions, attention has extended beyond academe to the broader social and popular level. Indeed, the COVID-19 pandemic in many countries, including the United States and Canada, has drawn attention to racialized health inequities.[25] This growing awareness stemming from the pandemic was further punctuated by the brutal murder, captured on video, of an unarmed African-American man, George Floyd, by Minneapolis police, on 25 May 2020. This broader social interest in responding to racialized injustice was also captured in the expansion of statements, public awareness, and school courses at every level on anti-Black racism following Floyd's tragic murder and related protests. As one recent American news article put it:

> Floyd's murder changed Black Lives Matter from a controversial social justice movement to an almost ubiquitous corporate mantra virtually overnight. Fortune 1000 companies poured billions of dollars into programs designed to address systemic racism and committed to fulfilling quantifiable racial hiring quotas after decades of resisting them.[26]

The murder of George Floyd and the related protests that followed were felt in numerous countries in Europe, Australia and in the Middle East; this was especially these case in Palestine where murals of Floyd painted on the wall express both solidarity and identification with the struggles of Black folks, and violence of policing, in the United States.[27]

The lingering absentce of discussions of race and racism in Israel/Palestine scholarship and commentary itself deserves explanation. In my collaborative work with Abigail B. Bakan we found it useful to extend the work of the late philosopher Charles Mills, as forwarded originally in his 1997 book *The Racial Contract*. Although Mills did not explicitly consider Israel/Palestine in his work; he gave considered attention to how an absenting of race from analysis and understanding stems from an 'epistemology of ignorance' that is typically very actively sustained by those with power.[28] As such, while Mills avers that 'race is the unnamed system that has made the modern world what it is today',[29] those holding power frequently do not see or understand the very system they created. Indeed, as Mills' conceptualization makes clear, even in formally 'race-blind' liberal polities like the United States, a metaphorical and unstated 'racial contact' works to ensure profound racialized inequality.

In the context of a dearth of scholarship that has made use of race in relation to Israel/Palestine,[30] our application and extension of Mills' framework to this part of the world has been aimed at explicating what we conceptualize as an Israel/Palestine racial contract, which works at the local and international levels to effectively render Palestinians as racialized, stateless, and victims of human rights abuses and repression, all while denying that racism has anything to do with these outcomes.[31]

In today's context there is more attention being paid to historic and contemporary expressions of anti-Black racism and anti-racist praxis, and this development also invites more close consideration of other forms of racism. Accordingly, it also makes sense to begin to name and identify the key elements of anti-Palestinian racism as a specific form of racism operating in local and global contexts.[32] Of course, as an Arab grouping comprised of both Christians and Muslims, Palestinians are subjected to Orientalism,[33] as well as anti-Muslim racism (also called Islamophobia) and anti-Arab racism.[34] But there is a relevance of naming anti-Palestinian racism as a form of racism distinctly experienced by Palestinians.[35] This perspective gains some further depth when considering how it is becoming a key contemporary site of mobilization against Palestinian oppression in ways that parallel and bolster the BDS movement and the naming and challenging of the practice of apartheid directed at Palestinians.

Resisting anti-Palestinian racism

By the early 2000s the complete failure of the Oslo Accords to deliver the promised peace was clear, and moreover life for Palestinians under conditions of occupation was increasingly deadly.[36] Additionally, the United Nations has proven to be unable or unwilling to actually do anything to change the status of the still lingering 'question of Palestine'[37] due to the fact that Israel has powerful allies, including the United States. Indeed, under US President Trump, not only was the problematically dubbed 'deal of the century' unserious as concerned bettering the lives of Palestinians, it was accompanied by the dramatic withdrawal of US support to the United Nations Relief and Works Agency (UNRWA) which supports registered Palestine refugees.[38]

Given the impasses as concerns states responding to the question of Palestine', the 2005 unified call from Palestinian civil society groups to global civil society was dramatic for ushering in a new moment of solidarity from civil society internationally. This includes labour unions, academic associations, student organizations and some churches and Jewish organizations, particularly in countries of the West.[39] While there is backlash against the movement, it is notable that it nonetheless continues to build strength and support. For example, in March 2022 members of the US-based Middle East Studies Association voted overwhelmingly in support of 'endorsing the Palestinian call for boycotts, divestment, and sanctions of Israel as a way to hold the government accountable for ongoing human rights violations'.[40]

The BDS call was also remarkable for putting on the table key demands pertaining to Palestinians in Israel, under occupation and in the diaspora. Specifically, these calls are directed at international civil society organizations and likened to the boycotts credited with ending apartheid in South Africa:

> We, representatives of Palestinian civil society, call upon international civil society organizations and people of conscience all over the world to impose broad boycotts and implement divestment initiatives against Israel similar to those applied to South Africa in the apartheid era. We appeal to you to pressure your respective states to impose embargoes and sanctions against Israel. We also invite conscientious Israelis to support this Call, for the sake of justice and genuine peace.
>
> These non-violent punitive measures should be maintained until Israel meets its obligation to recognize the Palestinian people's inalienable right to self-determination and fully complies with the precepts of international law by:
>
> 1. Ending its occupation and colonization of all Arab lands and dismantling the Wall
> 2. Recognizing the fundamental rights of the Arab-Palestinian citizens of Israel to full equality; and
> 3. Respecting, protecting and promoting the rights of Palestinian refugees to return to their homes and properties as stipulated in UN resolution 194.[41]

In addition, since the BDS call likened the solution for Palestinians to the solidarity that helped end apartheid (the policy of 'apartness' in operation in South Africa from 1948 to 1993), attention to the conditions experienced by Palestinians in Israel/Palestine and in the diaspora through an analysis of apartheid has also grown.[42] Consider here that a 2021 survey of Middle East scholars belonging to the Middle East Studies Association and the American Political Science Association found fully 59 per cent of those surveyed described the situation of Israel, the West Bank and Gaza as 'a one-state reality akin to apartheid'.[43] This focus on apartheid has also increasingly moved from simply being a way of placing other settler-colonies with racialized practices in comparison with South Africa under apartheid for which there is a tradition[44] to actually referencing the legal prohibition against apartheid as a crime against humanity.

The legal weight of the charge of apartheid stems from the combined weight of the 1973 *International Convention on the Suppression and Punishment of the Crime of Apartheid* – the first binding international convention on apartheid and racial segregation which came into force in 1976[45] – as well as the 1998 Rome Statute of the International Criminal Court. Today apartheid has come to extend beyond the temporal and geographic context of South Africa, and its now 'universal meaning' is understood to be 'applicable wherever it exists'.[46]

In this context where apartheid is understood to operate beyond South Africa's history, the number of reports coming from experts and non-governmental organizations invoking a legal understanding of apartheid and attaching it to Israel is growing exponentially. In addition to Palestinian organizations they include Richard Falk (former UN Special Rapporteur on the Situation of Human Rights in the Palestinian Territory Occupied since 1967),[47] the Israeli-based human rights organization B'Tselem,[48] Human Rights Watch (2021), Amnesty International (2022), and the report of Michael Lynk, the outgoing UN Special Rapporteur on the Situation of Human Rights in the Palestinian Territory Occupied since 1967.[49] Necessarily confining his analysis to occupied Palestinian territory from 1967, Lynk's report finds that

> the political system of entrenched rule in the occupied Palestinian territory which endows one racial-national-ethnic group with substantial rights, benefits and privileges while intentionally subjecting another group to live behind walls, checkpoints and under a permanent military rule "*sans droits, sans égalité, sans dignité et sans liberté*" satisfies the prevailing evidentiary standard for the existence of apartheid.[50]

However, the Amnesty International report is especially notable for finding apartheid to be practised against Palestinians in Israel, in the OPT and also in the diaspora:

> The organization has concluded that Israel has perpetrated the international wrong of apartheid, as a human rights violation and a violation of public international law wherever it imposes this system. *It has assessed that almost all of Israel's civilian administration and military authorities, as well as governmental and quasi- governmental institutions, are involved in the enforcement of the system of apartheid against Palestinians across Israel and the OPT and against Palestinian refugees and their descendants outside the territory.* Amnesty International has also concluded that the patterns of proscribed acts perpetuated by Israel both inside Israel and in the OPT form part of a systematic as well as widespread attack directed against the Palestinian population, and that the inhuman or inhumane acts committed within the context of this attack have been committed with the intention to maintain this system and amount to the crime against humanity of apartheid under both the Apartheid Convention and the Rome Statute.[51]

Both the BDS movement and the charge of apartheid have triggered forms of denial and resistance from the Israeli state and its allies including the charges that both BDS and the label of apartheid applied to Israel are anti-Semitic.[52] While antisemitism is a real and growing issue in the face of White supremacist revival in countries of the West, here the claim of antisemitism is spurious and it also does not address the fact that Jewish suffering can be used to suppress Palestinian claims including anti-Palestinian racism.[53] Indeed, both the BDS movement and the apartheid charge are critical avenues for mobilization which can include addressing the complex conditions, rights violations and racialized oppression that is specific to Palestinians across their fragmented geographies. In this regard, and given the fact that the specificity of racism Palestinians experiences is not completely covered by terms like Orientalism, anti-Arab racism or Islamophobia, the time seems especially ripe to be naming and organizing against anti-Palestinian racism.

Signs are already on the horizon that this is being pursued. Writing in the British context Chris Doyle, the Director of the Council for Arab-British Understanding, observes:

> Anti-Palestinian racism is at the heart of the conflict. It is Palestinians who are denied basic national and human rights, including the right to self-determination, to a state, to citizenship, to marry who they want, to land and water, and to a life of dignity. Their very presence is being erased, along with their history and culture. Nearly three-quarters of Palestinians can no longer live, and often even visit, what was their country.[54]

In the US context, and noting the attacks on Palestinian-American House Representative Rashida Tlaib and other members of 'the Squad,' Peter Beinhart argues that naming and making anti-Palestinian racism visible could help to transform current debates:

> since pro-Israel organizations in the US have made it nearly impossible to discuss Israel-Palestine without addressing questions of anti-Jewish bigotry, Americans of all backgrounds have a responsibility to ask why even blatant expressions of anti-Palestinian bigotry pass almost unnoticed. Because anti-Palestinianism is so invisible and so pervasive, introducing the concept could change the way Americans discuss what Israel does to Palestinians, and what America does to those who speak on their behalf. The notion of anti-Palestinianism might force politicians, pundits, and religious leaders who call the Squad bigots to reckon with the fact that the label applies far better to themselves.[55]

In the Canadian context, based on community input, the Canadian Arab Lawyers Association has also worked to name and describe anti-Palestinian racism:

> Anti-Palestinian racism is a form of anti-Arab racism that silences, excludes, erases, stereotypes, defames or dehumanizes Palestinians or their narratives. Anti-Palestinian racism takes various forms including: denying the Nakba and justifying violence against Palestinians; failing to acknowledge Palestinians as an Indigenous people with a collective identity, belonging and rights in relation to occupied and historic Palestine; erasing the human rights and equal dignity and worth of Palestinians; excluding or pressuring others to exclude Palestinian perspectives, Palestinians and their allies; defaming Palestinians and their allies with slander such as being inherently antisemitic, a terrorist threat/sympathizer or opposed to democratic values.[56]

This framework, understood as not exhaustive, reflects on the connections Palestinians and the Palestine solidarity movement have with other anti-racist and anti-settler-colonial movements.[57]

There is, as noted, in fact a long history to Palestinians identifying racism and attempting to have it brought into play in relation to politics. However, the recent attempts we are seeing now to grapple with naming and highlighting the features of anti-Palestinian racism as a specific form of racism are promising as they are occurring at a moment when there is more awareness and interest in different forms of racism. As well, the naming of anti-Palestinian racism, in combination with other developments around BDS and the apartheid charge, may go some way in further strengthening a broader anti-racist movement globally. Indeed, already on the ground there are fruitful discussions emerging on fighting antisemitism and anti-Palestinian racism together, while resisting the International Holocaust Remembrance Alliance definition of antisemitism which is problematic for equating antisemitism with criticism of Israel's policies towards Palestinians.[58]

Conclusion

The Google Scholar search engine reminds users they 'stand on the shoulders of giants' and over a long career with numerous scholarly contributions Elia Zureik is a giant in the fields of sociology, Palestine studie, and surveillance studies. His scholarly work, going back over five decades, has contributed to knowledge, and has enabled and will continue to enable new and different conversations amongst scholars. Through his works he has countered the power/knowledge nexus enabled by Orientalism, colonialism, settler-colonialism and the racialization of Palestinians and forged much needed epistemological space for Palestinian experience to be identified, heard and understood. This deserves celebration.

Building on the themes of settler-colonial racism, geographic complexity and resistance identified in the work of Zuriek, as I have tried to illuminate in this chapter Palestinians are also active agents in naming their oppression and claims, as well as in strategizing, forming larger alliances and forging solidarity across lines of difference. The United Nations, with its statist bias, has proven to be a necessary but insufficient space for resolving 'the question of Palestine', no doubt since it was also part of the problem – and before it the League of Nations with its mandate system. More than seventy years from the Nakba, Palestinians not only exist, but their collective experiences and knowledges are shaping and contributing to some of the most vibrant human rights movements and social justice struggles of the twenty-first century. This also deserves celebration.

Notes

1   Abu-Laban 2016; Henry et al. 2017.
2   Nadeau and Sears 2010; Thompson 2011; Drummond 2013; Gessen 2021.

3   See, e.g., Zureik 1971; Pike and Zureik, 1975; Zureik and Frizzell 1976.
4   Abu-Lughod and Sa'di 2007.
5   Abu-Laban and Bakan 2022.
6   Abu-Lughod and Sa'di 2007: 3.
7   Masalha 2012: 251–57.
8   Zureik 1977: 3.
9   Zureik 1974: 99.
10 Zureik 1983: 786.
11 Zureik 2002: 100,
12 Zureik 2003: 152.
13 Wimmer and Schiller 2003.
14 Zureik 2003: 152.
15 Zureik 2016, 2020; Zureik, Lyon and Abu-Laban 2011.
16 Zureik and Salter 2005; Zureik and Hindle 2004; Lyon and Zureik 1996.
17 Zureik 2020: 219.
18 Ibid.: 220.
19 Zureik 2016: 53.
20 Ibid.: 6.
21 Wolfe 2006: 388.
22 Bakan and Abu-Laban 2021: 2173–4.
23 George 2021.
24 Thompson 2008.
25 Abu-Laban 2021a.
26 Alcorn 2021.
27 Abu-Laban and Bakan 2021.
28 Mills 1997: 18.
29 Ibid.: 1.
30 Bakan and Abu-Laban 2021: 2172–3.
31 Abu-Laban and Bakan 2020.
32 Abu-Laban and Bakan 2022.
33 Said 1979b.
34 Abu-Laban and Bakan 2021: 143.
35 Abu-Laban and Bakan, 2021.
36 Gordon 2008.
37 Said 1979a.
38 United States White House 2020; Abu-Laban 2021b.
39 Abu-Laban and Bakan 2020: 147–71.
40 MESA 2022.
41 BDS 2005.
42 Abu-Laban and Bakan 2020: 225–9.
43 Lynch and Telhami 2021.
44 Abu-Laban and Bakan, 2020: 225.
45 United Nations General Assembly, 1973.
46 United Nations Human Rights Council 2022: 6.
47 Falk and Tilley 2017.
48 B'Tselem 2021.
49 United Nations Human Rights Council 2022.
50 Ibid.
51 Amnesty International 2022: 12–13, my italics.

52 Abu-Laban and Bakan 2020, 2021; United Nations Human Rights Council 2022: 5.
53 Abu-Laban and Bakan, 2021.
54 Doyle 2022.
55 Beinhart 2021.
56 Majid 2022: 14.
57 Ibid.: 14–18.
58 Bakan and Abu-Laban 2021.

References

Abu-Laban, Yasmeen (2016), 'Representing a Diverse Canada in Political Science: Power, Ideas and the Emergent Challenge of Reconciliation', *European Political Science* 15 (4): 493–507.

Abu-Laban, Yasmeen (2021a), 'Multiculturalism: Past, Present and Future', *Canadian Diversity* (Special Issue on 'Multiculturalism @ 50') 18 (1): 9–12.

Abu-Laban, Yasmeen (2021b), 'Re-defining the International Refugee Regime: UNHCR, UNRWA and the Challenge of Multigenerational Protracted Refugee Situations,' in Catherine Dauvergne (ed.), *Research Handbook on the Law and Politics of Migration*, 310–22, Cheltenham and Northampton: Edward Elgar Publishing.

Abu-Laban, Yasmeen, and Abigail B. Bakan (2020), *Israel, Palestine and the Politics of Race: Exploring Identity and Power in a Global Context*, London: I. B. Tauris.

Abu-Laban, Yasmeen, and Abigail B. Bakan (2021), 'Anti-Palestinian Racism: Analyzing the Unnamed and Suppressed Reality', *Project on Middle East Political Science (POMEPS) Studies* 44: 143–9.

Abu-Laban, Yasmeen, and Abigail B. Bakan (2022), 'Anti-Palestinian Racism and Racial Gaslighting', *Political Quarterly* 93 (3), https://doi.org/10.1111/1467-923X.13166

Abu-Lughod, Lila, and Ahmad H. Sa'di (2007), 'Introduction: The Claims of Memory,' in L. Abu-Lughod and A. Sa'di (eds), *Nakba: Palestine, 1948 and the Claims of Memory*, 1–24, New York: Columbia University Press.

Alcorn, Chauncey (2021), 'George Floyd's Death was a Wake-up Call for Corporate America: Here's What Has – and Hasn't – Changed', CNN Business. https://www.cnn.com/2021/05/25/business/corporate-america-anti-racism-spending/index.html (accessed 15 November 2021).

Amnesty International (2022), *Israel's Apartheid Against Palestinians: Cruel System of Domination and Crime Against Humanity* (1 February). Available at: https://www.amnesty.org/en/latest/news/2022/02/israels-apartheid-against-palestinians-a-cruel-system-of-domination-and-a-crime-against-humanity/ (accessed 1 February 2022).

Bakan, Abigail B and Yasmeen Abu-laban (2021), 'The Israel/Palestine Conflict and the Challenge of Anti-Racism: A Case Study of the United Nations World Conference Against Racism,' *Ethnic and Racial Studies* (Special Issue on Race and the Middle East) 44 (12): 2167–89.

Beinhart, Peter (2021), 'It's Time to Name Anti-Palestinian Bigotry,' *Jewish Currents* 16 July. https://jewishcurrents.org/its-time-to-name-anti-palestinian-bigotry (accessed 15 April 2022).

BDS (2005), 'Palestinian Civil Society Call for BDS'. https://bdsmovement.net/call (accessed 13 April 2022).

B'Tselem (2021), *This is Apartheid: A Regime of Jewish Supremacy from the Jordan River to the Mediterranean Sea,* 12 January. https://www.btselem.org/apartheid (accessed 15 January 2022).

Doyle, Chris (2022), 'Who Will Defend Palestinians from Racist Attacks,' *Arab News* 10 January. https://www.arabnews.com/node/2001521 (accessed 15 April 2022).

Drummond, Susan G. (2013), *Unthinkable Thoughts: Academic Freedom and the One-State Model for Israel and Palestine,* Vancouver: UBC Press.

Falk, Richard and Virginia Q. Tilley (2017), 'Israeli Practices Towards the Palestinian People and the Question of Apartheid', *Palestine and the Israeli Occupation* 1 (1): 1–65.

George, Janel (2021), 'A Lesson on Critical Race Theory', *American Bar Association Human Rights Magazine* 46 (2). https://www.americanbar.org/groups/crsj/publications/human_rights_magazine_home/civil-rights-reimagining-policing/a-lesson-on-critical-race-theory/ (accessed 13 April 2022).

Gessen, Masha (2021), 'Did a University of Toronto Donor Block the Hiring of a Scholar for her Writing on Palestine?', *The New Yorker* 8 May. https://www.newyorker.com/news/our-columnists/did-a-university-of-toronto-donor-block-the-hiring-of-a-scholar-for-her-writing-on-palestine (accessed 31 March 2022).

Gordon, Neve (2008), *Israel's Occupation,* Oakland: University of California Press.

Henry, Frances, Enakshi Dua, Carl E. James, Audrey Kobayashi, Peter Li, Howard Ramos and Malinda S. Smith (2017), *The Equity Myth: Racialization and Indigeneity at Canadian Universities,* Vancouver: UBC Press.

Human Rights Watch (2021), *A Threshold Crossed: Israeli Authorities and the Crimes of Apartheid and Persecution* (April 27) https://www.hrw.org/report/2021/04/27/threshold-crossed/israeli-authorities-and-crimes-apartheid-and-persecution (accessed 15 January 2022).

Lynch, Marc, and Sibley Telhami (2021), 'Biden Says He Will Listen to Experts. Here is What Scholars of the Middle East Think.' Brookings (19 February) https://www.brookings.edu/blog/order-from-chaos/2021/02/19/biden-says-he-will-listen-to-experts-here-is-what-scholars-of-the-middle-east-think/ (accessed 15 April 2022).

Lyon, David, and Elia Zureik (1996), *Computers, Surveillance and Privacy,* Minneapolis: University of Minnesota Press.

Majid, Dania (2022), *Anti-Palestinian Racism: Naming, Framing and Manifestations,* Arab Canadian Lawyers Association. Available at https://www.canarablaw.org (accessed 14 May 2022)

Masalha, Nur (2012), *The Palestine Nakba: Decolonising History, Narrating the Subaltern, Reclaiming Memory,* London and New York: Zed Books.

MESA (Middle East Studies Association) (2022), 'Middle East Scholars Vote to Endorse BDS: Press Release' (23 March). Available at https://mesana.org/news/2022/03/23/middle-east-scholars-vote-to-endorse-bds (accessed 14 April 2022).

Mills, Charles (1997), *The Racial Contract,* Ithaca: Cornell University Press.

Nadeau, Mary-Jo, and Alan Sears (2010), 'The Palestine Test: Countering the Silencing Campaign', *Studies in Political Economy* 85 (1): 7–33.

Pike, Robert M., and Elia Zureik (eds) (1975), *Socialization and Values in Canadian Society,* Toronto: McClelland and Stewart.

Said, Edward W. (1979a), *The Question of Palestine,* New York: Vintage Books.

Said, Edward W. (1979b), *Orientalism,* New York: Basic Books.

Thompson, Debra (2008), 'Is Race Political?' *Canadian Journal of Political Science* 41 (3): 525–47.

Thompson, Jon (2011), *No Debate: The Israel Lobby and Free Speech at Canadian Universities.* Toronto: Lorimer.

United Nations General Assembly (1973), *International Convention on the Suppression and Punishment of the Crime of Apartheid* (RES 3068 (XXVIII)), https://www.un.org/en/genocideprevention/documents/atrocity-crimes/Doc.10_International%20Convention%20on%20the%20Suppression%20and%20Punishment%20of%20the%20Crime%20of%20Apartheid.pdf (accessed 15 April 2022).

United Nations Human Rights Council (2022), *Report of the Special Rapporteur on the Situation of Human Rights in the Palestinian Territories Occupied Since 1967* (A/HRC/49/87) (21 March), https://www.ohchr.org/en/hr-bodies/hrc/regular-sessions/session49/list-reports (accessed 15 April 2022).

United States. White House (2020), *Peace to Prosperity: A Vision to Improve the Lives of the Palestinian and Israeli People,* available at https://trumpwhitehouse.archives.gov/peacetoprosperity/ (accessed 31 March 2022).

Wimmer, Andreas, and Nina Glick Schiller (2003), 'Methodological Nationalism, the Social Sciences, and the Study of Migration: An Essay in Historical Epistemology', *International Migration Review* 37 (3): 576–610.

Wolfe, Patrick (2006), 'Settler-Colonialism and the Elimination of the Native', *Journal of Genocide Research* 8 (4): 387–409.

Zureik, Elia (1971), 'Children and Political Socialization', in K. Ishwaran (ed.), *The Canadian Family*, 186–93, Toronto: Holt, Rinehart and Winston.

|Zureik, Elia (1974), 'Arab Youth in Israel: Their Situation and Status Perceptions', *Journal of Palestine Studies* 3 (3): 97–108.

Zureik, Elia (1977), 'Towards a Sociology of the Palestinians', *Journal of Palestine Studies* 6 (4): 3–16.

Zureik, Elia (1979), *The Palestinians in Israel: A Study in Internal Colonialism,* London: Routledge and Kegan Paul.

Zureik, Elia (1983), 'The Economics of Dispossession: The Palestinians', *Third World Quarterly* 5 (4): 775–90.

Zureik, Elia (2002), 'The Palestinian Refugee Problem: Diverging Interpretations', *Global Dialogue* 4 (3): 92–102.

Zureik, Elia (2003), 'Theoretical and Methodological Considerations for the Study of Palestinian Society', *Comparative Studies of South Asia, Africa and the Middle East* 23 (1 & 2): 152–62.

Zureik, Elia (2016), *Israel's Colonial Project in Palestine: Brutal Pursuit,* Milton Park and New York: Routledge.

Zureik, Elia (2020), 'Settler Colonialism, Neoliberalism and Cyber Security: The Case of Israel', *Middle East Critique* 29 (2): 219–35.

Zureik, Elia, and Alan Frizzell (1976), 'Values in Canadian Magazine Fiction: A Test of the Social Control Thesis', *Journal of Popular Culture* 10: 359–76.

Zureik, Elia, and Karen Hindle (2004), 'Governance, Security and Technology: The Case of Biometric's' *Studies in Political Economy* 73 (1): 113–37.

Zureik, Elia, and David Lyon (2022), 'Coronavirus Surveillance and Palestinians', *Jerusalem Quarterly* 89 (Spring): 51–62.

Zureik, Elia, David Lyon and Yasmeen Abu-Laban (eds) (2011), *Surveillance and Control in Israel/Palestine: Population, Territory and Power,* Milton Park and New York: Routledge.

Zureik, Elia, and Mark Salter (2005), *Global Surveillance and Policing: Borders, Security, Identity,* Cullompton and Portland: Willan.

Part Three

Zionist Settle-Colonialism: Surveillance

8

Secrecy as Colonial Violence

The Case of Occupied East Jerusalem

Nadera Shalhoub-Kevorkian and Abeer Otman

> *I realized that secrecy is there to destabilize Palestinians so they get sick . . . really sick, scared always and uncertain about their steps . . . their future . . . strange to their bodies . . . and even turn mad . . . real madness out of rage . . . real rage-Qaheir.*
>
> (Riyad)

Riyad, a Palestinian man in his sixties who lives in Occupied East Jerusalem (OEJ), uncovers the embodied workings of secrecy against the psychosocial wellbeing of the colonized. His insights expose some of the invisible and unseen spaces of state brutality apparent in the invocation of secrecy, and reveal its racism in wounding not only the present of the colonized, but also their futurity. Secrecy, as Riyad explains, is an intrusive mode of surveillance that creates physical, social, and psychological maladies. It is a maze of disciplinary technologies that produces and maintains not only fears, anxieties, ongoing trauma, uncertainty and threats but also refusal and rage among the colonized. Secrecy, as an intrusive mode of surveillance, creates a maze of disciplinary technologies that not only produce and maintain fears, anxieties, ongoing trauma, uncertainty and threats but also refusal among the colonized. More than simply a technology of power, secrecy's spaces of operation function psychologically to influence emotions, the mind and the psyche through the invocation of 'secret information', disrupt the psychological balance and play a crucial role in governing, incarcerating and dispossessing the colonized. Secrecy penetrates social and intimate relations and aspirations to generate mistrust between family members, friends and neighbours, resulting in familial and collective dismemberment.

The settler state and its regulatory surveillance regime control the colonized Other affectively and through specially engineered, securitized systems of classification, non-circulation and censorship. Various affective mechanisms of governance, erasure, denial and dispossession are part of the Israeli settler-colonial punitive context and its zealous politics,[1] which deny the traumatic history of the Nakba;[2] violate Palestinians psychosocially, spatially, and economically; and insist on hijacking the future.[3] By focusing on the invocation of secrecy as part of settler-colonial political behaviour apparent in draconian 'emergency' laws, acts and violent regulations, we hope to dig deeper into Zionists' de-territorialized and invisible machineries of surveillance. In doing so, we examine the state's use of secrecy in order to analyse its psychosocial affective operationalization, moving beyond the dichotomized political language of oppressed/oppressor to uncover fluid 'secretized' state manoeuvrings that aim at governing the colonized's existence.

Settler-colonial fear and insecurity, and its need to disavow the presence and existence of the colonized[4] will be examined through the prism of secrecy as experienced by Palestinian narrators from (OEJ) from May 2019 to May 2022. By analysing everyday 'secretized' technologies of the state and its machineries of surveillance, which recurrently engage with colonized bodies and psyches, these narrators reveal the activation of settler-colonial practices of affective wounding, incarceration, segregation and elimination. While the narrations about the actual, bodily and affective operationalization of secrecy could indeed be analyzed as technologies of incapacitation, punishment, and dehumanization, the state's use of secrecy can also be regarded as a political site where political awareness, actions and defiance are born. Riyad, a family physician living and serving Palestinians in OEJ, calls the state's use of secrecy 'an everyday politics of terrorizing Palestinian society'. He shares his own ordeal with the invocation of secrecy as a physician:

> When parents or youth share with me the way secrecy was used during their interrogation and arrest, the way the military invaded their homes in the middle of the night claiming they had secret information without formal proof, a court order, or even a photo, or stopped them while shopping, visiting relatives, or at school, I realized that secrecy is there to destabilize Palestinians so they get sick ... really sick ... I mean suffering from short breathing, chest pain, increase in their sugar level ... even stroke ... scared always and uncertain about their steps ... strange to their bodies, to their home ... and even turn mad.
>
> (Riyad)

Riyad explains how state secrecy becomes a permanent condition employed to make Palestinians believe they are always under surveillance – an infinite war.

Guided by voices encountering and countering state secrecy, this chapter argues that the marshalling of secrecy to maintain the violent dispossession of the settler state compels us to unpack its deployment of secrecy as a technology of surveillance, examine its bodily and psychological effects, and unmoor the state's use of it in order to rethink its 'surveillance' power. Historically, the use of state secrecy was observable in the role played by a host of state agents, such as secret services, popular conspirators, fake expositors, and professional accusers – what Debord calls 'networks of influence'.[5] Deleuze and Guattari (1987) break secrecy down into three components: the content in a box, an action (both in its effect and spread), and a perception – a game – in its shadowy power involving the spy, the revealer, the blackmailer, and the like.

This chapter will engage with Deleuze and Guattari's three components by first examining secrecy as colonial violence to explore how and why secrets are made, used, maintained, and broken. Second, the chapter will present secrecy as part of 'big data' used by the settler state and its securitized and secretized technologies of governance as an extension of the state's biopower. The third and fourth sections will look at secrecy and/ as psychological warfare and social dismemberment, probing the psychosocial effect of secrecy, its liveability within social and communal settings and institutions, and considering how 'secrets' die metaphorically and cease to exist. The chapter will reveal the power of state's politics of secrecy, and conclude with an examination of the colonized's modes of resistance and survivability to counter secrecy's psychological terrorism.

Secrecy and secret information as colonial violence

We define secrecy, and 'secret information', when invoked by the state, as an assemblage of concealed operations juxtaposing various forms of psychosocial invasion and dispossession. It is a carceral psychic and political strategy used to widen the scope of state domination. Secrecy and its political work are used and abused by the state security apparatus as a skilled concealment of showing, owing, or penetrating political subjects and entities. Secret information that is made up and/or obtained violently by the state supports, maintains and in some instances intensifies power, enhancing the political monopoly over the othered. The state's use of secrecy and its revelation increase the power of secrecy.[6] In the Palestinian context, secrecy dominates as surveillance, facilitating Zionist logic and policies of elimination.[7]

When state power and its structures use secrecy as a form of political violence, the legitimate use of secrecy constitutes a critical machinery for the state because it is connected to a system of power, with 'beliefs' and 'values', that guarantees the legitimacy of governance.[8] In combination, these factors establish norms and affective politics that empower the state and its agents to use secrecy and the claim of 'secret information' in order to act against the colonized without interruption. This normative validation of secrecy is rooted in affective politics embedded within the colonizers' beliefs, values and institutions, demarcating and reproducing the boundaries between national subjects and disposable others. Political norms capture how ongoing state political violence is not only normalized and carried out under the law but also anchored in perceptions and behaviour legitimized within social order, affective politics, structures and racialized hierarchies that produce exclusive sacralized entities against demonized others.[9] Emotions 'matter for politics', for they 'show us how power shapes the very surface of bodies as well as worlds'; affective politics intensify the binary between the 'we' and the excluded 'other' through emotional, gendered and racialized narratives that create hierarchies and preserve the governance of those perceived as the objective-rational hegemon over the inferior-irrational-emotional subordinated other.[10]

Psycho-political analyses of the politics and violence of secrecy are anchored in the work of liberation psychiatrists and psychologists that expose the complex dialectic of interpersonal and intra-personal structural processes, and racialized ideologies that constrain social transformation and decolonization. Psychiatrist Frantz Fanon (1963) resituates human psychology within sociopolitical and historical forces. He demonstrates how trauma from institutionalized and racialized colonial violence is linked to a profound experience of depersonalization. He illuminates the notion of depersonalization, defining it in relation to the ways colonizers individuated Blacks through dividing practices. Constantly being singled out and divided creates an ongoing questioning of oneself, forcing the colonized to query their reality. Fanon's insights reveal the thin line between the possibility of liberation through decolonization and the risk of intensifying rage and repressive violence. These resonate with social psychologist Ignacio Martín-Baró's (1989) argument that the state induces fear, anxiety and terror as a means of social control, thus creating a potent form of psychological warfare on both conscious and unconscious levels.

In the Palestinian case, scholars argue that the Israeli state's politics of surveillance facilitate its colonial logics of control, domination, uprooting and elimination.[11] Zureik (2016) shows how Israeli surveillance tactics expanded with time. Historically, Zionist settlers used surveillance and secret information to locate lands in Palestine that could be sold to them. After Israel was established in 1948, secrecy was used for militarized operations, political assassinations and manipulation. In today's context, scholars argue that Israeli surveillance and secrecy is deployed through 'intimate' bureaucratic surveillance and monitoring to ensure the state's power over Palestinian life.[12] In particular, this surveillance and secret information is used by the Israeli state to infiltrate and control the daily lives of Palestinians[13] and its most intimate aspects – the family and home.[14] Moreover, Israel's colonial technologies of secrecy penetrate the body and the psyche of the colonized Palestinian.[15] Shalhoub-Kevorkian and Wahab suggest that secrecy's logic unveils the political war in the settler colony Israeli state and works to maintain colonial psychological domination and violence through an affectual structure of entrapment, which operates through a legal system that favors the colonizer.

> Militarised secrecy's necrocapitalist assemblage takes us to one of the core dimensions of settler colonial ideology 'accumulation by dispossession' (Harvey, 2003), that is, the elimination of the colonized, demolition of life and the psychic in which the colonialist 'trades' and 'sells' the machineries of elimination as combat proven.[16]

Critical scholarship reveals that structures of entrapment within colonial and settler-colonial contexts are predicated on the use of various carceral technologies of surveillance which have resulted in social ruptures, theft of land and homes, and the attempted taming of the occupied.[17] When structures of entrapment are operationalized through secrecy and its psychological penetration, secrecy becomes a violent tool allowing state violence to infiltrate social affairs, familial ties, and deep intimate spaces as it attempts to discipline the affects and psyches of the oppressed,[18] which Sheehi and Sheehi term 'psychological foreclosure'.[19] Shalhoub-Kevorkian and Wahab make a parallel observation in their concluding remarks: '[s]ecret wars are not there to end the war, but rather to grant the activation of an unending psychological demoralization, psychosocial annihilation and socioeconomic control, insisting that "secrecy is the great necrocapitalist politic"'.[20]

In order to further comprehend the psychological consequences of secrecy and colonial technologies of surveillance, this chapter seeks to attain a bottom-up understanding of Palestinian Jerusalemites' experiences of the ways in which the state uses secrecy against them as a violent weapon, producing tangible suffering and injury and, at times, even death. The research will examine their narratives, the challenges they face, and how they cope with or confront those challenges while living in ongoing precarity. Conducting a margin-to-centre analysis,[21] the research utilizes critical feminist methodology[22] to highlight the importance of the lived experience of everyday life, with the goal of unearthing subjective knowledge.[23] Specifically, Palestinian feminist methodology stresses the importance of looking at the intimate,[24] at the everydayness of power and suffering, and at the epistemology of details to reveal voices of the oppressed, which shed light on narratives of violence and daily traumas of intrusion into intimate life.[25] The researchers interviewed Palestinian Jerusalemites who either experienced arrest themselves or the arrest of a family or community member and interrogation based on secret file between October 2020 and January 2022.

Big data and the datawars

Secrecy is something that one does not know how to comprehend and on what is it based. . . . I was arrested based on information they gather through algorithms. My arrest was not based on real information, but on algorithms. . . . They asked me about my work. . . . [T]hey interrogated me about my travels, I travel a lot for my work. . . . [T]hey asked me about people who are my friends on social media who I don't really know. . . . [T]hey saw a photo on Facebook, which I shared and they showed it to me. . . . [S]ecrecy is established based on people's movements . . . what they do on social media . . . travels . . . [T]hey [Israeli intelligence] construct assumptions that this person, while on his travels, will do certain things [involved with terrorists]. . . [T]his is how their system works.

Aadel

Aadel, who is 33 years old and lives in OEJ with his wife and their two little girls, was arrested two years ago. The Israeli police arrested him at work (at a prestigious Israeli institution). They coordinated his arrest with the security department of his workplace, which called Aadel and told him to leave his office and come to the security department outside the building. When Aadel arrived at the security department, he was arrested. He was taken out and searched in the street, in front of his colleagues, while in shock and unable to comprehend what was happening. To this day, Aadel doesn't know why he was arrested, humiliated, dragged from his workplace, his family and his life, locked in a cell and interrogated for a week. He explained, 'I never participated in any political action, not even a protest . . . [I]f there are any clashes [between the Israeli army and Palestinians], I stay indoors . . . I have never even ran a red light, so why was I arrested?'

Aadel's confusion and shock about being arrested speak to the ambiguity, doubt and uncertainty to which he is subjected as a colonized other existing under constant colonial surveillance. His mundane movements, actions and ties are subject to structured systems of observation and examination. Furthermore, he is at risk of facing criminal accusations and being treated like a criminal and a dangerous threat at any time and anywhere without ever knowing the reason, except to instil in him fear that the state is always watching. Aadel's voice reveals that secrecy is an intrusive mode of surveillance, comprised of the monitoring, counting and intersecting of random daily routines. He shows how ordinary life activities of work, travel and socializing are transformed into a secret file that leads to accusations of terror. In essence, Aadel is transformed from a colleague, friend, father and husband to a dangerous other – a 'legitimate target'[26] – in order to dehumanize, dominate, and incarcerate him as well as the Palestinian community. Aadel's voice reveals how secrecy produces and maintains a constant feeling of uncertainty and feeling threatened.

Big data is accumulated from mass, assembled surveillance and different sources,[27] including actions of or in relation to family members and neighbors, such as getting engaged to someone considered a political activist, travelling to a specific country, attending the funeral of a relative deemed questionable, and other mundane acts. Big data leads to social sorting, as citizens become profiles to be calculated, and accumulated information sorted into hierarchies that can be easily transferred and used.[28] When the algorithms are used by institutions perpetuating biases and prejudices, big data is threaded together with unclear, imagined assumptions, disguised as dangerous 'secret files' to further track and control peoples' movements and mobility.[29] This mode of producing imagined narratives to track subjects is an extension of the state's biopower.[30] In addition, in relation to the 'war on terror' there exists a 'Datawar'.[31] This Datawar 'echoes the architecture of war, yet works to conceal the violences of its classification, sorting, and banning of human lives'.[32] It is 'perhaps no longer a war that no one sees ... and the invisible violences of data-analytics remain obfuscated and responsibility is evaded.[33] The Datawar is a war by other means: it is proactive, embedded in large-scale information gathering and data exchange between hegemonic power holders.

In OEJ, the colonial state inscribes its power through a similar Datawar, equipped with a system of biopolitical surveillance that manages and calculates Palestinian life, birth, movement, and economy.[34] Aadel's voice illustrates the extent to which the state's Datawar and biopower produce imagined narratives through tracking, counting, and monitoring, which are used to incapacitate and inscribe power over the Palestinian movements and bodies. The Datawar's power (both actual and imagined) has the ability to incapacitate people via secrecy, since it is deeply entangled with the violence of secrecy and hidden strategies embedded in the settler state's ideological underpinnings. The Datawar and its systems of debilitation can be turned into a powerful, psychological military weapon. Secrecy as an extension of colonial big data, datawars, and its biopolitics penetrates time, as it can occur at 2:00 a.m. when children are asleep in their beds and families are taking refuge in their homes. It occupies bodies and psyches through militarized assemblages of big data, reaching deep into lives, as Nadia, a Palestinian woman from OEJ who was arrested based on secret information, reports: 'I started smelling their violence ... breathing it ... horrified by it ... I started dreaming fear ... questioning everything ... doubting even my own husband and mother.' The bio- and psycho-political invasion goes beyond incapacitation and creates psychic horrors, confusions, uncertainties, and deep sense of loss.

In Aadel's experience with Israel's secrecy of biopolitics, which is embedded in a settler-colonial context and its logic of elimination,[35] domination and subjection,[36] his personhood, work, travels, social relations, and personal movements were manipulated by surveillance algorithms and secrecy assemblages to dispossess him of his ability to control his life, body, and feelings – all under the guise that secret information is used for combat in the 'War on Terror'. Aadel framed it as 'algorithms data' technology. He explained that in algorithms data, his daily practices are misused and misinterpreted to recreate him as a threat: 'It's a system that has the power to pause your life, to turn it upside down, to drag you, to take you to court, to marginalize you, to define you as trivial ... all because the system found some intersections within your data.' The big data here creates new orders of knowledge, changes human understanding of mundane things, and offers different interpretations of local communal and personal details. It also carries major consequences for personal and social ties, networks, and interactions. Surveillance through big data requires the continuous collection of data on minute issues, body movements, social engagements, modes of shopping, acting, meeting, attendance of festivities and more. The aggregation of such computed data and its violent interpretations result in violent management that can result in the 'myth of big data'.[37] It could be the new form of social knowledge, a datafication with imagined narratives.[38] Couldry explains that the long-term consequences of the ideological shift toward big data as the new source of knowledge about the social could take one of two paths: the first allows those controlling, funding, and governing such data to recalibrate the possibilities of social existence. Here, the work of Oscar Gandy (1993) details how corporate data collection can be discriminatory. The second path relates to the risk of celebrating 'secret' knowledge acquired through automated processing. Aadel's voice decommissions the power of big data by stressing his own forms of social knowledge outside of the militarized hegemonic logic. His voice refuses his incarceration by way of the big data industry and insists on 'a refusal of discourse'.[39]

> The myth of big data is a fix of that sort: a society-wide rationalization of a certain state of affairs that works not just, or sometimes not even, through what we think, but always through what we do: what we go on doing, whatever we believe ('clicking like' and so on). The myth of big data is particularly broad in how it has emerged and is being played out, but is also particularly important in that it works to challenge the very idea that the social is something we can interpret at all. It works to disable other, older (and no doubt newer) forms of social knowledge.[40]

Scholars argue that algorithms come to affect security practices by creating "'dataveillance," or the systematic use of personal data systems in the investigation or monitoring of the actions or communications of one or more persons'.[41] Using such data is a powerful authority conferred by anti-terror legislation along with technologies and expertise of risk management that govern, police, surveil, monitor and profile subjects' and certain groups' everyday lives. This authoritative system enables the categorization of subjects and ethnic groups based on data derived from surveillance technologies.[42] In the context of political violence, 'dataveillance' technologies dehumanize and marginalize the surveilled as they are designed to recognize human beings in terms of their risk assessment scores rather than their humanity.[43]

Demonstrating how secret files, even if they contain fabricated information, are used to indicate the high risk and dangerousness of the subjected, Yasmeen recalled:

> With my parents' secret file, we were treated as if we were Bin Laden ... [T]hey were accused of military planning, funding military actions, supporting terrorism ... [T]hey tried to prove the charges but they didn't manage to prove all of the 47 accusations that were contained in my mother's file ... [T]hey had the most detailed information, like the exact money amounts and where they were transferred, clothing sizes ... [A]pparently, the state was monitoring my mother for so long ... they were waiting ... But my mother was only helping the needy, making Eid [holiday] cookies ... [T]hey had photos of my mother's cookies and presents ... [T]hey even considered the word 'cookies' as a secret code for the money, even though they had a photo of the Eid cookies ... [T]hey played with the information, tried to prove something but they didn't succeed ... but even this didn't save my parents.
>
> Yasmeen

This is how Yasmeen, a Palestinian Jerusalemite in her 20s, explained her understanding of the concept of 'secrecy'. Her parents were arrested based on secret files two years ago. Yasmeen's narration raises the question of how data about cookies, children's presents and charity for the needy is transformed into a secret file, generating accusations of military planning, funding military actions and supporting terrorism. For her, the secret file is fake. In the case of Yasmeen's parents, the state's colonial, secret technologies monitored and collected random and detailed data through mining and tracking[44] her mother's community-based charity for an extended period of time. The detailed, mundane data included photos of the mother giving out cookies, amounts of money transferred to families, and the sizes of the children's new clothes for holidays – weaving together a secret file indicating that she was 'supporting terror'. Data mining is allocated to specific state risk simulations that are defined as false or deceptive:

> Simulation technology is a new semiotic of control, one founded not on truth relations between a sign and the reality it purports to represent, but on the radical indeterminacy of those relations. The utopian goal of simulation...is not to reflect reality, but to reproduce it as artifice.[45]

For Yasmeen, collecting and using details about communal solidarity to create a secret file and the inability to prove such highly securitized accusations from a plethora of detailed data, speaks to the failure and the invalidity of the secrecy system and affirms that its accusations are fabricated, fictional and false.

Indeed, when the Eid cookies become code for money to support terrorism, it shows how the state's colonial surveillance power reproduces codes and models that try to predesignate and normalize a range of events and contingencies[46] to assemble secret files. The colonial violence of secrecy allows the state to pave pits for the colonized out of mundane movements and livelihoods and build a barbed and tangled assemblage without having real, true information about actual threatening activity. Therefore, secrecy becomes not a mere state security and surveillance tool, but rather a machine of colonial violence. The secrecy assemblage is woven from big data made of cookies, charity and presents for children, in the case of Yasmeen's parents, and work trips, social ties and workspace, in Aadel's story. Both cases show the ways in which secrecy wages a datawar on the colonized to produce a new, fabricated reality that nurtures the construction and application of colonial dispossession, entrapment, and incarceration.

Psychological warfare/foreclosure

Living in OEJ ... we all are restricted ... [W]e live in a closed space with surveillance cameras, movement detectors, and spies around you ... [W]e have no control ... their state secrets ... all based on unknown accusations ... but the occupiers plant fear ... mistrust ... sense of persecution ... we all are mutaradeen *[chased] ... and they surprise you with their attack ... [Y]our house belongs to a Jewish family ... your children participated in demonstrations ... your brother is Hamas and is under arrest ... your ID will be revoked ... your last baby won't be registered and won't have a birth certificate ...* mutaradeen.

Riyad

Riyad, the 63-year-old family physician mentioned above, points to the ways in which Palestinian Jerusalemites live under the constant persecution brought on by secret information – under what he calls the 'state's microscope'. The state's microscope represents technologies of surveillance and observation to oversee and record the occupied. For him, the state's secret system is always watching and waiting to attack.[47] Riyad's voice reveals how living under the state's persistent microscope gives the occupier multiple, close observations that provide various entry points to attack and penetrate the occupied with its secret, unknown accusations. The state uses secrets and secret information to allow for the possibility of attacking, penetrating, and uprooting the observed at any time and at any place. Intimate and mundane spaces of the home, family, children, living, and existence are all possible sources of secret accusations as well as possible sites for attacks to occur. Riyad's narration shows how the state creates an assemblage of secrets that results in a variety of attacks. Secrecy and secret information invoked by state's conceald operations juxtaposes various and multiple forms of invasion and dispossession that incarcerate the psychic and widen its control.[48] Listening to Riyad's voice speaking about secrecy, we learn that secret information provides a multiple-entry point into the lives of the colonized. The language of 'secrecy' carries strategic influence: waging a multi-front war against the colonized, allowing for infiltration into various layers of the colonized body, psyche and life.

Riyad said that living through the machineries of secrecy creates a reality and a constant feeling of persecution. Living with the sense of being persistently followed and watched and vulnerable to attack anywhere at any time plants fears and creates a sense of uncertainty while waiting for the unknown. This is also apparent in Yasmeen's comments: 'For 40 days, we knew nothing about my parents ... every day we heard something else ... even the lawyer didn't know anything. This gave me a sense that a catastrophe happened ... I cried for 40 days. [I]nside me, these 40 days never ended.' Once Yasmeen heard about her parents' secret file, she was terrified, imagining how a catastrophe would shatter and dismember her family even though she did not know what the accusations were about. The term 'secret file' kept Yasmeen and her family in an ongoing state of doubt, not knowing what to do. The state colonial system uses secret files to create a sense of mystery and dangerousness that incarcerates not only the accused but also their family and friends, who do not know how to act to help the arrested person, what to expect, what additional harm it might cause, or how to deal with the situation and what the consequences will be on the arrested person and on his family and friends. A state of 'psychological foreclosure',[49] like Yasmeen's case, incarcerates, holds and keeps the colonized in a constant state of helplessness while knowing that loved ones are facing the colonial violent system. The state's logic of secrecy produces a carceral assemblage packed with the 'spiral power of psychological warfare'[50] and creates a maze of disciplinary technologies that produces and maintains fears, anxieties, constant trauma, uncertainty, and threats.

This spiral psychological war is also apparent in Sameh's experience:

> I was arrested seven times based on secret files ... seven long interrogations all based on 'secret information' that was not substantiated ... I was arrested and tortured, not because I was a politically active man ... not at all, but because I live in an area with various political leaders and activists, and I was the tool used to terrify the area ... without touching the activists, until they managed to arrest them ... I go to a clinic just to sit for hours. I go to see a doctor, he knows about my inner wound ... a wound that is still bleeding ... [H]e helps me stop my bed-wetting ... I am a married man, a father ... that ends up cleaning up my own and my children's pee ... and the security agents collected the DNA of my children. I can still smell the same smell of the solitary confinement that drugged me and dragged me to expose all sorts of information about relatives and neighbors ... one of which was killed by the Israelis ... [S]ome nights, the smell is so strong ... I vomit all night long as if they made me smell poison.

Sameh is 38 years old man and lives in OEJ. During his last arrest, he was kept in interrogation for over a month and was released with no indictment or accusations, but with major psychological scars that never left him. Sameh's wounds illustrate how secrecy in OEJ, under the Israeli settler-colonial regime of control, is being used as a weapon to maintain the colonized as an enemy. It creates and recreates Palestinian lives and bodies as always and forever warzones. The psychological effect of the use of secrecy in Sameh's case reveals that policing in the Zionist police state produces moments of fascism, even in sleep (as when Sameh awoke while vomiting in his sleep and talking about poison), where dispossession is both material and psychological.

Sameh's 'inner wounds' show how secret files are severely traumatic. The ongoing trauma of secrecy's violations, incarcerations and penetrations of the colonized's life and body has deep psychological consequences. In Sameh's case, he experienced psychosomatic effects that violate his physical integrity as a father and as an adult. Secrecy's inscription of power on the bodies of the colonized,[51] as well as on their psyches,[52] indicates that operationalizations of assemblages of secrecy are wide, complicated, and deep within the colonized's inner body, affects and psychosomatics, senses, and DNA. For Sameh, his body and mind are poisoned by being trapped in the violent pursuit and observation of the secrecy system, while carrying the burdens of ongoing secret accusations, and confessing about one of his relatives that was later killed. Martín-Baró (1989) argues that political traumas of war take root in the body, manifested in a psychosomatic disturbance that develops into complex forms of psychotic alienation, such as loss of control over bodily fluids in Sameh's case.

Being a father makes Sameh's psychological burden harsher. His psychosomatic disturbance, in addition to his conviction that the state stole his children's DNA, made him sick. The psychological torture that Sameh faced made him frightened of his image as a father and his ability to protect his children.[53] As a father, he is expected to be there, escort, care for, and protect for his children. Yet, experiencing secrecy's continuous violence, un-fathers Sameh.[54] Secrecy shatter his image as a father, restrict his rules and modes of fatherhood, threaten his parental authority, and penetrate his family.

Listening to Sameh and Riyad's voices, we learn that secrecy carries with it a psychological war.[55] Its violent assemblages use various and multiple entry-points to hunt, trap, penetrate, dispossess, and poison not only the colonized's mind, but also his body, senses, and livelihood. This reality forecloses the occupied psychologically and keep him in a constant state of alertness, yet incapable of acting, handcuffed, choked, and shocked, creating psychological alienation.

Community dismemberment

When they arrested my parents and they said it's about the secret file, the closest family, friends, and neighbors, those who were supposed to be our backbone, stopped talking to us ... those who you need the most in such times 'raised their hands' [abandoned us], left us ... only one uncle and one aunt supported us, but everyone else distanced themselves as if we had scabs, you see it in their eyes ... I was at the center of it all and everything circled around me, suffocating.

Yasmeen

Yasmeen's voice shows how the state's secrecy penetrates the psyche and body of the colonized individual through their community. Fears, uncertainty, and anxiety generated by secrecy assemblages disrupt extended family, neighbours and the whole community – that is, the backbone of the colonized – to paralyse, asphyxiate, isolate and incarcerate them. Martín-Baró (1994) explains the psychology of the whole, considering the individual and collective effects of political violence, particularly the damage caused to social structures, institutions, and ties. Political violence undermines trust and respect among individuals in the community and prevents solidarity and consequently, collective capacity to cope with atrocities. Likewise. Yasmeen's experience shows how violent secrecy penetrates her family and her society to fragment and suffocate them[56] by distancing them, as if they were ill. The 'asphyxiatory' application of colonial power aims to make the Palestinian human collapse.[57] Political dismemberment and suffocation of communities generate deleterious consequences that include disputes, conflicts, failures, tensions and hostilities among community members.[58]

Martín-Baró (1989; 1994) argues that the state induces fear, anxiety and terror as a means of social control, thus creating a potent form of psychological warfare on both conscious and unconscious levels. People around Yasmeen were overwhelmed by rumours about the secret files without even being sure of the accusations. Fear and anxiety destroyed the community's support for the family; thus, Yasmeen insisted that it was the community that was sick, as she noticed it in people's eyes. Secret files wage war on the colonized community, disable the caring function of community and dismember communal ties, suggesting that community sickness creates additional burdens that suffocate and asphyxiate individuals who are nearest to the surveilled, like Yasmeen. Community dismemberment is a powerful psychological weapon in the state's hands to inscribe power on the colonized individual's body and psyche. The state's use of secrecy produces significant mistrust among even family members; thus, society is also shocked and wounded, and individuals react by distancing themselves because they suspect and mistrust each other. Such situations destroy the colonized's ability to access their community for support. Accordingly, dismemberment is a situation involving fragmentation of not only the Palestinian individual's body and psyche, but also the larger Palestinian social body of which he or she is a part. It is a mode of psychic-sociocide that cannot be overlooked.

Indeed, the community sickness caused by the dismembering powers of secrecy were apparent in Muna's voice, as she described community members as treating her '[l]ike I have leprosy' and asking, 'why are they [community members] afraid?' Her words reveal that the community around her was afraid to be infected by her sickness – the penetration of colonial secrecy. However, she explained that the community was already infected with violent colonial penetrations and disruptions. According to Muna, when the community denied her connectedness, it lost its meaning, power and purpose. As a result, the community that was afraid to be infected with secrecy was instead infected with ruptures, resulting in social paralysis, deep wounds and the cutting of its support and solidarity. According to Muna and Yasmeen, the colonial assemblages penetrate their familial and social bodies, cut the ties within them, and defuse and paralyse, hindering any chance of recovery. Yasmeen explains:

> If the community stood with us even only morally, it would be different ... [A]rresting my parents is like a knife in our bodies but when the community abandoned us, it was like a poisoned knife that we will never survive. I wish these years would be deleted from my life.
>
> Yasmeen

Yasmeen tells us that community support is vital for recovery from secrecy penetration; yet, when secrecy penetrates the communal body, they disperse its support networks and morality – a wound that cannot be healed. As Riyad said, secrecy's penetration 'is like poisoning the community, and what happens to a poisoned community? It starts to squirm'.

The voices of Yasmeen, Muna and Riyad indicate that secrecy not only poison the individual body and psyche, but also poison the communal body and its morality.

Scholars have described how colonial rule unleashes a deadly blow to the colonized community by disrupting the traditional machinery of moral homogeneity and practices with the immediate consequence of the individualism,[59] suggesting that state secrecy targets community responsibility,[60] collectivity, connectivity and solidarity. In the case of Israeli settler colonialism in particular, colonial surveillance and the industry of fear[61] aims at 'sociocide',[62] a state in which society barely exists as a positive agent of social action in the lives of its members.[63] In the state of 'sociocide', colonial powers attack the social fabric of the colonized, fracturing the community, penetrating the social fabric, disrupting daily life, dismantling basic human social services[64] and destroying local infrastructure.[65] Under such conditions, the colonized are forever questioning what is happening around them, for the entirety of their social relations.[66]

Survivability

Living in OEJ ... we all are restricted ... We live in a closed camp ... with surveillance cameras, movement detectors, and spies around you ... We have no control ... Still, when I think about how I studied or raised my kids ... with all the secrecy and secret policing ... we raised them with dignity ... we in the family – my wife, my aunt that lived with us – the family I mean ... we were the healers against the persecution of secrecy ... How else could have survived the constant threats?

Riyad

Riyad's description shows how Jerusalemites survive the dispersion of secrecy policing. Although secrecy assemblages trap the family using various, constant, unseen and, in some instances, unexpected technologies of surveillance, dispossession, wounding and control, Riyad, with the help of his family and his persistence in living with dignity, found ways to study, graduate, work, father, protect and repair what secrecy's violent persecution had dismembered.

Riyad explains the burdens of living under constant secrecy policing. Being trapped and chained by colonial and violent secrecy technologies make it difficult, almost impossible, to live with dignity. Hammami discusses the way in which Palestinians negotiate individual and collective ontologies of suffering. She argues that Palestinian men and fathers refuse to be identified with suffering; instead, they struggle in their everydayness, creating modes of survivability and domesticating them in their mundane living.[67] As a colonized and persecuted man and a father, Riyad told us how he resisted mundane, colonial and violent secretized psychological warfare by relying on two resistance powers: family and dignity. Lykes and Mersky (2006) argue that reparation and healing processes in the context of political violence require attention to their social and cultural context in order to be family- and community-oriented. They also argue that there must necessarily be a special focus on values and moral dimensions in order to move forward in meaningful ways. Otman argues that fathers living in the ongoing political violence of OEJ create new spaces, languages, and powers to protect their families and homes. A Palestinian father will ensure his children's psychological well-being through love, care and dignity as a means to survive colonial attacks, when other means are unavailable.[68] Riyad survived the ramifications of violent secrecy by maintaining and further connecting to his family, moving on in life, insisting on studying and fathering, and using the powers of dignity and family as his daily healing and medication against the wounding, sickening and paralysis of colonial secrecy assemblages and their surveillance technologies.

In the same manner, Aadel's comments show us how insisting on liveability and moving on thorough education is his counterstrategy against the incarceration of secretized warfare: 'I was back to my studies on the next day [after his release], I did my presentation in class, which I was supposed to do on the day I was arrested'. Aadel and his wife are students. They both go to the university with their child. Although Aadel was arrested, he never ceased his studies, indicating that pursuing and continuing his life, precisely where it was stopped, is an act of resistance against violent and sudden secrecy dismemberment. Continuity is Aadel's counterstrategy against colonial disruptions and dispersion. Additionally, Aadel, like Riyad, reveals that education served as a mode of survival against secrecy defusion: 'I heal myself with writing ... going back to my studies ... I also pushed my wife to do her master's, so if they [secrecy technologies] incapacitate me, she can move on.' Aadel suggests that his and his wife's education counters secrecy's brutality. They recover from colonial paralysis by gaining knowledge and perspective. Scholars suggest that higher education can aid in ending oppression and exploitation.[69] This encourages critical awareness,[70] developing enlightened witnesses.[71] Freire explains that education is liberating 'in that it enables people to overcome injustice, poverty and fear' and eventually brings about transformation.[72] Aadel indicated that education helps him not only to recover from his wounds and traumas, but also to strengthen his family resilience. He protects his family from future secrecy penetration and its psychological warfare by building up his wife's education and/as a psychosocial shield. Studies further show that trauma as discontinuity[73] ruptures both the continuity of the self and the community, while psychological connectivities, as seen both in Aadel's and Riyad's case, are positively correlated with psychological resilience,[74] precisely through continuing and connecting pre- and post-trauma lives.[75]

Both Riyad and Aadel exposed us to the way in which those that survived the violence of secrecy and its tools of dispossession and dismemberment (the psychological and social) insisted on their liveability, dignity, protection, familial connectivity and continuity;[76] Their strategies of moving on in life – whether through maintaining attachments to loved ones, education, or protecting family and dignity – are all modes of assembling the dismembered and continuing their psycho-social survival and connectivity amid the violence of secrecy.

'Secrecy' and the settler state: some concluding remarks

The very production and use of secrecy as a paranoid but creative violent weapon of the settler state manipulates the psyche, social cohesion, connectivity and continuity. Secrecy has become the modus operandi of Israel's invasive, securitized violent surveillance. As our chapter illustrates, such violence ranges from the use of big data and algorithmic calculations and detections/framings – or Datawars[77] – to the assemblage of militarized policing and securitized 'secrets', intimidating the colonized, while reassuring and empowering colonizers. Tracing the secret dialectics between exposure, revelation, and concealment to the violent murky zones of the settler state invites scholars to consider the politics, practices and brutality of secrecy.

Secrecy permeated the system of legal terror exercised by state governance, as it was used not only to help legitimize the racial exclusion on which Zionism was founded, but also to reinforce the settler-colonial logic of dispossession and erasure. Secrecy, Jerusalemites explained, became a mundane terror, and hence should be seen as a warning sign of racialized necroeconomies. Secrecy goes beyond surveillance and control, to act as a blockage to life: the more the colonizer uses and succumbs to the discourse of secrecy, the less living and breathing will be allowed in the Jerusalemite necrospatial context, and the less psychological and material foundations of liveability will be attained. Secrecy demarcates the ongoing affective surveillance regime and its brutal uprootings and dismembering. It exhibits the violent operationalization and affective workings of secrecy as surveillance not only on the communal and family connectivity and collectivity, but also on the home, the body, and the psyche of the colonized.

The voices of Jerusalemite Palestinians taught us four main lessons. First, studying secrecy – as surveillance apparent in the fusion of its visibility and invisibility, in 'a state of permanent war', with its shadowy network of spies – **targets affects** (both individual and collective ones). Secrecy is a politico-affective machinery of elimination (to bring about the death of psychological power too), cultivated and mobilized by the exclusionary ideologies of the state, aiming at situating colonial subjects in the dark, beneath the surface of living. The affective politics of exclusion apparent in secrecy were found to be central to the settler-colonial regime of control in OEJ. **Secrecy, we claim, rules through the psyches of colonized communities.** Affective politics exposed in the technologized surveillance of secrecy aims at empowering secrecy, as a technology of the settler state's power and control, in order to reproduce the state's politics of secrecy, dispossessing the colonized from their psychological serenity. Increasing mysteries when claiming secrets further justifies the barbarism of the state in waging a dark psychological war and its spy war.

Second, secrecy, beyond being a strategy of domination in the settler colony, **is imbedded in settler-colonial ideologies of exclusivity that justify the right to exclude the colonized and seize their liberty** when and while operating on affective spaces of living. Acts taken by state agents under the pretext of secret information are intimately connected to ideological tropes of Zionist biblical claims or their 'right to life', when the life and liveability, including the psycho-social liveability, of Palestinians stands in their face. Holding parents in jail for forty days while claiming to have 'data' and 'secret information' that cannot be disclosed, leaving family members in a precarious condition of fear of the unknown and uncertainty, may result in major psychological and communal disturbances. Using 'secrets' constructs an 'alien/dangerous/criminal/terrorist' enemy.

Third, secrecy operating under the umbrella of state security, as exclusion, **is a key machinery of erasure**. Secrecy, secret penetrations, and the use of 'secret security information' infiltrates the colonized's life and psyche, not only to control and surveil. We argue that its limits, effects and affects take us into the world of fascism. Casting one's life and social relations as something 'secret' that requires incarceration frames those dispossessed of liberty as terrorists. If there exists 'secret information', then there must be **an existential threat to the state**. Hence, when state agents claim they possess secret data and secret information, they immediately produce assumptions of existential threats. This is the core of the state's psychological fascism.

Fourth, secrecy, as an integral part of state governance, operating as a technology of psycho-social uprooting cannot be reduced only to an instrument of settler-colonial governance. Secrecy's circulation over the native's affects and society **gains additional power not only when incorporated by the colonizer, but also by the colonized.** For the colonized, secrets can also become a space of refuge, an enclave to innovate new modes of resisting state secrets. The voice of 23-year-old Rawan who was also threatened by the state's secret weapons summarizes our argument sharply when stressing that 'Zionists use secrecy as a psychological war debilitate us deeply … [I]t is an endless war that creates both in our minds and psychology an infinite insistence on confronting it.'

Notes

1. Lyon 2003; Zureik 2010; Grassiani 2016; Diphoorn and Grassiani 2016.
2. Masalha 2012; Sa'di and Abu-Lughod 2007.
3. Joronen 2019; Joronen and Griffiths 2019.
4. Veracini 2011.
5. Debord 1998: 69, 74.
6. Taussig 1999.
7. Zureik et al. 2011; Sa'di 2008; Tawil-Souri 2016; Zureik 2001.
8. Green and Ward 2000.
9. Shalhoub-Kevorkian 2015a.
10. Ahmed 2004: 12.
11. Abu-Laban et al. 2011; Sa'di 2008; Tawil-Souri 2016; Zureik 2001.
12. Zureik 2016; Shalhoub-Kevorkian 2015a; Tawil-Souri 2016.
13. Halabi 2011; Sa'di 2011, 2013; Shalhoub-Kevorkian 2015a; Tawil-Souri 2016.
14. Shalhoub-Kevorkian 2015a.
15. Shalhoub-Kevorkian, Otman and Abdelnabi 2021.
16. Shalhoub-Kevorkian and Wahab 2021: 1.
17. Saranillio 2010; Dhillon 2017; Grewal 2017; Kleinman 1997; Razack 2000; 2002; Shalhoub-Kevorkian 2015a; Simpson 2014; Thobani 2007.
18. Shalhoub-Kevorkian et al. 2021.
19. Sheehi & Sheehi 2022: 10.
20. Shalhoub-Kevorkian and Wahab 2021: 15.
21. Hooks 1984.
22. Hammersley 1992; Hooks 2009; Jaggar 2014; Lafrance and Wigginton 2019; Taylor et al. 2020.
23. Hesse-Biber 2007.

24 e.g., Abdo and Lentin 2002; Abu-Lughod 2016; Hammami 2015; Shalhoub-Kevorkian 2015a; Otman 2020, forthcoming.
25 Shalhoub-Kevorkian 2015b.
26 Suchman, Follis & Weber 2017.
27 Pasquale 2015.
28 Bennett et al. 2014.
29 Slade and Prinsloo 2013; Knight and Gekker 2020.
30 Amoore 2006.
31 Amoore and de Goede 2005.
32 Amoore and de Goede 2021: 425.
33 Ibid.: 426.
34 Shalhoub-Kevorkian 2015b.
35 Wolfe 2006.
36 Veracini 2019.
37 Boyd and Crawford 2012.
38 Couldry 2017.
39 Butler 2004: 36.
40 Couldry 2017: 237.
41 Clarke 1988: 499.
42 Amoore 2006.
43 Knight and Gekker 2020.
44 Bogard 2012.
45 Ibid.: 34.
46 Bogard 2012.
47 Shalhoub-Kevorkian et al. 2021.
48 Ibid.
49 Sheehi and Sheehi 2022: 10.
50 Shalhoub-Kevorkian, Otman and Abdelnabi 2021: 271.
51 Razack 2011.
52 Sayegh 1965.
53 Otman 2020.
54 Shalhoub-Kevorkian 2019.
55 Shalhoub-Kevorkian, Otman & Abdelnabi. 2021.
56 Englebert, Tarango & Carter 2002.
57 Salamanca 2011.
58 Englebert, Tarango & Carter 2002.
59 Igboin 2011.
60 Nowell 2010.
61 Shalhoub-Kevorkian 2015a.
62 Abdel Jawad 2001.
63 Doubt 2020.
64 Haj-Yahia 2007; Hamber 2009; Lykes and Sibley 2014.
65 Hammami 2015.
66 Shalhoub-Kevorkian 2015a,: 13.
67 Hammami 2015; see also Johnson 2007.
68 Otman 2020; 2022.
69 Abu-Rabia-Queder 2008; Ahmad 2004; Crenshaw 1989; Hooks 1984.
70 Martín-Baró 1994,
71 Hooks 1994; 1997.

72 Freire 2000.
73 McKinney 2008.
74 Shi et al. 2019.
75 Jackman et al. 2020.
76 Hamber 2009; Lykes and Mersky 2006; Lykes and Sibley 2014; Shalhoub-Kevorkian 2019; Otman 2020.
77 Amoore and de Goede 2005; 2021; Amoore 2013.

References

Abdel Jawad, S. (2001), 'War by Other Means', *Media Monitors Network* 16 May. https://www.mediamonitors.net/war-by-other-means/

Abdo, N., & R. Lentin (2002), *Women and the Politics of Military Confrontation: Palestinian and Israeli Narratives of Dislocation*, New York: Berghahn Books.

Abu-Laban, Y., D. Lyon & E. Zureik (2011), *Surveillance and Control in Israel/Palestine: Population, Territory and Power*, London: Routledge.

Abu-Lughod, L. (2016), *Veiled Sentiments: Honor and Poetry in a Bedouin Society*, Oakland, CA: University of California Press.

Abu-Rabia-Queder, S. (2008), 'Does Education Necessarily Mean Enlightenment? The Case of Higher Education Among Palestinian-Bedouin Women in Israel', *Anthropology and Education Quarterly* 39 (4): 381–400.

Ahmad, S. (2004), *The Cultural Politics of Emotion,* Edinburgh: Edinburgh University Press.

Amoore, L. (2006), 'Biometric Borders: Governing Mobilities in the War on Terror', *Political Geography* 25 (3): 336–51.

Amoore, L., & M. de Geode, M. (2005), 'Governance, Risk and Dataveillance in the War on Terror', *Crime, Law & Social Change* 43: 149–173.

Amoore, L. 2013. The Politics of Possibility: Risk and Security beyond Probability. Durham: Duke University Press.

Amoore, L., & M. de Geode (2021), 'Datawars: Reflections Twenty Years after 9/11', *Critical Studies on Terrorism* 14 (4): 425–9.

Bennett, C. J., K. D. Haggerty, D. Lyon & V. Steeves (2014), *Transparent Lives: Surveillance in Canada*, Athabasca, AB: Athabasca University Press.

Bogard, W. (2012), 'Simulation and Post-panopticism' in K. Ball, K. Haggerty & D. Lyon (eds), *Routledge Handbook of Surveillance Studies,* 30–8, London: Routledge.

Boyd, D., & K. Crawford (2012), 'Critical Questions for Big Data: Provocations for a Cultural, Technological, and Scholarly Phenomenon', *Information, Communication & Society* 15 (5): 662–79.

Butler, J. (2004), *Precarious Life: The Powers of Mourning and Violence*, New York: Verso.

Clarke, R. (1988), 'Information Technology and Dataveillance', *Communications of the ACM* 31 (5): 498–512.

Couldry, N. (2017), 'The Myth of Big Data' in M. T. Schäfer & K. van Es (eds), *The Datafied Society: Studying Culture through Data,* Amsterdam: Amsterdam University Press.

Crenshaw, K. (1989), 'Demarginalizing the Intersection of Race and Sex: A Black Feminist Critique of Antidiscrimination Doctrine, Feminist Theory and Antiracist Politics, *University of Chicago Legal Forum* (1): 139–67.

Debord, G. (1998), *Comments on the Society of the Spectacle,* London: Verso.

Deleuze, G., & F. Guattari (1987), *Thousand Plateaus* trans. B. Massumi, Minneapolis: University of Minnesota Press.
Dhillon, J. (2017), *Prairie Rising: Indigenous Youth, Decolonization, and the Politics of Intervention*, Toronto: University of Toronto Press.
Diphoorn, T., & E. Grassiani (2016), 'Securitizing Capital: A Processual-relational Approach to Pluralized Security', *Theoretical Criminology* 20 (4): 430–45.
Doubt, K. (2020), *Sociocide: Reflections on Today's Wars,* Lanham, MD: Lexington Books.
Englebert, P., S. Tarango & M. Carter (2002), 'Dismemberment and Suffocation', *Comparative Political Studies* 35 (10): 1093–1118.
Fanon, F. (1963), *The Wretched of the Earth*, New York: Grove Press.
Freire, P. (2000), *Pedagogy of the Oppressed*, New York: Continuum.
Gandy, O. H., Jr (1993), *The Panoptic Sort: A Political Economy of Personal Information,* Boulder, CO: Westview Press.
Grassiani, E. (2016), 'Commercialized Occupation Skills: Israeli Security Experience as an International Brand' in M. Leese & S. Wittendorp (eds), *Security/Mobility: Politics of Movement*, Manchester: Manchester University Press.
Green, P., & T. Ward (2000), 'State Crime, Human Rights, and the Limits of Criminology', *Social Justice* 27 (1): 101–15.
Grewal, I. (2017), *Saving the Security State: Exceptional Citizens in Twenty-First-Century America*, Durham, NC: Duke University Press.
Haj-Yahia, M. (2007), 'Challenges in Studying the Psychological Effects of Palestinian Children's Exposure to Political Violence and Their Coping with This Traumatic Experience', *Child Abuse and Neglect* 31 (7): 691–7.
Halabi, U. (2011), 'Legal Analysis and Critique of Some Surveillance Methods Used by Israel' in Zureik, Lyon & Abu-Laban (eds), *Surveillance and Control in Israel/Palestine: Population, Territory and Power,* 199–218, London: Routledge.
Hamber, B. (2009), *Transforming Societies after Political Violence: Truth, Reconciliation, and Mental Health,* New York: Springer.
Hammami, R. (2015), 'On (Not) Suffering at the Checkpoint: Narrative Strategies of Surviving Israel's Carceral Geography', *Borderlands* 14 (1): 1–17.
Hammersley, M. (1992), 'On Feminist Methodology', *Sociology* 26 (2): 187–206.
Harvey, D. (2003), *The New Imperialism,* Oxford: Oxford University Press.
Hesse-Biber, S. N. (2007), 'The Practice of Feminist In-depth Interviewing' in S. N. Hesse-Biber & P. L. Leavy (eds), *Feminist Research Practice: A Primer*, 111–48, London: Sage Publications.
Hooks, B. (1984), *Feminist Theory from Margin to Center*, Boston: South End Press.
Hooks, B. (1994), *Teaching To Transgress*, New York: Routledge.
Hooks, B. (1997), 'Revolutionary Black Women: Making Ourselves Subject' in B. Moore-Gilbert, G. Stanton & W. Maley (eds), *Postcolonial Criticism*, London: Routledge.
Hooks, B. (2009), 'Black Women: Shaping Feminist Theory' in F. S. Foster, B. Guy-Sheftall, and S. M. James (eds), *Still Brave: The evolution of Black Women's Studies*, 31–44, New York: Feminist Press.
Igboin, B. (2011), 'Colonialism and African Cultural Values', *African Journal of History and Culture* 3 (6): 96–103.
Jackman, D., J. Konkin, O. Yonge, F. Myrick & J. Cockell (2020), 'Crisis and Continuity: Rural Health Care Students Respond to the COVID-19 Outbreak', *Nurse Education in Practice* 48: 1–8.

Jaggar, A. M. (2014), *Just Methods: An Interdisciplinary Feminist Reader*, Boulder, CO: Paradigm Publishers.

Johnson, P. (2007), 'Tales of Strength and Danger: Sahar and the Tactics of Everyday Life in Amari Refugee Camp, Palestine', *Signs: Journal of Women in Culture and Society* 32 (3): 597–619.

Joronen, M. (2019), 'Negotiating Colonial Violence: Spaces of Precarisation in Palestine', *Antipode* 51 (3): 838–67.

Joronen, M., & M. Griffiths (2019), 'The Moment to Come: Geographies of Hope in the Hyperprecarious Sites of Occupied Palestine', *Geografiska Annaler* 101 (2): 69–83.

Kleinman, A. (1997), '"Everything That Really Matters": Social Suffering, Subjectivity, and the Remaking of Human Experience in a Disordering World', *Harvard Theological Review* 90 (3): 315–35.

Knight, E., & A. Gekker (2020), 'Mapping Interfacial Regimes of Control: Palantir's ICM in America's Post-9/11 Security Technology Infrastructures', *Surveillance & Society* 18 (2): 231–43.

Lafrance, M. N., & Wigginton, B. (2019), 'Doing Critical Feminist Research: A Feminism and Psychology Reader', *Feminism & Psychology* 29 (4): 534–52.

Lykes, M., & M. Mersky (2006), 'Reparations and Mental Health: Psychosocial Interventions Towards Healing, Human Agency, and Rethreading Social Realities' in P. de Greiff (ed.), *The Handbook of Reparations*, Oxford: Oxford University Press.

Lykes, M. B., & E. Sibley (2014), 'Liberation Psychology and Pragmatic Solidarity: North-South Collaborations through the Ignacio Martín-Baró Fund', *Journal of Peace Psychology* 20 (3): 209–26.

Lyon, David (ed.) (2003), *Surveillance as Social Sorting: Privacy, Risk, and Digital Discrimination*, New York: Routledge.

Martín-Baró, I. (1989), 'Political Violence and War as Causes of Psychosocial Trauma in El Salvador', *International Journal of Mental Health* 18 (1): 3–20.

Martín-Baró, I. (1994), *Writings for a Liberation Psychology*, Cambridge, MA: Harvard University Press.

Masalha, N. (2012), *The Palestinian Nakba: Decolonising History, Narrating the Subaltern, Reclaiming Memory*, London: Zed Books.

McKinney, K. (2008), '"Breaking the Conspiracy of Silence": Testimony, Traumatic Memory, and Psychotherapy with Survivors of Political Violence', *Ethos* 35 (3): 265–99.

Nowell, B. (2010), 'Viewing Community as Responsibility as Well as Resource: Deconstructing the Theoretical Roots of Psychological Sense of Community', *Journal of Community Psychology* 38 (7): 828–41.

Otman, A. (2020), 'Handcuffed Protectors? Palestinian Fatherhood-protection Unlocking its Chains', *International Journal for Applied Psychoanalytical Studies* 17 (4): 1–19.

Otman, A. (2022), 'Fathers in and against Pain: Father's Interruptions of Settler-colonial Technologies of Loss', *Affilia: Women and Social Work*.

Pasquale, F. (2015), *The Black Box of Society: The Secret Algorithms That Control Money and Information,* Cambridge, MA: Harvard University Press.

Razack, S. (2000), 'Gendered Racial Violence and Spatialized Justice: The Murder of Pamela Geore', *Canadian Journal of Law and Society* 15 (2): 91–130.

Razack, S. (2002), *Race, Space, and the Law: Unmapping a White Settler Society*, Toronto: Between the Lines.

Razack, S. (2011), 'The Space of Difference in Law: Inquests into Aboriginal Deaths in Custody', *Somatechnics* 1 (1): 87–123.

Sa'di, A. (2008), 'Remembering Al-Nakba in a Time of Amnesia', *Interventions* 10 (3): 381–99.
Sa'di, A. (2011), 'Ominous Designs: Israel's Strategies of Controlling the Palestinians during the First Two Decades' in Zureik, Lyon & Abu-Laban (eds), *Surveillance and Control in Israel/Palestine: Population, Territory and Power*, 83–98. London: Routledge.
Sa'di, A. (2013), *Thorough Surveillance: The Genesis of Israeli Policies of Population Management, Surveillance and Political Control Towards the Palestinian Minority*, Manchester: Manchester University Press.
Sa'di, A., & L. Abu-Lughod (2007), *Nakba: Palestine, 1948, and the Claims of Memory*, New York: Columbia University Press.
Salamanca, O. J. (2011), 'Unplug and Play: Manufacturing Collapse in Gaza', *Human Geography* 4 (1): 22–37.
Saranillio, D. I. (2010), 'Colliding Histories: Hawai'i Statehood at the Intersection of Asians "Ineligible to Citizenship" and Hawaiians "Unfit for Self-Government"', *Journal of Asian American Studies* 13 (3): 283–309.
Sayegh, F. (1965). Zionist Colonialism in Palestine. Palestine Liberation Organization.
Shalhoub-Kevorkian, N. (2015a), *Security Theology, Surveillance and the Politics of Fear*, Cambridge: Cambridge University Press.
Shalhoub-Kevorkian, N. (2015b), 'The Politics of Birth and the Intimacies of Violence against Palestinian Women in Occupied East Jerusalem', *British Journal of Criminology* 55: 1187–1206.
Shalhoub-Kevorkian, N. (2019), *Incarcerated Childhood and the Politics of Unchilding*, Cambridge: Cambridge University Press.
Shalhoub-Kevorkian, A. Otman & R. Abdelnabi (2021), 'Secret Penetrabilities: Embodied Coloniality, Gendered Violence, and the Racialized Policing of Affects', *Studies in Gender and Sexuality* 22 (4): 266–77.
Shalhoub-Kevorkian, N., & S. Wahab (2021), 'Colonial Necrocapitalism, State Secrecy and the Palestinian Freedom Tunnel', *Social and Health Sciences* 19 (2): 1–18.
Sheehi, L., & S. Sheehi (2022), *Psychoanalysis under Occupation: Practicing Resistance in Palestine*, London: Routledge.
Shi, L., J. Sun, D. Wei & J. Qiu (2019), 'Recover from the Adversity: Functional Connectivity Basis of Psychological Resilience' *Neuropsychologia* 122: 20–7.
Simpson, A. (2014), *Mohawk Interruptus: Political Life Across the Borders of Settler States*, Duke University Press.
Slade, S., & P. Prinsloo (2013), 'Learning Analytics: Ethical Issues and Dilemmas', *American Behavioral Scientist* 57 (10): 1510–29.
Suchman, L., K. Follis & J. Weber, J. (2017), 'Tracking and Targeting: Sociotechnologies of (In)security', *Science, Technology, & Human Values* 42 (6): 983–1002.
Taussig, M. (1999), *Defacement: Public Secrecy and the Labor of the Negative*, Stanford, CA: Stanford University Press.
Tawil-Souri, H. (2012), 'Digital Occupation: Gaza's High-tech Enclosure', *Journal of Palestine Studies* 41 (2): 27–43.
Tawil-Souri, H. (2016). Surveillance sublime: The security state in Jerusalem. Jerusalem Quarterly File, 68, 56–65.
Taylor, C. A., J. Ulmer & C. Hughes (2020), *Transdisciplinary Feminist Research: Innovations in Theory, Method and Practice*, London: Taylor and Francis.
Thobani, S. (2007), *Exalted Subjects: Studies in the Making of Race and Nation in Canada*, Toronto: University of Toronto Press.

Veracini, L. (2011), 'Introducing: Settler Colonial Studies', *Settler Colonial Studies* 1 (1): 1–12.
Veracini, L. (2019), 'Containment, Elimination, Endogeneity: Settler Colonialism in the Global Present', *Rethinking Marxism* 31 (1): 118–40.
Wolfe, P. (2006), 'Settler Colonialism and the Elimination of the Native', *Journal of Genocide Research* 8: 387–409.
Zureik, E. (2001), 'Constructing Palestine through Surveillance Practices', *British Journal of Middle Eastern Studies* 28 (2): 205–27.
Zureik, E. (2010), 'Surveillance and Control in Israel/Palestine: Population, Territory and Power' in E. Zureik, D. Lyon & Y. Abu-Laban (eds), 'Surveillance and Control in Israel/Palestine: Population, Territory and Power', 3–46, London: Routledge.
Zureik, E. (2016), 'Strategies of Surveillance: The Israeli Gaze. Strategies of Surveillance', *Jerusalem Quarterly* 66: 12–38.
Zureik, E., D. Lyon & Y. Abu-Laban (eds), (2011), *Surveillance and Control in Israel/Palestine: Population, Territory and Power.* London: Routledge.

9

Israel's Telecommunications Lines and Digital Surveillance Routes

Helga Tawil-Souri

Locating digital surveillance

Israel's prowess in technologies of surveillance is enthusiastically promoted by its proponents[1] and starkly exposed by its critics.[2] Meanwhile, news exposés often focus on what Mazzetti (2019) calls the digital nature of Israel's 'internet mercenaries': from the Israel Defense Force Unit 8200's digital espionage methods to MER Group's trawling of social media; from the Stuxnet computer worm and Checkpoint's real-time endpoint surveillance; from Vayyar's smart walls to NSO Group's mobile surveillance tools and the State's phone location-tracking during the COVID-19 pandemic.[3] The focus is often on the technological, digital, virtual or cyber, either celebrating surveillance's ubiquity and embeddedness within an assemblage of hi-tech military and security techniques, or critiquing how this system is built upon the exploitation and dispossession of Palestinians who are rendered simultaneously hyper-visible to a security regime while invisibilized and silenced in other ways.

What the focus on digital surveillance often advances is that it is de-territorial, taking place seemingly everywhere, through the ephemeral realm of mouse clicks, data extraction, pattern and discourse recognition, through software that doesn't leave a footprint, such as NSO's Pegasus software's self-destructive feature which removes traces of itself. Digital surveillance certainly occurs through texts, emails, within databases and social media platforms; on public wi-fi networks, organization-level surveillance camera systems and individual's mobile phones. Israel certainly limits Palestinians' internet access, curtails their privacy and freedom of expression, censors on-line material, deletes and blocks data, interrupts radio and television broadcasts, sends automated text messages and telephone calls on Palestinian phones.[4] But none of this means that surveillance is placeless and de-territorial.

First, all these activities rely and build on infrastructures which pre-date the digital era. In fact, the trajectory of digital surveillance can be traced along the phases of telecommunications: the telegraph, the landline telephone, the mobile phone and the internet. Each of these consists of three basic elements: a network of wires and channels, switching equipment to send and receive data, and terminal equipment which transforms electronic signals to other modes of information and vice versa. While we may imagine that the digital is virtual, in the ether or in the clouds, all digital information gathering, processing and circulation has to take place somewhere: inside computers, on filing systems and disks, through routers, stashed away in buildings and server farms, travelling along physical cables and wires. All of this has a perfectly identifiable geography, much of it following the routes and locations of previous communications networks. As a number of scholars argue, 'questions of electronic communication security and the nation as a whole go all the way back to the origins of the telegraph'.[5] Second, telecommunications infrastructure is necessarily territorial. It exists in specific locations and is dependent on the ability to fix things in place: to erect buildings, install towers and cables, connect wires, dig under the earth and land upon seashores. This infrastructure is the physical, material and territorial location from which digital surveillance is possible.

Much of Elia Zureik's work has demonstrated how the creation of geographical boundaries and spatial mechanisms have been at the core of Israel's surveillance apparatus, inseparable from techniques of population control; just as much of his work has also focused on digital forms of surveillance. Thus, while Zureik may not explicitly state it as such, his work makes clear that surveillance technologies play a critical role in the production of territory, or to put it another way, that territory is produced and mobilized by social-technical networks.[6]

Telecommunications has literally made and marked the expansion of Israeli colonization, serving as an early and continued form of territorial and distanced power, a way of centralizing and extending information control, an instrument for expanding and consolidating surveillance capabilities.[7] The development and placement of telegraph cables (later upgraded for telephone and internet traffic) and the control over early switches and terminals are the routes/roots of territorial colonization and new surveillance technologies. Israel's digital surveillance system is that which is built upon and depends on those territorially based networks.

By retracing the development of telecommunications infrastructure from the telegraph onwards, this paper locates Israel's digital surveillance. Unravelling those routes leads us to see how the State of Israel would emerge in spaces where it would control, own and manage telecommunications nodes, while simultaneously how Palestinian areas would be squeezed into corners with little telecommunications infrastructure, and where until today any such infrastructure remains territorially contained. To locate where Israel's digital surveillance capabilities are requires us to locate where original telecommunications systems first emerged and how Israel came to control these. This requires us to go back in time to the laying of the first telegraph cables during the Ottoman Empire.

Ottoman beginnings: centralizing and expanding telegraph lines

The telegraph – a device for transmitting and receiving messages over long distances, which traces its beginnings to inventions in the seventeenth and eighteenth centuries – remained the fastest mechanism for communication at a distance until the birth and expansion of radio and the regular telephone. With its instantaneous action thanks to wires crossing over diverse landscapes and oceans, the telegraph revolutionized communications and came to symbolize a new technological age: bringing people closer together, transforming connections between countries, marking the spread of global corporations and capitalism, and laying the groundwork for the accelerated changes and the surveillance forms of the twentieth century.

The first telegraph lines were laid in the 1830s and 1840s in the US and Europe, and by the 1840s and 1850s became intricately crucial for facilitating political and military communication.[8] Submarine telegraphs beginning in 1854 allowed for rapid communication between continents. Railroad and shipping companies, merchants, news outlets and postal services played a central role in shaping telegraphy, but its establishment as part of colonial control and later national control cannot be overstated. The strategic necessity of connecting to colonies, extending communications with naval fleets, accelerating diplomatic exchanges with allied governments, centralizing bureaucratic needs, responding to military needs and surveilling information flow were the political imperatives that drove telegraphic expansion. Telegraphic connection between Britain and India for example helped expand imperial power while contributing to the integration of the globe. 'The production, ordering and maintenance of a vast network of social and physical infrastructures not only required the establishment of new hierarchically interlaced institutions but was premised on, and constitutive of, a new colonial state form.'[9] The logic of communicative infrastructure – its building, placement, expansion, development and its absence – merged into the overall colonial project of the infrastructural production of the nation.

Because it made commercial sense to invest in places that already had material and institutional infrastructures and because communicative infrastructure strengthened existing infrastructure, cables tended to follow the same path. The initial cable systems of telegraphs thus followed an imperial and economic logic existing alongside colonial trading, railways and shipping lines. Similarly, today, fibre-optic lines follow political and economic logics which determine where they are laid and who can use them. As such, internet, mobile phone traffic and regular telephone traffic not only rely on physical cables, but cables that have been erected alongside original telegraph cables that wired much of the world in the mid-1800s.[10]

The Ottoman Empire was an early adopter of telegraph technology, drawing much interest during the reign of and reforms generated by Sultan Mahmud II (1808–39). But it would be an international war that ended up motivating the construction of the Ottoman telegraph line: in 1855, France laid an overland line from Bucharest to Varna, and Britain laid a submarine line under the Black Sea connecting Varna with Balaklava, its army headquarters in Crimea. The overlap between European and Ottoman interests highlights the telegraph's territorial and spatial importance. The wiring of the Ottoman Empire was driven by the financial gains the British would make, but ultimately, '[t]he driving force behind the British involvement in Ottoman telegraphy ... was the need for a telegraphic link with India',[11] serving to bind the British empire and enhance its political and commercial interests in the East. Meanwhile, the Ottomans 'exploited the advantages of electric communication to consolidate the control of their own empire'.[12]

Ottoman infrastructure expanded dramatically (by some accounts, more than 30,000 kilometres of lines) during the reign of Sultan Abdel Hamid II (1876–1909). By 1874 the Ottoman postal telegraph was described as 'enabling the central power in Constantinople to move the whole empire like a machine'.[13] The telegraph came to symbolize the Sultan's authority and reach: communicating with intelligence network within the empire and in exile, and tightening his grip on states far from the center of his rule. 'The empire, spanning parts of three continents, its cities and provinces separated by deserts, mountains, seas, and rivers, discovered in the telegraph an ideal system of communication and union'.[14] The telegraph proved to be a powerful instrument of control in the hands of a centralizing and territorially expanding government (see Fig.1); while for citizens it was 'an innovation that kept their empire united'.[15] As the Sultan's imperial territory shrank after the Congress of Berlin in 1878, telegraph communication became even more important for consolidating his rule and legitimacy.[16]

One of the telegraph's crucial features was its capacity to make communication instantaneous, and thus became critical as a 'tool of future intelligence operations and a temptation for control, especially during periods of tensions or hostilities'.[17] In other words, by assisting in the simultaneous centralization and expansion of power, through the telegraph – and later the telephone – the territory of surveillance could be extended, providing a 'new technology of control'.[18]

Palestine was connected through spurs and branch lines as a major cable extended from Anatolia down the Mediterranean coast through Akka, Haifa, Jaffa, Gaza and onto Egypt by the 1860s;[19] followed by submarine cables connecting Turkey, Cyprus and Tartous (in current-day Syria) in 1871, and Alexandria in 1878.[20] 'Palestine was a

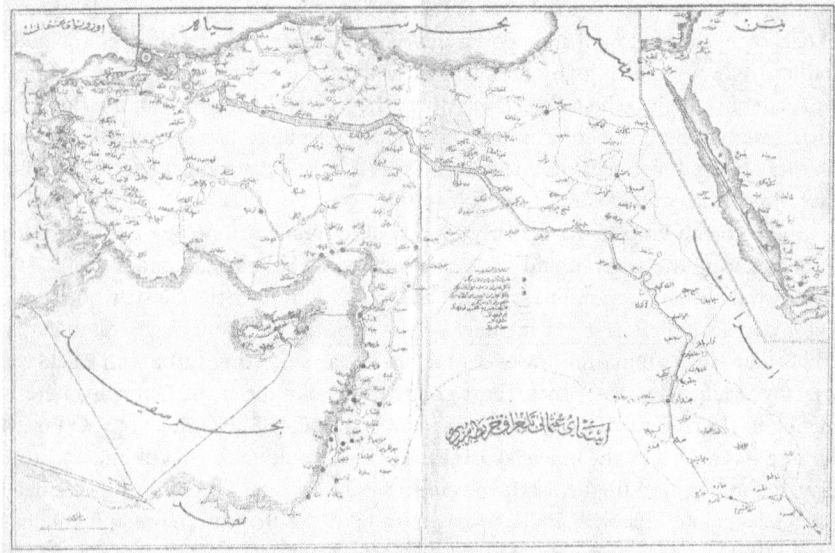

Figure 9.1 Imperial Administration of Post and Telegraph, Ottoman Empire. Istanbul: Mahmut Bey Matbaası, 1887.

central peripheral region, as well as a central Ottoman consideration. It was peripheral ... in the sense that it marked the southern flanks of the Syrian provinces and did not initially produce significant tax revenue, and that it was not strategically located along the pilgrimage route to Hijaz'[21] gaining importance as a gateway to the Suez and Ottoman Africa after the loss of Egyptian territory. Inland, the first telegraph line connected Jaffa and Jerusalem with Akka and Jaffa in 1865,[22] and in the 1870s smaller branch lines connected Safad, Nazareth and Bethlehem (see Fig. 2). It would not be until 1928 that the territory of Palestine would have a submarine cable, eventually connecting Cyprus and Haifa. With the increased centralization and control of the Tanzimat state apparatus, Palestine witnessed significant infrastructure development schemes that met military and economic designs.[23] By the end of the nineteenth century, a regional urban network emerged which 'involved a substantial amount of infrastructure (roads, railroads, and telegraphic communication) and created a complimentary system of defensive boundaries for the southern flank of the [Ottoman] empire'.[24] Existing globalization processes had of course already linked Palestine to the rest of the world through shipping lanes, overland trade routes, migration and pilgrimage. The telegraph built on these, but also extended and accelerated them.

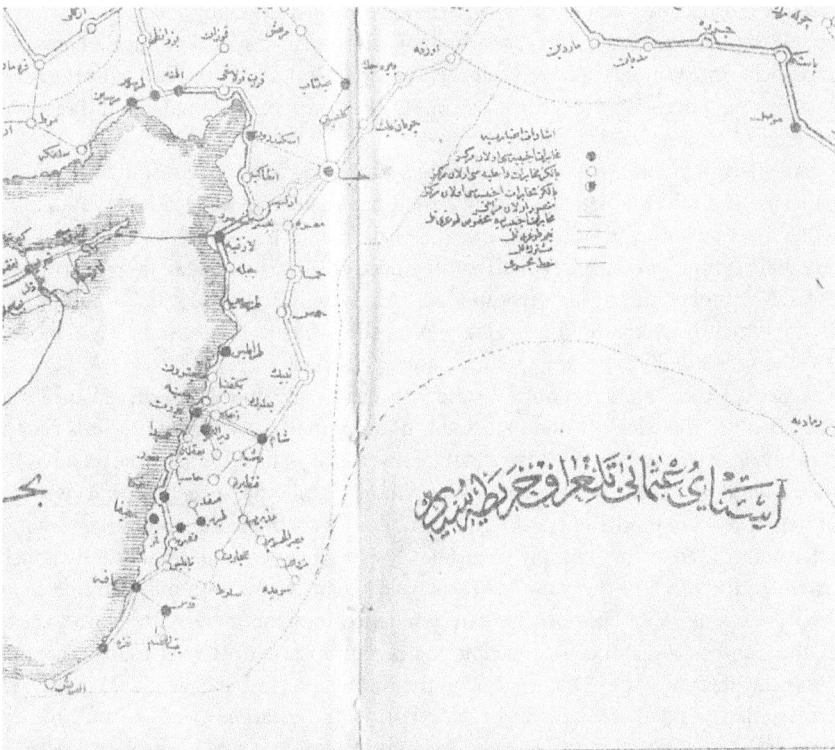

Figure 9.2 Imperial Administration of Post and Telegraph, Ottoman Empire. Istanbul: Mahmut Bey Matbaası, 1887. Detail.

Communications helped establish and consolidate imperial and international spaces of politico-economic orders. But telegraphs simultaneously co-created and challenged national containers. Early on, it was clear that ownership and control of the physical cable was important. The French and the British for example built their own infrastructure largely paralleling each other. 'Lines were strengthened and duplicated, as one imperial power avoided dependence upon the lines of another, using technology to "bypass" potentially unfriendly borders.'[25] Even the minute details of where to erect towers and posts had important political and economic repercussions on national or urban levels. Every wire strung was a prediction and a prescription about where information and commerce would travel, and about who should expect to connect to whom. Ideas about the telephone, and plans for its development, contained within them arguments about geographic scale.'[26] The telegraph thus did not just help expand and centralize empires, but nations and sub-national regions.

If telegraphy became important for binding together a nation and undergirding its centralizing power, it was also important for the opposite: in what, where and who was excluded. The geography of global telegraphy created particular understandings of the world that excluded significant portions of its population, reinforcing social orders based on concepts of race, gender and class. Communications had not just facilitated ties between powerful empires and nations, but also enabled uneven political and economic orders between the haves and the have-nots. 'Telegraphy affected many more people than its actual users by carving out non-congruent spaces of political, economic, and social interaction.'[27] As we shall see, the exclusion, bypassing of territories, and carving out non-congruent spaces would become of cardinal importance in developments in Israel/Palestine.

The telegraph network spread through the world in uneven and hierarchical patterns. The grid that would be built would be selective in its location, the logic of which, just as with the British in India, reveals 'that it was the requirements of the colonial regime for control, rather than the needs of Indian villages, that determined the development of the new communication system'.[28] While colonial authorities championed the telegraph for uniting people, the infrastructure ultimately advanced policies to instill divisions and fracture nascent alliances.

Skipping over territories however did not mean that control and surveillance was not possible. The telephone and telegraph underpinned what Penny Edwards calls 'a tyranny of proximity': allowing the state closer scrutiny of its subjects, while broadening the reach of government directives. In describing Cambodia, she explains: 'A network of new roads and modes of transport, telegraph wires and telephones replaced what is often referred to as the "tyranny of distance" with a new tyranny of proximity which extended the reach of the state ... While paved roads were commonly referred to as "routes of penetration" in colonial correspondence, they routinely bypassed vast tracts of the Cambodian countryside, facilitating communication between colonial centres while heightening the distance between officials ... and villagers.'[29] Whether in Cambodia or India, and later in Israel/Palestine, the creation of a new and uneven topological configuration through telecommunications was part of the very logic of a divide and rule strategy. From the telegraph onwards, technologies which radically altered global communication and their constituent surveillance capabilities were imbricated in, rather than removed from, existing systems of power which effectively contributed and constituted geopolitical entities such as empires, nations, regions and cities.

The lines of Israeli growth: telegraph, telephone and Tel Aviv

After the collapse of the Ottoman Empire, the British Mandate took responsibility for funding and maintaining activities such as road construction, telephone, telegraph, postal services and radio broadcasting through state revenues.[30] Private and entrepreneurial British interests would still be served such as in the building of the first submarine cable connecting Cyprus and Haifa in 1928. Although economic development was considered an integral part of the Mandated territories' path towards independence, given that Palestine was not as important to the British Empire as India or its African possessions the British invested minimally. Besides, the British were at this point experimenting with wireless and aerial technologies such as radio, aerial photography and balloons, as well as various forms of surveillance techniques. From an administrative point of view, the telephone was seen as an appendix to the telegraph, following the same routes and initially using the same cables. As with its other colonies, what the British developed in Mandate Palestine between 1920 and 1948 was in service primarily of communication among British administrators.

Mandate policy was to promote British exports and help British firms expand, and without any burden on British taxpayers to support the development of a capitalistic local economy. The latter pledge – a local economy, axiomatic as part of a Mandate's path towards independence – was primarily focused on ensuring the successful establishment of the Jewish National Home.[31] It was thus 'impractical to guarantee that equal facilities for the development of resources of the country should be granted to persons or bodies who may be activated by other motives, that is, to the Arabs'.[32] Moreover, as part of its promise to British taxpayers, the Mandate would only spend revenues generated by the Mandate territories themselves, most of which came from the landowning class which received its money from Zionist land purchases. As such, the Mandate 'viewed Jewish economic development as relieving them of their responsibility under the Mandate to develop the country' while also serving as the primary means by which the British could afford to rule.[33]

More importantly however, 'there was no real need for large-scale [British] Government sponsored development, since the Zionists were already seeing to it'.[34] The 1920s and 1930s were an era of Jewish state-building, which included many institutions and infrastructures, from media and telecommunications[35] and electricity,[36] to banking,[37] and military might,[38] and of course espionage and surveillance.[39] Thousands of Jews landed in Palestine, and hundreds of new Jewish settlements sprang up during this time, while Jewish workers and institutions, as well as military-cum-terrorist organizations and labor unions would provide the operational base for the new State of Israel. In other words, under the British Mandate, the institutional and organizational infrastructure for the State of Israel was laid.

In the realm of telecommunications various dynamics emerged. Jewish workers set up an International Railways, Post and Telegraph Workers' Union (RWU), with the support of the Labor Union party in 1919.[40] By the mid-1920s, the Haganah (a Zionist terrorist paramilitary group which would become part of Israel's military in 1948) was easily tapping telephone lines in Jerusalem and Jaffa, since both phone networks depended on a central exchange that was not automated. In some cases the Haganah purposely cut telephone wires.[41] By the early 1930s, Haifa was an economic, industrial and commercial hub: new telegraphy and telephones were laid in 1928, a new port built in 1932, and a pipeline from Iraq extended by 1934.[42] That the Jewish Agency and Jewish immigration institutions concentrated their efforts on encouraging Jewish immigration to Haifa was not without reason, as the goal was to benefit from the city's growing infrastructure. During the period of the Arab Revolts, Zionist organizations shadowed the British as they revisited security procedures to ensure that signals and telegraphs were in place to enable a military response.[43] By the time Palestine Broadcasting Station was opened in 1936, there were already multiple Jewish news agencies in Palestine. By 1939, there were already separate telephone directories for Jewish residents of Tel Aviv, Jaffa and other cities. In short, a great deal of telecommunications activity and infrastructure building was taking place well before 1948. Although meant in reference to the importance of the city, and playing on its name, Zionist leader Haim Weizmann – eventually Israel's first president – remarked that 'news from Jewish Palestine is transmitted by three agencies: by telegraph, by telephone, and by Tel Aviv'.[44]

Much of the writing on Zionist/Israeli infrastructure about the birth of the state generally posits two arguments: first, that it was the British that built the infrastructure upon which Israel established itself, exemplified in statements such as: 'The remarkable economic growth that enabled a tenfold increase in the Jewish population ... was made possible by the groundwork laid by the colonial government.'[45] Second, that all infrastructure and organization was 'inherited' from the British[46] as in 'if the land of Israel itself could speak, it would surely recall the twentieth century infrastructure introduced by the British'.[47] Both are only partially the case. The infrastructure during the Mandate period largely built on the existing infrastructure first introduced during the Ottoman period. Moreover, the infrastructure was placed by the colonial government not just haphazardly but to support a Jewish National Home, and Zionist organizations did the same.[48] If the land could speak, it would tell us where the State of Israel would emerge: the cities of Haifa, Jaffa and Tel Aviv (when the Partition Plan was proposed in 1947), and Akka, Nazareth, Safed and Beer Sheba (when those Lines were drawn in 1949): each a city from which collectively hundreds of thousands of Palestinians would be expelled, and each a city wired and connected with more robust and expansive infrastructure than would be found in, say, Nablus, Jericho, Bethlehem, Hebron and Gaza at that time. Telecommunications' territorial existence undergirded the territorial location of the State of Israel.

Digital surveillance relies on telecommunications, and traces its roots to more traditional forms of espionage, surveillance, and control. The history of Israel's military, security, and surveillance is well rehearsed:[49] from the Haganah's espionage service to the establishment of Sherut HaYediot (SHAY) which by 1940 was already headquartered in Tel Aviv with regional offices all around. SHAY was not only bribing British telegraph clerks to provide copies of communications to pass on to the Jewish Agency and penetrating British government and intelligence establishments, but also focused efforts on learning the use of wireless equipment and cryptography. SHAY, alongside other organizations, was built on the principle that it was 'not just for supplying information on current problems of the hour, rather as an auxiliary aid for the *expected political and military struggle in the near future*'.[50] Moreover, just as the interest between the British and the Yishuv overlapped in building infrastructure, so too intelligence gathering and interrogations centers were run jointly. The use of what would later be called 'Signals Intelligence' measures by Israeli intelligence services – wiretapping, encryption and decryption, and the plethora of intelligence disciplines deriving information from electronic devices[51] – can be traced back to the era pre-dating the formation of the state, as Jewish resistance movements operated comprehensive wiretapping operations, listening in on British officials and Arab leaders, as much as can be traced back to the location of the formation of the state.

In a historical reading that follows the infrastructure, Israel was established over parts of the land that were connected, where telegraph infrastructure was robust, where most of the switches and terminals existed, and where international connections, such as through submarine cables, had already been laid.

After 1948 Israel's telecommunications infrastructure would be operated by the state. Meanwhile, between 1948 and 1967, Jordan controlled telegraph and telephony provision for the West Bank and Jerusalem, while Egypt played the same role in Gaza. Egypt provided very little telecommunications upgrading to Gaza over the subsequent two decades. Jordan similarly invested very little in the West Bank, although, unlike Egypt, Jordan itself lacked much telecommunications infrastructure. The unevenness of telecommunications development between Israel and the Palestinian Occupied Territories would become more marked from this point onwards.[52]

On the Israeli side of the Armistice Line, telecommunications development reflected the new state's ideological, political and economic structure. This history is well documented.[53] Nonetheless, where new line installations occurred would foreshadow how the State of Israel would approach telecommunications after 1967 as it occupied the West Bank and the Gaza Strip and annexed Jerusalem. New installations focused on urban areas with high concentrations of Jewish populations such as Tel Aviv and Haifa, while 'development towns' where Mizrahi populations were settled were wired at much slower rates.[54] As demand for telephone lines grew, other political and economic factors (e.g. inflation, diminishing public expenditures) would also determine where they would be installed. Between the mid-1950s and early 1960s, government funds were directed towards telecommunications network expansion while also taking on a gradual liberalization approach.[55] During this boom period, the state focused on upgrading its network and its connections outside the region (primarily towards Europe); a new submarine cable connected Haifa to Marseilles in 1966.[56]

The occupation of the Occupied Territories starting in 1967 provided a cheap Palestinian labour force, allowing a shift of Israel's own labour force towards more advanced technology. In the meantime, Palestinians in the Occupied Territories would see very little telecommunications infrastructure growth, and lived under a strict military regime limiting most forms of communication from newspapers to fax machines. By 1972, Israel joined the INTELSAT network system and completed its modern satellite earth station. After the 1973 war, Israel increased its developments in hi-tech defence-related industries, especially in microelectronics, communications technology, weapons systems and aircraft manufacturing.[57] Military spending turned into a major fiscal tool, and by the time the Likud government launched its New Economic Policy in 1977, pro-business policies targeted the sales of government companies in fields such as energy, banking, manufacturing and transport and communication[58] – precursors to today's surveillance firms.

Influenced by similar tendencies in telecommunications across the world during the same period, in the early 1980s the Likud government launched a policy that telecommunications sector be managed by a quasi-private enterprise working under free market conditions to provide profits, eliminate shortages and establish conditions for domestic needs and international trade expansion. Bezeq, the Israeli Telecommunications Organization, was established in 1984, and a new Telecommunications Law was approved which transferred operational functions to Bezeq while maintaining regulatory functions under the Ministry of Communication. A second stage of telecommunications reform began in 1988 when customer-premises equipment, private switchboards and international long-distance services were liberalized; followed by another round in the 1990s when four commercial cellular licenses were awarded (and a cellular system installed in the military), accompanied by a shift from serving the public interest to serving government and corporate interests. At this point Israel expanded its development of its own telecommunications equipment, machinery and infrastructure, laying the groundwork for its future digital surveillance capabilities and global ascendency in those fields. In 1990 for example the first Israeli-built undersea cable, EMOS-1, connected Haifa and Tel Aviv with Turkey, Greece and Italy; and in 2012, another Israeli-built and Israel-owned submarine cable, Jonah (owned by Bezeq), further bolstered Israel's submarine connections. Over time, the routes of telecommunications became more deeply etched into the landscape.

Bezeq was in charge of building and maintaining telecommunications infrastructure in annexed Jerusalem and the Occupied Territories. This period can be described as one of active neglect of existing infrastructure (already dilapidated from the Jordanian and Egyptian period) on the one hand and focused on developing Jewish-only colonies with accompanying infrastructure, on the other hand. This was endemic across all infrastructural policy, from hospital beds to water, from roads to telecommunications. Even though Palestinians paid income, Value Added Tax (VAT) and other taxes to the Israeli government, Bezeq was neither quick nor efficient in servicing Palestinian users. Palestinian residents had to request official permission from the Israeli military apparatus governing the Territories for telephone service; many Palestinians waited up to ten years to obtain a line, and most never got one. The occupation did very little to develop telecommunications in Palestinian areas, if at all, rendering Palestinians subservient to Israeli infrastructure and controls. Overall, Palestinian areas remained underdeveloped: no new infrastructure was put in place, limitations on use were strict, leased lines were not permitted, everything was subject to surveillance and control. While some scholars have problematically tried to justify the unequal provisions of infrastructure and services as related to Palestinians' 'lower income and because they place a lower value on the telephone as compared with other goods',[59] there is no denying that the unevenness was a policy decision on the part of the Israeli government. For example, all switching nodes for telephony systems were built outside the areas that might possibly be handed over to a future 'sovereign' Palestinian state, so as to make it possible for Israel to control, surveil and limit all telephone traffic within, out of or into the Territories. For the few Palestinians who did have telephones, a call from Gaza City to Khan Younis was routed through Ashkelon, a call inside the West Bank was routed through Netanya or Afula. The same was true for inter-city calls, so that a call made within Nablus was also routed through Israel.

All limitations imposed on Palestinian telecommunications, whether on the level of infrastructure or individual use, were on the pretext of 'security', a term applied to any kind of event whether there existed any threat or not. For example, on the pretext of security, after the outbreak of the first Intifada, all international telephone and telex lines to the West Bank and the Gaza Strip were cut in March 1988, and by 1989 the Israeli military passed a law that prohibited the use of telephone lines for the sending of any faxes, emails or any form of electronic posting from the Territories. In the name security all kinds of limitations would be imposed on Palestinian telecommunications, well into the present day. Palestinians were telecommunicatively contained.

Containing Palestinians' lines

On the eve of the signing of the Oslo Accords in 1993, little more than 2% of all Palestinian households had fixed phone lines, compared to almost 75% of Israeli households (and 16% for Palestinian households within Israel).[60] The infrastructure that Israel handed over to the Palestinian Authority (PA) was in a debilitated state, made up of a public switched telephone and data network that consisted of only 80,000 lines and 14 exchanges relying on outdated copper wires. Only 5% of all Palestinian areas were wired for access to telecommunications, equivalent to 80 out of more than 400 villages.[61]

The PA handed management of telecommunication service provision to the newly established public shareholding company Palestine Telecommunications Company (Paltel) in 1995. Paltel opened the way for Palestinians to get phone and fax service (and eventually internet), increasing active lines in the West Bank and Gaza to 83,621 by 1996, using mainly the infrastructure available. As Paltel began to invest in expanding the infrastructure, telephone access quickly grew; 110,893 lines were installed by 1997; more than 300,000 by 2002; and 470,000 by 2018.[62] Paltel could not keep up. The demand demonstrated the lack of provisions under direct Israeli control.

But Paltel could not keep up because of more crucial infrastructural reasons. First, the PA and Paltel were only handed over responsibility over the infrastructure, and not control. All infrastructure had to maintain compatibility with the existing (and future) Israeli infrastructure, equipment orders and imports had to be pre-approved by Israel and in certain cases bought from Israeli suppliers, anything imported had to obtain the technical approval of Israeli standards, and even when approved would sit at Israeli ports accruing storage and customs fees. With the advent of cellular telephony, Palestinians would be allowed very limited spectrum allocation combined with stringent controls of what kind of infrastructure and machinery was allowed, even down to the details of what kind of broadcasting tower could be installed, and in which direction.[63] The constraints also entailed connection between the Palestinian Territories and the world, forcing all connections to physically pass through Israel and Israeli companies. The infrastructure was stunted from the beginning, not to mention the various times that the Israeli regime purposely destroyed Palestinian telecommunications infrastructure.[64]

Second, Bezeq had not wired or installed telephone exchanges over most of the areas with dense Palestinian populations (Jerusalem's infrastructure would remain under full Israeli control). Much of the existing network that Palestinians had relied on before Oslo had been built largely *outside* the West Bank and the Gaza Strip; as mentioned above, only 5% of Palestinian areas before the Oslo Accords were even wired.

Third, most of the infrastructure that was built inside the Territories after 1967 was largely in what was now called Area C, under Israeli sovereignty, and often in settlements, military outposts or along by-pass roads, and thus off-limits to Palestinians. As stated in the Accords: 'the Palestinian side shall enable the supply of telecommunications services to the Settlements and the military installations by Bezeq, as well as the maintenance by Bezeq of the telecommunications infrastructure serving them and the infrastructure crossing the areas under the territorial jurisdiction of the Palestinian side'.[65] Not only would Paltel have to allow Israeli providers access to Area C, but Paltel's infrastructure would have to rely on Israel's. This meant that where Palestinian infrastructure was allowed to be built would be territorially limited, determined by where previous infrastructure built by Bezeq existed and largely remained off limits to Palestinians, Oslo's maps and, over the ensuing years, Israel's territorial expansion of settlements, by-pass roads, buffer zones, checkpoints and the like. This translated into the permission to build a fragmented and contained telecommunications network that had to physically circumvent, at a minimum, more than 60% of the West Bank and 40% of the Gaza Strip and had to rely on Israeli networks for connections within and between these areas as well as beyond Israel/Palestine. Moreover, Areas A and B were not – and are still not – contiguous, so that to connect two towns in Area A often meant bypassing large swathes of Area C. As Patel moved ahead with building a telecommunications network, it would end up looking a lot like the 'Swiss cheese' map of the Territories itself.[66]

Area C's strategic location as the land that connects Areas A and B makes it ideal for central fibre-optic cables linking customers from all three areas to the system. Without permission to install any infrastructure in Area C, however, Palestinian cables must go through longer detours to bypass Area C, increasing the cost of installation and maintenance. Here is one example:

> To serve the residents of Qalqilya, the city had to be connected through a fiber transmission network in the city of Azun to the East. The most optimal route to establish a transmission path from Azun to Qalqilya would have been through a

9-kilometer road in Area C that extends in a straight line from the East to the West. The company, however, was not granted a license by the [Government of Israel] to dig this path. It, therefore, had to roll out fiber from Azun through various villages in Area B including Kafr Thulth, Ras 'Atiye, Habla to Qalqilya in order to limit its presence in Area C, and hence reduce the number of required approvals. This suboptimal transmission path extended over 15 kilometers and increased the cost of this operation by more than 60 percent.[67]

The essential territorial result can be stated simply as the fragmentation of the West Bank and Gaza. Paltel (and later other firms) cannot provide service in Area C, or much of Area B and A: in these and in cities such as Jenin, Tulkarm, Qalqilya and Bethlehem, Palestinians end up having to rely on or switching to Israeli providers. Far from offering a route out of dependency, telecommunications is a realm in which the Israeli colonial project is extended and centralized, and very much territorially so. The Palestinian infrastructure intended to make connection across distances possible ends up fragmented and contained.

During this same time, Israeli infrastructure and services in the West Bank expanded exponentially, driven by the need to wire military zones, settlements, and the many roads and highways that connect these to each other and to the other side of the 1949 Armistice Lines. In fact, settlements and outposts are often established by the installation of telecommunications infrastructure *first*, then followed by settlers.[68] These territories become part of Israel's network. Just as in colonial times, telecommunications infrastructure was not just reorganizing space but facilitating administrative, military, political and economic activity, supporting the spread of Israeli presence while also concentrating it, binding and gluing together Israeli spaces.[69] Telecommunications infrastructure literally marks the land, connecting Israeli areas (in the depths of West Bank settlements or downtown Tel Aviv) while excluding and dividing up Palestinian territory. This simultaneous expansion and exclusion is not a contradiction. Rather, it echoes how routes of telecommunications deepen their fixity, and how exclusion is part of the network. 'Networks are just as constituted by disconnection as by connection.'[70] Such exclusion, disconnection (what Supp-Montgomerie calls 'fracture') is intimately tied to the logic of surveillance.

By limiting Palestinian telecommunications infrastructure, Israeli digital surveillance is made easier in several ways. First, older technology infrastructure, for example 2G and 3G for cellular networks, or public switch networks for landline telephones, is easier (and cheaper) to limit, control and surveil, whether in terms of eavesdropping, detecting and monitoring data traffic, or the ability to shut it down.[71] Second, since all equipment for use in the West Bank and the Gaza Strip must first pass through Israeli customs and/or purchased directly from Israeli providers, the allegation that equipment is retrofitted with surveillance capabilities is not as outrageous as it sounds when one considers the known times when Palestinians have been tracked (and killed) through their mobile phones, even before GPS tracking became widespread.[72] Third, since the entire Palestinian infrastructure depends on the Israeli network, Israel has at its disposable the possibility of tracking, capturing and recording all voice and data traffic, uses and patterns. Fourth, Israel's telecommunications infrastructure exists all around, between, under and over Palestinian areas to bind settlements, military areas, bypass roads and checkpoints into one network, demonstrating Edwards' 'tyranny of proximity': extending the reach of the Israeli state and its surveillance capabilities, and extending the distance between Palestinians.

Digital surveillance's telecommunications routes/roots

One of the most fundamental aspects of telecommunications infrastructure is how it forms and deforms the fabric of space and time, organizing the possibilities for existence within them. Infrastructures locate us, as we negotiate and inhabit the material, symbolic and imaginative worlds they help to produce. The cables, wires, routers, towers, exchanges, switches and terminals, among the many other things necessary for a telecommunications network, create, define and delineate a state's centralized and distanced power, its means for consolidating as well as expanding that power.

The State of Israel came to exist territorially in the locations where a great part of an existing telecommunications network lay, at the time made up largely of a telegraph and telephone network. This was not serendipitous, but actively worked towards by the British Mandate, by Zionist organizations and eventually by the state itself. As infrastructures largely follow existing paths, Israel's state power deepened. 'Understanding information infrastructure as a problem of national sovereignty has given rise to infrastructure-building projects that literally materialize the boundaries of the state.'[73] Thus, while telecommunications infrastructure was one of the roots of state power, it also served as the means by which to extend territorial colonization. This infrastructure neither emerged out of nowhere nor continues unabated in a deterritorial sphere, but is identifiable and locatable in the cables, switches and terminals upon which all forms of digital communication depend. Telecommunications infrastructures are crucial sites in which power relations materialize.

The power of the contemporary state may no longer be (only) that of the telegraph and the telephone, but of computer science and network engineering. These are no less physical and territorial. They are territorialization projects that constitute and transform the state itself, as the telegraph and the telephone did before them.[74] With the digitization of information and the move towards systems of data-enabled mass surveillance, the information-based redistribution of authority has become even more embedded into telecommunications infrastructures.[75] In the case of Israel/Palestine, it is the State of Israel that ultimately controls the type of network possible, the strength and reach of that network, where it may lie, and who may or may not have access to it. It is equally the State of Israel that has access to all the data created and circulating on these networks. Israel's prowess in encoding systems, sensor and signal processing, software, passive and active electronic countermeasures, image processing, and display and surveillance systems, are ultimately matters of situated and embedded infrastructure.

Digital systems of surveillance materialize a state's territory. Populations and territories can be excluded and still be embraced by a surveillance regime. Israel has at its disposal a restricted Palestinian system that is dependent on Israel which is easier to surveil, and an advanced Israeli system that enacts all kinds of surveillance mechanisms onto Palestinians. The extent of Israel's surveillance is expansive, and within these spaces is where the containment of Palestinians takes place. Both are parts of the same strategy. Palestinians are thus not simply excluded, but differentially included. Surveillance 'penetrates differentially'.[76] But surveillance itself, even if digital, like state power, is ultimately concretized in telecommunications infrastructures.

Notes

1. Senor and Singer 2011.
2. Zureik 2001, 2015, 2016; Zureik, Lyon and Abu-Laban eds, 2010; Gordon 2008; Tawil-Souri 2016; Sa'di 2021; 7amleh 2019.
3. Kane 2016; Cahane 2021; Zureik and Lyon 2021.
4. Tawil-Souri 2012; Zureik 2016; 7amleh 2019.
5. Schwoch 2018: 18.
6. As Joe Painter (2010: 1093) states, territory must be interpreted principally as an effect: 'This "territory-effect" can best be understood as the outcome of networked socio-technical practices ... "territory" and "network" are not, as is often assumed, incommensurable and rival principles of spatial organisation, but are intimately connected.'
7. Varnelis 2004/200.
8. Osterhammel 2014: 3.
9. Goswami 2004: 45.
10. Starosielski 2015.
11. Bektas 2000: 676.
12. Ibid.: 700.
13. Ibid.: 695.
14. Bektas 2000: 669.
15. Ibid.: 670.
16. Siefert 2011: 101–2.
17. Ibid. 99.
18. Ibid.: 87.
19. Davison 1990.
20. The Eastern Mediterrenean was connected along the coast through underground cables. Submarine cables would provide direct connection to stations in Cyprus, Greece, to Egypt and eventually to points farther West. The Eastern Mediterranean would be relatively late in having its own submarine landing cables after those initially laid in Syria and Alexandria: Haifa in 1928, Beirut in 1938 with a French-built cable connecting it to Tunisia. Today along the Eastern coast, Syria's only landing point is still in Tartous, Lebanon three landing points (Tripoli, Beirut, Nahariyya), and Israel two landing points (Haifa and Tel Aviv). Israel however has a substantially higher number of cables (seven, compared to five for Lebanon and one for Syria) and is the only country of those three that has built and owns its own submarine cables. For an interactive map of submarine cables, see https://www.infrapedia.com/app
21. Tamari 2007: 38.
22. Meiton 2019: 44.

23 Tamari 2007: 38.
24 Ibid.: 64–5.
25 Siefert 2011: 99.
26 MacDougall 2013: 175.
27 Müller and Tworek 2015: 262–3.
28 Mann 2010: 198.
29 Edwards 2006: 427.
30 Kimmerling 2001: 62.
31 Sherman 1998.
32 Levine 1995: 103.
33 Ibid.: 103–4.
34 Ibid.: 103.
35 As Schejter and Yemeni (2015: 113) put it, 'flourishing media culture developed on the foundation set during the pre-state years'.
36 Meiton 2019.
37 Kimmerling 2001; Nitzan and Bichler 2002.
38 Kimmerling 2001.
39 Cohen 2010; Sa'di 2016; Zureik 2001; Zureik et al. 2010.
40 deVries 1994: 866.
41 Wagner 2019: 155.
42 Mansour 2006.
43 Wagner 2019: 157.
44 Azaryahu 2020: 47.
45 Tal 2002: 41.
46 Tal 2002; Schejter 2006; Schejter & Yemeni 2015; Soffer 2014.
47 Tal 2002: 41.
48 Tamari 2017; Meiton 2019.
49 Zureik 2001; Zureik et al. eds. 2010; Handel and Dayan 2017; Sa'di 2016; Black and Morris 1991; Cohen 2010.
50 Wagner 2019: 25; emphasis added.
51 Cahane 2021; Zureik and Lyon 2021.
52 An index that ranks countries based on their ICT development, ranked Palestine 123 out of 167 while Israel ranked 23 (ICT Development Index, 2017).
53 Rosenne et al. 1997; Schejter 2006; Schejter & Yemeni 2015.
54 Rosenne et al. 1997.
55 Nitzan and Bichler 1996.
56 Rosenne et al. 1997: 93–4.
57 Nitzan and Bichler 2002. This transformation in the Israeli economy was bolstered by a massive inflow of American capital and US permission to acquire and exploit advanced technological systems through US-Israeli joint ventures, such as Lockheed Martin, Boeing, Raytheon, General Dynamics and Northrop Grumman.
58 Nitzan and Bichler 1996, 2002.
59 Salomon and Razin 1988: 128.
60 PCBS 2004, 2010, 2014; Paltel Annual Report 2001; Israel Ministry of Communications 2008; Israel Central Bureau of Statistics 2008.
61 Paltel Annual Report 2001; personal interview, Paltel, March 2003.
62 Paltel Annual Report 2019.
63 Tawil-Souri 2015.
64 Tawil-Souri 2012; 7amleh 2019.

65 Oslo 2, Annex III, Article 36, D.3a.
66 Palestinian negotiator, Nabil Shaath, upon seeing Oslo II's map (which was only shown to the Palestinian negotiators twenty-four hours before the agreement was to be signed) exclaimed that the holes that made up the parts of a future Palestinian state looked like Swiss cheese.
67 World Bank 2014: 39.
68 Tawil-Souri 2015.
69 World Bank 2014: 39–40. While Israeli firms primarily serve settlements, military zones and highways, their presence has equally allowed these firms to sell services to Palestinian wholesale providers and customers, which is a form of illegal competition estimated to prevent more than $4.5million a year to Palestinian providers.
70 Supp-Montgomerie 2021: 23.
71 O'Brien and York 2015. As many critics point out, the potential economic losses and actual added economic costs (such as by having to circumvent large swaths of areas) stunt Palestinian economic growth (Tawil-Souri 2012, 2015; World Bank 2014; 7amleh 2019).
72 Tawil-Souri 2012.
73 Möllers 2021: 120.
74 Ibid.: 116.
75 Lyon 2014.
76 Browne (2015). Browne uses this term to mean that surveillance technologies have an embedded racial bias and operate according to a context which (re)produces forms of state control and racial social relations.

References

7amleh (2019), *Connection Interrupted: Israel's Control of the Palestinian ICT Infrastructure and Its Impact on Digital Rights*. Available online: https://7amleh.org/wp-content/uploads/2019/01/Report7amlehEnglishfinal.pdf

Azaryahu, M. (2020), *Tel Aviv: Mythography of a City*, Syracuse: Syracuse University Press.

Bektas, Y. (2000), 'The Sultan's Messenger: Cultural Constructions of Ottoman Telegraphy, 1847–1880,' *Technology and Culture* 41 (4): 669–96.

Black, I., and B. Morris (1991), *Israel's Secret Wars: A History of Israel's Intelligence Services*, New York: Grove Press.

Browne, S. (2015), *Dark Matters: On the Surveillance of Blackness*, Durham, NC: Duke University Press.

Cahane, A. (2021), 'Israel's SIGINT Oversight Ecosystem: COVID-19 Secret Location Tracking as a Test Case,' *University of New Hampshire Law Review* 19 (2): 451–90.

Cohen, H. (2010), *Good Arabs*, Berkeley: University of California Press.

Davison, R. H. (1990), *Essays in Ottoman and Turkish History, 1774–1923: The Impact of the West*, Austin: University of Texas Press.

deVries, D. (1994), 'Proletarianization and National Segregation: Haifa in the 1920s,' *Middle Eastern Studies* 30 (4): 860–82.

Edwards, P. (2006), 'The Tyranny of Proximity: Power and Mobility in Colonial Cambodia, 1863–1954,' *Journal of Southeast Asian Studies* 37 (3): 421–43.

Gordon, N. (2008), *Israel's Occupation*, Berkeley: University of California Press.

Goswami, M. (2004), *Producing India: From Colonial Economy to National Space*, Chicago: University of Chicago Press.

Handel, A., and H. Dayan (2017), 'Multilayered Surveillance in Israel/Palestine: Dialectics of Inclusive Exclusion,' *Surveillance & Society* 15 (3/4): 471–6.
ICT Development Index (2017), 'IDI 2017 Rank,' Available online: http://www.itu.int/net4/ITU-D/idi/2017/index.html
Israel Central Bureau of Statistics (2008), *Israel in Statistics 1948–2007*. Available online: http://www1.cbs.gov.il/reader
Israel Ministry of Communications (2008), *Telecommunications in Israel 2008*. Available online: http://www.moc.gov.il/139-en/MOC.aspx
Kane, A. (2016), 'How Israel Became a Hub for Surveillance Technologies,' *Intercept*, October 17. Available online: https://theintercept.com/2016/10/17/how-israel-became-a-hub-for-surveillance-technology/
Kimmerling, B. (2001), *The Invention and Decline of Israeliness: State, Society, and the Military*, Berkeley: University of California Press.
Levine, M. (1995), 'The Discourses of Development in Mandate Palestine,' *Arab Studies Quarterly*: 95–124.
Lyon, D. (2014), 'Surveillance, Snowden, and Big Data: Capacities, Consequences, Critique,' *Big Data & Society* 1 (2).
MacDougall, R. (2013), *The People's Network*, Philadelphia: University of Pennsylvania Press.
Mann, M. (2010), 'The Deep Digital Divide: The Telephone in British India 1883–1933,' *Historical Social Research* 35 (1) (131): 188–208.
Mansour, J. (2006), 'The Hijaz-Palestine Railway and the Development of Haifa,' *Jerusalem Quarterly* 28.
Mazzetti, M. (2019), 'A New Age of Warfare: How Internet Mercenaries Do Battle for Authoritarian Governments,' *New York Times*, March 21. Available online: https://www.nytimes.com/2019/03/21/us/politics/government-hackers-nso-darkmatter.html
Meiton, F. (2019), *Electrical Palestine: Capital and Technology from Empire to Nation*, Berkeley: University of California Press.
Möllers, N. (2021), 'Making Digital Territory: Cybersecurity, Techno-nationalism, and the Moral Boundaries of the State', *Science, Technology, & Human Values* 46 (1): 112–38.
Müller, S. M., and H. J. Tworek, (2015), '"The Telegraph and the Bank": on the Interdependence of Global Communications and Capitalism, 1866–1914,' *Journal of Global History* 10 (2): 259–83.
Nitzan, J., and S. Bichler (1996), 'From War Profits to Peace Dividents: The New Political Economy of Israel,' *Capital & Class* 60: 61–95.
Nitzan, J., and S. Bichler (2002), *The Global Political Economy of Israel*, London: Pluto.
O'Brien, D., and J. C. York (2015), 'A Slow Boat to Fast Data: Why Is Palestine Still Waiting for 3G?' *Electronic Frontier Foundation*. Available online: https://www.eff.org/deeplinks/2015/11/palestine-3g
Osterhammel, J. (2014), *The Transformation of the World: a Global History of the Nineteenth Century*, Princeton: Princeton University Press.
Painter, J. (2010), 'Rethinking Territory,' *Antipode* 42 (5): 1090–1118.
Paltel Annual Report. 2019. Available online: http://www.paltelgroup.ps/uploads/AnnualreportPG15MFinal.pdf
Paltel Annual Report. 2001. Available online: https://www.paltelgroup.ps/uploads/2001RA.pdf
PCBS (2004). Available online: https://www.pcbs.gov.ps/pcbs2012/Publications.aspx
PCBS (2010). Available online: https://www.pcbs.gov.ps/pcbs2012/Publications.aspx
PCBS (2014). Available online: https://www.pcbs.gov.ps/Portals/_Rainbow/Documents/e-Trans_Time%20seri_2014.htm

Rosenne, D., B. K. Erez and S. Hai (1997), 'Telecommunications in Israel: Advanced Technology, Evolving Competition' in Eli M. Noam (ed.) *Telecommunications in Western Asia and the Middle East*, New York: Oxford University Press.
Sa'di, A.H. (2016), 'Stifling Surveillance: Israel's Surveillance and Control of the Palestinians during the Military Government Era,' *Jerusalem Quarterly* 68.
Sa'di, A.H. (2021), 'Israel's Settler-colonialism as a Global Security Paradigm', *Race & Class* 63 (2): 21–37.
Salomon, I., and E. Razin (1988), 'The Geography of Telecommunications Systems: The Case of Israel's Telephone System,' *Tijdschrift voor economische en sociale geografie* 79 (2): 122–34.
Schejter, A. (2006), 'Israeli Cellular Telecommunications Policy,' *Telecommunications Policy* 30: 14–28.
Schejter, A., and Yemeni (2015), '"A Time to Scatter Stones and a Time to Gather Them": Electronic Media Industries Concentration Trends in Israel 1984–2013,' *Telecommunications Policy* 39: 112–26.
Schwoch, J. (2018), *Wired into Nature: The Telegraph and the North American Frontier*, Champaign: University of Illinois Press.
Senor, D., and S. Singer (2011), *Start-up Nation: The Story of Israel's Economic Miracle*, New York: Random House.
Sherman, A. J. (1998), *Mandate Days: British Lives in Palestine, 1918–1948*, London: Thames & Hudson.
Siefert, M. (2011), 'Chingis Khan with the Telegraph: Communications in the Russian and Ottoman Empires' in J. von Hirschhausen (ed.), *Comparing Empires. Encounters and Transfers in the Long Nineteenth Century*, 80–110, Göttingen: Vandenhoeck & Ruprecht.
Soffer, O. (2014), *Mass Communication in Israel: Nationalism, Globalization, and Segmentation*, New York: Berghahn Books.
Starosielski, N. (2015), *The Undersea Network*, Durham, NC: Duke University Press.
Supp-Montgomerie, J. (2021), *When the Medium was the Mission: The Atlantic Telegraph and the Religious Origins of Network Culture*, New York: NYU Press.
Tal, A. (2002), *Pollution in a Promised Land*, Berkeley: University of California Press.
Tamari, S. (2017), *The Great War and the Remaking of Palestine*, Berkeley: University of California Press.
Tawil-Souri, H. (2012), 'Digital Occupation: Gaza's High-tech Enclosure.' *Journal of Palestine Studies* 41 (2): 27–43.
Tawil-Souri, H. (2015), 'Cellular Borders: Dis/connecting Phone Calls in Israel-Palestine', in L. Parks & N. Starosielski (eds), *Signal Traffic: Critical Studies of Media Infrastructures*, 157–80, Champaign: University of Illinois Press.
Tawil-Souri, H. (2016), 'Surveillance Sublime: The Security State in Jerusalem,' *Jerusalem Quarterly* 68.
Varnelis, K. (2004/2005), 'The Centripetal City: Telecommunications, the Internet, and the Shaping of the Modern Urban Environment,' *Cabinet Magazine* 17 (Spring).
Wagner, S. B. (2019), *Statecraft by Stealth: Secret Intelligence and British Rule in Palestine*, Ithaca: Cornell University Press.
World Bank (2014), *Area C of the West Bank and the Future of the Palestinian Economy*. Available online: https://documents1.worldbank.org/curated/en/257131468140639464/pdf/Area-C-and-the-future-of-the-Palestinian-economy.pdf
Zureik, E. (2001), 'Constructing Palestine through Surveillance Practices', *British Journal of Middle Eastern Studies* 28 (2): 205–27.

Zureik, E. (2015), *Israel's Colonial Project in Palestine: Brutal Pursuit*, London: Routledge.

Zureik, E. (2016), 'Strategies of Surveillance: The Israeli Gaze,' *Institute for Palestine Studies* 66. Available online: http://www.palestine-studies.org/jq/fulltext/202338

Zureik, E., and D. Lyon (2021), 'Coronavirus Surveillance and Minority Groups in Israel/Palestine', *Middle East International Journal for Social Sciences* 3 (3): 197–215.

Zureik, E., S. Faris, I. Jillson, R. Baidas and B. Sartawi (2006), *Information Society in Palestine: The Human Capital Dimension*, International Development Research Centre, Ottawa. Available online: https://idl-bnc-idrc.dspacedirect.org/bitstream/handle/10625/31982/122296.pdf

Zureik, E., D. Lyon and Y. Abu-Laban (eds) (2010), *Surveillance and Control in Israel/Palestine,* London: Routledge.

Part Four

Palestine: Connections, Ruptures and Popular Resistance

10

Settler Colonialism in Palestine

Connections and Ruptures

Magid Shihade

Introduction

This chapter is part of my current research project on settler colonialism in Palestine. It builds on previous articles. The first (Shihade 2015a) focused on the local impact of Israeli settler colonialism. Through stories and voices of residents in Kafr Yassif, a Palestinian village in Galilee, it explored the impact of 1948, the creation of the Israeli settler-colonial state, and the imposition of military rule soon after on the sense of place, confinement, isolation and alienation that these Palestinians had felt since 1948, the rupturing of their connections to the rest of Palestinian society, and their connections to peoples and places in the neighbouring Arab states and beyond. It is an article about those Palestinians who remained on their lands after 1948 and became citizens of a state that was built on the destruction of their own society and how the restrictions on mobility within and without Palestine affected their sense of space and identity. It also explored different forms of connections they tried to create as a response to the new situation they found themselves in, their history of resistance to state policies filled with aspirations, hope, desires, and complicity. The article explored their histories and voices that challenge both Arab nationalist historiography that, in reaction to Zionism, claimed rootedness and indigeneity, and at the same time, it challenged Zionist myths about the un-rootedness of Palestinian Arabs representing them as un-rooted invaders/strangers to the land, and held them in contempt and saw them as a fifth column. Their stories and voices challenge the sense of presence and absence that they find themselves in both by Zionism and the Israeli State, but also by Arab nationalism that mirrored Zionism and Western modernity by focusing on the land/state and ignoring the human.[1]

The second article (Shihade 2015b) focused on the regional/continental impact and questions the place of Israel in Asia, a state that considers itself European/Western, as portrayed by its political and leadership, and it is also viewed as such by Western leaders and public, a point often publicly stated by Zionist and western leaders. By asking about the place of Israel in Asia, my approach in that article thus positions this cartographic question in the context of race, colonialism/settler colonialism, and modernity. The article also questioned the place of native Palestinians in Asia. That is, what political, economic, social and cultural consequences and connections are possible if one thinks of Palestinians as West Asians, or as Asians, rather than as 'Middle Easterners'. As such, the article was also about rethinking Asia and the meaning of Asia, how the geographic and political construct of Asia was developed, and who is included in this designation. It explores the cross-regional and trans-border connections within Asia that have been marginalized in academic work but also in public memory and knowledge about the peoples of the region and their long history of interaction; the cultural flows within the continent; and economic and political connections among peoples, groups and states within the continent of Asia. Thus Israel must be seen as a European project in Asia, it is at the heart of Europe, and it is not by accident that it receives massive support from Europe/West. One might also think of Canada, Australia and other settler-colonial cases as European/Western projects.

Building on the two articles summarized above, the third article (Shihade, 2015c) linked the local, regional/continental with the global by looking at the place of Israel in the globe, or what I call here 'global Israel'. Thinking about Israel in this way extends the question of the cartography of Palestine/West Asia and Israel-in-Asia to thinking about Israel in the world and to Israelization as a global process that has ramifications for those outside the region and continent.

I also want to make a brief note about my research method here, for I do not define my interviewees as those to be studied *or objects* of knowledge production, or as 'anthropos' as Walter Mignolo (2000) terms them, but as a source of knowledge and epistemology. It is from the conversations with these Palestinian villagers and workers that I was struck by the idea of a global Israel, and not just a local or an Asian/regional Israel. I realize that this concept was a more fitting one that would engage with the impact of the Israeli settler-colonial state on Palestine. I will gesture here to a few preliminary points that undergird the global nature of this settler-colonial project. One, the Israeli settler-colonial state triggered the dispersal of millions of Palestinians to Asia, Africa, Europe, Australia and the Americas and thus made them part of a global diaspora and exilic subjects who by nature have a deep attachment to their homeland and the people from whom they were separated. Two, the Zionist project also claims to represent Jews around the globe and indeed has recruited Jewish communities from all around the globe to manage this project. Furthermore, Jewish communities around the world continue to engage with the Israeli project either by critiquing it, or more commonly by supporting it and agitating against those who critique Israel. Finally, due to the significance of religious sites and histories, Palestine/Israel elicits strong feelings, attachments and interventions from people around the globe. Thus, it is very fitting to think of Israel/Palestine as a global question and of what I am calling 'global Israel'.

The major focus of that article is an argument for why the Israeli settler-colonial project in Palestine is better theorized as a global question and not just one that impacts the native Palestinian and local space or a regional question. This argument does not negate the local and regional impact of Israel, nor does it deny that the most staggering consequences of the creation of Israel were felt most by the native Palestinian society, but rather it conceptualizes the 'local' through its regional and global dimensions. On the one hand, Israel, world Jewry and their supporters, and on the other, Palestinians and their supporters engage in continuous battles over rights, ethics and politics. And the article is complementary to *Global Palestine* (Collins 2011), where Collins argues the global solidarity with Palestine is a response to global concerns about justice, rights, ecology, repression, racism and discrimination.

Theoretical framework

This chapter engages two presumably unrelated schools of thought: first, theories of nomadology and mobility by Deleuze and Guattari (1986) and their earlier, more expansive incarnation as theorized by the fourteenth-century Arab scholar Ibn Khaldoun; and second, theories of settler colonialism, especially as articulated by Fayez Sayegh (1965). The chapter also engages with the concept of Patrick Wolfe about the nature of settler colonialism as a structure rather than an event, and also Ibn Khaldun's ideas on the Nomad-Settler, whose presence in the new location and community can be only be sustained by mixing with the local culture. And finally, the chapter engages with the psychological impact of settler colonialism on the Native-Indigenous community utilizing ideas from Ibn Khaldun and Frantz Fanon (1968, 1969). By expanding the concept of rupture, I argue that settler colonialism in Palestine can be better understood in its global dimension and impact rather than as it is normally analysed as a purely local or even regional issue. This chapter thus contributes to work on settler colonialism, nomadology, Palestine and Arab Studies, studies of colonialism and Global Studies, and it aims at de-provincializing the question of Palestine and Palestine studies. It theorizes a new way of seeing Palestine by re-framing the Palestine question as a local, regional, continental and a global issue both in its origin and its current development, by examining how Israel has created local, regional and global ruptures for Palestinians and others.

In theories of Settler Colonialism and Palestine Studies, Sayegh's work (1965) is a pioneering one for it goes beyond the local implication of Israeli settler colonialism. Sayegh argues that the creation of the Israeli state led to the delinking of Palestine from Asia and Africa, as Palestine historically formed a link between these two continents.[2] Furthermore, the settler-colonial project undermines the sovereignty and self-determination not just of Palestinians but of *all* the peoples in these continents because it did not receive their consent.[3] According to Sayegh, the creation of the Israeli settler-colonial state was an imposition on the region by Western colonial powers against the wishes of the peoples of Africa and Asia and created a rupture between Africa and Asia that countered and undermined the decolonizing wave in these continents. My study builds on this argument by looking at the implications of Israel as a rupture beyond Asia and Africa. To begin with, Palestine is not only connected to continents but also to the Mediterranean and was always a link that connected peoples from countries around it; many from Greece and other places migrated to Palestine. Some of these migrants became leading figures in the Palestine national movement.[4] So, to limit the impact of the rupture of Israeli settler-colonialism to Africa and Asia limits our understanding of its implications globally.

Through interviews with elders in the village of Kafr Yasif, elders who lived before 1948 and experienced the rupture of 1948, the concept of rupture by Seyegh is expanded. To the question of what did the creation of the Israeli state mean for them, several talked about social, economic, and cultural rupture. Many people in Galilee before 1948 intermarried, visited, imported or exported goods to neighbouring countries. These social, cultural and economic connections were ruptured by the creation of the Israel state. They were unable to continue these connections after 1948. Legally Israel prohibited them from doing so. Also, neighbouring Arab states also did not allow legal interaction with them since they had become Israeli citizens. The concept of rupture was more than about political rupture. Even internally, Palestinians have been ruptured in every aspect of their lives. For most if not all of them, their way of life was ruptured by the Israeli state. Through confiscation of lands for example, farming became less possible. This can be also framed as a social rupture not just economic, because farming in the past created social gatherings that we hardly see today. There is also a legal rupture since Palestinians do not have the same rights as Jewish Israelis, who can, for example, marry anyone from any other place and get them Israeli citizenship. On the other hand, this is harder for Palestinians, especially if they marry another Palestinian from outside of the 1948 borders. This legal apartheid (and all settler states are apartheid states) creates an emotional rupture; Palestinian citizens of Israel cannot love and marry who they want. One can give several examples about the previous internal ruptures, and also talk about other aspects and other forms of rupture. In short, the concept of rupture is much wider than the political, and it affects every aspect of the lives of the Palestinians.

Furthermore, the Israeli settler-colonial project has been a global one from its founding and was supported and continues to be aided and defended by global empires. It was a project that defined itself as a global one – the 'ingathering' of Jews from all over the world – and continues to be claimed as a project that all Jews around the world must support. Furthermore, by the creation of Israel, millions of Palestinians today live all over the world and have an attachment to Palestine that remains restricted and shaped by Israeli policies of denial of the right to return, restriction on entry, and restriction on family unification.

Also, Israel/Palestine is a question that occupies so much attention at the United Nations, in world politics and in so many states, often exhausting energies and resources. It is a question that generates much solidarity all around the world for those who see the injustice done to the native Palestinians, a solidarity that is also met with attacks and repression in many parts of the world by pro-Israeli forces. In *Global Palestine*, John Collins (2011) argues that the Palestine question has created such a powerful global solidarity movement because of the many issues intertwined with it that affect people all around the world, such as access to water, access to land, the right to mobility, the right to education, the right to work, the right to self-determination, the right to freedom of speech and, indeed, the right to life – a life with dignity. In *Global Israel*,[5] I argue that Israel is the other side of the coin of Collins' analysis of *Global Palestine* as a signifier of global solidarity. *Global Israel* has infringed on all these rights locally, regionally, and globally, albeit with different intensity and outcomes.

Thus, in my view, it is through the study of this global rupture created by the Israeli settler-colonial state from 1948 to the present that one can better understand its global impact, which includes wars, displacement, refugees, invasions, air strikes, blockades, sanctions, repression, restrictions on movement and on entry, among other consequences. That rupture has become a permanent structure that has been impacting Palestinians and peoples from around the world, and it has also produced a global movement of solidarity.

To theorize the rupture produced by global Israel, I utilize the work of the fourteenth-century Arab scholar Ibn Khaldoun, especially his concept of the nomad, as a lens to understand mobility as a central aspect of human life. My work brings the theories of Sayegh and Ibn Khaldoun into conversation, as they both deal with rupture, but from different intellectual perspectives. Sayegh uses a Third Worldist prism and analysis of settler colonialism, while Ibn Khaldoun was thinking about questions of the nature of the human and the ways in which mobility, connections and cooperation, and labour and creativity are all central to being human in his analysis. I utilize Ibn-Khaldoun's work on nomadology/mobility as a corrective to its misappropriation by Deleuze & Guattari, who borrow the nomad concept from Ibn Khaldoun, with a marginal reference in their work. They argue that Ibn Khaldun's concept of the nomad is premodern, and specific to a certain culture and group, and theirs is modern and universal.[6] Yet, their work restricts the meaning of the nomad to one aspect, central as it is, that focuses on the relationship between the individual and the state, specifically in the context of violence and war-making.[7] Accordingly, their analysis is confined to the modern European state, in line with the work of Charles Tilly (1985), among others, that also views the individual through the prism of the modern state, a specifically Eurocentric approach. On the other end of the spectrum of the school of nomadology that developed from the work of Deleuze and Guattari, the nomad is presented as the human who is without roots, without connections, and continually roaming the earth unmoored from political structures or places of origin.[8] This romanticized version of the nomad has been criticized, and rightly so. Alex Young (2015), building on the work of critical Native American scholarship such as that of Jodi Byrd, argues that this idealized notion of the nomad in the Deleuzean school serves to erase both the Natives, who are excluded from such narratives, and their history and experience as a result of violent Western/European mobility/nomadology. Young sees this view of nomadology as based on 'a settler-colonial fantasy'. Thus, my theorizing of nomadology/mobility, as articulated originally by Ibn Khaldoun and later misappropriated by Deleuze and Guattari, can contribute to the ongoing debate about settler colonialism in different fields, and to the discussion of border studies and migration, among other issues.

Deleuze and Guattari's framing and exceptionalizing of the nomad, either as a violent conqueror or as world traveller, is in both senses a misconception of the original concept offered by Ibn Khaldoun, which is more universal. The nomad is part of Ibn Khaldoun's theory of social organizations that took place in the context of pre-modern nation-states. While mobile humans or nomads, in Ibn Khaldoun's understanding, might challenge the rule or government of territory during and through their mobility and can engage in violent resistance to that rule, there are other aspects of mobility that are central to being human. In contrast to the restricted analysis of nomadology and mobility, which also emerges from a Western privilege of movement, rootedness and mobility are dialectically related for Ibn Khaldoun. Nomadism is neither about invading Mongols nor the romance of Orientalized Bedouin sheiks. Ibn Khaldoun's Arabic term for the nomad, *badawi/badiw* (Bedouin/Bedouins), is primarily an economic category rather than an essentialized cultural trait. It references a mode of economic production or, as he described it, the way one person or group makes a living. The nomad's way of making a living is through raising animals and farming. Both forms of work require rootedness as well as mobility.[9] In the time of Ibn Khaldoun, which was a different historical context, rootedness was not viewed as in opposition to or a negation of mobility/nomadology, but rather each was connected with and constituted the other. Mobility is something that people do, not simply because of a *lack* of rootedness or a desire to roam the earth, but out of necessity.[10] So the fact that the original concept is not acknowledged but incompletely appropriated, and misappropriated, leads to further misrepresentation of the nomad.

In fact, for Ibn Khaldoun, nomadology is the norm, not the exception – it is not a trait that belongs to the few. Nomadism is not associated with a violent movement, and violence is not central to nomadism. Nomadism for Ibn Khaldoun is more about labour and sustenance, concerns that are central to any human or social organization.[11] He argues that all people, by nature, seek sustenance and so must move, to different degrees and in different ways, from one place to another in order to labour and survive. They move when there is a lack of resources in the areas they live in, or when their labour is not treated justly. They move because of their desire to explore, experience and connect. The nomad, for Ibn Khaldoun, is central to any human social organization,[12] rather than an exterior element in conflict with the city/state as Deleuze and Guattari argue. We also move because of emotional connections when we love someone who lives in a different place. We also move to study in other places. There are many reasons for people to move from one place to another. But in the concept of the nomad articulated by Ibn Khaldun, the nomad can sustain a life in the new place only when he mixes with the local culture. Thus, settlers, colonizers and occupiers sooner or later leave. And there are many examples in Al-Muqaddimah that Ibn Khaldun discusses to reflect that. Imposition, occupation, colonization, settler colonialism and oppression don't last for ever, because humans by nature are free, and they do not accept slavery and subjection for ever, as Ibn Khaldun argues.[13]

The important point here is that nomadology/nomadism is not strictly tied to conquest or violence, as Deleuze and Guattari theorize it. Nomadology/nomadism is about seeking refuge as well, as well as about creativity, and at its core is the ontology of a free human. After all, we are told again and again by Western thought that it is only 'natural' to be free as a human. Yet freedom and mobility have, since the rise and dominance of Western modernity, represented the privilege of some. In the case of Palestine, it is the settler who has the privilege of freedom of mobility, taking over the natural habitat of the native, while not only disrupting the natives' lives, but also rupturing the flow of movement and interconnectedness in the region and beyond. So what has disrupted this condition of being human – nomadology – is precisely Western modernity, racism, nation-states, colonialism and, acutely, settler-colonialism. One can conclude that it is the settler that has been the practitioner of violence, not the nomad.

It would have been more useful and original if Deleuze and Guattari had engaged the work of Ibn Khaldoun by taking into account this larger understanding of his concept of nomadology, and engage with its application to the modern state, especially the settler-colonial state, given his concept on the human nature of mobility, which for the modern state is an anomaly. In other words, if we follow Ibn Khaldoun's theory of human nature, the modern nation-state form goes against the grain of the human in restricting a constitutive element of human nature, that is, mobility. The settler-colonial state, in particular, has its own specific dynamic of rupture, which, as in Ibn Khaldoun's work, highlights the value of the insights offered by Sayegh into the Zionist colonization of Palestine. In the case of Palestine, the establishment of the Israeli settler-colonial state led to a shattering of the Palestinian community and its social organization as they existed prior to 1948, for it dismembered and detached pre-1948 Palestinian society from its Arab surroundings and beyond. Furthermore, through its wars against Arab states, Israel disarticulated the entire region that had for thousands of years been an important meeting point and a key node in the circulation of goods, humans, labour and ideas extending from Asia and Africa to the Mediterranean and beyond.

Furthermore, in this chapter, I also engage with Patrick Wolfe's concept of settler-colonialism as a structure rather than as an event. I argue that his argument is often misunderstood. It is often presented as a structure that is here to stay. But that is not how I understand it. I understand it as a way to theorize in the field of colonial settler studies compared to colonial studies. Colonialism comes to exploit resources and labour, not to displace people, and not rupture them as settler-colonial structures do. But that does not mean that settler-colonialism does not exploit local resources and labour. As Ross (2019) argues, the entire Israeli state was built by native Palestinians. One might say, it is the only settler-colonial state that was built by the labour of the natives. That is, in part, the Zionist Movement and the Jewish community had no little previous experience of construction or farming. Palestinians thus became the core labour force for the Israeli state in construction and farming. It is a tragic and a sad picture when natives, due to the necessity of survival, build the homes and work in the agricultural fields of the settlers. In this specific case, the settler is sustained by the native – a unique case of settler-colonialism.

One might also add to Veracini's (2011) work on settler-colonialism many points that were left out within the nature of settler colonialism, but also in restricting the comparison between colonialism and settler-colonialism. For example, one might also add an occupation to this theoretical definition. Occupation is short-lived. Among many examples is the German occupation of France during the Second World War. This was intended as a manoeuvre to win the larger war against the Allied Forces. All these (Occupation, colonialism, settler-colonialism) have things in common such as violence and destruction. While occupation is short-lived, colonization is a longer project, and settler-colonialism aims for an even longer period and has specific additional features that Veracini mentions, and there are more. If we make these comparisons, we might better understand Patrick Wolfe's concept of structure, which differs in nature and duration. However, connecting Wolfe with Ibn Khaldun, this should not mean that it is permanent. They will vanish sooner or later.

Finally, in this chapter, I bring in the insights of Frantz Fanon, whose insights into settler-colonialism and colonialism are often overlooked and not connected in studies of colonialism and settler-colonial studies. Fanon's insights have a lot in common with Sayegh, and with Ibn Khaldun. Sayegh's concept of rupture that I developed further to extend beyond the political, has a lot to do with Fanon's work on how settler colonialism also creates psychological rupture. That psychological rupture is also connected to ideas in Ibn Kaldun's work. Fanon's work drew much from his experience with French settler colonialism in Algeria. It talked about not only the political but also the social and cultural ruptures that French settler-colonialism created in Algeria. It is also connected to Ibn Khaldun on mimicry, the psychology of the oppressed.[14] Fanon further connects these ideas in his zero-sum game: it is either the settler or the native. I do not think that it is by accident that the Algerian solution to settler-colonialism (elimination of the settlers) is marginalized, if mentioned at all, in settler-colonial studies. Furthermore, his insights into the impact of colonization and settler-colonialism on the psychology of the native, which has much in common with Ibn Khaldun's idea on mimicry, is also absent. Thus, it is important to connect colonialism and settler-colonialism in many ways, one of which is the psychology of the oppressed. Long-term oppression creates a certain behaviour among the oppressed, which this chapter will briefly discuss, taking the Palestinian case as an example, and this connecting colonial and settler colonial studies, and what might people understand in post-colonial studies, which is better framed as neocolonial studies, because western colonialism never ended, it just took different forms of subjugation, exploitation, and violence. They all have in common the structures of rupture and connections.

As a way to illustrate my arguments in the following sections of this chapter, I will briefly clarify what I mean by mobility, connections and rupture in discussing the local, regional and global impact of Israeli settler-colonialism. Although the impact of global Israel is divided into three distinct categories, they share many connections.

Local ruptures: displacements and disconnections

A key point to note about local ruptures created by Israel is that the displacement of Palestinians started earlier than 1948, especially among farmers who used to live on lands they farmed and who became not only jobless but also homeless as a result of the waves of encroaching Zionist settlements in Palestine during the British colonial rule that began immediately after the First World War. This displacement happened in the context of the sale of lands to Jewish settlers by absentee Palestinian landowners, but more so due to policies of the British colonial government that took over common lands that existed during the Ottoman period and gave them to Jewish settlers. These common lands, or *masha'* in Arabic, were historically used by farmers who cultivated and lived on them, paying taxes to the Ottoman government.

Yet, the major event that led to mass displacement took place in 1948 when Zionist military groups who were fighting to establish the Israeli state drove out about 85 per cent of the Palestinian population from their lands, homes, villages, towns and cities. These Palestinians became refugees in areas outside of the control of the newly created Israeli state; in Gaza, the West Bank, neighbouring villages and towns within the state itself, and especially in neighbouring countries such as Lebanon, Syria, Jordan and

Egypt. This one-way exodus and forced mobility was, and remains, in contrast to the multi-way mobility on the part of the Israeli colonial settler regime and its privileged Jewish settlers. Israel allows and grants automatic entry to Jews from anywhere in the world and continues to prevent the return and entry of displaced and exiled natives. This Israeli Law of Return that privileges Jews is in contrast to the transfer of local native Palestinians, the denial of the right of return to Palestinian refugees, the restrictions on entry to Palestinians and the restrictions on family unification. While it is important to consider the question of class and gender in the way this displacement affected Palestinian society, the Zionist regime targeted the Palestinian population as a whole without any consideration of religious, social and economic distinctions within the targeted communities. Old, young, male, female, Muslim, Christian, rich and poor Palestinians faced the same fate. Yet, of course, each of these social and economic categories had an impact on the way displaced Palestinians fared after 1948.

This system or structure of displacement and restriction on mobility continued to take place and never stopped after 1948. Even after the war of 1948 ended, the Israeli military continued to push Palestinians out of their lands beyond the borders to neighbouring states, or within the borders of the state itself. Sometimes whole villages were emptied of their residents who sought refuge in nearby villages and towns, as happened in Iqrit and Kafr Bir'im in Galilee. People in these two Palestinian villages were asked to leave by the Israeli military on the pretext of 'caring for their safety', for the Israeli military claimed that it was fighting 'infiltrators' from the Lebanese borders and hence needed to evict those who lived in these two villages in order to clear the ground to fight those 'infiltrating' across the border. Even after this 'infiltration' ended, residents of these two villages have not been allowed to this date to return to their homes and continue to live as refugees in neighbouring villages and towns. Land confiscation and displacement targeting native Palestinians continue to take place from the north to the south of the country. At the same time, more land is given to Jewish settlements, and more Jews from around the world are brought in to take over land and resources.

Furthermore, several layers and forms of disconnection have taken place since 1948. Individuals from the neighbouring region who came to work in Palestinian cities like Haifa before the establishment of the rigid borders of the settler state, and who intermarried with locals, found themselves trapped. They could no longer travel back and forth across the region as they did before 1948 and they lost all connections to their families and friends in Lebanon and Syria. Those Palestinians who managed to remain on the land and became Israeli citizens over time became disconnected from Lebanon and Syria, with the severing of relationships through commerce and trade as well as historical and cultural ties. Many Palestinian families were dispersed and split as a result of the creation of the Israeli state. Those who were working in Lebanon or travelling in Lebanon and Syria around 1948 were never allowed to return. Some returned only as dead bodies after their families pleaded with the Israeli authorities to let them at least bury their relatives in the same family cemetery. Thus, their reunification with their families was only possible in death.

To this day, the Israeli state continues to issue different laws and regulations preventing its Palestinian citizens from intermarrying with Palestinians from Gaza, the

West Bank and elsewhere if they wish to remain citizens of the state, living on what remains of their land. The state thus has been active in disconnecting its Palestinian citizens from the rest of Palestinian society on many levels, including in the domains of emotions and desires. To fall in love with another Palestinian from elsewhere is something that must be carefully calculated for Palestinians inside Israel, because marriage could mean that one either has to leave family to live outside the borders of the Israeli state or have children who will live in legal limbo.

The same pattern of fragmentation and disconnection is taking place in Palestinian areas colonized by Israel in 1967 and more acutely in the last few decades. Those who live in Gaza find it almost impossible to have social relations with people who live in Galilee, Jerusalem or the West Bank due to the Israeli siege that has caged them into a narrow strip of land. The same is true for Palestinians who live in any of these other areas in relation to Gazans. Jerusalem is very close to Ramallah, yet it is incredibly difficult for two people living in each of these cities to fall in love and want to live together, because if they do, they cannot live in Jerusalem and would have to give up their legal right to live there. It is a huge problem for many Palestinians to just visit one another if they live in a different part of Palestine, for each area or Bantustan has a different legal status imposed on its residents by the Israeli settler-colonial state.

These policies of systematic dismembering of Palestinian society, disconnection from the natural environment and neighbouring states, forced removal/mobility and displacement, and depopulation is juxtaposed with the easy mobility afforded to Jewish settlers who can come from any corner of the world to live in Palestine and receive automatic citizenship and rights. They can fall in love and live with whomever they wish, marry freely, travel as they please, and in addition receive state grants, land and housing. Most have dual citizenship, so they can travel to all Arab countries, including places that native Palestinians used to visit and can no longer enter if they are Israeli citizens. They enlist in the Israeli military and different state security forces that enact different forms of repression and violence against Palestinians and Arabs. I argue that given these realities, the settlers are the true, violent nomads (as in Deleuze's definition), while the condition of the nomad/human, in the true sense of the word (as in Ibn Khaldoun's definition) has been wrested from the native Palestinians. What befell Palestinian society after 1948 has also had an impact on peoples living in neighbouring states, as I discuss next.

Regional ruptures

The rupture and fragmentation that devastated Palestinian society has also transformed and ruptured neighbouring societies in various ways. First, masses of Palestinian refugees suddenly descended on the adjacent countries and, in some cases, either outnumbered the local population, as in Jordan, or arrived in numbers that overwhelmed small states, such as Lebanon, with various social, political and economic ramifications. In both countries, the state entered into wars against the Palestinian refugees, whose political organization, the Palestinian Liberation Organization (PLO), attempted to fight the Israeli state in the hope of return to Palestine. Facing reprisals, invasions and wars by the settler-colonial state, the Jordanian state and powerful groups in Lebanon responded with violence against the PLO and the Palestinian refugees on several occasions, trying to survive next door to a powerful bully and aggressive military state supported by world powers and the global economic system.

Furthermore, due to the settler-colonial nature of the Israeli state, which by definition is a state with open frontiers, which never declared its official borders, the neighbouring states have experienced Israeli transgressions in different ways since 1948. In addition to the refugees that flooded these countries, they have faced wars, invasions, bombings and constant attacks. These waves of Israeli state violence have led to the occupation of neighbouring Arab lands, repression, destruction, and displacement of the populations living near the borders who moved away to avoid the death and destruction levelled against them by the Israeli military. To this day, Lebanese farmers who insisted on remaining on their lands that are near the border with Israel continue to face Israeli aggression, bombings, shelling and even kidnapping. But this was not the only impact, and I have not even mentioned Syrians who fell under Israeli occupation in the Golan Heights, nor discussed the impact on Egypt and Egyptian society; I have restricted the discussion mainly to Lebanon, and specifically around mobility, rupture and disconnections as a way to illustrate my argument about the regional impact of Israeli settler-colonialism.

The historical economic, social and cultural ties that connected people from around the region with Palestine were also ruptured as a result of the creation of Israel. The trade and commerce that linked the peoples in the region prior to 1948 was eroded, and the social ties that had existed since before 1948 were undermined. Cultural and religious ties that connected Christians and Muslims in the region with holy sites in Palestine were diminished. But this local and regional impact is not the end of the story and is in many ways linked to the global rupture.

Global ruptures

Palestine served for centuries as a crossroad between Asia, Africa, the Mediterranean and beyond. It was an important economic node as it lay on the trade route that merchants used to travel through Palestine to other destinations, bringing products from as far away as today's China and India to South Europe and further and linking regions and continents with social, economic and cultural flows and influences. That period of transnational migration and trade with all its flexible mobility ended in 1948. By waging war with Arab states and societies, Israel destroyed the historic route that linked all these locations and delinked these societies. Even when Israel tried to establish political and economic relations with states in Asia and Africa, as elsewhere, the main trade item it exported was its arms, technologies of surveillance, and expertise in repression. Israel is thus a key player in the global economy of violence and militarization.[15]

Palestine was also transformed from being an important cultural site for those who visited due to religious affiliations to a place that became inaccessible to many. While prior to 1948, anyone with the means to travel could visit religious sites in Palestine, after 1948 wealth became a non-factor in mobility and connections to the holy sites. The only factor that enabled travel was the nature of the diplomatic relations between the Israeli state and the state to which travellers belonged. Mobility for non-Palestinians wanting to visit Palestine became selective and restrictive for hundreds of millions of peoples around the world. This rupture was experienced not just by Arabs and Muslims but also by citizens of states that had no diplomatic relations with Israel after 1948 or cut their diplomatic relations in protest of Israeli aggression against Palestinians and Arabs. Many states who opposed Israeli participation in the 1956 invasion of Egypt severed their diplomatic relations at that time, and others did so in response to Israel's war against Arab states in 1967 and the colonization of the remainder of Palestine as well as areas in neighbouring Arab countries. The hopes of some and fantasies of others, of the possibilities and potential of the Oslo Accords signed by Israel and the PLO in 1993, ended very soon due to Israel's continuous settlements expansion and violence. To this day, with each Israeli invasion and war, more diplomatic ties with Israel are cut even by states as far away as Latin America, as during the 2014 invasion of Gaza. For states that re-established relations with Israel after Oslo, these ties remained based on security and intelligence cooperation and are mostly one-way circuits between countries in which Israeli arms, 'counterterrorism' techniques and surveillance are exported to these places, that is, technologies of death. Israeli tourists, many of whom flock annually to retreats in places such as India after ending their compulsory military service, use these locations in Asia as a therapeutic escape from their violent experiences as soldiers of a colonizing military force, involved in war after war, and in a constant state of repression of native Palestinians, and from a militarized and racist society. There is much more to be said here about the ways in which these flows of arms and tourists resituate Israel and Israeli culture in Asia, as a region that is Orientalized by many Israelis as a mystical and spiritual place, and how other societies are being Israelized, contributing to other kinds of ruptures of ties with Palestine as global Israel is consolidated in faraway locations.

These economic and cultural ruptures also have layered social dimensions. Due to the history of trade and cultural/religious tourism, Palestinian society was enriched by intermarriage with pilgrims and traders and was made ethnically and racially diverse as a result of migration. Older patterns of migration and mobility brought peoples from all around the world, reflected in the racial and phenotypic diversity and names common in Palestine; for example, Hindi for those whose ancestors hailed from India, Irani from Iran, Armani from Armenia, Turki from Turkey, Qatalani from Catalonia, Yanni from Greece, or Afghani from Afghanistan. There are many other examples of these histories of migrants/mobile subjects who came to live among the Palestinians, which ended in 1948. The genuine, more 'human' nomadology has been replaced since then by the mobility of settlers and those who claim to be Jews and can enter the lands and further displace the local, native Palestinians.

While Israeli settlers, many with dual citizenship, roam around the globe with relative ease, travellers to Israel-Palestine are profiled, interrogated and detained at Israeli borders, according to their Arab or Muslim-sounding names, in addition to their political allegiances and involvement. Individuals suspected of being in solidarity with the native Palestinians are always either harassed and detained at entry points or denied entry and deported. Even those who are allowed to enter are monitored and questioned before their departure by Israeli intelligence and authorities at the airport about the places they visited and the people they met, as a part of the Israeli strategy to restrict mixing and connecting with the native Palestinian community and exposure to the realities on the ground in Palestine. Of course, Palestinians who try to travel across Israeli borders are routinely subjected to this kind of treatment and much worse.

Thus, settler-colonialism in Palestine not only commands major attention around the globe, and the investment of resources from so many states around the world concerned with this issue one way or the other, but it also creates ruptures for those who feel solidarity with the Palestinian cause and the native Palestinians. One example of such rupture is the question of the Palestinian-led Boycott, Divestment and Sanctions movement and the growing movement for an academic boycott of Israeli institutions. For example, in the United States academics can exercise their right to freedom of expression in their intellectual work and can be publicly critical of any society and any state, including the United States itself, without any repercussions in general. However, the slightest criticism of Israel and Israeli society is faced with wholesale attacks, charges of anti-Semitism, and censorship. Academics who display a strong attachment to and solidarity with the Palestinians or express a public critique of the Israeli state can be blocked from getting an academic job or can lose their employment. At the least, they are often defamed, harassed and disciplined.

The recent case of Steven Salaita is one such example of censure and penalization for pro-Palestine speech and boycott activism. Salaita, who is a well-known Palestinian American scholar attempted[16] to link a similar dynamic of settler-colonialism both in the United States and in Israel, accepted and signed a job offer as a tenured professor from the University of Illinois at Urbana Champaign resigning from his position as an associate professor at Virginia Tech. But due to his critical scholarly work and vocal criticism of the Israeli state, especially during the 2014 invasion of Gaza, in his publications and media engagements, including social media, and his advocacy of the academic boycott, he was fired from his job, in effect, and left unemployed. After selling his house in Virginia, he and his wife and their child lived temporarily with his parents. Salaita and his family were forced to live in limbo just because of his strong critique of the racist and violent policies of the Israeli state. Similar patterns of rupture of scholars' lives due to their solidarity with Palestine take place in many other countries in Europe, Australia, Canada and elsewhere. Salaita's case is a good one to end this part with, as it demonstrates the working of many Zionist groups in repressing critics, and connects the three parts of the impact of settler-colonialism in Palestine.

Although there are many examples of academic censure and repression similar to the case of Salaita, his story illustrates the harsh consequences of the rupture created by the creation of the Israeli settler-colonial state. His personal story connects the local, the regional, and the global in an interesting way. He was born to a Palestinian family that was displaced by the creation of the Israeli settler-colonial state, becoming refugees who scattered all around the world, to Jordan, the United States and Latin America. His own connection to Palestine and its people was ruptured; his ability to travel to Palestine was restricted by the Israeli authorities; and his academic work was shaped by his roots in Palestine and his experience as an immigrant in the US, another settler-colonial state. Notably, Salaita's scholarship has always connected these two settler colonies and their indigenous peoples in a critical way. His writing expresses a form of attachment and connection to Palestine and caused him a further rupture of his life in the US. Now, Salaita's own move to another location to work at another university in the US and his own professional mobility has been disrupted. Salaita, like many others, drew the vengeful wrath of those who blindly support the Israeli state and who do not tolerate bold criticism of its policies. But his case also provoked an outpouring of support across the nation among those who felt solidarity and empathy for his fate and his intellectual and political work, sparking a vigorous campaign. Energies and resources are spent by both the Global Israel and the Global Palestine solidarity campaigns; one wishes to make the rupture in his life and his family life a permanent one, the other is mobilizing to bring back normalcy to his and his family life, and to highlight the assault on academic freedom.

Settler colonialism and its psychological impact

One aspect that is common between neocolonialism, colonialism and settler-colonialism is the question of the psychological impact of both on the colonized. Here, I aim to briefly connect these fields and connect Ibn Khaldun with Fanon. Fanon wrote about the non-Whites in France and Arabs in Algeria under the French settler-colonial structure, and Ibn Khaldun wrote about this issue in general or one might argue within each system; that is, the less empowered or the marginalized engages in mimicry of the dominant group. Both scholars spoke about how the oppressed, the dominated, or the colonized, due to the feeling of inferiority, engage in mimicry of the colonizer. Both scholars have written on how the subjugated try to fit in the hegemonic structure. Both wrote about how subjugated people think that their defeat, their subjugation, was due to the supremacy of the colonizers and the culture of the colonizer. Even though they did not call it such, and the world was not as globalized as it is today, it is, in essence, trying to fit into White supremacy. The global system has been especially so since the 1990s, a unilateral one dominated by the US and the West in general. People in the non-West want to be as White as possible so that White structure allows them entry into their system. Of course, that mimicry is always a bad copy of the original sick version, as Fanon argues. But in my view, it goes further. Those colonized who try to imitate the colonizer, the West in this case , rupture their connections to their local culture and reality, and by doing so they also open a space for further ruptures within their own communities. In their attempt to connect with the colonizers, in addition to the fact that the colonizers never accept nor respect these attempts, they further help in colonizing their communities. If Africans try to fit into the White system in France or the US, or if Arabs try to fit into the White system in France or the US, or Israel, not only do they never manage to do so, they further help deepen the sense of inferiority. This is especially so when the political, economic, social and cultural elites do so for the influence they have on the larger community.

Furthermore, in the settler-colonial structure it is impossible to understand any issue within the colonized subjugated communities without thinking about the psychological sense of inferiority. For example, when writing about the subjugated and the colonized, we need to think of two issues. One issue is the structure and its impact on them. Another is the local factors that feed into it. Violence within the Palestinian community cannot be understood without understanding the structure; the role of the state in promoting and condoning violence within the native community.[17] But that is not enough to explain what is taking place. The sense of inferiority also makes Palestinians direct their violence against one another. They know well that the state will not allow violence toward the Jews, the colonizers or the settlers.

It is not just in violence that the colonized are impacted in the way they conduct their lives economically, politically and culturally. There are also other issues that we can think of about the impact of colonialism and settler colonialism on the Native population and dominated groups' daily life and behavior. Doing so will help us in connecting fields such as colonial studies, settler colonial studies, and Palestinian studies and can help in healing ruptures that some are old but others that are the product of Western modernity.

Fanon wrote about the need to not mimic the sick, racist and violent West, not to try to fit into its economic, political and social structure, but to destroy it, and to work on creating a new society, a new economic system, a new political system, and help create a new humanity. In the colonial structure, Fanon argued this must come not by mimicry nor by clinging to the past, and the change cannot come from the polluted elites. It must come from the common people, and it will come through the constant work and struggle of the masses.

Ibn Khaldun wrote about the need to create a common Asabiyya, a common group feeling based on economic, political and social justice. In the globalized world of our time, the imperial, colonial, neocolonial, racist, neoliberal world system, our response is to create a new Asabiyya, a new world that doesn't aim at clinging to the past nor at mimicking the current system.

Conclusion

This chapter is to be seen as an exploration of an approach that aims at reframing and rethinking the question of Israel/Palestine. The Israeli settler-colonial case sets itself apart from all other settler-colonial cases by its local, regional and global impact. Mobility, connections, exchanges and normal life of the nomad/human have been since 1948 in constant trials and upheaval. The dominant form of mobility/nomadology that has taken place since then is the violent and repressive one, that of the settler. Hence, the claims that modernity brought ease in mobility and that Israel represents western modernity in the Orient, while pre-modern times are represented as restricting mobility, can be seen as false in this light.

As Collins (2011) argues in *Global Palestine*, Palestine can serve and has been serving several global questions and concerns and thus global solidarity for millions of people around the globe who are connected with needs that are normal or natural to every human being; the right to education, to health, to life, access to water, employment, and mobility which is central to all. *Global Israel*, on the other hand, is the other side of that coin, and it is a structure that ruptures mobility, normalcy and many basic needs and aspirations of peoples around the world.

The more dominant form of mobility since 1948 and as a result of the creation of the Israeli settler-colonial state that must be seen as a part of the global dominant West is the mobility of the settler with its borders of violence and repression, arms trade and technologies of surveillance and militarization that shape Israeli mobility locally, regionally and globally, accompanied by forced mobility and restrictions on mobility for the native Palestinians, as well as restrictions on mobility for peoples in the region and around the world who are deemed unwanted by the Israeli state and the Western-dominated global system.

Notes

1 Maira & Shihade 2012.
2 Sayegh 1965: v, 16, 17, 51.
3 Ibid.
4 Shihade 2015b.
5 Shihade 2015a.
6 Deleuze and Guattari 1986: 26, 27, with notes on p. 128.
7 Ibid.: 14, 17.
8 Ibid.: 15–17.
9 Ibn Khaldoun 2005: 309–17, 320–1.
10 Ibid.: 265, 270, 278, 285–7, 290.
11 Ibid.: 298.
12 Ibid.: 265, 270, 278, 285–7, 298, 342–3, 429, 456.
13 Shihade 2015b.
14 Fanon [1952] 1967.
15 International Jewish Anti-Zionist Network (IJAN) 2012.
16 Salaita 2006.
17 Shihade 2011.

References

Collins, J. (2011), *Global Palestine*, London: Hurst & Co.
Deleuze, G., and F. Guattari (1986), *Nomadology: The War Machine*, trans. B. Massumi, New York: Columbia University Press.
Fanon, F. ([1952] 1967), *Black skin, White masks* ed. C. L. Markmann, London: Pluto Books.
Fanon, F. (1968), *The Wretched of the Earth*, New York: Grove Press.
Ibn Khaldoun, M. (2005), *Al-Muqaddimah: An Introduction to History*, trans. F. Rosenthal, ed. and abridged by N. J. Dawood, Princeton: Princeton University Press.
International Jewish Anti-Zionist Network (IJAN) (2012), 'Israeli Worldwide Role in Repression', https://israelglobalrepression.files.wordpress.com/2012/12/israels-worldwide-role-in-repression-footnotes-finalized.pdf (accessed 24 April 2015)

Maira, S. and M. Shihade (2012), '"Hip-Hop from" 48: Youth Music, and the Present/Absent', *Social Text* 30 (3112): 1–26.
Mignolo, W. (2000), *Local Histories/Global Designs: Coloniality, Subaltern Knowledges, and Border Thinking*, Princeton: Princeton University Press.
Ross, A. (2019), *Stone Men: The Palestinians who built Israel*, London: Verso.
Salaita, S. (2006), *Holy Land in Transit: Colonialism and the Quest for Canaan*, Syracuse, NY: Syracuse University Press.
Sayegh, F. (1965), *The Zionist Colonization of Palestine*, Beirut: Institute of Palestine Studies.
Shihade, M. (2011), *Not Just a Soccer Game: Colonialism and Conflict among Palestinians in Israel*, Syracuse, NY: Syracuse University Press.
Shihade, M. (2015a), 'Global Israel: Settler, Native, Mobility, and Rupture', *Borderlands* 14 (1), http://www.borderlands.net.au/vol14no1_2015/shihade_israel.pdf
Shihade, M. (2015b), 'Not Just A Picnic: Settler Colonialism, Mobility, and Identity among Palestinians in Israel', *Biography* 37 (2): 77–99.
Shihade, M. (2015c), 'The Place of Israel in Asia: Settler Colonialism, Mobility and Rupture', *Settler Colonial Studies* 13 April, http://www.tandfonline.com/doi/abs/10.1080/2201473X.2015.1024379#.VTK1DyFVikohihade (accessed 24 April 2015)
Tilly, C. (1985), 'War Making and State Making as Organized Crime' in P. Evans, D. Rueschemeyer & T. Skocpol (eds), *Bringing the State Back*, Cambridge: Cambridge University Press.
Veracini, L. (2011), 'Introducing: Settler colonial studies"' *Settler colonial studies* 1 (1): 1–12.
Wolfe, P. (2006), 'Settler Colonialism and the Elimination of the Native', *Journal of Genocide Research* 8 (4): 387–409, DOI: 10.1080/14623520601056240
Young, A, (2015), 'The Settler Unchained: Constituent Power and Settler Violence', *Social Text* 33 (3 (124)): 1–18.

11

Popular Resistance in Palestine

Marwan Darweish

Introduction

The chapter will trace the thread of Palestinian unarmed resistance to Zionist colonization. Its first section will highlight resistance to the Jewish immigration to Palestine that took place under the Ottoman and British Mandate until 1948. The second section will discuss Palestinian resistance in the 1948–87 period and explore the everyday resistance of Palestinians in Israel to the military rule imposed on them after 1948 and up to Land Day in 1976; it will also examine the resistance in the West Bank and Gaza Strip that led to the first Palestinian intifada in December 1987. The chapter will then discuss the re-emergence of unarmed popular resistance to the apartheid Separation Wall. The last section will highlight grounds for hope arising from the increased involvement of international grass-roots solidarity movements with the Palestinians, inspired by recent events in Jerusalem.

The chapter is informed by a body of literature on civil resistance to tyranny and injustice which emphasizes that civil resistance as a mode of challenging oppression relies predominantly on the sustained use of nonviolent, unarmed, or non-military methods in pursuit of aims widely shared in society.[1] There has been a surge in publications about civil resistance in the last decade; however, much of this work draws on the original contributions of Gene Sharp, whose works (1973, 1980 and 2005) remain pivotal. Chenoweth and Stephan (2011) won attention for their additional claim that nonviolent forms of resistance to oppressive regimes are more likely to succeed than armed struggle due to their high levels of participation. Yet, most of the studies on unarmed civil resistance have focused on authoritarian domestic regimes, and research focused on colonisation and occupation has been limited. Sémelin contributed a crucial insight when he noted that the aim of unarmed resistance to Nazi occupation was never to defeat the occupier by nonviolent struggle but to deny the occupier's claims to legitimacy and 'find the strength to say NO'; in Sémelin's terms, the act of resistance to occupation is therefore an 'affirmation of the superiority of the de jure authority over the de facto one'.[2] Rings' (1982) study of civilian resistance to, and cooperation with, the occupier has informed this study's decision to categorize types of resistance to occupation and colonisation.

The basic assumption informing most studies of nonviolent civil resistance in pursuit of social political change is that all forms of domination are dependent on various sources of support to maintain the asymmetry of power, including the cooperation, willingly or by force, of sectors of the oppressed society. Repressive regimes depend not only on fear, intimidation and the coercive power of the state and military but also on the obedience of civilians and their preparedness to maintain the regime by contributing different forms of revenue.[3]

It is important to understand and identify the key pillars of support that function, externally and internally, to maintain the regime in power and then explore ways in which these pillars might be undermined and eroded to exercise leverage and change power relations.[4] Some scholars have emphasized the significance of strategies that raise the costs arising for the regime as a result of its oppressive policies and actions. These costs can be economic and political, but what Galtung calls 'shame power' is also significant as it can reduce the oppressor's moral legitimacy in the eyes of internal and external actors.[5] (Martin 2007). Galtung also developed the concept of a 'chain of nonviolence' to refer to the process whereby civil resistance, without being able to impact the oppressive regime directly, can sometimes forge links with others who can, in turn, influence the power structures that are being challenged.

Sharp's (2005) work and Rings' (1982) study of civilian resistance to occupation inform the framework for types of nonviolent action set out here, which will be used throughout this chapter:

1. Symbolic resistance: 'We remain who we are and communicate to others, by means of gestures, actions and dress, our continued allegiance to our cause and its values'.
2. Polemical resistance: 'We oppose the occupier by voicing protest and trying to encourage others of the need to maintain the struggle'.
3. Offensive resistance: 'We are prepared to do all that we can to frustrate and overcome the oppressor by nonviolent means, including carrying out strikes, demonstrations and other forms of direct action'.
4. Defensive resistance: 'We aid and protect those in danger and preserve human beings and values endangered by the occupier'.
5. Constructive resistance: 'We challenge the existing imposed order by seeking to create alternative institutions that embody our values'.

Palestinian resistance to the establishment of the Israeli state

This section traces the thread of Palestinian unarmed resistance against colonialism and the expropriation of Palestinians' land and the threat to their livelihoods posed by Jewish migration prior to the establishment of the state of Israel. What becomes clear is that the struggle against the Zionist project from the late nineteenth century to the middle of the twentieth century was dogged right from the start by factionalism and division that reflected, in part, the fractured nature of Palestinian society.

The Jewish migration to Palestine that occurred in order to establish a homeland commenced in the 1880s, at which time the Jewish community in Palestine numbered around 24,000 (five per cent of an estimated population of 500,000). By the end of the second wave of Zionist immigration in 1914, the Jewish population had risen to 85,000 and, as early as 1886, there were reports of clashes between Jewish settlers and the peasants evicted from their land.[6]

By the end of the Ottoman period of rule, a pattern of protest had formed. The traditional land-owning families saw Zionism as a threat to their position and responded by appealing to the Ottoman authorities to act as intermediaries. The more polemical forms of protest (newspaper articles, leaflets etc.) were the domain of the middle-class professionals, with journalists and students being particularly vocal in their opposition. The more directly confrontational modes of protest aimed at disrupting the territorial acquisitions of the incomers were primarily used by the direct victims of Zionist land purchases – the peasantry.[7] Kayyali summarized the situation prior to the establishment of British military rule in Palestine in 1917 effectively when he noted that 'within the ranks of the nationalist movement in Palestine, the notables performed the role of the diplomats; the educated middle classes that of the articulators of public opinion; and the peasants that of the actual fighters in the battle against the Zionist presence'.[8]

In November 1917, the British government affirmed in the Balfour Declaration its support for the establishment of a homeland for the Jews in Palestine, provided that nothing should be done to prejudice 'the civil and religious rights of existing non-Jewish communities in Palestine'.[9] When news of the declaration reached the Palestinians, it prompted a new awareness of the need to organize. A Muslim–Christian Association (MCA) was established with branches around the country to counter similar Jewish organizations, and a national day of protest to mark the declaration's first anniversary was held on 2 November 1918.[10]

A number of salient features characterize the first decade of British rule in Palestine when it is examined through the prism of unarmed resistance and mobilization:

'Spontaneous' clashes between peasantry and Jewish settlers

For the peasantry who experienced eviction through Jewish land purchases, the immediate response was anger and resentment that sometimes led to clashes with those directly responsible for their dispossession; but these clashes were localized, and at no point were there serious attempts to create a nationwide movement of active resistance based on the peasantry.

The absence of a coherent national leadership

The main reasons for the failure to develop a truly active national movement were twofold. First, the world-view of the peasantry was localized. They had no experience of coordinating collective action beyond their own villages. Secondly, there was no 'national leadership' to direct them along such a path. A major fracture between two of the most notable and influential Jerusalem-based families, the Husaynis and the Nashashibis, militated against the emergence of a unified leadership. Furthermore, the urban political elite and the peasantry occupied completely different social spheres: 'Not only did the indigenous ruling class have no experience of mass leadership, but the individual notable would never attempt such a course since it would only jeopardise his access to government'.[11]

The commitment to negotiation

Throughout the Mandate period, the main impulse of the Palestinian political elite was to continue in the role they had traditionally performed under the Ottomans, representing only their own interests to the authorities.

The prevalence of symbolic and polemical resistance

In the absence of any national-level popular movement of unarmed resistance, a plenitude of dispersed but collective forms of symbolic and polemical protest emerged. Regular items in the press urged people to oppose Zionists, imams spread the message in mosques at Friday prayers and strike days were observed to mark the anniversary of the Balfour Declaration and commemorate other days of national significance.

The timidity of the Palestinian political elite

In 1922, the British announced plans to establish a legislative council with very limited powers. At a congress held in Nablus in August 1922, it was resolved to boycott the upcoming elections. The boycott was effective and the legislative council never met. However, when, in the spring of 1923, it was proposed that further leverage should be exerted by withholding tax payments, land-owners rejected the move, fearing punitive British fines.

Religion helped to generate resistance

Religious tensions were on the rise in the run-up to 1928, as the Jews sought to extend their control and worship at Al-Buraq, adjacent to the al-Haram al Sharif. Reports abounded that the Jews had designs on the space and had erected a partition. On 15 August 1929 the presence of Zionist extremists at the Western Wall provoked a counter-demonstration by Palestinians, and Palestinian leaders mobilized people around the perceived threat to one of their most sacred spaces. On the following Friday, 23 August 1929, worshippers emerging from Al-Aqsa mosque clashed with Jews in the Old City, and 133 Jews and 116 Arabs were killed and over 500 wounded.[12] The violence spread, and, by the next day, 67 Jews had been killed in Hebron, despite the efforts of many Palestinian families who opened their homes to shelter Jewish residents.[13]

1930–36: from unrest to the first Palestinian uprising

The harsh measures meted out by the British, which included collective punishments for whole villages and neighbourhoods, fuelled bitterness and strengthened the hand of those calling for armed resistance. Tensions continued to rise throughout the

1930s, as a worsening economic situation and the suffering of the Palestinians was exacerbated by further increases in Jewish immigration and the Jewish boycott of Arab labour. Clashes between Palestinians and Jews grew in frequency and seriousness, and on 20 April 1936 the call went out for a national strike. To enhance its coordination, an Arab Higher Committee (AHC) was formed, headed by Haj Amin Husayni. This was the start of the first Palestinian Uprising which lasted from 1936 to 1939.

The uprising had two phases. In the first period, which lasted for six months from April to October 1936, unarmed forms of resistance including protest marches and demonstrations, strikes and boycotts and non-cooperation and civil disobedience were dominant. These activities were complemented by attempts to involve wider constituencies of support from neighbouring Arab countries. By July, the Nablus district was in full revolt, with Nablus at its centre. Matters were far beyond the control of the nominal Palestinian political leadership, which was coming under increasing pressure from citrus-growers to end the strike so that their harvest could be gathered.[14] It was agreed that, if the Arab leaders issued an appeal to end the strike, then their wishes would be followed. When the appeal was made on 10 October 1936, the AHC called for the strike to end that same day.

Following the strike's cessation, the British appointed a Commission of Inquiry led by Lord Peel and proposed partition, which was rejected out of hand by the AHC. This marked the outbreak of the uprising's second phase. A protest strike was called, and by mid-October armed groups were roaming the countryside attacking Jewish settlements and cutting communication lines.

An examination of the key factors that led to the collapse of the uprising reveals persistent and fundamental weaknesses that have continued to undermine the Palestinian struggle:

1. The notable families in Palestine had vested interests and so, as the revolt intensified, their paramount aim became to defend their property, wealth, status and influence. They prioritized the protection of their personal and family interests above those of the nation.
2. To a significant degree, the dominant political class that comprised the Palestinian leadership believed it was imperative to maintain good relations with the authorities, so that they might exercise their powers of persuasion at negotiating tables. Again and again, representations were made to the British, delegations sent to London and memoranda scripted. The Palestinian elites failed to grasp the absolute commitment of the British to the Zionist project of establishing a Jewish national home in Palestine.
3. The economic impact of the general strike was limited in part because there was a whole sector of society (the Jewish community) that continually worked to provide for the basic needs of the Jewish sector. The real suffering was borne by the strikers themselves.
4. The Palestinians were unable to rectify the severe asymmetries that limited their social and political leverage. Their appeals for interventions from Arab and Muslim leaders beyond Palestine fell on deaf ears.

5. Suppression of the revolt was brutal and extreme, and the British authorities ensured that Palestinians paid a high price for the revolt.

During the partition period, members of the AHC were in exile or jail, and the members of local-level cadres who were not in prison were exhausted and demoralized. The Zionists channelled Jewish refugees from Europe to Palestine in order to create 'facts on the ground' and prove the necessity of a Jewish homeland. On 25 February 1947, the British announced they were handing over responsibility for Palestine to the UN, which later created the Special Committee on Palestine (UNSCOP) to carry out its enquiries. UNSCOP was boycotted by the Arab League to which the enfeebled AHC had handed over its negotiating rights, and on 2 November the UN General Assembly passed Resolution 181 in favour of partition. By the end of 1948, the Nakba for the Palestinians was total: more than 400 villages had been destroyed; around 90 per cent of the Palestinian population had been displaced and dispossessed; and the social, economic and political fabric of their society had been destroyed.[15] In the new state of Israel, all immigration restrictions were lifted for Jews, who flooded in and occupied the land and properties of the indigenous Palestinians. When we review this period of partition, it seems as if the fate of the Palestinians had moved out of their hands. Bigger forces were at play, as the British and the United Nations allied with a vigorous and driven Zionist movement, granting legitimacy to its colonialist goal of creating a Jewish state.

Palestinian resistance: 1948–87

Zureik (2016), in his analysis of Israel's colonial project in Palestine, argues that its foundation is based on dispossession of the indigenous population through violence, repressive state laws and practices, and racial forms of monitoring. He demonstrates that territoriality determines individual (im)mobility and access to land, while economic viability highlights how territoriality and biopolitics intersect at various levels to advance the state's racial agenda.

Between the Nakba and the establishment of the Palestine Liberation Organization (PLO) in 1964, there was virtually no significant manifestation of organized public Palestinian resistance of any sort, and most of the forms of resistance they expressed were quiet and hidden in their nature for reasons that are not hard to find:

1. Colonialism, dispossession and division. Palestinian society had been devastated and fragmented by the Nakba.
2. The trauma of loss. Whilst they were scattered and separated from each other, Palestinians were also disempowered by the deep trauma and shock suffered by those with a deep attachment to place who found themselves uprooted, no longer a majority in their own homeland but relegated to minority and subordinate status.
3. The priority of economic survival. For most Palestinians reduced to poverty and subordination, the priority was survival and particularly economic survival.

Palestinians in Israel: quiet forms of resistance

After the establishment of the state of Israel, about 160,000 Palestinians remained within the borders of the newly established settler-colonial state living as an alien group. Zureik (1979) used the theory of internal colonialism to show how Israel destroyed Palestinians' socio-economic institutions and their way of life and subjected them to direct military control and surveillance for almost two decades. In many ways, Palestinians became a 'forgotten people', but it would be wrong to view them as mere passive victims of fate during those first decades of life in the new state. They engaged initially in quiet forms of resistance to preserve whatever autonomy they could find as they strove to survive in the face of the harsh living conditions that accompanied their displacement and dispossession.[16]

In many ways, the Palestinians in Israel in the years immediately following the Nakba could be described, to use Bayat's phrase, as a 'social non-movement' conducting the 'collective actions of non-collective actors'.[17] Activities that constituted types of 'quiet resistance' were undertaken by individuals and their families rather than by unified groups. However, some limited direct collective action was organized against military rule and in support of the pan-Arab movement[18] and it manifested itself in the following forms:

Determination to stay in their homeland

The destruction of hundreds of entire villages and the accompanying infrastructure resulted in a humanitarian crisis, and perhaps the 'quietest' form of resistance found expression in the determination and resilience of the Palestinians to stay in their homeland, whatever suffering they incurred.[19]

Resistance through cultivation

Large areas of land were confiscated or designated as closed military areas to which Palestinian entry was restricted, but local people found ways to circumvent these restrictions in order to cultivate their crops.

Culture, identity and resistance

Palestinians in Israel utilised various forms of symbolic resistance to the occupation aimed at preserving their culture and identity. For example, in 1949, the village of Umm al-Fahim was handed over to Israel by the Jordanian forces and the residents were instructed to celebrate the arrival of the Israeli army with singing and dancing. To express their resistance and defiance, older women made their faces black with charcoal and sang songs expressing their sorrow and anger rather than joy. This was an early instance of Palestinians in Israel expressing their opposition to Israeli military rule through songs and other cultural forms of resistance, and it indicates that Arab and Palestinian culture became a means to highlight national identity.[20]

Resistance to restrictions on movement

Israeli authorities imposed curfews and other measures to control the movement of Arab residents, and the targets of these measures explored ways to bypass these controls.

The PLO

In 1950, Cairo student Yasser Arafat set up a 'Union of Palestinian Students' with some friends. A short while later in Beirut, a medical student, George Habash, set up another student group known as the 'Arab National Movement'. Grass-roots organizations were also being established in the Gaza Strip, and by the mid-1950s a network of nationalist organizations was beginning to emerge. The main resistance organization, Fatah, grew out of this network to become the dominant force within the PLO, which was formed in 1964. In 1967, the occupation of the West Bank and Gaza rang the death-knell of Palestinian faith in pan-Arabism as a vehicle for liberation, and this boosted the fortunes of Fatah, which then became the prime agency of the Palestinian national movement.

Looking back on the period prior to the first intifada through the lens of unarmed popular resistance, a number of features can be highlighted:

The glorification of armed struggle

It was with the rise of Fatah and the PLO that the iconic figure of the Palestinian fighter with a Kalashnikov rifle became established as a symbol of Palestinian resistance that would hold sway in subsequent decades. A Palestinian state was to be achieved through 'armed struggle'.

Palestinians as victims

Palestinian history was presented as a narrative of heroic struggle undertaken against Zionism and by a people betrayed by traditional leaders and perfidious Arab states, a world-view which situated the asymmetrical power relationship between Israelis and Palestinians as the grounds for absolving Palestinians from responsibility for their failures.

The portrayal of defeat as triumph

Khalidi (1997) has pointed to a related peculiarity of the Palestinian experience: the manner in which failures came to be portrayed as victories or at least as examples of heroic perseverance against impossible odds.

Shifts in the Palestinian political centre of gravity

During the years when the PLO, and Fatah in particular, was a burgeoning force, the Palestinian political centre of gravity shifted. After 1967, this centre moved from

Palestine to the refugee camps in Jordan, and after 1970 it shifted to Lebanon. The PLO saw refugees as potential recruits for the armed liberation struggle, and its focus on the refugees distanced the organization from the Palestinians in the occupied territories, a separation heightened by the communication problems that worsened after the 1967 war and the ensuing Israeli occupation.

Palestinians in Israel: From quiet resistance to audible protest

By the early 1960s, Palestinians in Israel had started to move on from quiet and, to a large extent, hidden forms of resistance to more audible and open forms of protest. Sa'di, in his forensic study of the genesis of Israeli policies during this period, argues that the purpose of military rule was to maintain political and security control and social segregation of the Arab community in Israel.[21] Zureik (2016) further highlighted the relationship between colonialism and biopolitics as key to governance, demonstrating the importance of territory in the operation of surveillance and control.

The Israeli Communist Party (ICP), predominantly comprised of Palestinian members, was a key vehicle for early campaigns against the restrictions and discriminatory practices imposed on the Arab population within Israel. As such, the ICP and the *Al Arad* movement played important roles, not only in the struggle for full equality for the Arab minority, but also in the maintenance of an Arab national identity, and consequently they became the political home of leading Arab intellectuals, writers and poets.

The occupation of the West Bank and Gaza Strip had the paradoxical effect of uniting Palestinians from both sides of the Green Line after years of separation. It enabled Palestinians in Israel to renew family relations and commercial links that had been severed since 1948, but this new situation also exposed Palestinians in Israel to the Palestinian national movement and its PLO-led struggle in the occupied Palestinian territory. This so-called 'reunification' led to growing recognition of Palestinians' shared history, as well as to a burgeoning consciousness of the Palestinian national identity they held in common.[22] During the 1970s, Palestinians in Israel witnessed the emergence of new movements and civil society organizations which sought to articulate and represent their interests. One of the many groups that emerged was the National Committee for the Defence of Arab Lands (NCDAL) which was formed in 1975 as a coalition of various political groupings and community-based organizations in an effort to oppose land confiscations by the state. The NCDAL called for the first national strike by Palestinians in Israel on 'Land Day' on 30 March 1976, during which six protesters were killed by the Israeli police.[23] After years of military rule and relatively quiet resistance, Land Day represented the first act of mass, organized civil resistance by the Palestinians inside Israel.

After years during which Palestinians had been effectively ostracised by the PLO leadership and Arab states, the Land Day protests marked a significant acknowledgement that the Palestinians within Israel were part of the Palestinian nation. Their acts of hidden, uncoordinated and quiet resistance against military rule and oppression had been transformed into new forms of open, widespread, organized and nonviolent resistance that Israel, the PLO and the Arab states could no longer ignore.

Palestinians in the occupied territories prior to the first intifada

The message these developments embodied for the Palestinians in the occupied territories became clear: stay steadfast and eventually you will be liberated as a consequence of the pressure generated by the PLO and its external allies. In truth, their own allotted role was a passive one. The space available for organizing any form of collective resistance to the occupation was severely circumscribed, and any signs of opposition to the occupation were met with severe repression by Israel.

The emergence of any coordinated leadership that could organize resistance to the occupation within the Palestinian territories was hampered by the Israeli tactic of deporting any suspected resistance leaders, but it was also exacerbated by the PLO leadership's suspicion of any potential rivals to its own authority emerging in that space. Denied the opportunity to express themselves through any overtly political organization, activists within the occupied territories established other vehicles for education and mobilization. Student and professional associations, trade unions, women's societies, social and cultural associations and other grass-roots organizations were formed that served as agencies for both offensive and constructive resistance, organizing and mobilizing the people whilst also providing the basic services that were not provided by the Israeli occupiers. Consequently, these grass-roots organizations gained the allegiance of the majority of the Palestinian population and came to constitute the nucleus of an alternative structure of authority and power to rival that of the Israeli military government. In 1987, the Palestinian Communist Party was finally admitted into the ranks of the PLO. This display of unity provided the necessary basis for the kinds of coordination and cooperation between different nationalist factions within the occupied territories that became manifest with the outbreak of the first intifada.

The first intifada: December 1987–October 1991

When considering the first intifada through the lens of popular unarmed resistance and mobilization, it is useful to distinguish between two phases – the first from late 1987 through to early1990 and the second from mid-1990 to the Madrid Peace Conference of October 1991.

Phase one (December 1987–1990) – the struggle's horizontal escalation

The outbreak of the uprising came as a surprise to the leadership of the PLO in their headquarters in Tunis, and they were even more surprised by its scale and its coordinated nature, which had been enabled through the creation of a Unified National Command (UNC) that represented the different political factions. This clandestine body attempted to coordinate resistance through regular communiqués and leaflets. The UNC was supported by an organizational infrastructure of popular committees in villages, towns and refugee camps, and together they took on the character of an embryonic state, coordinating activities and administering the provision of basic services. In the months following the outbreak of the intifada, this organizational framework, organically linked to various groupings within Palestinian society, facilitated mass social mobilization and a horizontal escalation of the struggle which embraced all sectors of society.

The authority of the UNC and the popular committees became evident during the first phase of the intifada because of the solidarity demonstrated in response to strike calls and requests for merchants to restrict their opening hours to mornings only on non-strike days. As part of its attempt to undermine the authority of the Israeli occupiers, the UNC also called on all those Palestinians who worked for the Israeli administration to resign, prompting a significant positive response, and Palestinians referred to this process as 'cleaning out our national home'.[24]

Less visible, but just as powerful as these confrontations, were the constructive community actions that were integral to the first phase of the intifada. When people began to suffer economic hardship – as a consequence of disengaging from the Israeli economy, losing income through participation in strikes, and boycotting Israeli produce – families and communities began to become more self-reliant. Households cultivated vegetable plots and reared poultry, for example, and women's committees became highly active in promoting new forms of home-based economic activity. Homes also became bases for clandestine education classes that were held as a means of countering the Israeli closure of schools and colleges.

Phase two: post-1990 deterioration

By the summer of 1990, it was clear that much of the vigour and drive of the uprising had gone. Analysis of this phase suggests a number of reasons for this deterioration:

The relative failure of disengagement and non-cooperation

Palestinians hoped that their direct opposition and non-cooperation would raise the costs of the occupation to such a level that the Israelis would consider withdrawing. The weakness of this plan was that, historically, Israel has sought to control the territory of the Palestinians, not the people. Palestinian cooperation was not, therefore, required to maintain the occupation, and this seriously weakened the impact of the unarmed resistance.

The escalating costs of resistance

In many ways, the Palestinians were more dependent on Israel than the other way round. Israel could find replacements for the Palestinians who withdrew their labour, but the Palestinians could not find alternative sources of employment and income. Moreover, the Israeli economy remained the only source for many of the basic necessities of life within the occupied Palestinian territories and, as the months passed, the costs of resistance borne by everyday Palestinians rose.

Parallel emphases on 'shame power'[25] and 'vertical escalation'

Attempts to provoke shame and evoke sympathy from the Israeli public through suffering and efforts to force Israel to consider withdrawal by increasing the costs of continued occupation were ineffective. Conversion and coercion used as simultaneous strategies might even be said to have cancelled each other out, reducing the vulnerability of sympathetic Israelis to shame power.

The fragmentation of resistance and the weakening of political control

One of the strengths of the intifada lay in the coordination between the different political factions achieved through the UNC and the popular committees' structure. However, by 1990, not only were the tensions between the different factions increasing in the light of the perceived weaknesses of the unarmed struggle and the temptations of vertical escalation, but the majority of the experienced activists who had been able to maintain cohesion in the struggle had been apprehended and imprisoned (or deported) by Israel.

The apathy of third parties and the impact of external events

Palestinians lacked the power to impact on the self-interests of the US and other international actors and thereby push them to intervene constructively in the conflict. The Gulf War in 1990 intensified the hardship and the suffering of the Palestinians, as well as their bitterness. By mid-1991, more Palestinians were being killed by Palestinians than by Israel, as anger and resentment turned against those suspected of collaboration and 'betrayal' of the uprising.[26]

Palestinians within Israel were quick to show their solidarity with the Palestinians in the West Bank and Gaza Strip after the outbreak of the first intifada. A general strike designated as 'peace day' was called on 21 December 1987. The strike call met with a solid response in the Arab towns and villages and was accompanied by protest marches and demonstrations that led to clashes with the police and the arrest of over a hundred protesters. The strike actions and demonstrations continued throughout the intifada's early years, with the largest taking place in Nazareth and having a reported 50,000 participants.[27] Support also took on a more substantive form with people organising relief committees for the provision of humanitarian aid and supplies for delivery across the Green Line.

The intifada had a significant impact on the Palestinians in Israel. There was a deep sense of pride and admiration for their fellow nationals resisting the occupation, and this strengthened the sense of shared identity with those living in the occupied territories.

The Oslo process, September 1993 – September 2000

The peace negotiations commenced in October 1991 with a conference in Madrid which led, eventually, to the September 1993 signing of the 'Oslo Accords'. The rhetoric of the Accords' preamble was, in hindsight, hyperbolic – the reality that unfolded on the ground was a salutary experience for all those who dared to dream of the 'just and lasting and comprehensive peace settlement' alluded to in the declaration. As Said (2004) argued, the Palestinian flag flies over the Gaza Strip and Jericho without sovereignty, while Israel controls the borders, dictates security arrangements and controls the economy.

What followed was a cycle of violence fuelled on the Palestinian side by a growing sense of frustration at the lack of substantive progress towards the realization of any significant 'peace dividend'. On its part, Israel continued to negotiate from a position of strength, imposing its demands on its weaker partner and resorting to targeted assassinations, collective sanctions, new expropriations of land for settlements, and other 'facts on the ground', whilst ratcheting up the pressure on the Palestinian Authority (PA) to deal with the violence.

The result was an 'Interim Agreement', signed on 28 September 1995, that became known as 'Oslo II'. It divided the West Bank into three administrative divisions, categorized as Areas A, B and C, each of which was to enjoy a different degree of Palestinian self-government. The combined impact of these developments was to bring about a set of conditions that undermined the possibility of launching any new mass-participation unarmed resistance movement against the occupation.

1. The PA had been tasked by Israel and its international backers to act as the agent responsible for controlling dissent within the Palestinian community, and so it was directly involved in maintaining the occupation.[28]
2. People within the elite Palestinian political and socio-economic strata were developing vested interests in the occupation's status quo.
3. The break-up of the West Bank into different zones increased the socio-geographical fragmentation of the Palestinians, not least because of the obstacles to free movement created by the Israeli road-building programme.
4. The leverage that could be exerted over Israel by Palestinian non-cooperation was minimal, as Israel reduced its reliance on Palestinian labour and markets.
5. Potential leaders for any coordinated unarmed popular movement were lacking. Cadres that had been involved in the intifada followed different trajectories, but two career paths were common for their members. Some joined the new PA and others established or joined non-governmental organisations concerned with themes like democratisation and peacebuilding, invariably funded by foreign donors.[29]

The second intifada

The Al-Aqsa intifada began in September 2000, following Ariel Sharon's provocative entry into the Haram Al-Sharif area, but the deeper cause was the build-up of frustration, resentment, and anger resulting from seven years of a peace process that only served to deepen Palestinian dispossession and deprivation whilst strengthening the Israeli occupation. The malfunctioning of the PA and the cronyism that was its dominant feature only served to deepen the feeling that 'something must be done'.

The rapid militarization of the uprising reflected to some degree the emergence of a younger and more militant generation of activists who were influenced by the example of Hezbollah in Southern Lebanon, whose guerrilla tactics had succeeded in forcing Israel to withdraw in May 2000. Within a short while, every Palestinian faction, secular and Islamic, had spawned its own armed militia, each seeking to contribute to the collapse of the occupation through armed struggle. Among these groupings, the armed wing of Hamas re-emerged and took its fight beyond the borders of the occupied territories into Israel itself with suicide bombings that provoked massive Israeli retaliation. Amidst the carnage and the associated destruction of the socio-economic fabric of Palestinian society, there was none of the space there had been in the first intifada for any large-scale unarmed resistance.

The main points of contrast between the first and the second intifadas are summarized in Table 11.1.

On 30 September 2000, the Palestinian leadership in Israel called for a general strike to protest the killing of Palestinians in the Al-Aqsa compound the previous day. Demonstrations spread across the Arab towns and villages in the Galilee and Triangle areas over the following days. The response of the Israeli police was extreme and violent. They used live ammunition, resulting in the death of thirteen protesters.

> what pulled Palestinians out onto the streets of their villages was televised murder [sic] – relayed again and again on Arab TV – of 12-year old Mohamed Al-Dorra at the Netzarim junction in Gaza after 45 minutes of continuous Israeli army fire. And what put rocks into their hands was the lethal response of the Israeli police, for whom there has never been a Green Line as far as 'their' Palestinians are concerned.[30]

The strength of the response reflected the level of support for those Palestinians resisting the occupation but it also grew from the deep sense of frustration felt by the Palestinian minority at the racist discriminatory treatment they experienced as marginalized second-class citizens of Israel. Indeed, the lethal force used by the Israeli

Table 11.1 Main points of contrast between the first and the second intifadas

First intifada	Second intifada
Predominantly unarmed resistance	Predominantly armed/violent resistance
Mass civilian involvement	Civilians confined to 'support' functions
Cohesion and unity via popular committees	Fragmentation, with power falling to local militias
Predominantly secular	Increasingly religious in character
Attempts to influence the Israeli public through dialogue, shame power etc.	Attempts to influence the Israeli public through force, intimidation and fear
Active support from Israeli human rights and peace groups	Limited role for Israeli peace groups in the context of ongoing suicide bombings
Significant international support and third-party pressure towards ending the occupation	Particularly after 11 September 2001, resistance is viewed through the lens of the 'war on terror'

police only served to highlight the manner in which the whole community was discriminated against.[31]

> If one can summarize the Palestinian take on what lay behind October 2000, it would be to say that this was an institutional use of state power to deliver a message to a fifth of its population: be docile and accept your status as second-class citizens, or encounter the wrath of the army and security forces.[32]

A new development during this period was the emergence of Arab and Jewish groups in Israel opposed to the construction of the Separation Wall and in support of the Palestinian struggle to end the occupation.

The Apartheid Wall and the re-emergence of unarmed popular resistance

The suicide bombings and associated targeting of Israeli civilians provided the Israeli government with the rationale to justify its decision to embark on the building of a physical wall between the West Bank and Israel, which it claimed was designed 'to keep the bombers out'.[33] Construction of the Apartheid Wall commenced in the spring of 2002, and by September 2003 it had become a focus of international attention. It was clear that, whilst the Israeli government justified the construction of the wall in terms of Israel's security needs, its route was also determined by the desire to expropriate even more Palestinian land and impose an additional layer of suffering on the Palestinians. Within a very short time, the wall had impacted deleteriously on the lives of tens of thousands of Palestinians who were denied access to their fields, prevented from reaching their places of work and forced to travel circuitous routes and negotiate armed checkpoints either to get to their land, schools, universities or medical centres, or simply to visit family and friends. It was the imposition of this new, direct and visible challenge to their well-being that provoked a wave of popular unarmed resistance amongst those most directly affected.

An analysis of popular resistance between 2003 and 2014 makes it clear that at no stage was there anything comparable to a mass movement of protest. Instead, a series of local centres emerged for active unarmed resistance against the construction of the Apartheid Wall and land expropriation. At the height of the popular resistance during 2010 and 2011, there was some form of organized unarmed resistance against the ongoing occupation in a maximum of forty or fifty villages and neighbourhoods. The centres of resistance changed over time and, as the construction of the Apartheid Wall progressed, new 'hotspots' emerged. Some of these pockets of resistance, like those at Budrus and Bil'in, gained an international profile at the peak of their resistance but this declined with the passage of time.

In 2013, a senior political figure in the Bethlehem area identified some of the weaknesses of the unarmed protest aimed at ending the Israeli occupation of Palestinian territory:

Some of the leaders have a personal interest in the status quo ... So this is part of the cycle of mistrust. People want to see their leaders to the fore, as an example to people on the ground ... At the moment popular resistance is very localised – every Friday the same few villages, the same thing. It is not popular as it does not include the mass of people. If we were serious, we would make life hell for the settlers, blocking the roads, making the soldiers work. That would be popular resistance.[34]

Lack of social solidarity and the weakness of contemporary popular unarmed protest

Recent unarmed resistance has struggled to combat the expansion of the Israeli occupation, and it is clear that a major factor has been the erosion of any significant sense of social solidarity and cohesion amongst Palestinians during the first decades of the new millennium. There are many reasons for this deepening of horizontal and vertical divisions among the Palestinian people, but they include:

1. The geo-political fracturing that occurred as part of the Oslo process and with the division of the West Bank into Areas A, B and C.
2. The blockages that obstruct easy communication and movement between the areas, particularly between the West Bank and the Gaza Strip, and the siege of Gaza which has exacerbated their effects.
3. Political fractures, and particularly the division between Hamas and Fatah that reached its nadir in 2007 when Hamas took control of the Gaza Strip by force.
4. The economic impoverishment of large numbers of Palestinians who can no longer find employment in Israel, which has resulted in them prioritizing the satisfaction of basic needs above participation in a common struggle for a distant goal like the end of the occupation.
5. Widespread disillusionment with the cronyism and corruption that has permeated the Palestinian Authority and which has fed a country-wide lack of trust in those seeking to act as leaders.
6. Harsh Israeli punishments and sanctions enforced on activists who participate in the popular protest.

From Gaza to Jerusalem

Jerusalem has been the focus of several campaigns that seek to resist the eviction of Palestinians and the imposition of further Israeli control. The installation of electronic gates to regulate the entrance of worshippers to Al-Aqsa mosque triggered an outbreak of protest in July 2017 that lasted for three weeks, and generated mass mobilization of thousands of people who participated in the campaign's sit-ins. Palestinians from East Jerusalem and from Israel took leading roles in this struggle, which successfully forced Israel to remove the electric gates by the end of July.[35]

Another significant campaign, Gaza's Great March of Return, began on 30 March, 2018, and involved weekly demonstrations along the east border of the Gaza Strip. It inspired other Palestinians to organise similar events, and Palestinians in Gaza demonstrated every Friday to highlight the right of the Palestinian refugees to return. This ongoing campaign emphasised civil unarmed popular resistance and exposed the Israeli army's violent responses to unarmed protests.

The Al-khan Al-Ahmar campaign, near Jerusalem, aimed to prevent the displacement of the Bedouin community for a second time (they had resettled after been evicted from their original homes during the Nakba in 1948). This campaign, led by popular committees, is an example of an all-Palestinian protest carried out with the support of Israeli solidarity organisations and the diplomatic community in East Jerusalem, and in the end the Israeli authorities were forced to retract their plans.

The important role of third-party solidarity: grounds for hope?

Perhaps the most significant feature of popular resistance in the period following the second intifada has been the increased involvement of 'internationals' as accompaniers, co-participants in actions, and as 'activist-tourists' expressing their solidarity with Palestinians through their presence on the ground. The significance of the contribution made by these overseas activists has been threefold.

1. Their presence has created a kind of protective shield for Palestinian protesters. It serves as an act of witness that indicates solidarity, but it also puts the Israeli authorities under a type of surveillance.
2. They have established linkages between Palestinians and wider activist networks around the world.
3. On their return home, these international activists serve as powerful advocates of the Palestinian cause amongst networks and groupings in their own countries.

One outcome of this trend has been an expansion of the international grass-roots movement of solidarity with the Palestinian struggle. This loose 'movement of movements' has become one of the primary vehicles for implementing a Palestinian initiative that emerged out of a meeting of Palestinian civil society organisations in July 2005 – the call for a world-wide boycott, divestment and sanctions (BDS) campaign against Israel.[36]

There would appear to be increasing numbers of people and organizations around the world who agree that the continued Israeli occupation, the 'blockade', and the virtual imprisonment of the Palestinians in the Gaza Strip constitutes a gross and unacceptable violation of basic human rights and international law about which 'something must be done'.[37]

Despite the effects of the COVID-19 pandemic, which in many ways limited social and political interaction, 2020/21 saw accelerated growth in BDS campaigns, successful grass-roots actions and significant legal victories for Palestinian rights.[38] Writers, singers, artists and other celebrities endorsed the rights of the Palestinians, and pension funds around the world dumped Israeli firms from their investment portfolios over Israel's human rights abuses and international law violations. Cultural figures refused to cross the picket line, and the global ice cream manufacturer Ben & Jerry's pulled its products from illegal Israeli settlements. A wave of protests were carried out under the banner of #BlockTheBoat, and activists and workers in several ports around the world prevented Israeli cargo ships from docking.

In these acts, there are grounds for hope. On their own, the Palestinians lack sufficient leverage to shift the Israelis' stance and achieve a substantive and self-sustaining peace, but we are now in an age where transnational social movements exercise an influence on communities around the world and hence upon political leaders and decision-makers.[39] There is no reason why the BDS campaign and international solidarity movements cannot grow into a force for change that is capable of addressing the imbalance of power between Israel and the Palestinians.[40]

Notes

1 Schock 2005, 2013; Roberts and Garton Ash 2000.
2 Sémelin 1993: 27.
3 Sharp 1980.
4 Ackerman and Kruegler 1994.
5 Galtung 1989: 19; Martin 2007.
6 Kayyali 1970: 10.
7 Rigby 2010: 6.
8 Kayyali 1970: 61.
9 Khalidi 1997: 65.
10 Qumsiyeh 2011: 50–1.
11 Sayigh 1979:.14–15.
12 Qumsiyeh 2011: 67.
13 Omer-Man 2011.
14 Kayyali 1970: 292.
15 Pappé 2006: 131.
16 Darweish 2020; Darweish and Robertson 2021.
17 Bayat 2013: 15.
18 Dallasheh 2010.
19 Darweish 2020.
20 Darweish and Sellick 2017.
21 Sa'di 2014.
22 Ṣāyigh 1997; Rouhana and Sabbagh-Khoury 2011.
23 Darweish and Sellick 2017.
24 Rigby 1997.
25 Galtung 1989.
26 Rigby 1997: 54.
27 Darweish and Rigby 2015.
28 Roy 2007: 245.
29 Herzon and Hai 2005.
30 Usher 2000.
31 White 2012.
32 Pappé 2011: 234.
33 Darweish and Rigby 2015.
34 Ibid.: 2.

35 Beaumont 2017.
36 Barghouti 2011.
37 Darweish and Rigby 2018.
38 Barrows-Friedman 2021.
39 Keck and Sikkink 1999.
40 Darweish and Rigby 2018.

References

Ackerman, P. and C. Kruegler (1994), *Strategic Nonviolent Conflict: The Dynamics of People Power in the Twentieth Century,* Westport, CT: Praeger.

Barghouti, O. (2011), *BDS: Boycott, Divestment, Sanctions – The Global Struggle for Palestinian Rights,* Chicago: Haymarket Books.

Bayat, A. (2013), *Life as Politics: How Ordinary People Change the Middle East,* Stanford, CA: Stanford University Press.

Barrows-Friedman, N. (2021), 'What Were the Top BDS Victories of 2021?', *Electric Intifada,* 30 December. Available online: https://electronicintifada.net/blogs/nora-barrows-friedman/what-were-top-bds-victories-2021 (accessed 30 April 2022).

Beaumont, P. (2017), 'Israeli Security Forces and Palestinian Worshippers Clash Outside Al-Aqsa Mosque', *The Guardian,* 27 July. Available online: https://www.theguardian.com/world/2017/jul/27/israel-removes-further-security-measures-from-al-aqsa-compound (accessed 1 May 2022).

Chenoweth, E., and M. Stephan (2011), *Why Civil Resistance Works: The Strategic Logic of Nonviolent Conflict,* New York: Columbia University Press.

Dallasheh, L. (2010), 'Political Mobilization of Palestinians in Israel: The Al-'Ard Movement' in R. A. Kanaaneh and I. Nussair (eds), *Displaced at Home: Ethnicity and Gender Among Palestinians in Israel,* 21–38, New York: University of New York Press.

Darweish, M. (2020), '"This Is Our Home": Everyday Resistance of the Palestinians in Israel 1948–1966' in S. Murru and A. Polese (eds), *Resistances: Between Theories and the Field,* 96–116, Lanham, MD: Rowman & Littlefield.

Darweish, M., and A. Rigby (2015), *Popular Protest in Palestine: The Uncertain Future of Unarmed Resistance,* London: Pluto.

Darweish, M., and A. Rigby, (2018), 'The Internationalisation of Nonviolent Resistance: The Case of the BDS Campaign', *Journal of Resistance Studies,* 4 (1): 45–71.

Darweish, M., and P. Sellick (2017), 'Everyday Resistance Among Palestinians Living in Israel 1948-1966', *Journal of Political Power,* 10 (3): 353–70.

Darweish, M., and C. Robertson (2021), 'Palestinian Poet-Singers: Celebration under Israel's Military Rule 1948–1966', *Alternatives: Global, Local, Political,* 46 (2): 27–46.

Galtung, J. (1989), *Nonviolence and Israel/Palestine.* Honolulu, HI: University of Hawaii.

Herzon, S., and A. Hai (2005), 'What Do People Mean When They Say "People-to-People"?', *Palestine–Israel Journal,* 12–13 (4): 8–15.

Keck, M. E., and Sikkink, K. (1999), 'Transnational Advocacy Networks in International and Regional Politics', *International Social Science Journal,* 51 (159): 89–101.

Khalidi, R. (1997), *Palestinian Identity: The Construction of Modern National Consciousness,* New York: Columbia University Press.

Kayyali, A. (1970), 'The Palestinian Arab Reactions to Zionism and the British Mandate, 1917–1939, PhD diss., University of London.

Martin, B. (2007), *Justice Ignited: The Dynamics of Backfire,* Lanham, MD: Rowman & Littlefield.
Omer-Man, M. (2011), 'This Week in History: The 1929 Hebron Massacre', *Jerusalem Post,* 26 August. Available online: https://www.jpost.com/features/in-thespotlight/this-week-in-history-the-1929-hebron-massacre (accessed 1 May 2022).
Pappé, I. (2006), *A History of Modern Palestine,* Cambridge: Cambridge University Press.
Pappé, I. (2011), *The Forgotten Palestinians: A History of the Palestinians in Israel,* New Haven, CT: Yale University Press.
Qumsiyeh, M. (2011), *Popular Resistance in Palestine: A History of Hope and Empowerment,* London: Pluto Press.
Rigby, A. (1991), *Living the Intifada,* London: Zed Books.
Rigby, A. (1997), *The Legacy of the Past: The Problem of Collaborators and the Palestinian Case,* East Jerusalem: PASSIA.
Rigby, A. (2010), *Palestinian Resistance and Nonviolence,* East Jerusalem: PASSIA.
Rings, W. (1982), *Life with the Enemy: Collaboration and Resistance in Hitler's Europe 1939–1945,* Garden City, NY: Doubleday.
Roberts, A., and T. Garton Ash (eds) (2000), *Civil Resistance and Power Politics: The Experience of Non-violent Action from Gandhi to the Present,* Oxford: Oxford University Press, 2000.
Roy, S. (2007), *Failing Peace: Gaza and the Palestinian-Israeli Conflict,* London: Pluto.
Rouhana, N. N., and A. Sabbagh-Khoury (eds) (2011), *The Palestinians in Israel: Readings in History, Politics and Society,* Haifa: Mada Al Carmel Arab Centre for Applied Social Research.
Sa'di, A. H. (2014), *Thorough Surveillance: The Genesis of Israeli Policies of Population Management, Surveillance and Political Control Towards the Palestinian Minority,* Manchester: Manchester University Press.
Said, E. (2004), *From Oslo to Iraq and the Road Map: Essays,* New York: Vintage Books.
Sayigh, R. (1979), *Palestinians: From Peasants to Revolutionaries,* London: Zed Books.
Sayigh, Y. (1997), *Armed Struggle and the Search for State: The Palestinian National Movement, 1949–1993,* Oxford: Clarendon Press.
Schock, K. (2005), *Unarmed Insurrections: People Power Movements in Nondemocracies.* Minneapolis, MN: University of Minnesota Press.
Schock, K. (2013), 'The Practice and Study of Civil Resistance', *Journal of Peace Research* 50 (3), 277–90.
Sémelin, J. (1993), *Unarmed Against Hitler: Civilian Resistance in Europe, 1939–1943,* London: Praeger.
Sharp, G. (1973), *The Politics of Nonviolent Action, Part One: Power and Struggle,* Boston, MA: Porter Sargent.
Sharp, G. (1980), *Social Power and Political Freedom,* Boston, MA: Porter Sargent.
Sharp, G. (2005), *Waging Nonviolent Struggle: 20th Century Practice and 21st Century Potential,* Boston, MA: Extending Horizons Books.
Usher, G. (2000), 'Uprising Wipes off Green Line', *Al-Ahram* 503 (October): 12–18.
White, B. (2012), *Palestinians in Israel: Segregation, Discrimination and Democracy,* London: Pluto Press.
Zureik, E. (1979), *The Palestinians in Israel: A Study in Internal Colonialism,* London: Routledge.
Zureik, E. (2016), *Israel's Colonial Project in Palestine: Brutal Pursuit,* London and New York: Routledge.

Part Five

Issues of Bio-power

12

The Effect of the Separation Wall on the West Bank Labour Market

Sami Miaari and Đorđe Milosav

Introduction

At the time the decision was made by the Israeli cabinet to erect the separation wall[1] between Israel and the West Bank in 2002, the territory of the West Bank has been under a systematic closure regime for more than a decade. The closure regime was introduced in 1991 in the occupied Palestinian territories (oPt) which implied systematic restriction of movement of goods, labour and people.[2] It restricted the movement between the oPt and Israel, between the West Bank and Gaza, and international crossings between the West Bank and Jordan and the Gaza strip and Egypt. Lastly, the closure also included the restriction of movement within the oPts through an elaborate system of checkpoints.[3] This closure only applies to Palestinians living in the oPt; Israeli settlers and foreigners in the West Bank can move freely.

In the summer of 2003, Israel began the construction of a wall separating major Israeli and Palestinian population centres. The wall was officially devised by the Israeli government as a security policy in response to the violent events of the second intifada (2000–05). The separation wall is a mix of eight-metre-tall concrete walls, mostly built in the urban areas, and pyramid-shaped barbed wire fences surrounded by patrol roads. Overall, the wall runs parallel to the Green Line, a line created as an outcome of the armistice after the 1948 Arab–Israeli war which later became a separating line between Israel and the territories it captured in the Six Day War of 1967. Yet, for most of its route, the wall is built on the West Bank side, therefore creating the 'seam zone' – an area between the Green Line and the wall –which is now controlled by the Israel Defense Forces (IDF) and accessible only to Palestinians with special permits.[4]

Furthermore, the wall encompasses a number of the new (post-1967) Israeli settlements[5] in the West Bank which now lie on the Israeli side.[6] Due to the increase of the number of Israeli civilians in the settlements located in the West Bank, Israel has been accused to be in violation of the article 49 of the Fourth Geneva Convention which states that '[t]he Occupying Power shall not deport or transfer parts of its own civilian population into the territory it occupies'.[7] As the wall is being built inside the territory of the West Bank, the International Court of Justice issued an advisory opinion in 2004 stating that the construction of the wall is 'contrary to the international law' (ICJ 2004).

With the estimated costs of 2 million USD per kilometre,[8] the wall is one of the largest projects to have been carried out by Israel in the past few decades. By May 2011, Israel had completed 473km (61%) of the wall, 54 km (7%) was under construction while 247km (32%) were still in the planning-revision stage (see Figure 12.1 for map of the wall construction by 2008). Upon completion, the wall will end up isolating 733km² (733 thousand dunums) of the West Bank territory, effectively cutting out 13% of its total area (ARIJ 2011).

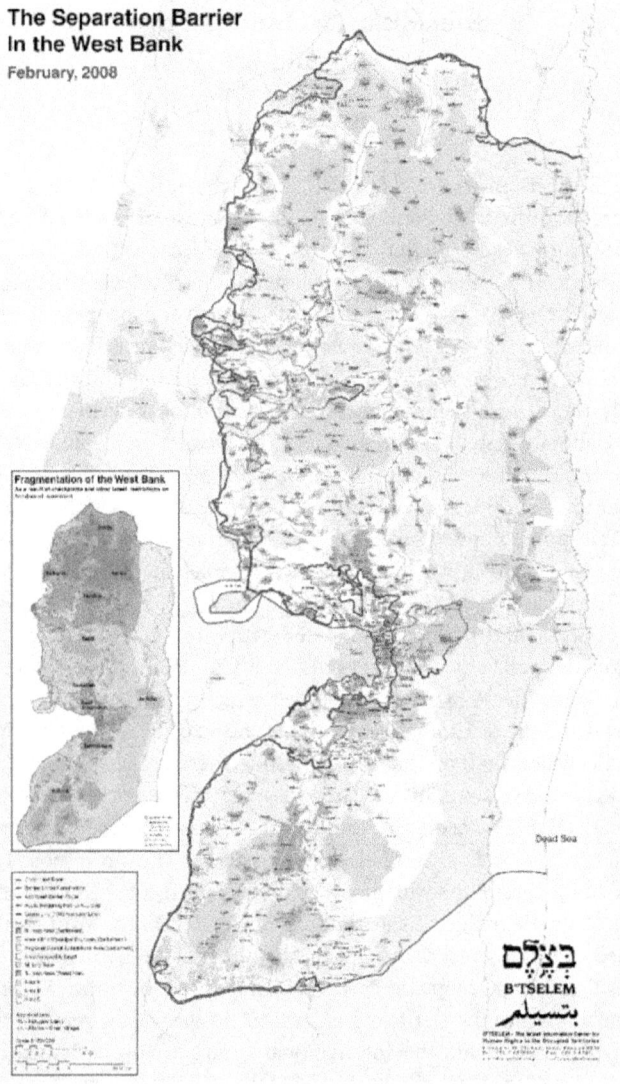

Figure 12.1 Map of the Separation wall in 2008 *Source:* B'Tselem

Indeed, the economic implications of the wall for the Palestinian population living in the West Bank are broad. The most notable implication is the Palestinian labourers being sealed off from entry into Israel. Prior to the second intifada Israel employed a quarter of the Palestinian labour force,[9] so the erection of the wall signals a possible effective end of Palestinian participation in the Israeli labour force. Furthermore, the wall separates Palestinian villages from their lands, often situated in the seam zone, thus impeding agricultural workers from working their lands as they have for generations, impairing their livelihoods and in turn reducing their standard of living.[10]

The effects of the wall are considerable in many other realms. Palestinians living in the West Bank have an increasingly restricted or no access to schools, universities and specialized medical care thus resulting in a severe reduction in knowledge, social capital and the overall health of the population.[11] By our estimates (see below), up until 2010, 224 out of 369, or almost 61% of all localities in the West Bank have been directly affected by the separation wall.

Following the existing descriptive evidence, the aim of this chapter is to investigate the effects of the separation wall on labour market outcomes among the Palestinian population in the West Bank. In order to estimate the effects of the wall on labour market outcomes we employ a differences-in-differences strategy. This identification strategy is based on a comparison of the changes that have occurred between the period before the construction of the wall and the period that succeeded it; and between localities near the wall and those at a distance from it. Thus, we compare localities that are directly affected by the separation wall to localities that are further from the separation wall and therefore not directly affected.

We run our analyses using panel data from the Palestinian Labor Force Survey (PLFS) collected by the Palestinian Bureau of Statistics. The information on the separation wall construction is taken from Applied Research Institute–Jerusalem (ARIJ) while the information on control variables such as closures over time comes from ARIJ and United Nations Office for the Coordination of Humanitarian Affairs (OCHA). We further utilize an array of other conflict related controls such as the number of Palestinian fatalities and settlement population taken from various data sources.

Overall, our results would suggest the wall caused a significant decrease in Palestinian hourly wages as well as a reduction on the number of days worked during the month. Palestinians living in the localities affected by the wall on average worked 5% days less for a 10% lower hourly wage in the month following the wall construction. Taking into account both reduced wages and the loss of working days, an average Palestinian worker living in the close proximity to the wall loses roughly 186NIS or 56$US per month due to the wall construction. Moreover, the results suggest that the wall has a gendered effect as females living in the close proximity to the wall on average worked a staggering 54% fewer days after the wall was constructed and men worked almost 21% fewer days. Lastly, the wall construction has a negative effect on the probability of employment for workers owning a permit to work in Israel and workers employed in the agriculture, construction and transport sectors. Interestingly, the probability of employment rose for Palestinians working in the manufacturing sector and services, most possibly as a result of the increase in the labour supply caused by the wall construction.

The remainder of this chapter is structured as follows:

- an extensive overview of the wall construction and background information for our study;
- a literature review;
- a description of the data;
- our estimation strategy;
- the results;
- conclusion.

Background

The wall's route and phases

The construction of the separation wall started during the second intifada (2000–05) in the summer of 2003. The separation wall was just one measure imposed by Israel out of security concerns and aimed to suppress the violence. The wall was built in the north and northwestern regions of the West Bank first, encircling Jenin, Tulkarm, Qalqiliya and Nablus districts, as well as Eastern Jerusalem.[12] The route of the wall was laid out in four phases. Phase A of construction was completed by the end of July 2003 and consists of approximately 140km from Salem to Elkana. Phase B, an 80km-long stretch from Salem to Bet-Shean, was completed in 2004 while Phase C included the section of the wall around Eastern Jerusalem. The initial 'Jerusalem Defense Plan' was approved in March of 2003, but due to legal complaints made both by the Israelis and the Palestinians, the decision was made in 2005 to build a temporary barrier around Jerusalem until legal matters were settled. As of 2017, the wall section around Eastern Jerusalem, also known as the 'Jerusalem envelope', cuts out Eastern Jerusalem from the rest of the West Bank by following municipal boundaries drawn up by Israel after the Six Day war in 1967.[13] Phase D consists of a 150km-long section from Elkana to Ofer and several 'special sections', such as the one protecting the road from Ben Gurion airport to Jerusalem and a number of other areas where the goal seemed to be to incorporate Israeli settlements such as Gush Etzion and Ariel on the west side of the wall.[14]

Therefore, the Israeli government made a number of changes to the wall route during the construction process. This was done in response to petitions by Palestinians and activist groups raising concerns about the illegality of the route. After the Israeli High Court of Justice (HCJ) stated that future expansion plans are not relevant when determining the route of the barrier, the government ordered a rerouting of the wall in at least four different instances in 2006, 2007 and twice in 2009. Yet, the ordered relocation usually occurs years after the order or it does not happen at all.[15] Out of more than 150 petitions questioning the wall in general and the route on specific sections of it, most were denied.[16] Furthermore, the route has changed in some areas not in response to these petitions but in order to bring more of West Bank territory or settlement areas into Israel proper.[17]

Regardless of these changes, 85% of the built and planned route of the wall runs inside the West Bank, putting 90 settlements such as Ma'ale Adummim and Ariel, as well as eight Palestinian localities and swathes of unused land appropriate for industrial and residential expansion on the west side of the wall.[18] According to OCHA, by September 2017, 460km (65%) had been completed, 53km (7.5%) were under construction and 200km were yet to be constructed.[19]

Upon completion, the wall will be 708km long – almost twice the size of the armistice Green Line between the West Bank and Israel.[20] As a result, according to various estimations almost 10% to 13% of the West Bank will be on the 'Israeli side' of the wall and practically unreachable to most of the West Bank Palestinian residents.[21] In their 2021 report, B'Tselem found that there were 280 settlements and outposts populated by more than 440,000 Israeli citizens without Eastern Jerusalem and that more than 2 million dunums have been 'de facto annexed' by official and unofficial means. By Israeli government and international estimates, each kilometre of the wall cost around 2 million $US, while the overall costs for the wall construction went from the planned $US 1bn to 2.1 bn.[22]

Although Israel created as many as 85 gates for purposes such as agricultural work and movement between Israel and the West Bank, in reality most of the gates are either closed, unmanned or operated for only a few hours a day or only during harvest seasons. Out of the 85 gates in 2016 only nine were open daily.[23] Moreover, the gates can only be crossed by West Bank Palestinians who have a permit, issued by the Israeli Civil Administration, a branch of the Israeli military which deals with the civil affairs of the West Bank area C.[24]

In respect to the legality of the wall construction, based on two most important court decisions written by Justice Aharon Barak from June 2004 on the case of Beit Sourik and from September 2005 about Alfei Menashe, construction of the wall has been justified on three main grounds: that the wall is officially 1) a temporary measure that will be dismantled when it is deemed no longer necessary, that it is 2) constructed solely based on security related concerns and that 3) it follows an internationally recognized legal principle of proportionality as it does not incur disproportionate harm to the local Palestinian population. These claims were criticized by many NGOs and the Palestinian Authority as well as by the International Court of Justice.[25]

The impact of the separation wall on human rights and quality of life

Adding to an onerous situation caused by the conflict and the existing closure regime, the building of the wall further aggravated the human rights of the Palestinians living in the West Bank, especially in terms of Palestinians' rights of freedom of movement. 'Urban localities near the path of the wall's construction are commonly subjected to increased movement restrictions … within and between Palestinian towns, villages and hamlets.'[26] Moreover, the wall caused an increase in movement restriction between the West Bank and Israel. Palestinians used to travel to Israel for work, education, health services, relative visits and religious reasons and the wall made that especially hard.[27] Due to the permit regime and the behaviour of the IDF soldiers stationed at checkpoints and wall gates,[28] crossing the wall became an expensive, time consuming and overall unpleasant experience. Moreover, as some portions of the wall cut through the inner West Bank, the wall contributes to the fragmentation of Palestinian society.[29] The wall seems to be negatively affecting the sense of Palestinian national identity by 'separating Palestinians from other Palestinians, and not Palestinians from Israelis'.[30]

Out of 85 wall gates in total, 66 are agricultural gates made to serve farmers accessing their land beyond the wall. Only a few gates are open daily, and only some landowners can access it by acquiring a permit from the Israeli Civil Administration. Moreover, all gates close every time a 'complete closure' is imposed, which happens after attacks or during Jewish holidays. The farmers who do obtain permits 'have trouble working their land because they generally are not allowed to bring in farm equipment or labourers to assist them. The procedure for obtaining a permit is cumbersome, and, to aggravate matters, the Civil Administration has yet to publish the criteria for obtaining a permit in Arabic'.[31] As a result, the availability of farming options is limited to cultivation of non-intensive crops such as olive orchards, thus reducing economic output.[32] Furthermore, the number of permits has been slowly decreasing: in 2016, only 58% of agricultural permits were approved, despite such measures being unlawful under international law.[33]

The wall and the closure regime have severe negative consequences on West Bank economic development as well. According to World Bank estimates, the West Bank economy suffered mostly due to limited access to land and international trade (World Bank, 2006; 2008a, 2008b) while poverty among Palestinians is rampant (World Bank, 2014). The negative economic consequences of the separation wall are prominently gendered, affecting both men and women but in different ways. According to a 2010 study conducted by the World Bank, the traditional roles of men as breadwinners are threatened by unemployment caused by the state of the West Bank economy and the shrinking Israeli market for Palestinian labour. As over 99% of Israeli working permit holders are men,[34] movement restrictions are disproportionally hitting men. As a result, men opt out for local private businesses or the informal sector, often with little success, or decide to work for the settlements.[35] In response to this financial shock, women sometimes take up work in agriculture and the public sector, thus adding an additional burden to their regular household roles. With unemployed men and overworked women, Palestinian families often experience frustration and animosity.[36]

Lastly, the wall construction caused infringement of the right to property through demolition and confiscation of Palestinian property and agricultural land.[37] Palestinian property has also been seized through military orders, declaration of state lands and evictions.[38] A considerable increase in land seizures happened during and after the second intifada. Out of 35,000 dunums of land seized in this period, over 25,000 dunums were seized for the wall construction.[39]

Literature review

The existing academic interest in the effects of the Israeli closure regime and the separation wall more specifically is growing. Yet, compared to various aspects of the closure regime such as checkpoints and the permit system, the effects of the separation wall are relatively understudied. Furthermore, the existing literature is mainly focused on the political implications of the wall, especially in regard to its implications for peace and international law.[40] Therefore, by examining the effects of the wall on the labour market outcomes we aim to contribute to the wider literature on the consequences of the Israeli closure regime. For the purposes of this chapter, we primarily present the results for the existing labour market research on the separation wall and closure regime effects and briefly touch upon the existing evidence on their political implications as well.

Economic consequences of the closure regime and the separation wall

Miaari and Sauer (2011) show that closures caused an increase in worker supply from abroad which in turn negatively affected Palestinian monthly earnings. Mansour (2010) corroborates their findings by showing that closures increased the supply of both skilled and unskilled workers in the West Bank which in turn reduced the wages, but only for unskilled workers. Etkes (2011) on the other hand shows a positive effect of Israeli employment permits on wages and employment but only for unskilled workers. Cali and Miaari (2018) showed that checkpoints negatively affected West Bank Palestinians' level of employment, wages and days worked, mostly through a reduction of labour demand caused by the restrictions on the mobility of goods across locations.

Roy (2001) and Farsakh (2002) show that many people moved across the Green Line for work and commerce before the buildup of the wall. Indeed, according to the data from B'Tselem (1999) in 1992 'more than one-third of Palestinian workers were employed in Israel and 42% of GDP was composed of the income of those workers'.[41] This is an important finding as cross-border movement prior to the construction of the wall is a key aspect of the West Bank labour market and, as will be shown, is an important element for our estimation strategy. When it comes to the wall effects, Sanders (2010) finds that the building of the wall cut the labour supply and induced low-skilled worker shortage in Israel which in turn resulted in an increase in non-Jewish foreign workers. Focusing on the West Bank side of the wall, Calì and Miaari (2018) find a positive effect of the wall on employment suggesting that the wall might be creating short-term work opportunities. Similarly, Oberholzer (2016) finds negative effects of the wall on unemployment rates but only for men. Yet, the economic participation of women declined significantly and more noticeably than for men. Furthermore, Oberholzer (2016: 4) found that the agricultural sector suffered considerably and argued that it was 'undoubtedly ... a result of higher transaction costs, the reduced access of some communities to their agricultural land and/or workplace, and the destruction and confiscation of agricultural assets'. Braverman (2009) and Di Cintio (2013) confirm these findings.

Indeed, to the best of our knowledge, Oberholzer's study is one of the most detailed analyses of labour market effects of the separation wall. Yet, as the author notes herself, the study fails to control for variables such as the number of Palestinian fatalities, the availability of credit and ownership of the Israeli working permits and variables related to the closure regime, most of which we are able to control for in our study. Moreover, we have individual level data on the local level, as opposed to the governorate level used in Oberholzer's study. Lastly, we employ a dif-in-dif estimation strategy thus accounting for unequal effects of the wall between the period before its construction and the period that succeeded it and on areas in the West Bank that are close (treated) and further away (not treated) from it.

The existing research on political implications of the wall

Taking a historical perspective, Cohen (2006) argues that the construction of the wall serves two Israeli political goals: 1) the officially proclaimed and justified need of the Israeli government to protect its citizens and 2) the promotion of a territorial strategy in line with its political ideology. As a result, Cohen concludes, by taking up the West Bank territory east of the Green Line and de facto including it in Israel, the wall is undermining the viability of a Palestinian state, and consequentially the two-state peace solution.

El-Atrash (2016) presents a detailed account on how the construction of the wall is impeding the possibility of a two-state solution. The author discusses the implication of the wall on several key issues. By constructing the wall east of the Green Line Israel is 'de facto annexing' Israeli settlements around East Jerusalem and elsewhere in the West Bank, thus violating 'internationally recognized border between the Palestinian territory and Israel' as well as 'perpetuating the Greater Jerusalem Plan'.[42] Furthermore, the author documents that the wall is severely affecting the West Bank water supply as well as the amount of available land for infrastructural development. Altogether, the author concludes that 'all facets of Palestinian socio-spatial and physical development have been adversely affected by the construction of the "wall," in a way that makes envisioning sustainability and viability of the coming Palestinian statehood a dim possibility'.[43]

The more formal empirical analyses of political implications of the closure regime and wall construction is scarce. Longo, Canetti and N. Hite-Rubin (2014) exploit an 'easement' of checkpoint policies as a natural experiment and find that less restrictive movement policies cause a decrease in the support of violence among the Palestinian population in the West Bank. Furthermore, by relying on original panel data they were able to tease out the mechanism behind such an effect and argued that the easement of checkpoints reduced the perceived humiliation among the Palestinians thus reducing their readiness to support violence. Thus, by including various set of indicators measuring the levels of political violence, we aim to control for conflict on labour market outcomes.

Data

In order to examine the effects of wall construction on labour market outcomes, ideally, we would use geo-referenced individual-level panel data on the labour market outcomes with a time span including the period before and after the construction of the wall. Secondly, we would require time-series data on the construction of the wall.

In addition, in order to account for competing factors that might influence labour market outcomes, we would require data on other aspects of the closure regime such as checkpoints, entry permits and the presence and location of the Israeli settlements. Lastly, in order to account for the effects of conflict we would require geo-referenced data on the type and intensity of the conflict. Luckily, all of the above-mentioned data requirements are met. In this section, we describe the data and present our estimation strategy in the next section.

Labour market outcomes

For the information on the labour market outcomes, we rely on the data from the Palestinian Labor Force Survey (PLFS) collected by the Palestinian Bureau of Statistics. We utilize the statistics on daily wages, employment status, number of days worked in the previous month, number of hours worked in the previous week as well as the information on the type of occupation and the industry one is employed in. The PLFS data are available from 1995 to 2010 at the individual level. One household is surveyed 4 times over the period of 6 quarters, in the first two and the last two quarters. Furthermore, the PLFS data include information on the type of community (city/village/refugee camp) where the subjects of the study reside. Most importantly, the survey includes the exact location coordinates of each household as well as the location of the workplace of each household member if employed. This information is crucial in order to identify the effects of the separation wall. We exclude individuals from the Gaza Strip as we are interested in the wall effects on the West Bank labour market and restrict the sample to individuals of legal working age (15 years and above). Descriptive statistics on key sociodemographic variables are presented in Table 12.1.

Table 12.1 Descriptive Statistics for individual level variables

		Obs.	Mean	SD
Employment		215,663	0.342	0.421
Hourly Wage		57,775	84.902	54.413
Work days per month		59,422	21.672	6.109
Work hours per week		196,981	16.325	20.135
Female		215,663	0.492	0.499
Age		215,663	34.542	16.652
Years of school		215,659	9.006	16.241
Married		215,663	0.554	0.494
Locality type	City	215,663	0.41	0.491
	Village	215,663	0.47	0.496
	Refuge Camp	215,663	0.12	0.325

Source: Authors' elaboration of Palestinian Labor Force Survey

Separation wall

The information on the separation wall construction is taken from Applied Research Institute–Jerusalem (ARIJ). This data is available for every other year from 2002 to 2016. To obtain data on the length of the wall for the missing years, we use linear interpolation. This data contains information on (a) the length of the wall for each West Bank locality that crosses the path of the wall, (b) the location of the locality relative to the wall (e.g. behind the wall, outside the wall, circled by the wall, and divided by the wall), and (c) the distance of the locality from the wall.

Physical barriers

The information on closures over time comes from ARIJ and OCHA,[44] which has been monitoring the barriers within the West Bank since 1995. As noted, the closure regime is a complex system of movement restrictions imposed by the IDF which includes a multitude of physical barriers of various types. The Israeli army has been constructing permanent and partial checkpoints, road blocks, earth mounds, road gates, all of which restrict the movement *within* the West Bank. Regardless of the type, the barriers are prolonging the travel time between localities within the West Bank, are imposing greater costs of traveling and are often reported as places of humiliation by the IDF towards Palestinians.[45]

For each type of barrier, we have information on the position of the barriers for each locality in every year according to the road distance in kilometres. We construct a weighted count of the number of barriers within 20km via existing roads, from the locality's centroid, weighted by the inverse of the distance. This weight captures the idea that the more distant a checkpoint is, the less it will affect mobility to and from a certain locality.

Conflict

Palestinian fatalities

This dataset contains information on all Palestinian fatalities due to politically-motivated violence in each year since the outbreak of the first Intifada in 1987 for each locality. This data is collected by the B'Tselem, the Israeli Information Center for Human Rights in the Occupied Territories, and is considered to be accurate and reliable by both Israelis and Palestinians.[46]

Settlement data

This dataset is provided by the Applied Research Institute of Jerusalem (ARIJ) and contains information on the location of Israeli settlements in the West Bank. This data allows us to calculate the road distance between the settlement and various Palestinian localities. Using this information, we follow Cali and Miaari (2018) to construct an index of the total population of the Israeli settlements within a 20km road distance from the locality's centroid, weighted by the inverse of their distance. The weighting ensures that settlements further away the locality have less of an effect on the index.

Estimation strategy

Our main estimation strategy is based on the differences in differences design where we utilize the timing of the wall's construction adjacent to each locale as our treatment variable. The empirical model we use to measure the effect of construction of the West Bank wall on Palestinian labour market outcomes is:

$$Y_{ijt} = \alpha_0 + \alpha_1 Barrier_{tl} + \alpha_2 locality_{il} + \alpha_3 (Barrier_{tl} * locality_{il}) + \beta X_{itl} + \varepsilon_{ilt}$$

where Y_{ilt} is the labour market outcome of individual i in locality l and quarter t. Y_{ilt} is either a dummy indicating employment, natural logarithm of hourly earnings, natural logarithm of the number of days worked in the previous month or the natural logarithm of the number of hours worked in the previous week [dependent variables]. $Barrier_{tl}$ is a dummy variable equal to 1 if the observation is taken from the post-barrier construction in locality l, which is located near the barrier; or zero otherwise. Using the ARIJ data on the separation wall construction, we calculate the distance between the locality's centroid from the wall and assign a value of 1 if the distance is less than 5km. $Locality_{il}$ is equal to 1 if the individual i is from locality j (located near the barrier, i.e., 'treated' by the barrier), and zero otherwise (localities not in proximity to the barrier). X_{itl} is a vector of individual characteristics that include years of schooling, age and age squared, experience, as well as dummies indicating personal status, residence in an urban area/refugee camp, gender and industry type. ε_{ilt} are the error terms.

Parameter α_3 measures the difference-in-differences effect of the West Bank wall on the labour market outcomes of a locality situated near the barrier; it measures the causal effect of the West Bank barrier on labour market outcomes. We discuss the overall effects of the wall as well as examine the heterogeneity of the wall's effects by gender, industry, skills and having a working permit.

In order to control for the effects of the internal closure regime and violence, we include our closure regime index and measures on the number of Palestinian fatalities in the preceding quarter. Lastly, we add the settler population index. As noted, physical proximity between Israeli settlements and Palestinian localities may affect Palestinian political attitudes and the intensity of conflict, which can in turn affect labour market outcomes.[47] Furthermore, as many Palestinians find work in the settlements[48] as well as due to the notions that the trajectory of the wall seems to be built in order to ease the access of the settlement population to Israel. As the location of settlements might affect both the location of wall construction and labour market outcomes, we include our settlement population index as an additional control in our baseline estimation. More formally, we expand on our baseline estimation in the following way:

$$Y_{ijt} = \alpha_0 + \alpha_1 Barrier_{tl} + \alpha_2 locality_{il} + \alpha_3 (Barrier_{tl} * locality_{il}) + \beta X_{itl} + \delta Closure_{tl} + \gamma Fatalities_{t-1l} + \theta Prisoners_{t-1l} + \mu Demolitions_{t-1j} + SetPop_{lt-1} + \varepsilon_{ilt}$$

Results

Main results

The results of the main analysis are presented in Table 12.2. All models include individual and time fixed effects and robust standard errors using the Huber-White method clustered at the locality level. Note that due to our coding approach where we coded the distance of the locality from the wall by referring to the distance obtained in 2016, the distance variable was omitted from the regression output as it is fixed for each individual throughout the panel rounds. In models 1, 3, 5 and 7 we present the results of our benchmark estimation with employment, logged hourly wage, logged days worked in the previous month and logged hours worked in the previous week, respectively, where we only include individual level controls. In models 2, 4, 6 and 8 we include additional locality level conflict related controls – closure index, settlement population index and the number of Palestinian fatalities in the preceding year – to further test the effect of the wall construction on each of our labour market outcomes.

Across all models, the expected mean change caused by the wall construction between the treated and untreated individuals is negative. Yet, it is statistically significant only for hourly wage ($p<0.05$) and the number of days worked in the previous month ($p<0.01$). The coefficients and the significance of the effects of the wall construction on hourly wage and days worked in the previous month does not change in a meaningful way and remains statistically significant after the introduction of conflict related controls in models 4 and 6. Lastly, the effect of the wall on employment in both models is negative and significant at 10% while the p value for number of hours worked in the previous week is >0.10.

When it comes to the effect size, following the output of model 4 from Table 12.2 with all controls, the difference in wages between the treated and untreated localities after the wall has been constructed is around 10% (10.1%). This indicates that the construction of the wall, on average, caused a 10% decrease in hourly wages for the Palestinians living in the localities closer to the wall. As the mean of the hourly wage for Palestinians across the West Bank is around 11NIS according to the data provided by PLFS, the wall caused an additional loss of 1NIS per hour, or roughly 176NIS per month, according to a West Bank average of 22 working days. Following the current exchange rates of 2022, the wall caused a loss of roughly US$53 to each Palestinian worker every month. Yet, this loss is likely to be much higher as the number of days worked was also reduced. As it is shown in models 5 and 6 of Table 12.1, the difference in the number of days worked in the previous month between Palestinians living in treated and untreated localities after the wall has been constructed is around 5% (5.56%) indicating that Palestinians living in the localities closer to the wall on average worked 5% days less in the month following the wall construction. As the average number of days worked during the month for the whole of West Bank is around 22 days (PLFS), a 5% decrease would indicate that the wall is costing each affected Palestinian on average just over 1 day worth of work per month. Taking into account the reduced wages and the loss of working days, an average Palestinian worker loses roughly 186NIS or US$56 per month due to the wall construction.

Table 12.2 Main Effects of the Wall Construction on Labour Market Outcomes

	(1) Employment	(2) Employment	(3) Wage	(4) Wage	(5) Days Worked/ Month	(6) Days Worked/ Month	(7) Hours Worked/ Week	(8) Hours Worked/ Week
Distance								
Wall Dummy	0.0441** (0.0177)	0.0439** (0.0178)	0.0996** (0.0449)	0.0997** (0.0447)	0.335*** (0.0768)	0.332*** (0.0749)	0.123 (0.0779)	0.119 (0.0806)
Distance x Wall Dummy	−0.0330* (0.0189)	−0.0332* (0.0190)	−0.105** (0.0477)	−0.106** (0.0475)	−0.332*** (0.0770)	−0.326*** (0.0752)	−0.119 (0.0790)	−0.112 (0.0816)
Female	–	–	–	–	–	–	–	–
Years of School	0.00539*** (0.000492)	0.00538*** (0.000491)	0.0117*** (0.00227)	0.0117*** (0.00227)	0.00353*** (0.00127)	0.00355*** (0.00127)	0.00487*** (0.00126)	0.00487*** (0.00126)
Age	0.0121*** (0.00134)	0.0121*** (0.00134)	0.0401*** (0.00758)	0.0401*** (0.00758)	0.0139*** (0.00440)	0.0140*** (0.00441)	0.00570 (0.00434)	0.00613 (0.00432)
Age squared	−0.000138*** (1.38e-05)	−0.000138*** (1.38e-05)	−0.000412*** (0.000113)	−0.000412*** (0.000113)	−0.000162*** (5.71e-05)	−0.000163*** (5.72e-05)	−9.49e-05* (5.10e-05)	−0.000100** (5.07e-05)
Engaged	0.0211*** (0.00443)	0.0212*** (0.00443)	0.0326** (0.0140)	0.0326** (0.0140)	0.0201** (0.00864)	0.0197** (0.00863)	0.0181** (0.00792)	0.0178** (0.00791)
Married	0.0152** (0.00591)	0.0152** (0.00591)	0.00599 (0.0185)	0.00612 (0.0185)	−0.0210* (0.0115)	−0.0214* (0.0115)	−0.0155 (0.00974)	−0.0159 (0.00977)
Divorced	0.0366*** (0.0104)	0.0366*** (0.0104)	0.0622 (0.0399)	0.0623 (0.0398)	−0.0118 (0.0255)	−0.0124 (0.0256)	−0.0509* (0.0302)	−0.0515* (0.0302)
Widowed	0.00965 (0.00733)	0.00969 (0.00732)	0.0214 (0.0542)	0.0219 (0.0543)	−0.0205 (0.0299)	−0.0212 (0.0297)	−0.0674** (0.0340)	−0.0683** (0.0340)
Separated	0.00434 (0.0120)	0.00442 (0.0120)	−0.0307 (0.0654)	−0.0299 (0.0655)	−0.0394 (0.0310)	−0.0390 (0.0309)	0.0486 (0.0427)	0.0480 (0.0428)

(continued)

Table 12.2 Continued

	(1) Employment	(2) Employment	(3) Wage	(4) Wage	(5) Days Worked/ Month	(6) Days Worked/ Month	(7) Hours Worked/ Week	(8) Hours Worked/ Week
Other	0.00909 (0.00905)	0.00870 (0.00903)	0.0426 (0.0563)	0.0427 (0.0562)	-0.0236 (0.0269)	-0.0235 (0.0269)	-0.0815* (0.0439)	-0.0835* (0.0437)
Refuge	-0.000982 (0.0100)	-0.000994 (0.0100)	-0.0143 (0.0431)	-0.0146 (0.0431)	-0.0185 (0.0229)	-0.0178 (0.0227)	-0.0164 (0.0219)	-0.0159 (0.0217)
Rural	0.00243 (0.00872)	0.00189 (0.00867)	0.0459 (0.0308)	0.0448 (0.0306)	-0.00593 (0.0164)	-0.00443 (0.0163)	-0.0200 (0.0277)	-0.0178 (0.0273)
Camp	0.00755 (0.00950)	0.00912 (0.00936)						
Manufacturing	0.0204 (0.0138)	0.0203 (0.0138)	0.108*** (0.0242)	0.108*** (0.0242)	0.132*** (0.0172)	0.132*** (0.0172)	0.176*** (0.0162)	0.175*** (0.0162)
Construction	-0.106*** (0.0121)	-0.106*** (0.0121)	0.152*** (0.0214)	0.152*** (0.0214)	-0.0395** (0.0161)	-0.0395** (0.0161)	0.0905*** (0.0158)	0.0904*** (0.0158)
Commerce	0.0553*** (0.0140)	0.0553*** (0.0140)	0.0780*** (0.0216)	0.0779*** (0.0216)	0.164*** (0.0172)	0.164*** (0.0172)	0.209*** (0.0166)	0.209*** (0.0166)
Transport	-0.00835 (0.0146)	-0.00846 (0.0146)	0.0487** (0.0231)	0.0486** (0.0231)	0.137*** (0.0200)	0.138*** (0.0199)	0.203*** (0.0175)	0.203*** (0.0175)
Services	-0.550*** (0.0124)	-0.550*** (0.0124)	0.147*** (0.0204)	0.147*** (0.0204)	0.176*** (0.0165)	0.176*** (0.0164)	0.145*** (0.0169)	0.144*** (0.0169)
Checkpoints Index (20km)		-0.00219*** (0.000672)		-0.00479 (0.00555)		-0.00265 (0.00292)		-0.00156 (0.00177)

	(1)	(2)	(3)	(4)	(5)	(6)	(7)	(8)
Settlement Index (20km)		1.388		2.476		−8.712***		−15.50***
		(1.042)		(5.235)		(2.610)		(3.176)
Palestinian Fatalities (lagged)		0.0210***		0.0317		0.0750***		0.0601***
		(0.00584)		(0.0468)		(0.0195)		(0.0169)
Constant	0.455***	0.441***	0.835***	0.809***	2.650***	2.752***	3.446***	3.598***
	(0.0292)	(0.0319)	(0.155)	(0.170)	(0.0805)	(0.0836)	(0.0889)	(0.0980)
Observations	702,469	702,469	125,673	125,673	137,450	137,450	230,084	230,084
R-squared	0.269	0.269	0.014	0.014	0.027	0.027	0.017	0.018
Number of individuals	215,656	215,656	56,167	56,167	58,356	58,356	94,796	94,796

Note: Robust standard errors (Huber–White method) clustered at locality level in parentheses; * significant at 10%; ** significant at 5%; *** significant at 1%. All regressions include individual and time fixed effects. Variables for distance between the locality and the wall, gender and camp residence are omitted as they are fixed though time.

In the next section we present the heterogeneity of effects of the wall construction by taking into consideration individuals' gender, skill level, permit ownership and the type of industry that the individual is working in.

Heterogeneity of effects

In Tables 3, 4, 5 and 6 we present the results of a set of heterogeneity effect estimations on employment, hourly wage, logged numbers of days worked in the previous month and the logged number of hours worked in the previous week, respectively. Yet, for brevity, we discuss the results by the type of heterogeneity in question while taking into account all labour market indicators. The estimations are constructed by running the baseline difference-in-difference while subsetting for the variables for gender, skill level, ownership of a permit to work in Israel and the type of industry one works in. In all models we include the full list of controls. Thus, this provides estimates of the heterogeneity of wall effects across these categories. All models include individual and time fixed effects and robust standard errors using the Huber-White method clustered at the locality level.

Gender

According to this analysis where we subset for gender (Table 12.3), both genders experienced a drop in days worked in the previous month and hours worked in the previous week, while women suffered substantively more. Moreover, this analysis would suggest that only females suffered from a drop in the hours worked ($p<0.01$) while males additionally suffered from a drop in wages as well ($p<0.05$).

In terms of the size of the effects, females on average worked a staggering 54% fewer days after construction of the wall while men worked almost 21% fewer days. Moreover, females on average experienced a 55% drop in the number of hours worked during the week while the effect of the wall on the number of hours worked was statistically insignificant for males. Lastly, only males experienced a drop in wages of roughly 10%. Therefore, it seems that the wall did not cause a loss of jobs or changes in wages among the females but it did affect their time spent at work. These results are consistent with the idea that the economic and psychological tension in the household caused by male members of their household getting less work and being paid less pushed women to deflect work in order to stay at home and care for the household.

Skill

Subsetting for skilled and unskilled workers suggests that although the number of days worked dropped for both skilled and unskilled workers, the effect is much stronger for the skilled workers (see Table 12.4). For the skilled workers, the number of working days dropped by 39% while the unskilled workers experienced a drop of 15%. Furthermore, the number of hours worked dropped only for the unskilled while the corresponding coefficient for the skilled workers is statistically insignificant.

Table 12.3 Heterogeneity of Wall Effects on Labour Market Outcomes: Gender

	(1) Employment Females	(2) Employment Males	(3) Wage Females	(4) Wage Males	(5) Days/Month Females	(6) Days/Month Males	(7) Hours/Week Females	(8) Hours/Week Males
Wall Dummy	0.0168	0.0659	−0.0238	0.106***	0.769***	0.242***	0.843***	0.0826
	(0.0200)	(0.0506)	(0.0501)	(0.0400)	(0.0175)	(0.0354)	(0.290)	(0.0658)
Distance x Wall Dummy	−0.0126	−0.0488	0.0112	−0.110**	−0.782***	−0.233***	−0.807***	−0.0820
	(0.0210)	(0.0514)	(0.0558)	(0.0444)	(0.0220)	(0.0371)	(0.291)	(0.0669)
Constant	0.378***	0.500***	1.053*	0.804***	3.112***	2.714***	3.488***	3.621***
	(0.0340)	(0.0532)	(0.553)	(0.178)	(0.268)	(0.0911)	(0.275)	(0.0958)
Observations	345,762	356,707	20,458	105,215	24,055	113,395	43,182	186,902
R-squared	0.385	0.229	0.016	0.015	0.021	0.030	0.017	0.021
Number of individuals	106,808	108,848	9,451	46,716	9,972	48,384	21,748	73,048

Note: Robust standard errors (Huber–White method) clustered at locality level in parentheses; * significant at 10%; ** significant at 5%; *** significant at 1%. All regressions include individual and time fixed effects and a full set of controls including years of schooling, age, age squared, marital status, urban area / refugee camp residence dummies, industry type dummies and a set of conflict related controls: closure index, settlement population index and number of fatalities in the previous year. Reference category for industry is manufacturing. Distance and camp dummies are excluded as they are fixed through time.

Table 12.4 Heterogeneity of Wall Effects on Labour Market Outcomes: Skill

	(1) Employment Unskilled	(2) Employment Skilled	(3) Wage Unskilled	(4) Wage Skilled	(5) Days Worked/ Month Unskilled	(6) Days Worked/ Month Skilled	(7) Hours Worked/ Week Unskilled	(8) Hours Worked/ Week Skilled
Wall Dummy	0.0649**	−0.00267	0.131	−0.0122	0.181***	0.490***	0.181***	−0.106
	(0.0271)	(0.0309)	(0.0859)	(0.0987)	(0.0330)	(0.0809)	(0.0587)	(0.0656)
Distance x Wall Dummy	−0.0531*	0.00746	−0.114	−0.0138	−0.166***	−0.498***	−0.171***	0.0994
	(0.0279)	(0.0324)	(0.0919)	(0.101)	(0.0380)	(0.0816)	(0.0609)	(0.0676)
Constant	0.576***	−0.172**	0.722***	1.058***	2.735***	2.828***	3.589***	3.564***
	(0.0308)	(0.0675)	(0.231)	(0.311)	(0.120)	(0.126)	(0.116)	(0.197)
Observations	512,585	189,884	72,478	53,195	77,309	60,141	151,174	78,910
R-squared	0.303	0.166	0.016	0.016	0.032	0.024	0.020	0.015
Number of individuals	163,494	65,176	34,559	23,353	35,905	24,377	65,314	32,775

Note: Robust standard errors (Huber–White method) clustered at locality level in parentheses; * significant at 10%; ** significant at 5%; *** significant at 1%. All regressions include individual and time fixed effects and a full set of controls including years of schooling, age, age squared, marital status, urban area / refugee camp residence dummies, industry type dummies and a set of conflict related controls: closure index, settlement population index and number of fatalities in the previous year. Reference category for industry is manufacturing. Distance and camp dummies are excluded as they are fixed through time.

Permit

The heterogenous effect on Palestinian workers who own and do not own a permit for work in Israel is one of the main and most interesting results provided by our analyses. Note that by default, all individuals included in the models on heterogenous effects of permit ownership work in Israel. These workers should be directly affected by the wall construction as the wall figures as an additional obstacle on their way to work. Subsetting for workers with and without a permit suggests that the wall construction has a negative and statistically significant effect (p<0.01) on the probability of employment but only for workers owning a permit to work in Israel. The probability of employment for workers without a permit is unaffected by the wall construction as the coefficient is statistically insignificant (but also negative). This is probably caused by the notable reduction and erratic procedure in issuing working permits after the wall construction. As Palestinian workers need to acquire sponsorship for their permit by their employee, the Israeli employers might be more reluctant to sponsor the permits as the wall would further complicate commuting to and from Israel, thus providing an unreliable labour force. Moreover, the Israeli employers might be further incentivized to hire workers without permits as the administrative procedure could be avoided and the undocumented workers provided with comparatively lower wages than for Palestinian workers with permits.

This understanding is widely supported by the extensive report on working conditions among the Palestinian workers working in Israel conducted by ITUC (2021). Moreover, this is further supported by our data as the probability of employment among the workers without a permit was not affected after the wall construction. The number of days and number of hours worked was negatively affected only for the workers with the permit (p<0.01). This is consistent with the understanding that the wall is causing delays when crossing to and from Israel but only through official wall gates and with clean paperwork. Workers without permits would have been crossing to and from Israel through unofficial channels so the commuting obstacles caused by the wall construction would not have an effect on their commuting time and overall access to Israeli working places. This is supported by the ITUC report (2021) which suggests that illegal workers spend more time in Israel, often in hiding, in order to reduce the number of times they are required to cross the border and thus risking in getting caught. In terms of wages, the wall caused an increase in wages among the workers with permits and a decrease in wages among the workers without a permit, with both coefficients being statistically significant (p<0.01).

Industry type

Subsetting for different industry types provides us with further insight into the heterogeneity of effects (see Table 12.6). For brevity, we report only statistically significant results and focus on employment. The probability of employment after the construction of the wall for Palestinians working in the agriculture, construction and transport sectors dropped dramatically, with the agriculture sector being hit the strongest. On the other hand, the probability of employment rose for Palestinian

Table 12.5 Heterogeneity of Wall Effects on Labour Market Outcomes: Permit

	(1) Employment W Permit	(2) Employment W/O Permit	(3) Wage W Permit	(4) Wage W/O Permit	(5) Days Worked/ Month W Permit	(6) Days Worked/ Month W/O Permit	(7) Hours Worked/ Week W Permit	(8) Hours Worked/ Week W/O Permit
Wall Dummy	0.511***	0.119***	−0.221***	0.457***	0.344***	0.0253	0.462***	0.137**
	(0.0332)	(0.0341)	(0.0596)	(0.0888)	(0.0450)	(0.0895)	(0.0380)	(0.0551)
Distance x Wall Dummy	−0.413***	−0.0425	0.278***	−0.467***	−0.284***	0.0120	−0.479***	−0.0811
	(0.0573)	(0.0785)	(0.107)	(0.126)	(0.0667)	(0.102)	(0.0568)	(0.0953)
Constant	0.545	1.164***	4.610***	2.186*	3.877***	2.820***	3.471***	3.209***
	(0.598)	(0.439)	(1.127)	(1.248)	(0.786)	(0.748)	(0.802)	(0.612)
Observations	12,704	20,499	8,149	9,937	8,698	10,779	9,321	12,325
R-squared	0.137	0.186	0.047	0.045	0.057	0.078	0.033	0.063
Number of individuals	7,045	12,204	4,893	6,976	5,170	7,470	5,503	8,372

Note: Robust standard errors (Huber–White method) clustered at locality level in parentheses; * significant at 10%; ** significant at 5%; *** significant at 1%. All regressions include individual and time fixed effects and a full set of controls including years of schooling, age, age squared, marital status, urban area / refugee camp residence dummies, industry type dummies and a set of conflict related controls: closure index, settlement population index and number of fatalities in the previous year. Reference category for industry is manufacturing. Distance and camp dummies are excluded as they are fixed through time

Table 12.6 Heterogeneity of Wall Effects on Employment: Industry

	(1) Employment Agriculture	(2) Employment Manufacturing	(3) Employment Construction	(4) Employment Commerce	(5) Employment Transport	(6) Employment Services
Wall Dummy	0.510***	−0.0682***	0.223***	0.00730	0.105**	−0.0101*
	(0.0207)	(0.0149)	(0.0200)	(0.0102)	(0.0499)	(0.00520)
Distance x Wall Dummy	−0.492***	0.0843***	−0.171***	−0.00130	−0.120*	0.0131**
	(0.0572)	(0.0254)	(0.0394)	(0.0168)	(0.0522)	(0.00572)
Constant	0.713***	1.031***	0.463**	1.143***	0.575*	−0.101***
	(0.223)	(0.173)	(0.223)	(0.100)	(0.347)	(0.0249)
Observations	60,183	40,302	56,571	50,976	13,808	480,629
R-squared	0.031	0.023	0.080	0.017	0.028	0.004
Number of individuals	31,810	17,929	24,928	22,941	6,149	169,062

Note: Robust standard errors (Huber–White method) clustered at locality level in parentheses; * significant at 10%; ** significant at 5%; *** significant at 1%. All regressions include individual and time fixed effects and a full set of controls including years of schooling, age, age squared, marital status, urban area / refugee camp residence dummies, and a set of conflict related controls: closure index, settlement population index and number of fatalities in the previous year. Reference category for industry is manufacturing. Distance and camp dummies are excluded as they are fixed through time.

working in the manufacturing sector and services, although the effect in terms of the effect size is not as strong. These results are consistent with the idea that the wall is cutting access to the Palestinian land on the other side of the wall, thus limiting employment opportunities in the agriculture. Furthermore, as the majority of Palestinian workers in Israel work in the construction sector, a drop in the probability of employment in this sector is expected as well. Finally, as the West Bank is highly reliant on Israel for trade,[49] the wall is causing a drop in employment for the transport sector as the wall is very likely further complicating the transport of goods between the West Bank and Israel. It is possible that the limited increases of the probability of employment in the manufacturing and the service sector mirror the Palestinian efforts to find alternative jobs in response to the loss of their previous employment in the sectors of agriculture, construction and transport.

Conclusion

In this chapter we examined the effects of the West Bank wall construction on labour market outcomes of Palestinians living in the West Bank. In spite of the extensive research on the effects of the closure regime,[50] the consequences of the construction of the West Bank separation wall received comparatively less academic attention.[51] By employing a difference-in-difference estimation strategy on fine grained individual level panel data and taking into account an extensive set of both individual level and locality level controls we provide first causal evidence of the wall effects on labour market outcomes.

Overall, the wall caused a significant decrease in Palestinian hourly wages as well as a reduction on the number of days worked during the month. Palestinians living in the localities closer to the wall on average worked 5% days less for a 10% lower hourly wage in the month following the wall construction. As the average number of days worked during the month for the whole of West Bank is around 22 days (PLFS), a 5% decrease would indicate that the wall is costing each affected Palestinian on average just over 1 day worth of work per month. Taking into account both reduced wages and the loss of working days, an average Palestinian worker loses roughly 186NIS or US$56 per month due to construction of the wall.

We further examined the potential complexity of wall effects by testing whether the construction had a differential effect across gender, skill, permit ownership and industry type. According to our analyses, the wall has a gendered effect as females on average worked a staggering 54% fewer days after the wall has been constructed while men worked almost 21% fewer days. Moreover, females on average experienced a 55% drop in the number of hours worked during the week while the effect of the wall on the number of hours worked was statistically insignificant for males. Secondly, both skilled and unskilled workers were affected negatively by the wall with the effect being much stronger for skilled workers. Our analysis would suggest that the number of working days for the skilled workers dropped by 39% while the unskilled workers experienced a drop of 15%.

Thirdly, focusing on the workers employed in Israel, we provide evidence that the wall construction has a negative effect on the probability of employment only for workers owning a permit to work in Israel. This, coupled with other results on the heterogeneity of wall effects on Palestinians with and without permit ownership would suggest that the wall is causing delays when crossing to and from Israel but only through official wall gates and with clean paperwork. Workers without permits would have been crossing to and from Israel through unofficial channels so the commuting obstacles caused by construction of the wall would not have an effect on their commuting time and overall access to Israeli working places.

Finally, our analysis of the heterogenous effects of the wall on Palestinians working in different industries would suggest that employment in the agriculture, construction and transport sectors were hit the strongest while the probability of employment rose for Palestinian working in the manufacturing sector and services. It is possible that the limited increases in probability of employment in the manufacturing and the service sector mirror the Palestinians' efforts to find alternative jobs in response to the loss of their previous employment in the sectors of agriculture, construction and transport. This is consistent with qualitative evidence provided by various NGOs and international organizations which so far have mainly focused on agriculture. Thus, the mechanism behind a drop in employment in the construction and transport sector and an increase in the manufacturing and service sectors warrant further research.

Notes

1. For the purposes of this study, we use the terms 'wall' and 'separation wall' interchangeably. Following Rogers and Ben-David (2010) the term 'separation wall' figures as a middle ground as it is occasionally used by both sides. Formally, the state of Israel calls it a 'security fence', Palestinians use the term 'apartheid wall' while the International Court of Justice uses the term 'West Bank wall'. For an in-depth discussion on terminology see Rogers and Ben-David (2010).
2. Roy 2001.
3. Roy 2001; Cali and Miaari 2018.
4. Jones, Leuenberger and Wills 2016.
5. The settlement policy began in 1967 under the leadership of Israeli Deputy Prime Minister Yigal Allon; for details see Zertal and Eldar (2009).
6. Cohen 2006.
7. Amnesty International 2019.
8. Kershner 2005.
9. Miaari, Zussman and Zussman 2014.
10. UN OCHA, 2006.
11. Ibid.
12. Cohen 2006.
13. B'Tselem 2017.
14. https://www.jewishvirtuallibrary.org/background-and-overview-of-israel-s-security-fence (last entry: 28.04.2022)
15. B'Tselem 2012, 2017.
16. Ibid.
17. B'Tselem, 2012.
18. B'Tselem, 2011; see also reports from Karem Navot by Etkes (2013, 2015 and 2018).
19. UN OCHA 2017: 10.

20 B'Tselem 2011: 44.
21 B'Tselem 2017; ARIJ, 2011.
22 B'Tselem 2017.
23 UN OCHA 2017.
24 B'Tselem 2011.
25 B'Tselem 2017; Palestinian Authority 2016; ICJ 2004.
26 Roy 2001: 377.
27 Miaari, Zussman and Zussman 2014.
28 Longo, Canetti and N. Hite-Rubin 2014.
29 Roy 2001.
30 Dana 2107: 905.
31 B'Tselem 2011: 46.
32 B'Tselem 2011.
33 UN OCHA 2017.
34 ITUC 2021.
35 ITUC 2021; World Bank 2010.
36 World Bank 2010.
37 Roy 2001; Etkes 2013.
38 Etkes 2013.
39 Etkes 2018: 7.
40 For an overview see Jones, Leuenberger and Wills. 2016.
41 Cited in Oberholzer 2016: 7.
42 El-Atrash 2016: 376.
43 Ibid.
44 Data for the years 1995, 2000, 2001, 2003, 2005, 2008, 2009 and 2010 are collected by ARIJ and data for the years 2004, 2005 and 2007 are collected by the OCHA. For the years when data on physical barriers is missing (1998 –99) we match the test score data with physical barriers data in 1995. This assumes that there were no changes in the number and location of checkpoints between 1995 and 1999.
45 Longo, Canetti and N. Hite-Rubin 2014.
46 Mansour and Rees 2012.
47 Calì and Miaari 2018.
48 ITUC 2021.
49 World Bank 2006, 2008a, 2008b.
50 Calì and Miaari 2018; Etkes 2011; Sanders 2010.
51 Oberholzer 2016; Braverman 2009; Di Cintio 2012.

References

Amnesty International (2019), *Destination: Occupation: Digital Tourism and Israel's Illegal Settlements in the Occupied Palestinian Territories*, London: Amnesty International, available at https://www.amnesty.org.uk/files/2019-01/Destination%20occupation%20online.pdf?R44FHd4Tzm2nuui9DO1btMFOIYgsTdvT= (accessed 5 January 2023)

ARIJ (Applied Research Institute-Jerusalem) (2011), 'Status of the Environment in the Occupied Palestinian Territory: A Human Based Approach', Jerusalem: ARIJ.

Braverman, I. (2009), *Planted Flags: Trees, Land, and Law in Israel/Palestine*, Cambridge: Cambridge University Press.

B'Tselem (1999), *Builders of Zion: Human Rights Violations of Palestinians from the Occupied Territories Working in Israel and in the Settlements*, Jerusalem: B'Tselem.

B'Tselem (2011), *Human Rights in the Occupied Territories, 2011 Annual Report*, Jerusalem: B'Tselem.

B'Tselem (2012), *Arrested Development: The Long Term Impact of Israel's Separation Barrier in the West Bank*, Jerusalem: B'Tselem.

B'Tselem (2017), *Annual Report*, Jerusalem: B'Tselem.

B'Tselem (2021), *This is Ours – And This, Too: Israel's Settlement Policy in the West Bank*, Jerusalem: B'Tselem.

Calì, M., and S. H. Miaari (2018), 'The Labor Market Impact of Mobility Restrictions: Evidence from the West Bank', *Labour Economics* 51: 136–51.

Cohen, S. E. (2006), 'Israel's West Bank Barrier: An Impediment to Peace?' *Geographical Review* 96 (4): 682–95.

Dana, K. (2017), 'The West Bank Apartheid/Separation Wall: Space, Punishment and the Disruption of Social Continuity', *Geopolitics* 22 (4): 887–910.

Di Cintio, M. (2013), *Walls: Travels along the Barricades*, Berkeley, CA: Counterpoint.

El-Atrash, A. (2016), 'Implications of the Segregation Wall on the Two-state Solution', *Journal of Borderlands Studies* 31 (3): 365–80.

Etkes, D. (2013), 'Israeli Settlers' Agriculture as a Means of Land Takeover in the West Bank', Israel: Kerem Navot.

Etkes, D. (2015), 'A Locked Garden: Declaration of Closed Areas in the West Bank', Jerusalem: Kerem Navot.

Etkes, D. (2018), 'Seize the Moral Low Ground: Israeli Land Seizure for "security needs" in the West Bank', Jerusalem: Kerem Navot.

Etkes, H. (2011), 'The Impact of Employment in Israel on the Palestinian Labor Force', *Peace Economics, Peace Science and Public Policy* 18 (2), doi:10.2139/ssrn.1974213.

Farsakh, L. (2002), 'Palestinian Labor Flows to the Israeli Economy: A Finished Story?' *Journal of Palestine Studies* 32 (1): 13–27.

ICJ (2004), *Advisory Opinion Concerning Legal Consequences of the Construction of a Wall in the Occupied Palestinian Territory*, International Court of Justice, 9 July 2004, available at: https://www.refworld.org/cases,ICJ,414ad9a719.html (accessed 6 June 2022)

ITUC (2021), 'Workers' Rights in Crisis: Palestinian Workers in Israel and the Settlements', available at https://www.ituc-csi.org/workers-rights-in-crisis-palestine (accessed 6 June 2022)

Jones, R., C. Leuenberger and E. R. Wills (2016), 'The West Bank Wall', *Journal of Borderlands Studies* Leuenberger and E. R. Wills 31 (3): 271–9.

Kershner, I. (2005), *Barrier: The Seam of the Israeli-Palestinian Conflict*, New York: Palgrave Macmillan.

Longo, M., D. Canetti and N. Hite-Rubin (2014), 'A Checkpoint Eeffect? Evidence from a Natural Experiment on Travel Restrictions in the West Bank', *American Journal of Political Science* 58 (4):1006–23.

Mansour, H. (2010), 'The Effects of Labor Supply Shocks on Labor Market Outcomes: Evidence from the Israeli–Palestinian Conflict', *Labour Economics* 17 (6): 930–9.

Mansour, H., and D. I. Rees (2012), 'Armed Conflict and Birth Weight: Evidence from the al-Aqsa Intifada', *Journal of Development Economics* 99 (1): 190–9.

Miaari, S. H., and R. M. Sauer (2011), 'The Labor Market Costs of Conflict: Closures, Foreign Workers, and Palestinian Employment and Earnings', *Review of Economics of the Household* 9 (1):129–48.

Miaari, S., A. Zussman and N. Zussman (2014), 'Employment Restrictions and Political Violence in the Israeli–Palestinian Conflict', *Journal of Economic Behavior & Organization* 101: 24–44.

Oberholzer, F. (2015), 'The Impact of the West Bank Wall on the Palestinian Labour Market', *International Development Policy Revue internationale de politique de développement* 6 (2), available at https://journals.openedition.org/poldev/2002 (accessed 5 January 2023).

Palestinian Authority (2016), *National Policy Agenda 2017-2022*.

Rogers, R., and A. Ben-David (2010), 'Coming to Terms: a Conflict Analysis of the Usage, in Official and Unofficial Sources, of 'Security Fence', 'Apartheid Wall', and other Terms for the Structure between Israel and the Palestinian Territories', *Media, War & Conflict* 3 (2); 202–29.

Roy, S. (2001), 'Palestinian Society and Economy: The Continued Denial of Possibility', *Journal of Palestine Studies* 30 (4): 5–20.

Sanders, E. (2010), 'Israel to Deport Hundreds of Migrant Workers' Children', *Los Angeles Times* 2 August.

OCHA (United Nations Office for the Coordination of Humanitarian Affairs) (2006), *Humanitarian Impact of the West Bank Barrier Crossing the Barrier: Palestinian Access to Agricultural Land*.

OCHA (United Nations Office for the Coordination of Humanitarian Affairs) (2017), *Occupied Palestinian Territory: Humanitarian Facts and Figures*.

World Bank (2006), 'An Update on Palestinian Movement, Access and Trade in the West Bank and Gaza'. World Bank.

World Bank (2008a), 'West Bank and Gaza Update', *The World Bank Group: A Quarterly Publication of the West Bank and Gaza Office*.

World Bank (2008b), 'West Bank and Gaza: Palestinian Trade: West Bank Routes', The World Bank: Report No. 46807.

World Bank (2010), 'West Bank and Gaza: Checkpoints and Barriers: Searching for Livelihoods Gender Dimensions of Economic Collapse', World Bank: Report No. 49699.

Zertal, I., and A. Eldar (2009), *Lords of the Land: the War over Israel's Settlements in the Occupied Territories, 1967-2007*, London: Hachette UK.

13

Palestinian Refugee Archives

UNRWA and the Problem with Sources

Salim Tamari and Elia Zureik

The United Nations Relief and Works Agency (UNWRA) was established following the war of 1948 as part of General Assembly Resolution 194 as caretaker of Palestinian refugees. It employs over 30,000 employees involved in the fields of health, education and welfare administration in Lebanon, Syria, Jordan, the West Bank and Gaza. UNRWA's partly digitized archives is one of the richest sources of sociological data on any refugee population in the world, covering demographic, economic, household, health and educational attributes. It is also comprehensive and diachronic covering the shifting features of the Palestinian population over seven decades since the inception of UNRWA (1951–2022). The family files described below contain a unique document for each refugee family describing the conditions under which each family became a refugee in the war of 1948, and listing family belongings left in the village or city of origin. The following essay is derived from a 2000 report titled *Reinterpreting the Historical Record: The Uses of Palestinian Refugee Archives for Social Science Research* (Institute of Jerusalem Studies, 2001). It integrates two chapters which summarize the authors' contributions on the problem with refugee data sources, with particular reference to UNRWA sources. The authors conducted a field survey of the data sources in Lebanon, Syria, Jordan and the Palestinian Territories during 1999–2001. In addition to the survey of the UNRWA Archives which is presented here, the full study includes contributions by Martina Rieker (on policy analysis), Bassem Serhan (Lebanon archives), Jaber Suleiman and Manar Rabbani (on Syrian archives), Julie Peteet (on American Friends Service Committee (AFSC) archives), Michael Fischbach (the United Nations Conciliation Commission for Palestine (UNCCP) records). The figures listed in this essay refer to the situation as it existed in 1991–2001.

Introduction: data sources on Palestinian refugees

While UNRWA is the main depository of data on registered Palestinian refugees, it is not the only such source. A sister UN organization, the United Nations Conciliation Commission for Palestine (UNCCP), possesses in its archives extensive data on confiscated Palestinian refugee property. The archives of the International Red Cross (IRC) Geneva and Bern, and the American Friends Service Committee (AFSC) offices in Philadelphia contain valuable information about Palestinian refugees that predate UNRWA's establishment in 1950.

In an effort to preserve a major segment of Palestinian history for national and research purposes, the Institute for Jerusalem Studies (IJS) undertook an assessment of the feasibility of digitizing available archival data stored in paper form in 2000. The IJS also contracted a multimedia specialist to prepare a pilot study to estimate the cost and ways to electronically link various aspects of the UNRWA archival system including text and graphics.

UNRWA's archives: a historical note

UNRWA is the successor to the short-lived United Nations Relief for Palestine Refugees (UNRPR), which was established on 11 December 1948 by a United Nations General Assembly Resolution 194 (III) and existed from January 1949 to May 1950. The purpose of the UNRPR and its successor UNRWA is to alleviate the hardships faced by the close to three-quarters of a million Palestinians who became refugees in 1948 and their descendants. For more than half a century the refugees, now into their fourth generation, have been prevented by Israel from returning to their homes. UNRWA, which is the longest serving refugee organization dedicated to one specific group, has been caring for Palestinian refugees through thick and thin, in a region that has seen five major wars (in 1948, 1956, 1967, 1973 and 1982), as well as numerous other internal upheavals, including two major Palestinian uprisings against Israeli occupation in 1987 and 2000. Throughout this entire period, UNRWA strove to maintain a functioning organizational and bureaucratic structure spanning the locations of refugee camps in five fields of operations in the West Bank, Gaza, Jordan, Lebanon and Syria. Until l995, UNRWA's administrative headquarters were located in Vienna, after which they were moved to Gaza.

Like any other organization of its size, employing in excess of 20,000 people consisting of doctors, teachers and administrators, UNRWA has become a depository of vital information akin to census data chronicling the genealogy of Palestinian refugee life from the time of their dispersal up to the present. The purpose of this chapter is to describe the scope and nature of information stored on Palestinian refugees, with a view to recommending ways to improve access to and storage of millions of documents, which if not properly transferred to electronic medium soon, are bound to decay and become degraded thus rendering their future use in doubt.

As a start, the two authors prepared in 1996 Phase I of the feasibility report on the conditions of the UNRWA archives in Amman, Gaza and the West Bank. The report is reproduced in this chapter and details the structure of UNRWA's archives. The archives consist of the original family documents deposited by the refugees with the Agency; basic 'family fact sheets' containing interviews carried out by the Agency with the refugees in1948;socio-economic database containing information about families classified as hardship cases; basic information about individual refugees; administrative records of the Agency; health and education records which extend back to no more than five years; and the audiovisual holdings which contain still pictures, films, slides, videos, posters and maps.

Two years later, in 1998, Phase II of the UNRWA fieldwork commenced to complement the 1996 UNRWA site visits. Two researchers, Basim Serhan and Suleiman Jaber, were contracted to prepare reports on the UNRWA archives in Beirut and Damascus, which serve as headquarters for UNRWA's fields of operation in Lebanon and Syria. These three reports provide the most thorough description of UNRWA's archival structure.

International Red Cross and American Friends Service Committee

Prior to the arrival of UNRWA on the scene, and immediately after the 1948 war, the IRC conducted the first systematic registration and provided emergency services to the refugees in the West Bank, Lebanon and Syria, while the AFSC did the same for the refugees in Gaza. Both organizations compiled data on Palestinian refugees at the time, all of which was turned over to UNRWA when it was established in 1950.

United Nations Conciliation Commission for Palestine

The UNCCP was established by the United Nations General Assembly Resolution 194, the same resolution that governs the UNRWA mandate. The UNCCP was instructed by the UN to facilitate the repatriation of the refugees, their resettlement, rehabilitation and economic compensation. Implicit in this mandate was the need to carry out a valuation of refugees' property. For over a decade, between 1951 and 1964, the UNCCP undertook to document the extent of Palestinian property losses and come up with a value figure for this property. In the process, the organization produced close to half million documents. Recently, efforts were made to digitize the paper documents as part of the UN efforts at modernizing its records.

Two overriding themes concern us in this essay. One is to describe in detail the organizational structure and the practices which evolved over more than half century to monitor, administer and provide essential services to a refugee population that numbers in excess of four million people and is scattered in different geographical areas. The second is to provide the reader with a sense of how this information, all of which practically exists in archival format, could be preserved as an integral part of Palestinian history, and eventually utilized to carry out policy-related research and academic analysis.

The first organized attempts made at assisting Palestinian refugees immediately after the 1948 Nakba were undertaken by the AFSC and the ICRC. In the closing months of 1948, the AFSC was asked by the United Nations to offer assistance to the 200,000 Palestinian refugees who ended up in Gaza after their expulsion and flight from their homes and villages. The archives of the AFSC in Philadelphia, started in January 1949, when the AFSC established field offices in Gaza, to May 1950, when the AFSC handed over its refugee files to the newly established UNRWA. The organization of the archives is meticulous. The AFSC kept detailed records on the administration of Palestinian refugees, and reflections and impressions of the AFSC's relief workers at the time. In addition to the statistical data which was turned over to the UNRWA and is not available in Philadelphia, the archives contain a wealth of qualitative information which captures the operation of the largest refugee NGO at the time in an environment where the local population in Gaza numbering around 80,000 was overwhelmed and ill equipped to handle a flood of 200,000 refugees. For researchers, the administrative material is useful in highlighting the process of organizational decision making under highly stressful conditions. In her report on the AFSC archives Julie Peteet describes the archives as a classic example of object instruction. She remarks that 'refugee voices are completely absent from these archives', and goes on to say that 'For those interested in the construction of the refugee as an object of intervention and management, these documents are exceedingly enlightening'. Parallel to the AFSC activities, the ICRC offices were set up in December 1948 in Amman, Beirut and various parts of Palestine. On behalf of the UNRPR, the ICRC provided medical and relief assistance to Palestinian refugees until May 1950, when their services were transferred to the UNRWA.

When the ICRC terminated its refugee assistance operation in 1950, it shipped only one-tenth of its estimated ten tons of documents to its Geneva offices. The rest were destroyed in Beirut. Jalal al Hussaini, investigating the ICRC archives, discovered that none of the personal information about refugees was available in Geneva, even though the ICRC had registered between February and April 1950, 331,000 refugees in 'Arab Palestine' (i.e., outside the Israel armistice border of 1948), and an additional 28,000 internal refugees in what became Israel. In all likelihood, these records were passed on to UNRWA with the transfer of responsibility between the two organizations. As with what the AFSC archives revealed, here too the bulk of the material in Geneva deals with the administrative and organizational functions of the ICRC, and chronicles reports from its field offices in various locations in the Middle East. To the extent that these records dealt with individual refugees, they related to the limited number of family reunification cases, where basic information about the applicant was preserved. However, these application forms did not include the full range of demographic and background data on the applicant. In some cases, the ICRC files contained information about the circumstances surrounding the expulsion and displacement of refugees. In other cases, the ICRC was singled out by its own functionaries for not having provided sufficient assistance to refugees to curtail their hasty departure from Palestine. The definition of what constitutes a refugee seems to be guided by administrative criteria than by any universal definition. Thus, the ICRC definition of refugees hinged on losing their domicile as a result of the 1948 war. This definition did not accommodate those who lost their livelihood but remained in their domicile, such as the residents of Tulkarem and the Bedouins of Beersheba region. In spite of any shortcomings, the ICRC did manage to set up 36 refugee camps and provide preliminary educational, health and relief services until UNRWA took over the task of looking after the 'Refugees of Palestine'.

Our estimate, after visiting UNRWA Headquarters in Amman, Gaza and the West Bank, is that close to 70 million documents are stored in these sites. The survey of the UNRWA offices in Syria, covered the family files, hardship cases and educational and health data. It is estimated that there are 5.3 million documents in total. The survey count of documents in UNRWA's Lebanon fields of operation carried out produced a figure of 6.3 million sheets of paper. The count for Syria and Lebanon did not include administrative records, since most of these administrative documents are stored in the Amman headquarters. Altogether we can say that there are around 80 million sheets of paper of direct interest to the digitization project, in addition to the audiovisual material.

There are important variations in the administrative practices, depending on the site in question. For example, in Syria the government kept close tabs on the refugee population from the outset. the Syrian Ministry of Labour and Welfare maintains close coordination with UNRWA, so much so that the registration number given to Palestinian refugees by the Syrian government appears on the refugee file maintained by UNRWA, and vice versa. Any changes in the family status of the refugee (birth, marriage, death etc.) must also be coordinated between the two agencies. This is in contrast to Lebanon where although the government set up a separate administrative unit in charge of the refugees, the chaotic situation in the country made such close coordination between the UNRWA and the Lebanese government impossible to maintain. Jordan too maintains a separate department dealing with Palestinian refugee affairs which is affiliated with the Prime Minister's office. Unlike Syria, Lebanon and other Arab countries, Jordan granted Palestinian refugees of 1948 full citizenship status, and it coordinates with UNRWA routine monitoring of the camps. Even in the West Bank and Gaza where the rest of the refugees are located, the Israeli Civil Administration carried out in 1967 its census of the occupied territories and maintained the population registry until it was turned over to the Palestinian Authority (PA) in the wake of the Oslo agreement. Even here, the PA, in accordance with the Interim Agreement with Israel, continues to provide the Israeli government with all updates to the population registry. At least this was the case until the outbreak of the Second Uprising following the collapse of the Camp David talks in September 2000.

The UNRWA registration forms contain historical and current information dating to the pre-1948 period. For example, the pre-1948 information (contained in the family files) covers things such as birth and marriage certificates, property deeds, land registration, tax receipts etc. The registration coding scheme makes it possible to trace changes in family and individual member status across four generations, covering social and geographic mobility of the refugees. It is thus possible to construct a demographic profile of Palestinian refugees for policy and research purposes. Through proper linkages with other documents in the files one should be able to examine relationships between health factors, education and other demographic variables, bearing in mind that the educational and health data extends back only five years. The process of linkages through creating a standardized coding system for the various types of documents in UNRWA's archives is yet to be achieved. This is in spite of UNRWA's valiant attempts to create a uniform registration system. In instances when UNRWA contemplated substituting the current family/household system with an individually based registration system, the host governments reacted with unease, fearing that such a system would imply undertaking a census and as such poses 'a threat to their national statistical sovereignty'.

On occasions one comes across data revealing information that has been little known so far. For example, the UNRWA archives in Syria contain information about two depopulated villages near the Syrian-Israeli border containing the Baqqarah and Ghannameh tribes. Although they first became refugees in 1948, to be later allowed to return to their villages in 1949 after the signing of truce agreement between Israel and Syria, Israel moved some of them in 1951 to other locations within the Green Line; and in 1956, on the eve of the invasion of Egypt, Israel expelled them to the Syrian Golan heights, and they eventually moved to other locations within Syria in the wake of the 1967 war. As of this date UNRWA refuses to register them as refugees, after numerous attempts were made by the refugees themselves.

Although the UNRWA archives contained information about refugee property ownership, the extent of this information was rather limited. A more comprehensive source is the database compiled by the UNCCP and stored in New York. There is no doubt that there is an overlap between the UNRWA and the UNCCP data. The UNCCP did not distinguish between refugee and non-refugee in its survey. It thus included data about Palestinians who became refugs in 1948 but did not register with the UNRWA, as well as information about non-Palestinian owners of property in Palestine, and Palestinians who remained in what became Israel. Michael Fischbach states that the UNCCP records contain 'the most complete and most reliable source of data indicating the number of refugee landowners and the scope of their losses available in the world'. The shortcoming of these archives is due to the fact that the UNCCP did not take into account collectively owned land, Waqf land, built-up areas, publicly owned land, and movable property. In short, the UNCCP records must be used with care, particularly in calculating Palestinian losses for compensation purposes in any future settlement between the Palestinians and Israelis.

In addition, UNCCP records have major flaws, pointed out both by Fischbach and Abdul Raziq. One of these is the absence of all records pertaining to land in the Beersheba region, where communal and nomadic usufruct was preponderant. That land constituted a very substantial area of Arab property in pre-1948 Palestine. The inclusion of these properties will be a major task involved in the updating of these files.

One main objective of this archival document is to initiate both policy and scholarly studies on how best to use refugee records in a manner that will relate to the current debate about the future of refugees. Most pressing among them is to help in a concrete way to address the issues of claims for restitution and compensation of refugee property, and the issue of repatriation of refugees. We hope that these documents will contribute to create the basis of an integrated corpus of data which cross-references material from UNRWA, UNCCP, IRC and AFSC archives. Another task would be to enhance the internal usability of each of those registries. In the case of UNRWA we are proposing that future input be made in three areas:

- The expansion of the Unified Registration System (URS) to include regular input from the various health and education field offices so that the demographic profiles are more comprehensive. This will allow not only for regional comparisons about the conditions of refugees but will also give us time series comparisons about changes in their conditions.

- The incorporation of historical material located mainly in the family files, as well as in other data from the Central Registry of UNRWA archives, into the computerized system.
- This also entails transforming the URS from a current database into a historical database, allowing for the accumulation of biographical data over four generations of refugees.

With such horizontal and vertical expansion of the UNRWA database, the researcher can begin to examine regional differences among refugee communities, and address in a more systematic manner the tasks of rebuilding refugees' lives once schemes for repatriation are undertaken. Material is suggested in this chapter about the utility of such investigations using existing data. For example, we show how the URS can be effectively utilized for tracing place of origin of refugees before the 1948 war and correlating this geographic information with their current residence, refugee camp status, material condition of the family, and the demographic profiles of its members. With the enhanced incorporation of the family files, and with effective linkages to the UNCCP files, we can expand these correlations to assess losses during the war, property claims, and existing skills obtained by family members. With the preparation of claim files such data will prove to be indispensable.

But for this type of research and policy programmes to be effective we should also focus on the question of linkages. As they were constituted since 1950, UNRWA family files are not the proper source for establishing systematic documentation for material and non-material claims by refugee household. Their utility is limited in giving a partial picture about the social conditions about the refugee household, their habitat before their exile, and the conditions that led to their expulsion from Palestine. Only by linking these files to the Refugee Property 1 (known as RP1) forms (covering the bulk of private property entries) that constitute the basis of the UNCCP data does one begin to acquire a holistic picture about the material conditions of the refugee families and the magnitude of their losses.

It is hoped that these collected papers will provide a modest but useful basis for the researchers and policy makers seeking sources and methods to establish a linkage between the four main data sources on Palestinian refugees.

UNRWA archives on Palestinian refugees

The United Nations General Assembly decision to move the United Nations Relief and Works Agency (UNRWA) Headquarters from Vienna to Gaza, and eventually wind down its operations, had serious consequences for the future of Palestinian refugees on two levels.

First, regarding the existential future and legal status of Palestinian refugees and with it the future of the camps. Second, which is our primary concern here, is the future of the organization and the wealth of information stored in it, estimated to be in the millions of documents. Current information and historical data on more than 3.2 million Palestinian refugees and spanning close to half a century of operation are stored in various UNRWA archives and fields of operation. This information, the bulk of which is stored on paper, deals with personal, familial, administrative, legal and organizational matters. If not transferred to another medium and preserved properly, this information is likely to further erode with the passage of time and render the medium on which it is stored inaccessible to further use and preservation.

In cooperation with UNRWA, the Institute for Palestine Studies (IPS) prepared a feasibility study proposal which was submitted to possible donors for the purpose of funding. Partial funding of the feasibility proposal necessitated dividing the work into two phases. The present report is the outcome of phase I of the feasibility study. It concentrates on surveying the conditions of the UNRWA archives in three of its five fields of operations: Jordan, the West Bank and Gaza. The archives in Lebanon and Syria will be dealt with in phase II of the project. Additionally, the American Friends Service Committee's archives in Philadelphia, which contain data on the initial displacement of Palestinian refugees in Gaza, will be covered in phase II.

Gaps in the records

It is important to bear in mind that the above information does not cover the entire Palestinian refugee population, let alone the Palestinian people. With regard to the former, the UNRWA family archives do not include information about Palestinian refugees, who qualified for registration under UNRWA's definition of 'Palestine refugees' but were excluded from its mandate because they did not originally settle in any of UNRWA's designated Five Fields of Operation.

From 1993, UNRWA began to accept applications from these refugees for inclusion in its registry. In addition, Palestinian 'internal refugees', who were displaced during the 1948 war but remained in what became Israel, have been excluded from UNRWA's registry of refugees, even though the ICR and the AFSC carried out an enumeration of these internal refugees. During its visit, the feasibility study team (FST) discovered that the UNRWA archives contain uncatalogued basic information about this group. They will be incorporated in the universe of refugee population. Third, well-to-do Palestinians who were displaced during 1948, or those who were outside Mandatory Palestine when the 1948 war broke out, do not appear in UNRWA's list of refugees. Finally, Palestinians displaced for the first time during the 1967 war do not formally fall under UNRWA's jurisdiction, even though the organization assists them in conjunction with the host governments of Jordan and Syria.

Amman headquarters and field offices

The feasibility study has several objectives. First, it intends to recommend ways to preserve the only systematic information available on close to half of the estimated seven million Palestinians worldwide. Second, it assesses the feasibility and possibility of eventual transfer of these archives to the Palestinian Authority (PA) where they will be stored in a national Palestinian archive. Third, to organize the data in such a way so as to make it available for research and policymaking. Fourth, to maintain the operational use of the data as long as UNRWA maintains its functions vis-à-vis the refugees. Fifth, to establish levels of access depending on the type of user in question, e.g., administrator, policy maker, researcher or lay person.

In order to achieve these objectives, the feasibility study proposed to use the latest technology in order to preserve UNRWA's millions of documents electronically through the use of hypertext and multimedia technology where text, sound, graphics and pictures will be stored on a CD-ROM.' This will give the user simultaneous and easy access to a variety of types and levels of information and at various levels of linkages between the data. Moreover, the information will be stored in such a way so as to enable future users to manipulate it for research and policy purposes, and, as long as UNRWA remains in existence, to update its information for operational purposes.

This necessitated the designing of data bases with open architecture in order to facilitate their constant updating and classification. An elaborate coding scheme will be developed in the future to facilitate easy use of the stored information. Additionally, and depending on the type of usage, different access methods will be developed to conform to standards of confidentiality.

In specific terms, the feasibility study aimed at linking electronically, for the first time, the main data sources available at UNRWA. They consisted of the following:

- The Central Registry, which contains records related to various legal and administrative matters pertaining to programs, agreements with governments and international organizations, and information about UNRWA personnel.
- The Unified Registration System (URS), presently operated from the Amman Headquarters, which integrates data stored in UNRWA's archives with data gathered regularly from the Field Offices.
- The Socio-Economic Database, which contains information profiling individuals and families who qualify for hardship assistance.
- The Demographic Database, which encompasses background information about refugee families and their members.
- The Family Files, which are distributed in UNRWA's five Fields, but so far have not been computerized.
- The Health Files, located at the various Field Offices and clinics in each of the five Fields of UNRWA's operation, and contain detailed information about the health conditions of refugees.
- The Educational Files, which are located at the various schools and Field Offices in each of UNRWA's five Fields of operation.
- The Films, videos and still pictures, which date back to the early fifties, if not earlier, and are currently stored in Gaza and UNRWA's Amman HQs.

Compared to the rest of the data bases and because of their historic nature, the Family Files and the Central Registry contain the most systematic information stored on Palestinian refugees. Their information provides the basis for policy and research analysis. For example, data stored in the Family Files provide in some cases the most detailed information on the demographic background of Palestinians at the individual and family levels. Age, generation, gender, family size, occupation and marital status, to name a few of the possible codes to be used in classifying the information contained in the Family Files, provide us with rich material on Palestinian refugees spanning across three generations. Longitudinal analysis of the data, through comparing educational levels of members of the same family across generations is a unique opportunity to assess the relationship between demographic background and educational attainment.

Similarly, by linking the Family Files to data available in the departments of Health and Education one can obtain a reliable picture of the determinants of the well-being of Palestinian refugees. It is possible to learn from the rich experience of UNRWA and the wealth of the available data to apply this information to Palestinian society as a whole.

In addition to demographic data, the Family Files contain in some cases information about land and property ownership in Palestine prior to the dispersal, certificates of birth, marriage and death, place of origin and destination of the refugee, and the circumstances surrounding their exodus.

The Central Registry Files document the workings of the organization by preserving, for example, documents pertaining to the various projects undertaken by the agency since its inception, the legal, financial and administrative aspects of the running of the agency, including information on its more than 20,000 employees the overwhelming majority of whom are Palestinian refugees themselves. While so far this has not been explored, these archives contain the experience of the agency, its so-called institutional memory, and could very well provide useful information for the nascent Palestinian state in the areas of administration, and delivery of health and education services. Whether it is research, policy, or sheer interest, information in these files will prove to be of immense importance for preserving the collective memory of the Palestinian people and their travails over the last half century.

In November 1995, UNRWA distributed a project proposal aimed at computerizing and developing a Unified Registration System which at that time was estimated to cost $3.2 million, aiming at integrating three of its databases:

- a database on individual registration containing 3,322,210 registered Palestinian refugees.
- a database on 676,025 family files; and
- a database on 181,437 hardship cases.

The advantage of this system, from UNRWA's point of view, is that it furthers the efficient running of the agency and the operation of its various functions, and eventually would link the agency's various social programs such as health education, and social services.

Subsequently UNRWA prepared a proposal for a pilot study to assess in more concrete ways means of storing on optical disk data derived from its Family Files. This pilot project, budgeted at around $50,000, focused on Jordan only. It was proposed, by using the same indexing method common to several of UNRWA databases, to link these files to other components of the URS, which include the Registration Database and the Socio-Economic Database.

Finally, while the first two proposals were intended to focus on the efficient running and delivery aspects of UNRWA, there was a third proposal whose purpose is mainly research-oriented with some policy implications. The French Centre d'Etudes et de Recherches sur le Moyen-Orient Contemporain (CERMOC) proposed to approach UNRWA as a prototype of an international organization with a view to analysing its administrative culture and mode of interaction with its outside environments, be they refugees or other international actors.

By drawing upon political science, sociology, and anthropology, CERMOC proposed to assess the means by which it is possible to transfer the knowledge and expertise gained by UNRWA over the years to Palestinian society at large, including the PNA. This objective was achieved through in-depth interviews with representatives of the agency and by carrying out documentary analysis of its archival material. In an effort to tap the organization's institutional memory, CERMOC was hoping to capture an important element of Palestinian history.

The projects of UNRWA, IPS and CERMOC converge in certain aspects and diverge in others. First, UNRWA is primarily concerned with facilitating the operational side of the organization. Thus, of the various attributes we associate with the UNRWA data, UNRWA is interested in a subset of these. Whether it is the demographic, socioeconomic, health or educational background of the individual refugee, UNRWA's focus is on the operation of the organization. As such it has not attempted to tap the historic dimension of the so-far uncatalogued family files and link them to the various databases. CERMOC was primarily interested in the administrative attributes of the organization, i.e., its Central Registry and how these reflect the culture of the organization and its relationship to the outside environment.

The IPS project aimed at establishing linkages among the various data sources available at UNRWA. The linkages were to be carried out by means of 1) identifying and classifying the various documents; 2) developing a coding scheme which renders the documents amenable to analysis; and 3) deploying an appropriate software which makes possible the physical transformation of the documents from hard to soft medium through imaging and optical character recognition.

Inventory of UNRWA archives

Since its inception UNRWA has accumulated a vast number of documents, data files and archival sources that present a challenge to classification. For the purposes of this study we have chosen to identify these documents under three main headings: data files; archival documents; and visual and mapping documents. The data files include the Unified Registration System, the family files, and the hitherto unclassified files on internal refugees. They also include the data files derived from the education and health departments.

The archival documents are mainly concentrated in the records of the central registry which cover the active and inactive files accumulated (previously) in Vienna (now in Amman and Gaza) and the field offices. The visual and mapping documents include the photo archives, video and 16mm films, and maps prepared by the field engineering units. A fourth source of archival data that is not dealt with here, but is of potential significance, is the routine reports that are daily transacted in the field offices, schools and UNRWA clinics.

Only the aggregate data derived from these reports eventually appear in periodic and annual UNRWA publications. Many of these transactions (such as procurement records, and individual health reports of patient visits) are periodically destroyed. The ability of UNRWA to computerize field activities (especially in health and education) may allow future researchers to include even those activities in permanent databases.

We will now deal in some detail with the contents of these archival sources:

The Unified Registration System

At the heart of the UNRWA databases is the system of family and individual data entry and retrieval system known as the Unified Registration System (URS). It is a unique informational system which has the most comprehensive social and demographic data on Palestinian refugees, unmatched – in terms of size or attributes – by any similar system anywhere.

URS began in 1979 when a registration data base system was established in Vienna on an ffiM mainframe. Since that date the Relief and Social Services Department initiated a process of conversion through which all its registration data acquired from the field was integrated into the URS. Advances in the technology and costing of computerization allowed the system to be decentralized so that data could be gathered in regional computers and then transferred periodically to the Central system in Amman. These field registration systems are quite recent: 1993 in Syria, 1994 in Jordan, 1995 in Gaza and the West Bank, and March 1996 in Lebanon. In April all data was transferred from the Vienna mainframe to the Amman central computer (a UNIX/Sybase platform). Only backup files from the old IBM mainframe remain in Vienna. This backup data is significant since it contains historical information not incorporated into the present URS.

The URS has three major components, and a fourth potential data base (for internal refugees), which will be discussed below.

The Demographic Database

This database contains two kinds of documents: Household demographic data on all refugee families who have active registration for UNRWA services, altogether about 670,000 families (known as Family Demographic Files, or FamDem); and record of individual members of these households (known as Individual Demographic Files, or IndDem), covering as of 1995 about 3.3 million Palestinian refugees. This data is continuously being updated.

The Socio-Economic Database (SEDB)

Based on a much more detailed and comprehensive informational output this database is derived from the Special Hardship Cases; refugees who fall below a certain income level, require services not available to the bulk of refugee households. Data on SEDB began in 1991 and contain family attributes since that date, but not before.

The SEDB covers three sets of data: demographic data on households that are eligible for assistance under the special hardship cases (FAM-SOC), additional statistical attributes of such families (FAM-SHC); and extensive data on individuals in those categories. The Socio-Economic Database is linked to the Demographic Database so that correlations, for administrative and research purposes can be established.

Input for the Demographic Database comes from the Field Registration System, including the family files, field investigations, and upgrading of those data by case workers. Information for the Socio-Economic Data comes from the Special Hardship Cases Questionnaire, and from the Family Fact Sheet. These sets of information then feed into three data bases:

- The FAM-SHC (basic data on Special Hardship Cases): the core information for SHCs: Number of Case, no. of rations, SHC category (elderly, widow, disabled etc.) and the date of investigation.
- Socio-Economic Database: more general family and individual demographic attributes (address, family income, forms of assistance, health status, education and economic status).

Table 13.1 indicates the total number of files available for the five major data categories in the unified registration system.

All five categories of data in the URS are derived from two main sources: The basic data sheet in the Family Files (see below), and continuous update provided by the field offices on the basis of field investigations on the part of UNRWA case workers, and requests made by individual refugees to obtain services. Thus the information contained is based on living and operational transactions.

The family files

The family files contain the non-computerized basic information from which the demographic data is ultimately derived. It contains the most extensive data on the attributes, composition and changes in the status of almost three quarter of a million refugee families.

There are some 644,543 family files in the five regional offices of UNRWA containing, for all fields except Gaza, a basic 'Family Fact Sheet' recording the original circumstances

Table 13.1 Unified Registration System, Data Files by Category, August 1996

Field of UNRWA Operations	Demographic Data Base		Socio-Economic Data Base		
	Families	Individuals	SHC	Families	Individuals
West Bank	132,664	534,413	8.2*	7,706	26,729
Gaza	150,160	719,269	13.3	2,491	56,593
Lebanon	84,596	353,945	9.2	8,778	33,996
Syria	78,535	348,504	6.8	6,396	20,117
Jordan	230,070	1,366,087	8.6	8,209	33,129
Total	676,025	3,322,218	46.2*	43,219	170,564

Source: UNRWA HQ Amman (August 1996); (*) Figures in thousands

of the refugee family and supporting documents of the family's pre-1948 status. The fact sheet contains the names of family members, sex, their date of birth, occupation (if any), current residence, conditions which led to their leaving their original homes in Palestine, education (selective), and the relationship of the family member to the head of household. The supporting documents are varied. Most files contain birth certificates, marriage certificates, reference to property deeds, references to occupation in pre-1948 Palestine, and so on.

Because family files were originally opened with the objective of providing relief services, the criteria of eligibility for material support were established by UNRWA field staff in 1950. UNRWA family files constitute a continuity with the system of registration that was initiated by the IRC (in the West Bank, Syria, and Lebanon) and the AFSC (in Gaza) in the aftermath of the 1948 war. Contrary to common perception however, the data contained in the current (1950) files was not transferred from the IRC/AFSC files but contain data that was reentered by UNRWA staff between 1950 and 1952. In this process many initial applications for registration were dropped since they no longer met the newly established for UNRWA registration. Others were also dropped because they left the five regions (or 'fields') of UNRWA operations. These became known as 'dead files' for administrative purposes. Theoretically however refugee families whose files were dropped from the active register were retained in inactive files, which were no longer eligible for the agency's services. Table 13.2 indicates the number of family files and their proportional distribution by region:

In 1992 UNRWA's former Commissioner General, Iliter Turkman, reopened the process of registration for Palestinian refugees without any condition of 'need' as a prerequisite. The new objective was simply to document claims to refugee status for those Palestinians who were formerly denied registration as a result of the 'need' standards. The new files, amounting to about 400 files annually for all five regions (altogether less than 1,500) are better documented than the earlier files in terms of pre-1948 family property. They contain extensive supporting evidence of title deeds, professional status, rent and tax records, school records etc. The older files on the other hand have better documentation on the current (at the time of registration) status of the refugee family, since the purpose of registration was to establish eligibility for services. On average the older files tend to reflect the social status of Palestine's poorer and destitute refugees, while the 'Turkman' files tend to reflect the conditions of the professional and middle classes among refugees.

Table 13.2 Family Files and their Regional Distribution by Field (1996)

Region	Number of Files	Percentage
Jordan	230,070	34.1
Gaza	150,160	22.2
The West Bank	132,664	19.6
Lebanon	84,596	12.5
Syria	78,535	11.6
Total	676,025	100.0

Source: Derived from UNRWA data on URS, Amman August 21, 1996

In terms of classification the prospective researcher should think of these files as falling into three categories:

- Active family files: the vast majority – the files which constitute the raw data for UNRWA's URS and other demographic data.
- Inactive ('Dead') family files – the files withdrawn either because their respondents no longer fulfil eligibility criteria, or because they moved out of UNRWA's field of operations. Data from these files do not appear in the URS, except by mistake.
- Reactivated family files – the ongoing entries by refugee families who were so far denied registration as refugees because of the need eligibility criteria (i.e., poverty), or because they were so far outside UNRWA area of operations. Data from these files are not entered into the URS. It is quite possible that there is some overlap between the inactive files and the reactivated files.

The key link between the family files and the demographic data base is the initial registration code (known as the EX-Code), and the current registration number which supplanted the ex-code in1956 to accommodate the need for standardization of recording the expanded number of refugees. [See historical note below.]

When a member of a refugee household separate from his or her original family, and start a new household, a new file is opened which is connected1D the original household by the ex-code. Thus, every single refugee has an individualized registration number, a family registration number and a family ex-code – the latter two items being common to all household members. The possibilities inherent in this coding system for establishing linkages over time, as well as within the demographic attributes among household members are enormous.

Family Files and their supporting their supporting documents are currently outside the computerization system of the URS. They are classified and handled manually in the five Fields of Operation. The condition of historical documents attached to the files are fair to poor, but will deteriorate with time. The main problem for establishing a feasibility for processing these documents (for example, scanning them) as a prelude to classification is their volume. The current UNRWA estimate of these documents is 25 million, based on an average count of 40 papers per document. Since new entries are being made, particularly by reactivated family files, and since the new files are likely to be larger in size, this estimate would have to be upgraded. A count of 100 papers (as an upper limit) would yield an estimate of 67 million papers.

Historical note: the evolution of refugee registration

Since the UNRWA system of registration is becoming increasingly standardized, particularly digitization of data and the establishment of the URS, it would help the researcher to delineate here the manner in which the system evolved. According to Lex Takkenberg, who has done a systematic examination of the registration system, the system is typified by a large degree of adaptation to problems of administering refugee aid in each region. In Gaza fur example UNRWA registration records, which are based on AFSC earlier records for 1948 to 1950, are most accurate and complete. In Lebanon, due to local conditions, they are the less so. Takkenberg suggests that because the earlier UNRWA records from Lebanon included several thousand Lebanese migrant workers who lost their livelihood as a result of the 1948 war, UNRWA introduced the well-known criteria of continued residency in Palestine (1946–48) as a precondition for refugee status, in order to eliminate these workers from the roll. Here we have delineated a schematic chronology of the registration phases:

1948–50: The initial registry

The International Committees of the Red Cross (ICRC) and the American Friends Service Committee, establish a registry of all refugees in Gaza (AFSC) and the other Arab host countries (also performed by the ICRC). We have been unable to find traces of this registry in the archives. Serial coding is used using a combination of alphabets (for region) and serial number (for family code).

1950: Master cards

UNRWA takes over the registration based on eligibility (means test) from AFSC and ICRC. Contrary to common perception UNRWA re-registers refugees. Registration was based on a standardized Pink Forms (Grey for Gaza) known as the 'Master Cards'. These cards still exist in the Gaza registry, but not in the West Bank or Jordan. They may have been destroyed.

The Ration Registration Card was established as a six-digit identification number for each family, replacing the AFSC/ICRC numbers. Each region was given a range of potential registration number which allowed future growth of the refugee families to be added. A Fact Sheet was included in the family file of each refugee family (except in Gaza) which summarized the results of field investigation of the status of that family

1956: IBM punch cards

In 1956 the six-digit ration number was replaced by the eight-digit Family Registration Number. This was entered on IBM 8x32 punch cards for the mechanical enumeration of refugee family attributes. The old Ration Card became known as the EX-Code. Each family had one unique registration number (see note on ex-code in the historical section below).

1958: Index cards

The punch cards were further simplified and entered onto index cards which provided a typed standardized summary of each family's attributes (see the 'logical structure of UNRWA registration' below). Nuclear families that 'split' from the parent families were given new ex-codes.

1979: Registration database

The beginning of computerization of family demographic data for all fields on an IBM mainframe computer in Vienna.

1994–96: Unified registration system

A centralized system of data entry from the Relief and Social Services (but not from health or education) was developed. The system relies on systematic and periodic data entering the central computer from the five fields and processed in Amman. The URS utilizes both the ex-code (the eight-digit family registration number) and a ten-digit registration number for each individual refugee. It contains data on 3.2 million Palestinian refugees.

The logical structure of the enumeration system

Both the unique Family Registration Number (RN), and the Code of Origin (CO), which appear in each data sheet in the URS, contain a logical structure which is of immense use to the researcher.

The eight-digit registration number (RN) identifies the family alphabetically by the first name of the head of household and his serial number in his family, the region they live in, and their habitat (big city, small city, village, camp, out of camp). Thus, the number 25101573 refers to a family from Gaza District (2), living in Deir al Balah (5), in an out of camp location (10), followed by the alpha group name of this particular beneficiary (Arabi Abdallah Doleh).

The ex-code which appears next to the RN links the computerized demographic data of the RN sheet with the non-computerized family file which includes the accumulated documentation of all family members (marriage certificates, birth certificates, changes in family economic status, educational career etc.), and with the computerized socio-economic data if the family falls into the Special Hardship Cases. In the latter case an SHC number, appears next to the RN. If there is a blank next to the SHC number it indicates that this family is not classified as an SHC case, and therefore no socio-economic computerized data is available for it.

The replacement of ex-codes by the new registration number was necessary for technical and administrative reasons: technical because the six digits did not accommodate the amount of information required, and administrative because UNRWA wanted to streamline its records.

Until 1993 a new ex-code was given to newly established nuclear families, upon the production of a new marriage contract. Since this created a lot of confusion in the coding system among members of the same extended family it was decided to restore the old ex-code to the new families, beginning in 1993. But this was done unevenly in different areas. The process is called 'Amalgamation of Ex-codes'. In Syria the process is about 85% complete, meaning that the same ex-code now refers to the same extended family in the majority of cases. In Lebanon the completed files are 70% of the total. In Gaza, the West Bank and Jordan the process of amalgamation is still proceeding.

The five-digit Code of Origin (CO) which appears next to each registration number indicates the origin of the refugee family in pre-1948 Palestine. This is a valuable historical piece of information that exists for all 3.2 million refugees. In the example cited above the CO code is 30007. This indicates that the Doleh family comes from Jaffa city (30), from the Old Quarter of the city (007). Jaffa and Jerusalem are the only two cities for which details of original habitat are provided. We asked the URS staff to

Table 13.3 Palestinian Refugees Who Come From Jaffa by Quarter (1948)

District Code	Sub-District Code	Location	Name	No. of Families
3	0	001	Jaffa (general)	36,567
3	0	002	Tel Aviv	47
3	0	003	Petah Tiqva	14
3	0	004	Abu Kabir	2,204
3	0	005	Ajami	4,196
3	0	006	Manshiyyeh	4,552
3	0	007	Old City of Jaffa	1,570
3	0	008	Nuzha	3,227
3	0	010	Jabaliyyeh	4,290
3	0	011	Saknet Darwish	4,894

Source: UNRWA URS 'Number of Registered Families per code of Origin', Amman HQ, 21 August 1996

provide us with a breakdown for Jaffa refugees. Table 13.3 is an example of what the URS system can provide.

A few observations are in order here. The number of families in the last column indicates the current number of families in all regions whose ancestors lived in Jaffa on the eve of the 1948 war. 'Jaffa General' refers to families who did not indicate living in a specific location in the city and may include villagers who gave Jaffa city as their location of origin. There is a bias in this table, as in all URS data, in favour of poorer refugees. Thus, the Ajami Quarter, which was an exclusive, wealthy quarter, is probably underrepresented in this table, while Manshiyyeh and Saknet Darwish, both working-class quarters, are probably overrepresented.

Some problems in the UNRWA registration system

From the point of view of research and policy analysis the main weakness of the registration system derives from the fact that it was established for the purpose of administering aid to needy refugees, and not for purposes of enumeration. This is no fault of its designers obviously but in preparing the data for research functions one must bear in mind these limitations. These limitations can be highlighted by the following features:

Heterogeneity in the system of field entry

Despite attempts at centralization and standardization of data entry systems, each UNRWA field (region) of operation has its own specificities. Part of this variation is due to historical conditions: for example in Gaza the transfer of AFSC registry to Family files did not go through the procedure of 'Investigation Fact Sheets' which are standard in the West Bank and Jordan and possibly in Syria and Lebanon, where the Red Cross preceded UNRWA as a refugee 'caretaker'. The civil war in Lebanon, and the transfer of family files from the Sheikh Jarrah (Jerusalem) HQ to Jordan for tens of thousands of families, also disrupted the codification systems in these regions.

Multiplicity of ex-codes

In 1993 it was decided to restore the old ex-codes to nuclear family members who split from their parent families. Since this process is uneven it meant that in some fields (Syria and Lebanon) the ex-code records have a different meaning than in other fields. This problem will be solved when all ex-codes are amalgamated- but this is likely to take time.

The registration system is not a census of refugees

The system is based on voluntary reporting by prospective refugees. Confirmation of registration itself (except for New Registration since 1993) is based on criteria of eligibility for aid. As a result a large number of refugees are excluded from the system:

- Refugees with independent income or property.
- Refugees who did not reside in UNRWA areas of operation.
- Refugees who were dropped from the record due to budgetary limitations which set an upper ceiling for refugees receiving aid.
- Refugees who were the offspring of a refugee mother and a non-refugee father, and therefore not eligible for registration.
- Refugees whose dignity prevented them from registering.
- Refugees whose status improved and who moved out of the eligibility criteria.
- Refugees who lost their home and property but who remained in Israel and became Israeli citizens (about 30,000 'internal' refugees in 1948).
- First-time displaced persons in the war of 1967 (e.g. uprooted residents of the West Bank who sought refuge in Jordan). Only second-time refugees continued to be registered in their new areas.

On the other hand, there were a number (admittedly small) of Lebanese, Gazan and Jerusalem citizens who, because their lives were affected drastically by war and occupation, were allowed to register as refugees eligible for UNRWA aid. In short, the registration system is biased towards poorer refugees and is confined to those living in countries neighbouring Palestine.

The URS is linear, in the sense that it 'freezes' the profile of the refugee family at one point in time. Changes over time have to be gleaned from previous (mostly non-standardized) documents in the family files. This makes it difficult, but not impossible, to study patterns of mobility and social change among refugees. While the master cards (of 1950) contain names of refugees in English and Arabic, modern computerized updating of files is exclusively in English which leads to considerable confusion in tracing some family names and could lead to double entries.

The Health and Education Department data

So far, the Unified Registration System (URS) has excluded data emanating from these two departments from their data entry system. Both departments yield crucial services to refugees that constitute significant complementation to a proper profile of refugee families. Furthermore, services to students (in UNRWA schools) and patients (in UNRWA clinics) are provided systematically to camp and non-camp refugees seeking such services. In Lebanon, Syria, and Gaza this amounts to over 90% of registered refugees. In Jordan and the West Bank (where alternative services are available in the public and private sectors) the number drops to about 60-75%. All educational and health services provide operational data on refugee beneficiaries which can be linked to the URS through the individual registration system. Such linkages are not made currently because, for administrative reasons, these fields are autonomous. Also, the technical feasibility of processing the data from the field school and clinic to the field office and then to the central computer at HQ has to be worked out both conceptually and operationally.

But the instruments of this integration already exist. In the health department for example, all beneficiaries must fill an UNRWA Department of Health Family File (Green Card) which contains the UNRWA registration numbers, the names of family heads and members. It also contains a list of chronic and/or family diseases. Each green card has a 'Clinic Card' (white) attached to it containing the medical history and records of each adult family member. It has a section on hospitalization of family members; dates and summary of physician's diagnosis; laboratory tests with positive findings. These cards are permanent and have been kept over the years. Similar records are kept for male (blue cards) and female (rose cards) children who are 0–3 years old, and for students in primary and intermediate schools, including data on immunization and screening for vision, height, weight, hearing and dental condition. All of this data is recorded on forms which can trace their recipient to his family through the RIC number and eventually to the Ex-Code. UNRWA maintains one of the most systematic recordings of the health status of its beneficiaries in the Middle East, possibly in the third world. It would thus be a substantial enrichment for the unified-registration system to have this information base incorporated into it. It would be a great loss if such integration is not done.

Internal refugees: a forgotten batch of records

One of the findings of this study was the uncovering of six boxes of data cards which contain the initial registration data of Palestinian refugees who remained in Israel. These victims of the 1948 war are those refugees, then estimated to be around 30 thousand individuals, who remained in the area occupied by the state of Israel during the war, and in its aftermath, but who lost their homes and livelihood due to forceful migration or inability to go back to their towns and villages. Ultimately most of these refugees became Israeli citizens but (with rare exceptions as in the case of Kufr Bar'am and Iqrit villages in Galilee) were not allowed to reclaim their homes or land. For many years they were denied citizenship and became known as 'Absent-Present' – present in the state, absent from their homes.

The recovery of these boxes is likely to shed important historic light on the origin and status of this forgotten community. The boxes found contain yellow (original) and pink (correction) filing cards containing typed and handwritten data on each refugee family. Each card contains names, ages, sex, occupation, past address and present

Table 13.4 Internal Refugees (1948)

Box No.	Estimate of Entry Cards for Families	
	Family Cards	Correction Cards
1	2,140	–
2	2,420	329
3	2,397	846
4	–	1,856
5	1,480	1,880
6	2,867	235
Total	11,304	5,155

Source: Authors' Count of 'Master Cards' in Central Registry (Inactive Files), UNRWA HQ, Amman

'distribution centre' to which the family is attached. The cards also contain indexing slots which can be detached for easy visual recognition and computing of the occupational status of the refugee (farmer, skilled worker, unskilled worker), and whether the refugee had property in Palestine. However, these latter two categories (occupation and property) are not systematically recorded for all cases. The refugees whose names are registered are mostly from Galilee but contain many refugees from Jerusalem, Lydda and Jaffa. The majority are Muslim and Christian Arabs, but the list contains hundreds of Jewish, Armenian, Greek and Italian families. Unfortunately, no dates are provided for the entry card, but the corrections indicate that these entries were made between 1948 and 1951. We conducted a rough estimate of the number of cards (i.e. families) which yielded Table 13.4.

The UNRWA Central Registry archives: a primary source for Palestinian history

In August 1996, the UNRWA headquarters moved from Vienna to Gaza. A few departments, including the central archives, moved to Amman (with the exception of the film department, and the CR active files). Our team visited the central archives and made the following inventory of what exists.

In 1960 the older rudimentary system of classifying the archives was replaced by a standardized UN system which is currently in operation. The archives can be generally divided into the new operative files (active files), and the old inactive files. The main problem facing the researcher is that there is no substantive consistency between the contents of these files and the label describing them. Sometimes this correspondence has to do with administrative logic internal to UNRWA bureaucratic procedures, but which does not lend itself to the objectives of the external researcher. For example, we found that much of the social surveys commissioned by UNCTAD, ESCWA and FAFO on socio-economic conditions in the occupied territories and some of the host countries are classified under 'Organizational Files'. The explanation for this was that these surveys contained data (probably less than 1%) that pertained to the organization of UNRWA.

One of the rare studies conducted on the UNRWA archives (the only one we found) was undertaken in 1970 by Peter Hawkins, a senior UNRWA director, and then a personnel officer. At the time Hawkins estimated that there were 'at least' twelve independent systems of documentation operating in UNRWA departments. He suggested that future reorganization be geared towards 'centralization of the records in four or five registries', and 'to centralize the control for all in the hands of a records management administrator'. Many of his recommendations for standardization and planning of registry files seem relevant today, except perhaps for the technical section, which has been superseded by modern technology.

New classification system

The new classification system was introduced into the central registry in 1960 to integrate UNRWA documentation system with UN and international standards of archiving. What separates it from the former system above is both dates and subjects. Some files, for which there is an ongoing administrative relevance, were reclassified and continued under a new series. A code reference was introduced into the old filing system to indicate that the file has been transferred to the new system. Most files from the 1950s however were relegated to the inactive files and retained their older designation. Following is a list of the codes and contents of the new classification system. The total number of files in the UNRWA Central Registry Archives (Amman) are 823. This total covers the files of the old classification system (inactive files); the registration cards of internal refugees; the old administrative files; and the new administrative files (active files) using the standard UN protocol of classification. Most of the inactive files are today housed in the Amman HQ of UNRWA, while the bulk of the active files are in the new headquarters in Gaza. We estimate the total number of paper documents they contain to be 2.5 million.

The film and photographic archives

UNRWA files contain a very rich archive of photographic, film and video documentation of Palestinian refugee history. The archives span the last fifty years of UNRWA, Red Cross and AFSC services. Unfortunately, the system of classification that regulates the central registry archives does not include the photo and film archives, and the system developed here is very rudimentary and tentative. In August 1996, along with the central registry, the film and photo collection were moved to Gaza HQ, and to Amman.

Until 1957 UNRWA had no permanent photographic section. Photographing was either commissioned on an assignment basis or was acquired from other sources such as the Imperial War Museum in London. Between the years 1976 and 1996, the Assignment Book became the main source of the photo cataloguing in UNRWA. All UNRWA photographs exist in two photo libraries. Photo Collection A (1948-96), which includes all prints classified by camp and year, are in special drawer files in Gaza HQ. Most of these photographs are identified on the back, but there is no general catalogue. Photo Collection B includes all the negatives of the above (in Gaza) and contact sheets (in Amman), classified by date and location only. The prints (collection A) contain a small fraction of the negatives. The UNRWA film library is scattered and unclassified. The 16mm films produced before 1978 were boxed and shelved in the Palestinian Film Institute in Beirut. When the Israeli army invaded the city in 1982 all those films were confiscated. Attempts were made to regain these films by UNRWA after the Oslo agreement was signed, but the Israeli government was unresponsive. All films (16mm negatives and prints) are today in the Amman HQ. Old video films are stored in Amman, new ones in Gaza. In 1982 the UNRWA's film library was confiscated by the Israeli army and has not been regained so far.

The ethnographic collection

UNRWA has a modest ethnographic museum which was established in Gaza in 1995. Its collection includes a large number of regional costumes, peasant agricultural implements, village pottery, swords and daggers, coffee and entertainment paraphernalia, household items, women's and men's jewellery, smoking implements, musical instruments, a number of Palestinian passports and travel documents from the Ottoman period to the present, Ottoman and Mandatory stamps, and currency. The passport collection includes rare documentation issued by the Government of All Palestine to citizens of Gaza in the years 1948-52.

The collection is on public display but there is no catalogue or a system of labelling. The costumes are inferior to the collection of the Bireh Ethnographic Museum, or to Widad Ka'war's collection in Amman. However, the agricultural implements are varied and interesting. The museum could do with better documentation of the refugee experience, as opposed to social life in Palestine in general. There is no display of any urban culture, and the collection has an orientalist flavour to it.

Transfer of the UNRWA archives to the PA

There is a considerable interest within the Palestinian Authority in creating a National Archive which will eventually house the UNRWA archives. In September 2000, Arafat announced the intention of the PA to establish a National Library and named the committee in charge of preparing the grounds for it. He indicated that there would be a manuscript and archival section to this library.[1] Dr As'ad Abdul Rahman, the newly appointed head of the Refugee Commission in the PA, also indicated to us the interest of the PA in acquiring the UNRWA archives 'when the time is appropriate'.[2] Both Mr Turkman, the former ComGen of UNRWA, and Mr Hansen, the former directors, indicated that they see the natural fate of the archives to be in PA hands.

It is our assessment that the archives contain invaluable material on the social conditions of the Palestinian people, both in Palestine and in the Arab diaspora. They also contain historical records with no parallel anywhere else. This includes the family files (which should remain confidential), the computer data basis, the historical archives, as well as the photo and film archives. It is natural and necessary that preparations be made to transfer these files to a national Palestinian Depository.

Arrangements should be made to start with this transfer. It is our feeling however that certain conditions should be met for this transfer to succeed and be productive:

- Smooth transfer should be negotiated with UNRWA so that the transfer is made by mutual consent. Full credit should be given to UNRWA staff for their historical role in establishing this archive. UNRWA staff should be involved in all phases of the transfer to ensure proper classification or reclassification of data, as well as in the training of PA personnel who will administer the data. It might be useful to hire UNRWA staff to administer the Archives within the PA national depository.
- Proper guarantees should be given to ensure the confidentiality of the sensitive data in the archives, particularly data pertaining to personal details of family histories, and the privacy of those family members. Proper grantees should be given to ensure future access to this data by bone fide researchers and analysts. It is one of our tasks in this study to establish guidelines for different degrees of clearance to UNRWA archives depending on the status of the researcher.

Preservation of UNRWA archives

There is no automatic scanning process that could be applied efficiently to transfer these paper documents into electronic images. The fastest and cheapest way to preserve these documents on electronic media would be through camera scanning. This process uses expensive tools (although they are getting cheaper every day) and requires less manpower compared to the traditional and cheaper scanners which are more labor intensive since they are not equipped with automatic feeding capability. The extra time spent during the traditional scanning process could be used for additional coding and indexing of the scanned documents.

Some of these documents, such as those in Central Registry files, are fit for Optical Character Recognition (OCR) technology. This will allow the use of an open retrieval and access system with hypertext search and content search capabilities. Coding and classification systems could be developed to extract useful information automatically where the documents are in a standardized format. Once a system of coding and indexing is developed, the bulk of the work will consist of identifying the new codes from the hard copies and embedding them in the new electronic system. Some of these indexes, may be somehow automated, but the major part will have to be done manually. These codes will form (together with the hard copies), part of the new database that will be of use to policy makers and researchers. It is important to maintain the historical depth of the data. Currently, UNRWA's main interest is in the operational utility of the data, and as such the transfer of the historical data to electronic format has a low priority.

To sum up, there is a wealth of data available. To make it useful for research purposes it should be easily accessible. The more effort spent into preparing and structuring the data at the entry phase, the more accessible the data would be for future use. Furthermore, integration and linkages of all modules of the databases in the system, including the URS, will widen the horizon for the eventual comprehensive use of the information.

Security levels and levels of access are an integral part of the new system. The more the data is structured, the more specific the allocation of levels of access is. Partial data could be made accessible for specific users at certain levels, e.g. the page, record or field, and on some forms a mask could be applied to block access to particular users. Additionally, users will not have access to the identity of individuals in the various UNRWA databases. Thus, the coding system developed must use numeric identifiers (such as the ex-codes) which will enable users to link records belonging to the same family members, establish family trees and correlate various attributes for the purpose of research and policy making. Overall, data should be secured against alteration.

Notes

* This refers to the situation in 2001. Obviously, the technology of data processing and preservation has been superseded since this report was written.
1   *al-Ayyam* 19 September 1996.
2   Interview, Amman, 19 August 1996.

In Lieu of Afterword

14

Liminal Lights in Dark Places

Elia Zureik's Sociological and Critical Contribution to Palestinian and Surveillance Studies

David Lyon

Behind his well-known bluster was not only a skilled scholar and project leader but a man deeply committed to progressive values that, above all, helped us to give voice to the voiceless.

Vinny Mosco, colleague and co-researcher, mid-1980s[1]

The above comment from Vincent Mosco neatly sums up many memories of Elia Zureik, relating to his long and fruitful career as a critical sociologist. Zureik himself says very little about how he came to be the person that Mosco describes, although when he does, it is very illuminating. We are all products of cultural borrowings – a sense that he ascribes to Edward Saïd – but, asserts Zureik, 'The fusion of cultures... is carried out against a backdrop of the borderline intellectual's liminal status as an émigré, expatriate, exile, or refugee... Liminality is crucial to the borderline intellectual' allowing someone like him 'to move between spaces and time periods, testing the threshold of survival'.[2]

This contribution to the well-deserved festschrift considers Zureik's work in sociology in a place geographically distant from his childhood home, Akka, the ancient walled port city on the coast of Palestine. But though he has lived since 1991 in Kingston, Ontario, in Canada, the lives of Palestinians always remain close to his heart and his academic interests. Intellectually, the story shows how Zureik's training at SFSU, SFU and Essex gave him the tools to conduct sociological research in a number of fields, including two strands in particular: new information technologies and latterly, surveillance, on the one hand, and the sociology of Palestinians on the other. Interestingly, these two eventually coalesced into one, seen especially in his study of *Israel's Colonial Project in Palestine* (2016) and the earlier co-edited collection, *Surveillance and Control in Israel/Palestine* (2011). But the interest in surveillance also led to a major gift to international sociology, *The Globalization of Personal Information*.[3]

But academics do not live disembodied lives and there is much more to the story than only the intellectual. The tale I tell derives from my own experience as a colleague of Zureik, with whom I first corresponded, from the UK, in 1984, just before he and

Mosco received the grant for their study of telephone workers in the transition to Information Technology, that we shall come to in a moment. I arrived in Kingston in 1990 and in the 2020s we are still collaborating on one or two projects. At the same time, it's a story liberally laced with the memories and reflections of others who were Zureik's students and colleagues, who learned from him but – of course – sometimes clashed with him. This determined academic can on occasion erect fortifications worthy of Akka, but those who know him also know that he will mellow in time.

A note on biography and sociology: anyone can read a CV but it gives only limited understanding of the person-in-context. This chapter on Elia Zureik places weight on the relation between Palestinian origins and vignettes of the life-work accomplished – mainly in Canada – but cannot evade, for example, the intellectual impact of North American and British sociology, the challenge to sociology of appropriately researching and theorizing the advent of information technology in the 1980s, and, increasingly, surveillance from the 1990s, or the shaping effects of the particular university department – Queen's Sociology – on the subject. My title draws attention to just three aspects of Zureik's scholarly contributions, and while these are significant, I do not claim that they tell anything like the whole story.

Three themes from Zureik's work hold this little essay together: One, Zureik's early life in Palestine and his experience of a ruptured life, with the establishment of the state of Israel in 1948, before seeking higher education in the US, Canada and the UK and then studies in the sociology of the Palestinians and their struggles both inside and beyond Palestine. Two, social research on communication and information technologies, conducted from the early 1980s, and shifting towards surveillance and control from the 1990s. Three, the merging of research interests between Palestinian life and new technologies in projects on the use of surveillance within the settler colonialism of Israel.

An émigré Palestinian sociologist

Born and raised in the Palestinian town of Akka on the Mediterranean coast in 1939, Zureik was a 9-year-old when the *Nakba* occurred, the war of 1948 driving many thousands from their homes, creating a massive refugee population both inside and, mainly, outside of Palestine and forming a two-tier society within Israel, in which Palestinians were decidedly disadvantaged. He went to a private Catholic high school in Akka. A postdoc, Lynda Harling Stalker, recalls that she 'enjoyed hearing his stories of school and the pranks he used to play when he was growing up – he would get a mischievous twinkle in his eyes'.

He chose to leave Palestine in 1960 to study at San Francisco State University. The attraction was its combined programme in sociology, politics and anthropology. He switched to sociology for his MA at Simon Fraser University in British Columbia, Canada, because British sociologist Tom Bottomore[4] – who recognized Karl Marx's contribution to sociology – was head of department (1965–68). At SFU Zureik was in the same MA class as Anthony Giddens, who would later become the doyen of British sociology.[5] Lastly, Zureik went to a flagship new university, Essex, at Colchester in the UK, for his PhD. Essex was known for its 'radical bent' and Zureik's PhD work was supervised by Fred Greenstein, an expert on political socialization (and would be famous for his studies of the US presidency). Zureik's dissertation was on 'Politics and the English Child', which among other things questioned how far 'deference' described the political attitudes of children in the UK. He actually began teaching sociology at Queen's University in Kingston, Ontario, Canada, in 1972, before completing his PhD.

Throughout this time abroad, he was of course, a Palestinian émigré, carrying with him memories of another life, with its profound memories and ongoing commitments. This is seen in his first book, *Palestinians in Israel*, which came out in 1979, preceded by a special issue of *The Journal of Palestine Studies*,[6] edited by him and containing a preview of the book's thesis. These writings drew attention to the unique situation in which Israel engaged in the 'settler-colonialism' of Palestine and indicated several ways in which previous Zionist accounts of Palestine had failed to do justice to the actual Palestinian predicament and subsequent struggles. The arguments raised at this time are dealt with in other parts of this book, but two striking features showed what kinds of sociology Zureik was committed to writing. On the one hand, these works are carefully and even-handedly empirical, based on a variety of sources. And on the other, they are emphatically critical. In the *Palestine Studies* article, for instance, he observes that the author's stance cannot ultimately be separated from their own being. He cites Paulo Freire's *Pedagogy of the Oppressed* to underscore his point.[7]

While engaged in Palestine-related research, Zureik also worked collaboratively with colleagues at Queen's, early on with Robert (Bob) Pike - building on his PhD research - producing a book on *Socialization and Values in Canadian Society* (Zureik and Pike 1975). But other research interests were piqued by the development of the silicon chip in 1978 and the subsequent development of other microprocessors that prompted popular - and inflated - claims of a new social formation shaped by the 'microelectronics revolution' in computing.

These led to other collegial collaborations, with Vincent (Vinny) Mosco, on telephone workers (1989), with Diane Hartling on an extensive bibliography of work on *The Social Context of Information and Communication Technologies* (1987), and with Vincent (Vince) Sacco, a criminologist, on computer crime (1990) and, also with Fouad Moughrabi, on equality, law and democracy in the Middle East (1993).

Interestingly, the piece co-authored with Sacco did not follow standard methodological practice of examining law enforcement agency records or organizational surveys. The two researchers chose a self-reporting survey of Canadian university students, finding that social characteristics did not play much part, but that students' beliefs about ethics and about the prevalence of misuse did affect their own in involvement. It would be most interesting to compare this study with a contemporary one, more than a generation later. Equally, Zureik, Moughrabi and Sacco's (1993) study of 'Perceptions of Legal Inequality in Deeply Divided Societies: The Case of Israel' questioned the tendency of such matters to be discussed in abstract ways in political philosophy. They countered with the argument that an experiential - real life - dimension of the law is equally important, especially when Israel's treatment of minorities might be compared with experience in neighbouring countries. Elia and colleagues were intellectual adventurers, willing to try new ideas and to question taken-for-granted ones.

Studies in communication and information technology – and surveillance

It was not just the *sociology* of new technologies that interested Zureik. In 1981, says David Neice, recently arrived from Harvard, he found Dr Zureik quite excited: 'I was wondering what had him so elevated. It turned out that he had just bought one of the earliest models of the IBM personal computer and as someone who loved to learn he was busy mastering its functions.' But, he continued, 'Elia had played around with that computer for enough time to have also considered where "being digital" for the general population might trend. He had already begun to think about the potential large-scale effects of the so-called "micro-electronic revolution" on society. It was just part of his nature to speculate far out into the future of technological change.'

Neice was close to Zureik when 'he proposed that we initiate a research group called Studies in Communication and Information Technology or SCIT'. They moved quickly and soon had an office, were writing research proposals and hired Dianne Hartling to prepare an annotated bibliography. Soon the Canada Council agreed to support the work and a conference was arranged in May 1982, on 'Micro-electronic Technology and Canadian Society'. Margaret Boden, a multi-disciplinary scholar from the Cognitive Science Group at Sussex University, UK, was the keynote speaker. One of the key themes arising from that conference, says Neice, was the notion of a potential digital divide between those with and without access to the benefits of the new technologies – a theme that continued to concern Zureik in the ensuing years.

The social impacts of the new technologies were seen for example in that telephone workers – especially women – were, as Zureik's co-investigator Vincent Mosco puts it, 'very unhappy with soul-destroying use of new technologies to measure or monitor their every move. It was rank Taylorism, and Elia made certain it occupied a major place in our report'. The two had obtained funding from the Ministry of Labour, via the Communication Workers of Canada (union), for an ambitious, multi-province, bilingual study using both qualitative and quantitative research. The Union actually asked them to withdraw some of the criticisms which, Mosco suggests, came from union leadership 'bias in favour of more skilled male technicians'. Zureik flatly refused. This would not be the last time that Zureik helped to plan and execute a complex, multi-faceted research project. In Mosco's judgement, this was because 'he led the project with great skill, whether this involved motivating graduate students or applying his considerable ability to carry out both quantitative and qualitative research at the highest level. As a result of his tenacity, we completed the project, producing a voluminous report and several published articles.'

The SCIT program was a very successful multidisciplinary research and seminar programme at Queen's University, led by Zureik, along with several colleagues from political studies, computing, law, policy studies and business, as well as sociology. The group was pioneering a new area of study that would, before long, see many similar such groups, journals and research centres emerge around the world. The programme found funding to print the texts of the seminar papers – there being no such thing as a public 'internet' or circulation of 'online' papers in the early years of SCIT. This group also brought together those in the social sciences who were beginning to create courses in this area, that would eventually become part of the standard curriculum in sociology, political studies and film studies at Queen's. It would run in tandem with the early work on surveillance, conducted at Queen's, as seen in the first research workshop, presented jointly by the sociology department and SCIT.

Zureik's first joint project with the author, which turned out to be highly consequential, was to apply to the Social Sciences and Humanities Research Council of Canada (SSHRC) to support a research workshop on Surveillance and New Technology, held in 1993. It was a low-budget, high-quality event that brought together just about everyone we could think of who might be able to contribute. Although the post-structuralist Mark Poster and the symbolic interactionist Gary Marx simply could not understand each other, it was nonetheless an auspicious and stimulating meeting of minds on a common project. Its fruit was not only the edited collection, *Computers, Surveillance and Privacy*[8] but also an embryonic international community of interdisciplinary scholars – including, notably, law and computing – that became the core of many similar projects over the next three decades.

During the 1990s, I increasingly came to respect Zureik's work, discovering repeatedly how thorough was his approach, and how reliable were many of his judgements. True, he could be dismissive of some authors that I might have relied on, but overall, his assessments were worth considering. He and I were complementary to each other in leadership and as the research projects grew in number and scope, we learned – without ever mentioning it out loud – to share tasks according to skillsets. But I recall one striking event in the 1990s that drove home to me the stature of my senior partner's sphere of influence. Zureik gave the welcome and introduction to a public lecture at Queen's, by Edward Saïd. As the author of the book that launched postcolonial studies rose to speak, his first words were in praise of *Zureik's* scholarship, and in recognition of his role in redirecting Palestinian studies.

By 1999 Zureik and I were ready for further joint endeavours, this time a research project under the SSHRC Knowledge-Based Economy programme. The research project, which ran from 2000 to 2003, examined 'Surveillance, Risk and Social Ordering in Global Information Societies'. We invited a co-leader, Yolande Chan, a MIS scholar in the Queen's School of Business, which also helped to tip the scales to more workplace-related research. Several products were generated by this project, including an edited collection on *Surveillance as Social Sorting: Privacy, Risk and Digital Discrimination* (Lyon 2003) including Zureik's fine chapter on 'Theorizing Surveillance: the Case of the Workplace'. His ability to plough his own furrow is very clear in this piece, which remains both careful and critical. He eschews simplistic Marxist and Foucaldian analyses and uses empirical evidence to question each. In particular, he notes the new opportunities for agency and resistance among the surveilled, even as new electronic modes of deskilling and discipling labour proliferate.

However, another kind of product emerged from this project; the consolidation of a research group that both included members of the 1993 workshop and added to the roster of new ones who were to take this research more definitively into the twenty-first century. At Queen's, the group became known as the Surveillance Project, a name that it retained until 2009 when Queen's officially approved the creation of the Surveillance Studies Centre (SSC). Zureik was very much at the core of each, as a leader, an assiduous scholar, a conscientious contributor and, from time-to-time, a controversial and contentious colleague.

But while Zureik delved into project after project at Queen's, he was equally immersed in teaching and student supervision. While research was tremendously important to him, he always had an eye to those who, like him, had been displaced or were otherwise struggling. In the late 1990s, the sociology PhD programme was approved and, soon after, a 'displaced' student, Steve Marmura, relates that he 'contacted Elia following a television debate he had participated in about the Israeli/Palestinian conflict'. He explained: 'I wanted to congratulate him on a job well done and ask him some follow up questions.'

Their conversation led to Steve being challenged to consider studying for a PhD and Zureik recommended three books to whet his appetite: *Jihad vs McWorld* by Benjamin Barber, *The Clash of Civilizations* by Samuel Huntington and *Modernity at Large* by Arjun Appadurai. Despite his self-doubt, and fear of being involved with 'technology', Marmura read the books and was intrigued. 'At a time when I felt somewhat lost,' he explained, 'Elia provided me with a light at the end of the tunnel. I will always be grateful to Elia for calling me back to my true path.' Marmura's dissertation was about the uses of new media by Palestinians. As things turned out, Marmura would also become involved in yet another major project.

That project, running from 2003 to 2007, was The Globalization of Personal Data, this time under the Initiative on the New Economy at SSHRC. It was a multi-disciplinary and collaborative project, again, with a number of dimensions. One of these weighted the project heavily in Zureik's direction. Emily Smith, who was previously a MA student of Zureik's, and was to become an indefatigable Research Associate with the Surveillance Project and then the SSC at Queen's, picks up the story: 'Elia took on the international survey component of the Globalization of Personal Data project, which was a huge undertaking to say the least ... He was not one to back down from a challenge, and when Colin Bennett[9] and Charles Raab mentioned in the opening chapter of *The Governance of Privacy* (2003, 2006) that there was no comprehensive global survey on privacy and surveillance, he took up the cause'. As she also observes, it was after his work on this project that Zureik received the Queen's University Award in Excellence in Research in 2008.

Zureik was quite clear that the burgeoning field of surveillance studies should pay more attention to empirical studies. Alongside initiating theoretical contributions of stature, Zureik always stressed the need for adequate evidence. This was his background, not only as a Palestinian but also in studies of new technologies and surveillance.[10] He noted in a review article, for instance, that 'the study of surveillance, which is heavy on theorizing and light on empirical research, could benefit if researchers pay more attention to the types of personal data and their relationship to surveillance, and if in the context, more attention is paid to subjectivity'.[11] This he accomplished in his leadership of the global survey – and it led in turn to further reflections on the theme when the dust had settled.

That collaborative SSHRC project – The Globalization of Personal Data – was intended to demonstrate that by the start of the twenty-first century, issues raised by surveillance were distinctively global. The project was intended to probe the reality that surveillance was no longer simply a matter of personal data collection-and-use *within* nation states. The very character of the rapidly growing digital economy, centred in Silicon Valley but increasingly challenged in particular by Chinese technology entrepreneurialism, was global in scale. To achieve its aims, the project focused on several areas – surveillance in border and airport security, national identification systems and location-tracking. It produced no less than three edited books, one sole-authored book, and a research report for the Office of the Privacy Commissioner of Canada. But the most time-and-resources-consuming dimension of all was the massive public opinion research operation overseen primarily by Zureik.

Using external agencies – for several countries, the Ipsos-Reid public opinion research company, based in Canada – this project examined, comparatively, the respective surveillance-privacy situations in Brazil, Canada, China, France, Hungary, Mexico, Spain and the United States. A Chinese company, Millenriver, in Beijing, along with the Chinese Academy of Social Sciences, ran the poll in China, although local help was also required in all countries that were examined, especially in Japan. We used interviews, focus groups and vignettes to ensure good coverage, so at every stage the challenges were enormous. Characteristically, as Smith also notes, 'When working for Elia on the GPD survey, he would often present us with massive background research projects.' She and other team members would be in the office, 'and he would come in regularly and say "Are we winning?"' She goes on, 'When working intensely on projects, he would have difficulty sleeping, and we would often get messages from him when he was awake working at 3 a.m.' Eventually, the edited collection saw the light of day in 2010.[12]

Zureik thrived on this gargantuan project, even though it kept him from sleep. That he was also able to be flexible, in a pinch, was also manifest. For example, to run a huge project in a medium-sized university,[13] meant that suitable assistance was limited. The project needed extra help, at a time of a relative paucity of potential postdocs in Kingston. A key lack was for quantitative researchers. Lynda Harling-Stalker came on the scene: 'Even though I was a *qualitative* researcher doing work on crafts in Newfoundland, Elia (and David!) took a chance on me as a lead writer for the international survey. What I remember is that Elia said, "Well, Lynda, at least you are not allergic to numbers!"' And she was grateful: 'I only got to work with Elia for two years, but I learned a lot from him during that time. He taught me that good scholarship can have real impact on people's lives.'

Palestinian studies meets surveillance studies

Like any good scholar, Zureik believes in the cross-fertilization of one area of research by another. Tracing his oeuvre over several decades, and switching metaphors, one notes how distinct research streams appear, but also how their banks can soften, allowing for confluence. As well, what was once thought of as a single stream can divide, delta-like, into separate and distinct channels. So, while his earliest work on Palestinian life hinted at the surveillance activities of the Israeli state, Zureik's many years working directly in surveillance studies, in parallel to critical studies of Israel–Palestine relations, meant that his later studies of those conflicts include some of the most stimulating understandings of surveillance. Theoretically, they also encompass, for instance, more sympathetic readings of Foucault than had earlier been evident.

Let us begin to explore this phase by considering the role played by yet another major SSHRC project Zureik helped to lead – in its early years – on The New Transparency: Surveillance as Social Sorting (2007–14). The project explored the ways in which surveillance was increasingly making ordinary citizens, consumers and others, more visible to organizations, related either to government or commerce. As it did so, new modes of categorizing were being developed, that allowed for more tightly construed, and consequential modes of social sorting. The upshot, the team suggested, was not only that ordinary people were increasingly legible to political and economic institutions of power. It was also that they were seen in sometimes prejudicial ways, affecting their basic choices and life-chances, but that at the same time they had less and less means of knowing what was happening or what to do about it.

During that project, the research team decided that a Middle East focus would be appropriate as a stream within the wider research. Until then, much of what passed as surveillance studies related to the global North, in countries in which structural inequalities – especially economic – were often exacerbated by developing forms of surveillance, in which the primary focus of surveillant discipline was human behaviour, and where colonialism was all-too-frequently considered as something relating to an historical 'past'. The surveillance aftermath of 9/11 was still strongly felt, however, which served – negatively – to raise the profile of persons from the Middle East as they had become the primary targets of international border and airport scrutiny and monitoring. Why not rotate the lens of surveillance studies to examine surveillance *within* one of the most intensively surveilled strips of land in the world – Israel/Palestine?

In order to ensure that participants *from* Israel/Palestine and from countries of the Palestinian diaspora could be present, the research workshop was held in Larnaca, Cyprus, in December 2008. It was a unique event that began like no other I have ever attended, with palpable tension, a friable atmosphere of suspicion, doubt and fear. For some, it was the very first face-to-face meeting with the stereotyped hostile Other. As someone who had become accustomed to explicating the realities of settler-colonialism in the state of Israel and in the Palestinian territories, and able to communicate with both Arabic and Hebrew speakers, Elia Zureik was the ideal host and mediator. By the end of the event, much taut strain had given way to a relieved interchange, deepened mutual understanding and even laughter and a multicultural night swim in the Mediterranean. (I cannot recall if he was in the water!)

The grounded intellectual business of that workshop was to explore the relationship between surveillance and control in relation to the classifying and controlling of populations with grossly different citizenship rights, and the contested territory, with its confiscated lands and rapidly extending illegal settlements. Running through all were the questions – as Edward Saïd noted, classically – of the fraught relations between 'knowledge' and 'power,' in which novel modes of surveillance are inflected in fresh ways.[14] Several of these were discussed in the course of the workshop, particularly as they relate to Foucault's work – which, as many have noted, and despite his having taught at the University of Tunis (1966–68), in what was a former French colonial protectorate, was surprisingly silent on colonialism. Other themes included the fascinating and poignant treatments of everyday surveillance, for example in the required use of ID cards to negotiate everyday life, especially in the oppressive checkpoint system that frames Palestinian existence. And the ways that not only behaviour but also consciousness, memory and quotidian use of time are subject to surveillance in this colonial setting.

Zureik's studies of settler colonialism as the core of the Zionist project were shown to have extensive surveillance ramifications in the workshop and the book it spawned and that he co-edited.[15] While he modifies some of his original insights from 1979, he also anticipates the fuller treatment that he would give to this theme in his *magnum opus, Israel's Colonial Project on Palestine: Brutal Pursuit* (2016). Whereas the ID cards, biometrics and other familiar forms of electronic surveillance are important for maintaining Israeli control, there are also forms of bureaucratic and informal surveillance that, as Zureik observes,[16] resemble the Stasi system used in Eastern Europe during Soviet domination. But it is not only visibility but also *invisibility* that is ensured by surveillance, in the form of racialized zoning laws separating colonizers and colonized in Israel. For Zureik, colonialism operates as and through surveillance, a notion that he found resonated more in the humanities than the social sciences.[17]

While it was in a sociology department that Zureik found many of his most engaged students of colonialism as surveillance, he also met another student, Tabasum Akseer, from cultural studies. She recalls first meeting Zureik as a graduate student in 2012. She noticed him at talks in the SSC, sociology and gender studies, and wondered about his sharing multidisciplinary interests in security, surveillance, the Middle East and gender. Puzzled, she observed that 'we would often smirk or laugh sarcastically at the same comments'. She felt 'fascinated by a Palestinian Christian who was so passionate and informed about the complex issues across the Middle East, including Afghanistan. After a few encounters I finally spoke with Prof. Zureik and felt an instant bond. One that surpassed academic boundaries, and felt more familial. Elia reminded me often of a sharp, witty uncle who would share frank and honest feedback about your professional career and personal life, sincerely and unapologetically. And with an unmatched wickedly funny sense of humour.'

While Zureik was still completing the *magnum opus*, a PhD student from Turkey, Özgün Topak, reflects, 'I was fortunate enough to be in one of the first cohort of students who took Elia's famous course on Colonialism and Surveillance (it must be 2010 or 2011). I recall Elia's expertise on the topic and his devotion to the Palestinian human rights, one of the most significant human rights problems in the world. Elia's course helped developing my understanding of settler-colonialism in various contexts, Israel/Palestine, Canada and others. His interventions helped shaping my understanding of surveillance as a grounded everyday reality of oppressed populations (whether it is irregular migrants at borders of Europe or Palestinians), not something that can be simply captured by abstract concepts (such as Panopticon).'

And a decade later, when that course was disrupted by COVID-19 – and Elia was over eighty years old – Midori Ogasawara, a postdoc from Japan, also felt privileged to be present: 'Because there had been few studies to connect surveillance and colonialism even after the war on terror, I think that his contribution to shape this area of study is enormous. It is very interesting that he did it in the last decade or so after his retirement by putting his life experiences and scholarly knowledge together. So, in my view, it's an art of his life. The art tells the importance of scholar's life experience and social position, especially as the vulnerable, and encourages us to be bold to pursue new directions in research.' No wonder I noticed, one day, that Elia took a short nap before class!

Between these two versions of the Colonialism and Surveillance course, Zureik spent from 2014 to 2016 as Department Head, setting up the Department of Sociology and Anthropology at the new Doha Institute for Graduate Studies (DIGS) in Qatar. This was a 'retirement' project (he had retired from Queen's in 2005) for which his services had been sought – one obvious connection being that for years Qatar had been a financial supporter of Palestinian rights and had helped to foster better relations between Fatah and Hamas.[18] Indeed, the DIGS was itself an example of Qatari support for Palestine; eligible students obtain tuition and accommodation at no cost to them. My own collaboration with Elia continued for a few weeks when I was a guest professor on surveillance issues – in the only DIGS building that had been completed at that time.[19] This period that Zureik spent in Doha is clearly of a piece with his main trajectory – using the social sciences to illuminate our understanding of Palestinian society and politics, even though he was now in retirement.

And there is still energy for research today! The recent mention of COVID-19 brings up to date the parts of the story that have been our focus. The interplay between Palestinian studies and surveillance studies has been prominent in this chapter and became significant once more as the global pandemic that broke out in 2020 reached Israel/Palestine. For not only was the spread of sickness viral, the spread of surveillance to track the course of the pandemic also became viral (Lyon 2022). How this affected Israel and the Palestinians was typical of the settler-colonialism that had engaged Zureik's attention for more than fifty years.

So it happened that our most recent collaboration concerned the ways that the Coronavirus crisis was dealt with by the Israeli authorities. Public health initiatives directed towards the mitigation of COVID-19 did of course vary tremendously from country to country, depending on social-historical and political-economic factors. But in the case of Israel/Palestine, already existing health disparities were reproduced more starkly in COVID-19 conditions. However, Israel's colonial project in Palestine also appears in sharp relief, seen most clearly in the controversial involvement of the Israeli Security Authority (Shin Bet) in mass surveillance, digital contact tracing, and related high-tech policing of quarantine orders. As in some other countries, security and policing forces were brought in, and in Israel this meant racialized distinctions affected who obtained what treatment. Moreover, by extending the reach of 'security' in this way, the infiltration of public health by security may well continue after the pandemic.[20]

Reflections on a liminal scholarly life

Reflecting on someone's life, over many years, one is obliged to ask questions about their motivation, their drive, their fads and foibles, perhaps their roads-not-taken; and regarding their work and its legacy, about what was really achieved and for whom. As the author of this chapter, and someone who has had close contact with Elia for almost forty years, I also reflect on the difference Elia has made in my own life and how my own thinking and commitments have been affected by working with him. Some of this ground has already been covered in what I have written; what follows are aspects of Elia Zureik's life and contributions that stand out for me – and no doubt these will have resonance with others' experiences.

First and foremost, Zureik has persisted with a passionate concern for the Palestinian plight. This is not merely a strand of his scholarly contribution. It is the guiding thread that runs through the whole, that gives coherence to the complete corpus of his work and explains the stance that he takes on many aspects of his research. I know nothing about the subjects of his graduate studies essays, but it is clear that, not long out of graduate school, he was set on writing sociologically about Palestinian life under occupation – as it came to be understood. And, interestingly, views of his pioneering early work have been modified, gaining greater respect over the years, especially as others, including Israeli scholars, have produced similar diagnoses of the central issues of settler-colonialism and its subjugation of Palestinian life.

Secondly, his dogged commitment to the Palestinian cause notwithstanding, Zureik's concern to be a careful sociologist has never wavered. He seeks solid evidence, both qualitative and quantitative, in order to craft his conclusions. And he frames his research using the theoretical work of a wide range of scholars, to which he adds over time. Naturally, given what has just been said about his commitment to Palestinians, such theories must always relate to the view from the margins, that by definition will question hegemonic Western views. Zureik's own life qualified him to follow such a path and to use his tenacious pursuit of adequate evidence to throw light in dark places.

Following on from this, thirdly, students – especially international graduate students – benefitted hugely from Zureik's concern for the displaced, the marginalized, the minority. Several such students have told me of their being welcomed to Elia and Mary's home for dinner or for special events like (Canadian) Thanksgiving. One, Çagatay Topal, a Turkish student, found Zureik 'witty and caring'. He also recalls discussions in thesis meetings: 'We were both stubborn in defending our positions at the beginning; but, in the end, he always found something reconciling (OK, with a little bit of help from David) and we reached a point where we could both be contented.'

Çagatay's comments remind me, fourthly, of the more angular dimensions of Elia's exchanges, that could also be matched by accounts of his kind and gentle moments. In his memoirs of his colleague, David Neice described Elia as *both* 'irascible' and 'gracious'. Sadly, it is often for the former that colleagues and professors are remembered, so it is worth recalling that many benefitted from Elia's generosity and willingness to come alongside the lonely, sad, troubled, mistreated or misunderstood. Tabs Akseer, quoted above, notes that 'More than a decade later, we continue to stay in touch, despite the many changes in personal and professional trajectories. My respect and admiration for Elia and Mary continues to grow over the years. It is an honour to count Elia as a close confident, friend and fellow conspirator.'

Fifthly, I note with interest that while Zureik collaborated on Middle East issues with colleagues far and wide – in Israel/Palestine itself as well as in the far-flung

Palestinian diaspora – the same was scarcely true of his general sociological or particular surveillance studies work. He worked jointly with *local* colleagues – other professors, postdocs, and PhD students – over most of his years at Queen's, and with others only occasionally, for instance with Abbe Mowshowitz, a computer scientist at City University of New York.[21] This also indicates his keenness to work interdisciplinarily, as he also did with SCIT, and the SSC, at Queen's.

Sixthly and finally, Elia engages bigheartedly with friends and family. Several people have stressed the warmth with which he speaks of his family, especially his grandchildren. This is something that has struck me, too, and also echoes what I have experienced of Palestinian families in Canada and in East Jerusalem and in various Palestinian towns in the West Bank. I should record here, appropriately, that I have been honoured to be treated as a friend as well as a colleague by Elia Zureik. Without him, for instance, I'm not sure that I would have become actively involved with a Christian Palestinian peace movement. I too have seen the grumpy *and* the gracious but much more than that, I have been privileged to spend time with a very creative and knowledgeable critical sociologist, from whom I learned much through our research on surveillance issues. He is someone who is ready to talk with and listen to anyone – including supporters of the occupation – a faithfully fervid critic of settler-colonialism and unfaltering defender of Palestinian rights.

Notes

1. I am very grateful to several former colleagues, postdocs and students who responded to my request for comments and memories relating to their knowing Elia Zureik. All quotations are taken from emails sent in response to my request.
2. Zureik 2016: xiv.
3. Zureik, Lyon and Abu-Laban (eds) 2011; Zureik et al. (eds) 2010.
4. As I write, I hear echoes of my own journey. In the UK, I digested – and debated – Bottomore's *Introduction to Sociology* to gain entry to university in 1968.
5. It is interesting to see how Giddens' work was to influence Zureik's research on the ways that Palestine was 'constructed' by surveillance practices – see Zureik 2001. For the record, my contact with Giddens was his being my commissioning editor at Polity Press.
6. Nakleh and Zureik 1977.
7. Ibid., citing Freire 1970.
8. Lyon and Zureik 1996.
9. Bennett (University of Victoria), along with Kirstie Ball (then with the Open University UK, now at St Andrews University, Scotland), and Kevin Haggerty (University of Alberta) were on the team with Zureik and Lyon.
10. Zureik, Mosco and Lochhead 1989.
11. Zureik 2007: 113.
12. Zureik et al. 2010.
13. Harling-Stalker notes that Zureik often sarcastically refers to Queen's as the 'Harvard of the north', underscoring his disavowal of the inflated claims that are sometimes made for the university or that its graduates are 'better than others' because they were taught at a prestigious institution.

14 Saïd 1978.
15 Zureik, Lyon and Abu-Laban (eds) 2011.
16 Zureik 2016: 28.
17 Ibid.: 96.
18 Zureik 2018.
19 The third university setting where we each spent time was Bir Zeit, in Ramallah. But there, our visits were separated by two decades. Zureik was a visiting professor in 1995; I taught a course at BZU in 2015.
20 Zureik and Lyon 2022.
21 Mowshowitz and Zureik 2005.

References

Bennett, C. J., and C. Raab (2003), *The Governance of Privacy: Policy Instruments in Global Perspective*, Aldershot: Ashgate; later (2006) Cambridge, MA: The MIT Press.
Freire, P. (1970), *Pedagogy of the Oppressed*, 30th anniversary edition 2000, New York: Bloomsbury.
Lyon, D. (2022), *Pandemic Surveillance*, Cambridge: Polity Press.
Lyon, D. (ed.) (2003), *Surveillance as Social Sorting: Privacy, Risk and Digital Discrimination*, London: Routledge.
Lyon, D., and E. Zureik (1996), *Surveillance, Privacy and the Globalization of Personal Information*, Minneapolis: University of Minnesota Press.
Mowshowitz, A., and E. Zureik (2005), 'Consumer Power in the Digital Society', *Communications of the ACM* 48 (10): 46–51.
Nakleh, K., and E. Zureik (1977), 'Sociology of the Palestinians', *Journal of Palestine Studies* 6 (4): 3–16.
Said, E. (1978), *Orientalism*, New York: Pantheon.
Zureik, E. (1979), *The Palestinians in Israel: A Study in Internal Colonialism*, London: Routledge and Kegan Paul.
Zureik, E. (2001), 'Constructing Palestine through Surveillance Practices', *British Journal of Middle Eastern Studies* 28 (2): 205–27.
Zureik, E. (2007), 'Surveillance Studies: from Metaphors to Regulation to Subjectivity', *Contemporary Sociology* 36 (2): 112–15.
Zureik, E. (2016), *Israel's Colonial Project in Palestine: Brutal Pursuit*, London: Routledge.
Zureik, E. (2018), 'Qatar's Humanitarian Aid to Palestine', *Third World Quarterly* 39 (4): 786–98.
Zureik, E., L. Harling-Stalker, E. Smith, D. Lyon and Y. E. Chan (eds) (2010), *The Globalization of Personal Information: International Comparisons*, Montreal and Kingston: McGill-Queen's University Press.
Zureik, E., and D. Hartling (1987), *The Social Context of the New Information and Communication Technologies: A Bibliography*, New York: Peter Lang.
Zureik, E., and D. Lyon (2022), 'Coronavirus Surveillance and Palestinians', *Jerusalem Quarterly* 89: 51–62.
Zureik, E., D. Lyon and Y. Abu-Laban (eds) (2011), *Surveillance and Control in Israel/Palestine: Population, Territory and Power*, London: Routledge.
Zureik, E., V. Mosco and C. Lochhead (1989), 'Telephone Workers' Reaction to the New Technology', *Relations Industrielles/Industrial Relations* 44 (3): 507–31.

Zureik, E., F. Moughrabi and V. Sacco (1993), 'Perception of Legal Inequality in Deeply Divided Societies: The Case of Israel', *International Journal of Middle East Studies* 25: 423–42.

Zureik, E., and R. M. Pike (1975), *Socialization and Values in Canadian Society*, Toronto: McClelland and Stewart (2 volumes).

Zureik, E., with Vince Sacco (1990), 'Correlates of Computer Misuse: Data from a Self-Reporting Sample', *Behaviour and Information Technology* 9 (5): 353–69.

Index

Note: References in *italic* and **bold** refer to figures and tables. References followed by "n" refer to endnotes.

ABD. *See* accumulation by dispossession
Absentee Properties Act 118, 151, 152
Absentee Property Laws 152
Abu-Basma 124–5
Abu El-Haj, Nadia 54, 101
Abu-Laban, Baha 169
Abu-Lughod, L. 26, 170–1
Abu-Saad, Ismael 39
Abu-Sitta, Salman 43
accumulation by dispossession (ABD) 149, 155–8, 162
Ackerman, B. 86n32
Adalah 135–6
ADRID. *See* Association for the Defense of the Rights of the Internally Displaced
afforestation 18, 131, 133, 134
    Holocaust and 59
AFSC. *See* American Friends Service Committee
Agamben, Giorgio 102, 107
agency/agentic power 104–6
    Campbell's differentiation 105
    Giddens' structuration theory 105
Agricultural Bank 17
Akka (Acre) 1
Akseer, Tabs 333
Al-Aqsa 259–60, 262
Al-Araqib village/villagers 129–30, 137–8, 153
Alatas, S. H. 21
al-Baladuri 44
Al-Haq 137
al-Khalil (Hebron) 26, 28
Al-khan Al-Ahmar campaign 263
Allon, Yigal 58
Al-Muqaddasi 44

American Friends Service Committee (AFSC) 296, 297–8, 300, 302, 308, 310, 312, 316
Amnesty International 176
anti-Arab racism 3, 174, 177
anti-Black racism 174
anti-colonial writings 23–6
anti-Muslim racism 3, 174, 177
anti-Palestinian racism 2–3, 174–8
    apartheid 175–7
    BDS movement (*see* BDS (boycott, divestment and sanctions) movement)
    Beinhart on 177
    Canadian Arab Lawyers Association on 177
    Doyle on 177
anti-Semitism 16, 84, 176–7
apartheid 24–5, 175–7
Apartheid Wall. *See* separation wall
Appadurai, Arjun 106, 328
Applied Research Institute–Jerusalem (ARIJ) 271, 278
Arab Bureau of the Jewish Agency 16
Arab Higher Committee (AHC) 251
Arabic language 40
    Israeli Nationality Law 59
Arabic place (space and sites) names 4, 43–5
    appropriation and Hebraicization 38–9, 55–6, **56–7**
    biblical names 50
    displacements and replacement of 41, 50
    Hebrew names 47–8, 50
    road signs transliterated from Hebrew 59–60, **60–1**
    Talmudic names 50, 51

Arab–Israeli war of 1948 8, 18, 21, 116, 117, 118, 135, 151, 152, 237, 269, 295, 297, 298, 301, 302, 308, 310, 312, 314, 324
Arab National Movement 254
Arafat, Yasser 254, 317
archaeological parks in Israel 55
archives 9
   AFSC (*see* American Friends Service Committee (AFSC))
   International Red Cross (IRC) 296, 297, 300, 308
   UNCCP 297–301
   UNRWA 295–7, 301–16
   Vatican library 43
Area C 218–19
Arendt, Hannah 102, 154
Arikha, Yaakov 46
Arlosoroff, Haim 25
Armistice Line 215, 219
Arnold, M. 76
'Arraf, Shukri 62
Asabiyya 243
Ascalon/Asqalan/Ashkelon 45
Ashkenazi Jews 19, 63
Association for Civil Rights in Israel. *See* Meretz
Association for the Defense of the Rights of the Internally Displaced (ADRID) 160
attachments
   ethics of 76
   of particular 76–7
   value of 76
Avineri, Shlomo 22, 104

Bakan, Abigail B. 174
Balfour Declaration 8, 249, 250
Balibar, Etienne 101
Barakat, R. 26
Barber, Benjamin 328
Battle of Hattin 51
Bayt Jibrin (Bayt Jubrin) 51
BDS (boycott, divestment and sanctions) movement 3, 170, 174, 175, 176–7, 263–4
Bedouin Advancement Authority 124
Bedouin population 4, 18, 56. *See also* Naqab Palestinians

confiscation of lands 5, 118–19
cultivation 117, 119
declassified government records 118–19
ghettoization 5, 121–6
nomadism 5
planned towns 123
Beinhart, Peter 177
Ben-Gurion, David 46, 47, 50, 116, 117, 120, 130–1, 133, 134
Ben-Gurion University of the Negev (BGU) 133–4
Ben Gvir, Itamar 134
Ben & Jerry's 263–4
Bennett, Colin 328
Ben-Tzvi, Yizhak 46
Berda, Y. 101
Bezeq (Israeli Telecommunications Organization) 216, 218
Bhabha, Homi 98
biblical archaeology 40, 53–5
   educational system 39
   Israeli-Jewish identity 54
   Zionist nation-building 54
biblical excavations 40
biblical landscape 54–5
biblical memory 41
biblical names 46
big data and datawars 189–93
Bitan, Hanna 48
Blaut, J. M. 13
#BlockTheBoat 264
Boden, Margaret 326
Book of Joshua 63
Bottomore, Tom 324
Bourdieu, Pierre 105
Brenner, Yosef Haim 19
British Mandatory Palestine 7
   land survey 17
   name changing among Zionist settlers 46
   Naqab Palestinian land ownership claims 127
   population surveys 14
   renaming place names 41
   telecommunication and transport infrastructure 7, 213–15
B'Tselem 176
bureaucracy 101

Burke, E. 76, 85n7
Byzantine administration 44

Cali, M. 275, 278
Campbell, Colin 105
Canada 1, 2, 28, 99, 173, 230, 241, 323, 324–7, 339, 331, 334
   academic freedom 169
   higher education institutions 169
Canadian Arab Lawyers Association 177
Canetti, D. 276
Cangh, Jean-Marie van 43
capitalism 156. *See also* accumulation by dispossession (ABD)
captive mind 21
Carmel National Park 58
cartography 37
causal mechanisms 100
Central Registry 303, 304, 315–16
Chatterjee, P. 19
checkpoints 25
Chowers, Eyal 104
Christian(s) 3, 38, 54, 58, 62–3, 77, 127, 159–60, 174, 237, 239, 315, 331, 334
Christianity 16, 18, 44, 63
Churchill, Winston 16
citizenship 150
   accumulation by dispossession (ABD) 155–8
   indigenous population 150
   settler colonial societies 150
   sociological perspective 150
Citizenship Law 136–7
citizenship of Palestinians in Israel 4, 134–7
   Citizenship Law 136–7
   concatenated dynamics 154
   dispossession 154–5
   Internally Displaced Persons (IDP) 151–3, 158–60
   Nation-State law 135–6
   redrawing boundaries 158–62
   right of return 134–5
   theory of indigenous refusal 158
civil resistance. *See* resistance
The Clash of Civilizations (Huntington) 328
closure regime 269, 273–7. *See also* separation wall

Code of Origin (CO) 311
Cohen, Abner 19
Cohen, S. E. 276
Cold War 22
collective action. *See also* resistance
   electronic media and 106
Collins, John 231, 232, 243
colonialism 235. *See also* Israel; Palestine; settler colonialism
   as a disputed theoretical framework 96
   foundational concerns 98
coloniality of being 26–9
colonization 16–17. *See also* Palestine
   East Jerusalem 7
   utilitarianism 2, 16
communication infrastructure 7–8. *See also* telecommunications
Communication Workers of Canada 326
community dismemberment 195–7. *See also* secrecy
   as psychological weapon 196
Computers, Surveillance and Privacy (Zureik and Lyon) 327
constitutional theory 81–2
constructive resistance 248. *See also* resistance
costs of separation wall 270. *See also* economic implications of separation wall
Couldry, N. 191
COVID-19 pandemic 129, 170, 172, 173, 207, 263, 331–2
Crenshaw, Kimberle 173
The Critique of Practical Reason (Kant) 85n5
cultural identity of Palestine 61–4
cultural memoricide 49
cultural talk 84

Dahamshe, Amer 61
Daher-Nashif, S. 28
dataveillance 191
Datawar 190, 199. *See also* big data and datawars
Davis, U. 24
Dayan, Moshe 41–2, 118, 121
Debord, G. 186
decolonial epistemology 1–2

defensive resistance 248. *See also* resistance
dehumanization of Palestinians 101
Deleuze, G. 186, 231, 233–5
Delta Force 28
democracy 20
    ethnic 20–1
    liberal 83–4
    meaning 83
    universal commitment 78
Demographic Database 303, 306. *See also* UNRWA archives
depersonalization 187
digital surveillance 6, 25, 207–21
    de-territorial 207
    telecommunications and (*see* telecommunications)
Dignity Uprising of May 2021 153
discursive institutionalism 100–1
dismemberment 196. *See also* community dismemberment
displacement of Naqab Palestinians 118–26
    dispossession and 118–19, 138
    urbanization plan 121–6
dispossession 78, 80, 82, 83, 84, 96, 97
    accumulation by dispossession (ABD) 149, 155–8, 162
    indigenous populations 18
    Israeli citizenship 154–5, 158–62
    Naqab Palestinian displacement and 118–19, 123, 125, 128
    settler colonial citizenship 150, 151
Doha Institute for Graduate Studies (DIGS) 332
Doyle, Chris 177
dual citizenship 238, 240

economic implications of separation wall 271, 275–6
Educational Files 303, 313–14
educational system 21–2
    Abu-Saad on 39
    biblical archaeology 39
    Palestinian students 21–2
    scriptural geography 39
Edwards, Penny 212
Egypt
    Israeli invasion of 240
    telecommunications 215

El-Atrash, A. 276
electronic media 106
Elon, Amos 58–9
environmental colonialism 18
epistemology 230
    colonial 96–100
    decolonial 1–2
    modernization 96
    standpoint 94, 98, 99
Epstein, Yitzhak 17
equal universal rights 77
ethics 76
ethnic democracy 20–1
ethnographic collection/museum 317. *See also* UNRWA archives
ethnographic studies 106
eugenics 25
European-style forests 58–9. *See also* Jewish National Fund (JNF)

Facing the Forests (Yehoshua) 58
Falk, Richard 176
Falleti, T. 106
Family Files 303–4, 307–14. *See also* UNRWA archives
Fanon, Frantz 7, 97, 108, 187–8, 231, 235–6, 242–3
Farsoun, Samih 63
Fatah 254
Filastin. *See* Palestine
film and photographic archives 316–17
first intifada 256–8
First World War 17, 236
Fischbach, Michael 295, 300
Floyd, George 173–4
forests
    European-style 58–9
    pine 54–5
Foucault, Michel 23, 26, 101, 106, 107, 330–1
freedom
    academic 99, 169, 242
    equality and 74
    of expression 241
    Kant on 85n5
    as a principle 75
Freire, Paulo 198, 235
frontier settlement 119–20

Galston, W. A. 76
Gandy, Oscar 191
Gans, C. 77
Gavison, Ruth 104
Gaza 8, 240. *See also* UNRWA archives
   grass-roots organizations 254
   Great March of Return 262–3
   UNRWA ethnographic museum 317
Generation Z students 169
Geographic Sites in Palestine ('Arraf) 62
ghettoization 5
Giddens, Anthony 105, 107
Ginat, Joseph 19
Global Israel (Shihade) 232, 242, 243–4
The Globalization of Personal Data 328–9
The Globalization of Personal Information (Zureik) 323
Global Palestine (Collins) 231, 232, 243
global ruptures 232–3, 239–42
God–TV Forest network 18
Goldberg, David Theo 101
Goldberg Committee 125
The Governance of Privacy (Bennett and Raab) 328
Granott, Abraham 17
Great March of Return 262–3
Green Patrol 122
Greenstrein, Fred 325
Guattari, F. 186, 231, 233–5
Guerin, Victor 38, 41
Gulf War (1990) 258
Gunther, Hans 25

HaAretz 130–1
Habash, George 254
Haganah 214–15
Hamas 260
Hamid II, Abdel 210
Hammami, R. 197
Harding, Sandra 98
Hartling, Diane 325
Hashomer Hatza'ir 51
Health Files 303, 313–14
Hebrew 40–1
Hebrew literature 58
Hebrew names 4, 41–3, 47–8
   family or personal names 46–7
   Israeli army officers and soldiers 42

   Naqab landscape 47
   road signs transliterated into English and Arabic 59–61
Hebrew Names Committee 42, 46–7
Hegel, G. W. F. 76, 77, 85n8
Herodotus 44, 45
Herzl, Theodor 3, 74, 78–80, 96, 104
   Altnueland 3, 79
   Der Judenstaat (the Jewish State) 16, 79
   as secular liberal Zionist 74
Hezbollah 260
Histories (Herodotus) 44
Hite-Rubin, N. 276
homo sacer 102
Huber-White method 280
human rights, separation wall impact on 273–4
Huntington, Samuel 328
Husayni, Haj Amin 251
Husaynis 249
Huxley, Aldous 13

IBM 8x32 punch cards 310
Ibn Khaldoun, M. 231, 233–5, 238, 242, 243
ICRC. *See* International Committees of the Red Cross
index cards 310
indigenous peoples 138
   European white settlers 48–9
   liberal citizenship rights 158
   refusal 158
   views 49
Indur 51
Institute for Jerusalem Studies (IJS) 296, 302
   Reinterpreting the Historical Record 295
INTELSAT network system 216
Interim Agreement 259
internal colonialism 24–5, 73
Internally Displaced Persons (IDP) 128, 151–3, 158–60. *See also* Palestinians in Israel
   citizenship rights 151
   incidental membership 155
   population management 152–3
International Committees of the Red Cross (ICRC) 297, 298, 310

International Convention on the Suppression and Punishment of the Crime of Apartheid (1973) 176
International Court of Justice 269, 273, 291n1
International Holocaust Remembrance Alliance 178
International Railways, Post and Telegraph Workers' Union (RWU) 214
International Red Cross 9
International Red Cross (IRC) 296, 297, 300, 308
interrogations 6–7
The Invasion of America (Jennings) 48–9
IRC. *See* International Red Cross
Islam 44, 62–3, 84
Islamophobia. *See* anti-Muslim racism
Israel 73–84. *See also* Palestine; separation wall
  as an apartheid regime 24–5
  archaeological parks 55
  closure regime 269, 273–7
  constitutional structure 80–1
  cultural discourse 77–8
  establishment in 1948 7–8, 40, 54, 324
  European-style forests 58–9
  as Jewish and democratic 4, 73–5, 78
  land 81
  as land west of the Jordan 54
  liberal movement 80–4
  military rule 152–3
  Palestinian resistance to (*see* resistance)
  planning laws 82
  reforestation policies 59
  self-definition 4
  settler-colonial nature 78–9, 94–6
  surveillance policies (*see* surveillance)
  Zureik's epistemological framework 97–100
Israel Department of Antiquities and Museums. *See* Israeli Antiquities Authorities
Israeli Academy for the Hebrew Language 46
Israeli Antiquities Authorities 61

Israeli army
  Hebrew Names Committee 46–7
  Hebrew names of officers and soldiers 42
Israeli Civil Administration 274
Israeli Communist Party (ICP) 255
Israeli Government Names Committee 40, 42–3, 47–8
Israeli High Court of Justice (HCJ) 272
Israeli Independence Day 160
Israeli Information Center for Human Rights in the Occupied Territories 278
Israeli Nationality Law 59, 81
Israeli place names and landscape 58–9
Israeli Security Authority (Shin Bet) 332
Israeli-Zionist renaming of Palestinian geography
  biblical academy 40
  British colonial biblical explorations 38, 39
  educational policies 40
  Government Names Committee (*see* Israeli Government Names Committee)
  Hebrew names (*see* Hebrew names)
  post-Nakba period strategies 46
  pre-state period strategies 45–6
Israel Land Authority 51
Israel Museum 61
Israel Nature and Parks Authority 55
Israel's Colonial Project in Palestine (Zureik) 323, 331
Israel Technology and Education Campus 133

Jabotinsky, Vladimir 103
Jackson, Andrew 16–17
Jaffa 27–8
  as export-import port 17
Jerusalem 26–7, 61
  pine forests 54–5
Jerusalem Day 27
Jerusalem Light Festival 27
Jewish immigration from MENA 119
Jewish National Fund (JNF) 17, 18
  afforestation 18, 59, 131, 133, 134
  European-style forests 58–9

Jewish National Home 213
Jihad vs McWorld (Barber) 328
Joint List of non-Zionist Palestinian parties 135
Jones, Robert Trent, Jr. 51
The Journal of Palestine Studies 325
Judaism 84

Katorza, Michal 18
Katz, Yisrael 59
Kayyali, A. 249
Kedar, Alexandre 128
Kelsen, H. 86n31
Khalidi, M.-A. 79
Khalidi, R. 254
Khalidi, Walid 52–3
Kimmerling, B. 24
Kitaigorodsky, Shmuel 42
Kremnitzer, Mordechai 135
Kufr Qassem massacre in 1956 160
Kymlicka, W. 76, 85n10

labour market outcomes, separation wall and 271, 275, 276–90
  estimation strategy 279
  gender 284
  heterogeneity effects 284–90
  industry types 287, 290
  main effects **281–3**
  permit for work in Israel 287
  skilled and unskilled workers 284
land claims of Naqab Palestinians 117–18, 137–8
  Al-Araqib villagers 130
  Israeli Supreme Court decision 127–8
  legal efforts 126–8
Land Day 247, 255
language 76–7
Lapid, Yair 136
Lebanon 237, 239, 299
The Legal Center for Arab Minority Rights in Israel. *See* Adalah
legal ruptures 232
Lentin, Ronit 101
Levy, Gideon 51–2
liberal democracy 83–4
liberal states 76–7. *See also* state
Living with the Bible (Dayan) 41

Li Xiaolin 18
local ruptures 236–8
logic of elimination 150
Longo, M. 276
Lorde, Audre 14
Lykes, M. 197
Lynch, J. 106
Lynk, Michael 176
Lyon, David 1, 103

MacIntyre, A. 76, 85n13
Madrid Peace Conference 256
Maggio, Jay 23
Mahmud II, Sultan 209
Maldonado-Torres, N. 26
Mandel, N. 15
Marj Ibn Amer Kibbutz Ein Dor 51
Marmura, Steve 328
Marshall, T. H. 4
Martin-Baro, Ignacio 188, 195–6
Martyrs' Forest 18
Marx, Emanuel 19
Marx, Gary 327
Marx, Karl 77, 324
Marxism 23
Masalha, Nur 79
Master Cards 310
Mathewson, K. 13
Mazzetti, M. 207
Mbembe, Achille 102
Memmi, Albert 97
memoricide 49
Meretz 135, 136
Mersky, M. 197
methodological nationalism 172
Miaari, S. H. 275, 278
Middle East and North Africa (MENA) 119, 120
Middle East Studies Association 175
Mignolo, Walter 230
Mills, C. Wright 5
Mills, Charles 174
Mishna 38
Modernity at Large (Appadurai) 328
modernization theory/discourse 19–22
Mosco, Vincent 323, 324, 325
Moughrabi, Fouad 325
Mowshowitz, Abbe 334
multicultural epistemology 97–8

Muslim–Christian Association (MCA) 249
Muslims 3, 14, 44, 52, 54, 62–4, 84, 174, 234, 239, 240, 249, 251, 315
Nakba (catastrophe) 18, 27, 29, 39, 40, 45–6, 47, 49, 50, 51, 55, 58, 59, 77, 118, 129, 152, 160, 161, 170–1, 178, 185, 252, 253, 263, 297, 324
Namier, Lewis Bernstein 46
Naming Committee of the Jewish National Fund 41
Naqab 5, 115–16
   Al-Araqib 129–30, 137–8
   Ben-Gurion on 117–18, 120
   environmental conditions 116
   illegal Jewish outposts 116
   Israeli state efforts for sovereignty over 130–4
   Jewish immigrants 119–21
   land surveys 117
   land under cultivation 119
   as 'No Man's Land 117
   tribes 117
   Zionist settlement efforts 116–17, 119–21
Naqab Palestinians. *See also* Palestinian(s)
   absent presentees 137
   confiscation of lands 118–19
   current conditions 128–37
   declassified government records 118–19
   demolition of house and village 129–30
   displacement and dispossession 118–19, 138
   land ownership 117–18, 126–8, 137–8
   NGOs supporting rights of 125
   Prawer-Begin plan 125–6
   present absentees 118, 137
   restoring land holdings 126–8
   as trespassers and invaders 127, 137
   urbanization and 121–6
Nashashibis 249
National Committee for the Defence of Arab Lands (NCDAL) 255
nationalism
   methodological 172
   Palestinian 62–4
   place names 37–8

Nationality Law. *See* Israeli Nationality Law
national leadership 249–50
Nation-State law 135–6
Nation State of the Jewish People 21
Negev Coexistence Foundation (NCF) 129
Neice, David 326, 333
neo-racism 101
networks of influence 186
Neuman, Boaz 104
The New Transparency: Surveillance as Social Sorting 330
New York Times Magazine 15
NGOs supporting rights of Naqab Palestinians 125
Nimtsa-Bi, Mordechai 46
nomad/nomadism/nomadology 233–5
   Deleuze and Guattari on 233, 234–5
   Ibn Khaldun on 233–5
nonviolent civil resistance 247–8. *See also* resistance
Nora, Pierre 3–4
North, Robert 43
Nozick, R. 83

Oak, Amos. *See* Elon, Amos
occupation of senses 27
occupied East Jerusalem (OEJ) 185–200
   Arabic road signs and toponyms 59–60
   Jewish colonial settlements 60
   Nation-State law 135
offensive resistance 248. *See also* resistance
Ogasawara, Midori 331–2
Old Testament 38, 39, 42, 44, 45, 53–4
   literary imagination 39
   Western biblical scholarship 54
Orientalism (Said) 6, 23, 170
Orshalim 59
Oslo Accords 174, 258–9
Oslo II. *See* Interim Agreement
Otman, A. 197–8
Ottoman Empire 6, 41, 117, 127, 128, 156
   Agricultural Bank 17
   Naqab Palestinian land ownership claims 127
   population surveys 14
   protest 249
   renaming Palestinian place names 41
   telegraph cables 208–13

Oxford, Lord 117
Oz, Amos 2

PA. *See* Palestinian Authority
Paicovitch, Yigal. *See* Allon, Yigal
Palestine. *See also* Israel; Naqab;
    Palestinian(s)
  afforestation (*see* afforestation)
  agriculture 17, 43
  as 'a land without a people for a people
    without a land' 14–15, 117
  archaeological exploration 54
  coloniality of being 26–9
  de-Arabization 41, 54
  economy 17, 43
  as a geographical unit 84
  Herodotus 44, 45
  Herzl's plan 15–16
  Jewish migration to 248–9
  land, claim over the 17–18
  making the desert bloom 17–18
  maps/cartographic materials on 43
  modernization discourse 19–22
  multi-layered cultural identity 43,
    61–4
  physical disappearance 49
  population 43
  population surveys 14–15
  as *terra nullius* (empty land) 2, 15–16
  toponym 44
  as 'white man's burden' 2, 19
  writings/scholarship on 23–6
  Zionist colonial representation 14–21
  Zureik's epistemological framework
    97–100
Palestine Archaeological Museum 61
Palestine Broadcasting Station 214
Palestine Exploration Fund 38
Palestine Land Development Company
    117
Palestine Telecommunications Company
    (Paltel) 217
Palestinian(s). *See also* Israel; Naqab;
    Palestinians; Palestine; separation
    wall
  Arabs (*see* Arabs)
  Christian Arabs 62–3
  discriminatory policies against 96–7
  dispossession (*see* dispossession)

internet access 207
Muslim population 62
nationalism 62–4
subjugation 94–5, 97
surveillance (*see* surveillance)
as trespassers or resident aliens 54
Palestinian Authority (PA) 259, 262,
    273
  telecommunication service 217–20
  UNRWA archives 302, 317–18
Palestinian Bureau of Statistics 271, 277
Palestinian Communist Party 256
Palestinian(s) in Israel 150–3
  audible and open forms of protest
    255
  citizenship 153–62
  Internally Displaced Persons (IDP)
    151–3
  laws of appropriation 152
  military rule and policies 152–3
  population management 152–3
  quiet forms of resistance 253–4
  redrawing boundaries of citizenship
    158–62
Palestinian Labor Force Survey (PLFS)
    271, 277
Palestinian Liberation Organization
    (PLO) 238–9, 252, 254–6
Palestinian place names 38–64
Palestinian refugees. *See also* archives;
    UNRWA archives
  data sources on 295–301
Palestinians: From Peasants to
    Revolutionaries (Sayigh) 23–4
The Palestinians in Israel (Zureik) 23, 24,
    25, 170, 325
Palestinian villages 18, 41–2, 49–56, 58, 62,
    159, 162, 229, 230, 237. *See also*
    Naqab
Palmon, Yehoshua 119
Pappe, Ilan 49, 50, 52, 102
Parekh, B. 76
peasantry and Jewish settlers 249–50
Pedagogy of the Oppressed (Freire) 235
Peel, Lord 251
Peel Commission 116
Pegasus 133, 207
Peled, Nurit 101
Peled, Y. 154

Perceptions of Legal Inequality in Deeply Divided Societies (Zureik, Moughrabi and Sacco) 325
Peres, Shimon 2, 15
Peretz, D. 20
permit for work in Israel 287
Peters, Joan 14
photographic archives. See film and photographic archives
physical barriers in West Bank 278
Pike, Robert (Bob) 325
place names 37–8. See also Israeli-Zionist renaming of Palestinian geography; Palestinian place names
   historical and cultural heritage 37
   naming and renaming 37
   nationalism 37–8
   significance 42
polemical resistance 248. See also resistance
population management 152–3
Poster, Mark 327
Prawer-Begin plan and Naqab Palestinians 125–6
psychological rupture 236, 242–3
psychological warfare/foreclosure 193–5. See also secrecy

quality of life, separation wall impact on 273–4
Queen's University in Kingston, Ontario, Canada 325–8, 334
quiet forms of resistance 253–4
Qumsiyeh, Mazin 63

Raab, Charles 328
Ra'ad, Basem 48
racialization 101, 173
racial Palestinianization 101
Rahat 56, 122
Ration Registration Card 310
Reinterpreting the Historical Record (Institute of Jerusalem Studies) 295
Relief and Social Services 311
renaming strategies 37. See also Israeli-Zionist renaming of Palestinian geography
resistance 247–64
   Al-khan Al-Ahmar campaign 263

   audible and open forms 255
   to establishment of the Israeli state 248–50
   first intifada 256–8
   first Palestinian uprising 250–2
   Great March of Return 262–3
   Naqab Palestinians 122
   Oslo Accords 258–9
   quiet forms 253–4
   second intifada 259–61
   third-party solidarity 263–4
   types 248
   unarmed 261–4
road signs 59
Robinson, Edward 38, 41, 44, 50
Rockefeller Museum. See Palestine Archaeological Museum
Rome Statute of the International Criminal Court 176
Ross, A. 235
route of separation wall 272–3
Rubinstein, A. 77
Ruppin, Arthur 25
ruptures 231–3
   concept 232
   global 232–3, 239–42
   legal 232
   local 236–8
   psychological 236, 242–3
   regional 238–9
   social 232

Sacco, Vincent (Vince) 325
Sa'di, A. H. 101
Sa'di-Ibraheem, Y. 27, 28
Said, Edward 259, 323, 327, 330
   epistemology 96, 97, 98
   on exile 1
   Orientalism 6, 23, 170
   The Question of Palestine 23, 24, 169–70
   resistance culture 98
Salaita, Steven 241–2
Sandel, M. 76
Sauer, R. M. 275
Sayegh, Fayez 231, 233, 235, 236
Sayigh, Rosemary
   Palestinians: From Peasants to Revolutionaries 23–4

Schmidt, Vivien 100–1, 105–6
Second Intifada 259–61
Second World War 1, 22, 23, 76, 235
secrecy 6, 185–200
   big data and Datawars 189–93
   as colonial violence 187–9
   community dismemberment 195–7
   as machinery of erasure 199–200
   psychological warfare/foreclosure 193–5
   racialized necroeconomies 199
   strategic influence 193
   as strategy of domination 199
   survivability 197–8
   as technology of psycho-social uprooting 200
secular/secularism/secularization 77
securitization 102
SEDB. *See* Socio-Economic Database
Segal, Rafi 55
'Select for Yourself a Hebrew Family Name' 46–7
separation wall 247, 261, 269–91
   costs 270
   economic implications 271, 275–6
   human rights and quality of life 273–4
   labour market outcomes 271, 275, 276–90
   literature review 274–6
   map *270*
   political implications 276
   route and phases 272–3
   as a security policy 269
settler colonialism 25–6, 94–6. *See also* Israel; Palestine
   epistemology (*see* epistemology)
   Fanon on 235–6, 242, 243
   Ibn Khaldun on 242, 243
   psychological impact 242–3
   ruptures (*see* ruptures)
   Veracini's work on 235
   Wolfe on 26, 80, 155, 173, 231, 235
Settler Colonial Studies 26
Shafir, G. 154
Shaked, Ayelet 136
Shalhoub-Kevorkian, N. 27
Shamir, Yitzhak 22
Sharon, Ariel 122, 259
Sharp, Gene 247, 248

Shenhav, Y. 101
Sherut HaYediot (SHAY) 214–15
Signals Intelligence 215
Simpson, Audra 158
Six Day War of 1967 269
Smith, Emily 328
Smith, Linda Tuhiwai 49, 115
Smooha, Sammy 20–1
Smuts, Jan 25
Social Context of Information and Communication Technologies (Zureik and Hartling) 325
Socialization and Values in Canadian Society (Zureik and Pike) 325
social knowledge 191
social ontology of colonial surveillance 100–4
social ruptures 232
Social Sciences and Humanities Research Council of Canada (SSHRC) 327, 328–9
sociocide 197
Socio-Economic Database (SEDB) 303, 306–7
sociological imagination 5
sociology of the occupation 25
South Africa 25
   apartheid 24, 175
Spivak, G. 23
Stalker, Lynda Harling 324
State of Israel. *See* Israel
Sternbach, Amos. *See* Elon, Amos
Sternhell, Zeev 104
Stirner, M. 76, 85n9
Studies in Communication and Information Technology (SCIT) 326–7
Sukenik, Yigael 42
Supreme Court of Israel 160
surveillance 2, 6–8, 94, 95, 98–9. *See also* telecommunications
   agentic power 104–6
   digital 6, 25, 207–21
   racialization 101
   secrecy (*see* secrecy)
   securitization 102
   social ontology 100–4
   as tool of governance 99
Surveillance Studies Centre (SSC) 327

surviving, secrecy policing 197–8
symbolic resistance 248. *See also* resistance
symbolic violence 4–5
Syria 237, 298–9, 300

Takkenberg, Lex 309–10
Talmudic names 38, 50, 51, 60
Tamir, Y. 77
TAVO. *See* Tubingen Atlas of the Near and Middle East
Taylor, C. 76, 85n11
Tel A-Seba 122
telecommunications 7–8, 207–8
   British Mandate policy 7, 213–15
   Ottoman Empire 209–12
   Palestinian infrastructure 217–20
   telegraph/telegraph lines 208–13
   Zionist/Israeli infrastructure 214–17
Telecommunications Law 216
telegraph/telegraph lines 208–13
   Ottoman Empire 209–12
   submarine 209
telephone 213
   directories 8, 214
   tapping 214
A Theory of Justice (Rawls) 76
theory of modernization 19
Thompson, Thomas 43
Tilly, Charles 233
Tlaib, Rashida 177
Topak, Ozgun 331
Topal, Cagatay 333
Trail of Tears 16
Tubingen Atlas of the Near and Middle East (TAVO) 43
Tubingen Bible Atlas 43
Turkman, Iliter 308

UNC. *See* Unified National Command
UNCCP. *See* United Nations Conciliation Commission for Palestine
UN Human Rights Council 130
Unified National Command (UNC) 256–7
Unified Registration System (URS) 300, 301, 303, 304, 306–15
   Demographic Database 306
   Family Files 307–14

Socio-Economic Database (SEDB) 306–7
United Nations Conciliation Commission for Palestine (UNCCP) 295–6, 297–301
United Nations Office for the Coordination of Humanitarian Affairs (OCHA) 271, 278
United Nations Relief and Works Agency (UNRWA) 9
   administrative headquarters 296, 298
   digitized archives (*see* UNRWA archives)
   employees 295, 296
   foundation 295
   General Assembly Resolution 194 295
   registration forms 299
   successor to UNRPR 296
   Syria and Lebanon offices 298–9
United Nations Relief for Palestine Refugees (UNRPR) 296
United Nations Special Committee on Palestine (UNSCOP) 252
United Nations (UN) 173, 174–5, 232
United States 173, 174–5
UNRPR. *See* United Nations Relief for Palestine Refugees
UNRWA. *See* United Nations Relief and Works Agency
UNRWA archives 295–7, 301–16
   Central Registry 303, 304, 315–16
   data sources 303
   Demographic Database 303, 306
   Educational Files 303, 313–14
   ethnographic collection 317
   Family Files 303–4, 307–14
   film and photographic archives 316–17
   gaps in records 302
   Health Files 303, 313–14
   inventory 305–15
   new classification system 316
   preservation 318–19
   refugee registration 309–11
   Socio-Economic Database 303, 306–7
   transferring to Palestinian Authority 317–18

Unified Registration System
(URS) 300, 301, 303, 304,
306–15
urbanization, Naqab Palestinians
displacement and 121–6
Abu-Basma 124–5
Goldberg Committee 125
housing 122
Prawer-Begin plan 125–6
Rahat 122, 123
sewage system 123
social non-cooperation 122
Tel A-Seba 122
URS. *See* Unified Registration System

Veracini, Lorenzo 26, 235
villages. *See* Palestinian villages
violence 106, 243. *See also* secrecy; surveillance

Wadi al-Hawarith 41
war of 1948. *See* Arab-Israeli war of 1948
Weizman, Eyal 55
Weizmann, Chaim 46, 214
West Bank 8
Jewish colonial settlements 60
physical barriers 278
separation wall 247, 261, 269–91
White, Hayden 28
Wisner, B. 13
Wolfe, Patrick 15, 26, 80, 155, 173, 231, 235
World Bank 274
World Zionist organizations 116

Yehoshua, A. B. 58
Yerushalayim 59
Young, Alex 233

Zangwill, Israel 14, 116
Zionism 1, 14, 77–8. *See also* Israel; Palestine
built-in violence 74
ethno-religious discourse 74
goal of 3
political 1, 3, 172
Western states 1, 13
Zionist collective memory 41. *See also* Israeli-Zionist renaming of Palestinian geography
Zionist liberal movement 80–4
Zureik, Elia 1–2, 3, 6, 7, 73, 78, 80, 95, 96, 149, 154, 162, 164n1, 169, 178, 188, 208, 253, 255
colonial epistemological framework 97–100
curriculum vitae (CV) 1, 324
early life 324–5
friends and family 334
The Globalization of Personal Information 323
Israel's Colonial Project in Palestine 323, 331
Mosco on 323
The Palestinians in Israel 23, 24, 25, 170, 325
on racialization 101
reflections on liminal scholarly life 332–4
on securitization 102
self-imposed exile 1
settler-colonial model 26, 115
sociology of the Palestinians 171–3, 323
Surveillance and Control in Israel/Palestine 323
surveillance studies 25, 101–8, 172, 208, 323, 329–32
training 323

www.ingramcontent.com/pod-product-compliance
Lightning Source LLC
Chambersburg PA
CBHW050331230426
43663CB00010B/1812